2005

WE'LL ALWAYS HAVE PARIS

We'll Always Have Paris

AMERICAN

TOURISTS

IN FRANCE

SINCE 1930

HARVEY
LEVENSTEIN

The University of Chicago Press
Chicago and London

HARVEY LEVENSTEIN is professor emeritus of history at McMaster University in Hamilton, Ontario. He is the author of a number of books, including *Revolution at the Table*; *Paradox of Plenty*; and *Seductive Journey: American Tourists in France from Jefferson to the Jazz Age*, the first volume of the two-volume study of American tourists in France, published by the University of Chicago Press.

The University of Chicago Press, Chicago 60637
The University of Chicago Press, Ltd., London
© 2004 by The University of Chicago Press
All rights reserved. Published 2004
Printed in the United States of America

13 12 11 10 09 08 07 06 05 04   1 2 3 4 5
ISBN: 0-226-47378-3 (cloth)

Library of Congress Cataloging-in-Publication Data

Levenstein, Harvey A., 1938–
    We'll always have Paris : American tourists in France since 1930 / Harvey Levenstein.
        p. cm.
    Includes bibliographical references and index.
    ISBN 0-226-47378-3 (alk. paper)
        1. Americans—France—History—20th century.   2. Tourism—France—History—20th century.   3. France—Foreign public opinion, American.   4. United States—Foreign public opinion, French.   5. National characteristics, French.   6. National characteristics, American.   7. France—Social life and customs—20th century.   I. Title.
    DC34.5.A44L49 2004
    914.404′81′08913—dc22

                                                                          2004003493

For Mona

CONTENTS

I sent the completed manuscript of this book to the publisher in April 2003, some days after American troops occupied Baghdad. I kicked myself, of course, for not finishing the book earlier. Not only did it help explain the virulence of the wave of Francophobia prompted by the French refusal to support the United States in this venture; it also showed, I thought, how there was little chance that the crisis would dim the special allure that traveling to France has always had for many Americans.

My previous book, *Seductive Journey: American Tourists in France from Jefferson to the Jazz Age*, shows how in the nineteenth and early twentieth centuries American tourists to France would often return with tales of how the French played fast and loose with morality. World War I saw such negative views reinforced, as many of the over 1 million American troops—the so-called doughboys—who served in France returned from there convinced that the French were immoral, dishonest, and ungrateful for their help. The wave of American tourists who flooded into France during the 1920s helped reinforce these convictions as, particularly in Paris, they encountered a host of people who seemed out to cheat them at every turn. In this volume I show how these ideas, along with disgust over French people's standards of personal hygiene and their apparent propensity to eat revolting foods, persisted through the Great Depression of the 1930s and blossomed again after World War II. Many GIs returned from France full of unkind stories that were not unlike those of the doughboys, and a new wave of tourists revived many of the complaints of their prewar predecessors.

Added to this was the widespread belief that the French were inveterate anti-Americans, a conviction buttressed by such things as French politicians' attacks on Coca-Cola and the appearance of "Yankee Go Home" graffiti on French walls. Although the American media usually linked these to pro-Communism, in fact much of this French anti-Americanism echoed ideas that had arisen in the nineteenth and early twentieth centuries, long before the rise of the French Communist party.[1] Indeed, by the 1930s the basis for what became the standard French critique of America was already solidly in place. People on all sides of the political spectrum saw the United States as a country dominated by the values of industrial production. They called it a place with little in the way of culture, whose people were crude and materialistic in the extreme, where family, community, and the finer things of life took a backseat to the relentless accumulation of wealth. Its tourists were regarded as reflecting this and were often portrayed as uncultured and insensitive, relying on fistfuls of dollars rather than language and knowledge to manage their way through France.

The irony is that during and after the Depression successive French governments, including the Gaullists, came to realize just how important the American tourist dollars were to their economy. Anxious to encourage American tourism, they mounted campaigns to eliminate the practices, shady and otherwise, that so annoyed Americans and made repeated attempts to have the French learn to smile and become more welcoming. We shall see how, for the most part, not only did these campaigns fail to change the French; they also did little to placate American tourists, most of whom still thought that the French reserved a particularly mean-spirited welcome for them.

Yet Americans still continued to visit France in ever-increasing numbers. It remained their top overseas destination until the late twentieth century, when England edged it out, mainly because it was a more convenient jumping-off point for tours of Europe. Why, then, did they flock to a country whose people were widely regarded as hostile to them? Part of the answer lies in another vision of France, one that also dates back to the earliest years of the American Republic: the idea that it was the epicenter of high civilization and sophisticated pleasures. Sometimes this attractive view coexisted in the same minds as the negative one, but in the twentieth century the positive and negative views came to be associated with different social classes, regions, and genders. In general, the unfavorable images persisted among the lower and middle classes, especially males. On the other hand, the upper-class social elite and upper-middle classes, particularly on the East Coast, continued to view France as a beacon of civilization and refinement. They returned from visits there with their self-images as worldly, stylish, and sophisticated people reinforced. Upper-middle-class women in particular thought that gaining a familiarity with European high culture and French taste would elevate them culturally and socially.

The generation of young writers and artists who flocked to France in the 1920s reinforced another attraction: its reputation as a place that respected personal freedom. This would recur again in the 1950s, when America again seemed oppressed by the forces of conformity and repression. During those years France also regained its reputation among African Americans for another kind of freedom: liberation from the day-to-day racism that dogged black people's existence in the United States. The rest of the century saw the playing out of these competing visions on an increasingly large stage, as the age of mass tourism swamped France, bringing in millions of American tourists who were increasingly diverse in their origins, attitudes, and what they wanted from their trips abroad.

The book is therefore about much more than Franco-American political relations. It also tries to explain why foreign tourism has become the world's largest international industry and its most common form of cultural interaction.[2] Why this has come to pass is not as obvious as it may seem, for surely Madame de Staël was not far off the mark when she called foreign travel one of life's "saddest pleasures." Being deposited in unfamiliar locales where people with strange customs speak incomprehensible languages can be a surefire recipe for disorientation, insecurity, and worse. For many Americans in France, this has not just meant being bewildered by bidets and puzzled by pissoirs. It has also meant trying to decipher mysterious charges on hotel and restaurant bills and enduring a succession of cheating cab-drivers, grasping bellhops, sullen salesclerks, and haughty waiters. We shall see how this was a major reason that prearranged package tours were so popular with Americans, especially in the 1950s and 1960s, when the United States was on the cutting edge of something that is now happening in the rest of world: the steady opening up of foreign travel to people progressively lower on the class ladder.

In *Seductive Journey* I used the distinction made in the tourist industry between cultural tourism and leisure tourism. Tourists involved in the former usually expect some kind of self-improvement to come from being exposed to a place's historic, architectural, and artistic heritage. Leisure tourists, on the other hand, see travel as an opportunity to experience the pleasures that they cannot have in the course of their everyday life at home—lying on a sandy beach, sipping drinks in an outdoor café, or watching bare-breasted women parade across a Parisian stage.

At first glance, it might seem that the key difference between the two is that only cultural tourism is regarded as a form of self-improvement. However, these days the distinction is not so clear-cut. As I said in *Seductive Journey*, I think that in the 1920s the spread of a kind of pop-Freudianism helped persuade many well-off Americans that overcoming one's inhibitions, jettisoning one's puritan baggage, and having enjoyable experiences abroad were beneficial to one's mental health. In this book I show how these lines became further blurred. The Depression of the 1930s hardly changed upper-class tourism, which continued to revolve around social engagements in Paris and France's luxury resorts and spas. However, few of the upper-middle-class Americans who continued to travel to France did so just to "have a good time." They tended to justify their now-expensive trips in terms of cultural uplift of some sort. So did most of the upper-middle-class tourists of the post–World War II era and the middle classes who began arriving in large numbers in the 1960s. They managed to do this, though, by turning sightseeing—especially seeing the world-renowned celebrity sights—into their central cultural pursuit.

Traditional leisure tourism persisted as well, as France continued to be regarded as the quintessential land of joie de vivre. Well into the 1960s, drinking at all-night bars and nightclubs, watching risqué stage shows, ogling prostitutes, and buying "dirty books" were standard features of tourists' visits. The millions of younger tourists who began flocking overseas in the 1970s were little interested in either the Louvre or the Folies Bergère, yet they represented a major step toward the merging of the two kinds of tourism. Reflecting the culture of narcissism that prevailed among much of the middle class, these members of what Tom Wolfe called the "Me Generation" tended to regard pleasurable (or even painful) experiences of almost any kind as expanding one's personality and therefore culturally uplifting.

While the 1970s saw the triumph of mass tourism, the years thereafter saw its fragmentation. Although great masses of people were now engaged in overseas tourism, they were by no means doing the same things. In this regard, I discuss changing attitudes toward French food (some readers may be surprised at the fear and trembling it often evoked among Americans) and the rise of gastronomic tourism. I also show how one of the ironies of the recent surge in Francophobia in America is that it came at the heels of a two-decade period during which French anti-Americanism declined markedly and the French seem to have treated American tourists better. Indeed, although the Iraq crisis led to massive French disapproval of American foreign policy, there was no evidence of any negative consequences for American tourists.

It is unlikely, then, that the repeated calls for Americans to shun France and all of its products will have a lasting impact on tourism there.[3] They resonate mainly, as we shall see, among people who never have and never wanted to visit France anyway. Similar calls in the late 1960s, prompted by President Charles de Gaulle's defiance of the United States, had little long-term impact, for the historic American attraction to France simply ran too deep for the flow of tourism to be stanched. Since then France, with its delicious combination of attractions for both pleasure and self-improvement, has managed to maintain the special place it has always had in the hearts and minds of an extraordinary number of Americans. Like Rick in the movie *Casablanca*, recalling to Ilsa the happy days they spent there, they, too, can say, "We'll always have Paris."

— —

I would like to thank the Social Sciences and Humanities Research Council of Canada for the research grant that enabled me to travel to archives and libraries in the United States and France and to do a number of very useful interviews there. My wife, Mona, helped me with some of the archival research and was indispensable for the English-language interviews, arranging many of them and asking excellent questions. She then read over the first draft of the manuscript and made useful suggestions for revision. I was also lucky that my daughter Lisa was working on her dissertation at the same time as I was researching this book. She alerted me to useful Web sites on women's and African American history and sent me photocopies of items she came across in her research. Their usefulness is attested to in the many references to the Philadelphia African American newspapers. James C. Hill of the University of Illinois at Chicago was also of great help in this regard, responding to my e-mail query about African Americans in France with a number of suggestions for sources. I am grateful as well to the many people who allowed Mona and me to interview them, and to Patricia Laplante-Collins, whose invitation to speak at her "salon" in Paris led to our encountering a number of them. They are mentioned by name in the text and the notes, although, because of the nature of their jobs in the tourist industry, a few of them thought it wiser to be referred to by pseudonyms. Some interviewees were also kind enough to share diaries they kept during their trips to France. Doug Mitchell continued to be a fine editor, supportive and encouraging. It was good to see him finally get to Paris while I was writing this book, so he could appreciate, without envy, the tales of my gastronomic adventures there.

I did not receive Chris Endy's recent dissertation on American tourism to France during the cold war until I had completed much of the first draft of this book.[4] Fortunately, I had met him while we were both doing research on the topic in the Bibliothèque Nationale in Paris, and it became clear that his emphasis, which is on the role of tourism in foreign policy, would be much different from mine. However, there is inevitably some overlap, and we do sometimes refer to the same sources. When this has occurred, I have tried scrupulously to give him credit for those that I came across first in his work. On another point regarding references: I often used the Canadian editions of weekly magazines, whose content and pagination frequently differ from the American ones. To avoid confusion, I have therefore not used article titles (which also sometimes differ) and page numbers when referring to them.

GREAT DEPRESSION FOLLIES

1

It Sometimes Rains in Nice

On July 13, 1931, a rather sad-looking couple, Gerald and Sara Murphy, took the train from Paris to Cherbourg, boarded the liner *Aquitania*, and sailed for New York City. For much of the past ten years they had been one of the most glamorous American couples in France. When the wealthy young pair arrived in Paris in 1921, they were brimming with self-confidence and ambition. He was tall, lithe, and handsome; she was vivacious and beautiful. At first, they both took art lessons, and Gerald soon made a mark as an accomplished modern artist. Before long, though, they began spending more time partying with creative people than creating their own art. In the end, their main claim to fame became the champagne-drenched parties they threw for other creative people, such as F. Scott Fitzgerald, Ernest Hemingway, Cole Porter, and Pablo Picasso, in their villa on the Côte d'Azur, the sunny strip of Mediterranean coast that Americans call the Riviera. It was these all-night parties that Fitzgerald later immortalized in his novel *Tender Is the Night*, in which the central character, patterned after Gerald, ultimately forsakes his creative talents for the bottle. The athletic-looking couple who had initially frolicked on the beach ended up avoiding it, spending the last years of the decade shuffling around their house in corpulence-concealing beach pajamas.[1] Ultimately, along with Fitzgerald, they came to symbolize the downside of what another American expatriate in France, Gertrude Stein, called the "Lost Generation."

In 1931, the same year that the Murphys returned, Fitzgerald published "Babylon Revisited," a short story about a man who had been on the same kind of party circuit as the Murphys. He returns to Paris hoping to recover his nine-year-old daughter, who had been taken from him when his wife died because, like Murphy, he had become a drunk. He is stunned to find that, because of the Great Depression, Paris seems devoid of Americans. His first stop is the practically empty bar of the Ritz hotel, long a popular watering hole for well-heeled American tourists. "It was not an American bar any more. . . . It had gone back to the French." Montmartre, the famed artists' quarter whose bars and nightclubs had been crowded with American tourists, was also forlorn. "The Poet's Cave had disappeared, but the Café of Heaven and the Café of Hell still yawned—even devoured, as he watched, the meagre contents of a tourist bus—a German, a Japanese, and an American couple who glanced at him with frightened eyes."[2] The Paris of the Jazz Age, which since the end of World War I had been a magnet for hundreds of thousands of American tourists, was no more.

— —

During the 1920s many other young Americans with creative ambitions had, like the Murphys and Fitzgeralds, flocked to Paris and, like them, ended up just doing a lot of drinking. A depressed franc helped Paris's Left Bank replace New York's Greenwich Village as a magnet for young Americans with bohemian aspirations. Prohibition, which banned the sale of alcoholic beverages after January 16, 1920, fueled the process, turning France into a literal as well as a figurative oasis. Travelers would begin drinking the moment their ships left New York Harbor and continue until the boat train pulled into Paris's Gâre du Nord. Those with bohemian inclinations would make for the sidewalk cafés of the Left Bank's boulevard Montparnasse, which were packed with carousing American artists, writers, and musicians. The better-heeled would stay in the wealthier parts of the Right Bank and search out famous watering holes like Harry's New York Bar. Tourists of both kinds would also make for the Riviera, hoping to join in on the kind of fun so famously had by people such as the Murphys and Fitzgeralds.

Endlessly flowing booze buttressed the old idea that France was a land that was free from American puritanism, where the pursuit of pleasure reigned supreme. In the newly popular Freudian lexicon, it was a place where people could shed their inhibitions. Although Paris teemed with prostitutes, most American tourists were happy to get their sexual titillation from more vicarious pursuits such as "Paris by Night" tour buses that took them to see bare-bosomed women on the stage of the Folies Bergère and prostitutes plying their trade in Montmartre. They would also gawk at the crowds on the sidewalk terraces of the Montparnasse cafés and fantasize about the naughty carryings-on of artists and their "models."

Of course, tourists also came to see the world-famous sights: the Eiffel Tower, Notre-Dame, the Arc de Triomphe, the Champs-Elysées, and so on. Moreover, France's long-standing reputation as a center of high culture continued to attract many tourists. They would be awed by Paris's incomparable architectural beauty and overwhelmed by its art treasures, particularly those in the Louvre, the immense palace housing the world's largest and most impressive collection of Western art.

Female schoolteachers on their summer holidays were a ready market for this kind of cultural tourism.[3] The diary of Jan Gelb, a twenty-six-year-old New York City schoolteacher on her first trip to France in the summer of 1929, is filled with uplifting cultural experiences. Notre-Dame Cathedral, she wrote, "affected me like the most profound and noble symphony." She spent an entire day at the Louvre, after which she "staggered out, cleansed of soul." During the next few weeks, she visited it many more times, calling it "a feast—banquet—orgy." At the Opéra, she was impressed by the magnificent building as well as the opera itself, but was especially taken by the "exquisite" ballet, an art form that she, like most Americans, had never seen before.[4]

In the mid-1920s, summer "educational" tours of Europe for middle-class college students had become very popular. The large groups usually started and ended their trips in Paris, where they would be herded through the major sights and galleries before being allowed to add their exuberant presence to the mobs of Americans in its bars and cafés. In addition, each year over five thousand American undergraduates would register in eight- to ten-week summer courses in Paris. There were even touring programs for children aged twelve to fourteen. One observer called the whole process "the greatest student migration in history."[5]

This combination of France's sensual and cultural attractions—what Clifton Fadiman later called the idea "of a Europe possessing some magical secret, some snake oil Happiness-and-Culture, unpurchasable within domestic boundaries"—helped make France by far the most popular destination for Americans abroad.[6] It was, said one observer at the end of the 1929 summer tourist season, "the center of the American tourist's universe . . . the Super Mecca of travelers."[7]

— —

Two months later the Great Crash practically leveled the New York Stock Exchange. As Fitzgerald's alter ego discovered, the Great Depression that followed seemed to turn this American Mecca into a ghost town for American tourists and expatriates. Many, like the Murphys, depended on stock dividends for much of their income, and in 1930 and 1931 these began to dry up.[8] To make matters worse, while the American economy imploded, France experienced a brief respite, something that encouraged the French government to shore up the value of the franc, making France even more expensive for Americans.[9] In January 1930 a young American woman on Smith College's junior-year-abroad program wrote home from Paris, "They say all the Americans are leaving Paris to go home . . . and the shops and hotels have no more business. The Riviera is almost empty."[10]

In fact, though, the exodus of Americans expats was just beginning. Within a year it had turned into a wholesale flight. In February 1932 a resident American wrote in her diary about an artist friend who was in "a fine fix."

> He has just had a letter from his father saying that his business in Nebraska is bankrupt . . . and he can't send him another cent. Ward now has only a few francs in his pocket—his rent isn't paid and he doesn't know what to do. He has gone up to see the American Aid Society this morning to see if they will send him home. . . . He's going to try to get his few belongings out of his studio tonight after dark so they won't be seized because he hasn't paid the rent.[11]

By mid-1933 the dollar's value had fallen yet again and the expatriate population had dropped to 13,500, less than half of what it had been before the Great Crash. American churches, schools, and community centers were shuttered and closed. Many of their staff and clientele boarded the same boat trains for home as had the Murphys, or headed for Italy, where the living was cheaper.[12] By 1935 revenue from user fees at the American Library in Paris had shrunk to 8 percent of what it had been in 1930. Unable to pay its rent, the library was evicted from its fine building near the Champs-Elysées.[13]

The French lamented the exodus' impact on the luxury trade. In late 1934 the newspaper *Le Temps* said there were not ten buildings in the wealthy Right Bank quarter where these families used to live "without the fateful 'apartment for rent' sign."[14] In mid-1935 another observer said, "They were the best clients of French resorts and the most faithful luxury-lovers in France. How many bankruptcies of luxury establishments in Paris, in the spas, the seaside, and high commerce have been caused by this exodus of resident Americans?"[15]

However, it was the Depression's impact on American tourism, which provided over one-third of all of France's tourist income, that most preoccupied the French.[16] In November 1929, just two months after the Crash, the *New York Times* reported that people in the French tourist industry were "begin[ning] to wonder whether American tourists would ever come again to Europe."[17] In March 1930 the chamber of commerce of Cannes, the Riviera's most fashionable town, officially complained to the American ambassador about that winter's falloff in the American tourist trade, as if the ambassador could do anything about it. The *Times* reported from Paris that the French now regretted having jeered at American tourists in 1926, a reference to the riots that had broken out in reaction to American tourists rubbing French noses into the lamentable value of the franc.[18]

That summer did not quite bring the much-feared disaster—the number of tourists actually remained steady. However, there was a nasty omen: their spending dropped by about a third.[19] The next year, 1931, more than fulfilled the gloomiest predictions. The distress calls began in mid-June, when the eastbound transatlantic liners, which would normally be packed with summer tourists, reported that passenger traffic was only 30 to 50 percent of that of the previous year.[20] In late August a reporter in Paris said, "The summer now drawing to a close will be known in Europe as the American Tourist Season Without the American Tourist." Those few who did come "refused absolutely to be lavish." Only a few years ago, he said, an American friend in Paris would show visitors the elegant place Vendôme and facetiously call it "the most beautiful square in America." Recently, looking over the same square, the friend said, "I never realized the population of Paris was French!"[21]

The world's fair held that year in Paris, the Colonial Exposition, was of little help. Its theme, the benefits of colonialism, was hardly one to attract Americans. The American pavilion was a reproduction of Mount Vernon, the house on George Washington's slave plantation, with music provided by what the *Paris Herald* called a band consisting of "college-educated Indians."[22] Only the spectacular reproduction of the temple at Angkor Wat, Cambodia, seemed to have piqued the interest of the relatively few Americans who went there.[23] At the end of the year, the French national tourist office gloomily announced that tourism from the United States was down two-thirds from the previous year, and that those Americans who did come had spent much less.[24]

—·—

As soon as the economic crisis had struck, spokesmen for the French tourist industry demanded that their government stop relying solely on France's undoubted charms to attract tourists and mount a publicity campaign in America. They said that they were particularly concerned about competition from Germany, which, "with characteristic efficiency," was spending large sums to attract American visitors.[25] The government had responded by opening a tourist office in New York and beginning a new promotional campaign to win back the tourist dollars.[26] But there was much more to

France's American problem than the worsening Depression and a lack of publicity. There was also the French reputation for being miserly, greedy, and rapacious with Americans, whom they regarded as a nation of millionaires.[27] This stereotype of the French had been fueled by the over 1 million American troops stationed in France during World War I, many of whom returned to America with tales such as that French peasants had tried to charge rent for the land in which the Americans dug their trenches. Even during the mid-1920s, when the dollar was soaring, Americans constantly complained about being defrauded and overcharged, in some cases resorting to their fists to settle the consequent disputes.[28] Even resolute Francophiles expected to be cheated at every turn. When Jan Gelb first arrived in Paris, she took it as a matter of course that she was "cheated atrociously by the taxi driver."[29]

Reports of the falloff in tourism thus prompted considerable crowing in America. The acerbic theater critic George Jean Nathan said that "the French have killed the goose that laid the golden egg." Not only did French hotels add a host of extra charges to Americans' bills, but restaurants had two sets of prices for the same menus, one for the French, the other for Americans. As a result, he said, Americans were now taking their custom to London and Berlin.[30] An article in the *Saturday Evening Post* said the French thought "Americans will pay anything" and treated them "as ripe, ingenuous suckers who, while *en voyage* at least, will allow the bleeders to fasten onto us and stay there until we are as flat and bloodless as a lemon sole."[31]

Many of the problems arose from the myriad supplements and taxes that were commonly added to French bills. In April 1930, when it was announced that a new high commissioner of tourism would visit the United States, the *New York Times* suggested that he interview returned tourists about "complaints of excess taxes, exorbitant charges and a general inclination to make tourists pay in proportion to the supposed wealth of their country of origin." High on the list was Paris nightspots' infuriating practice of charging almost as much for bottled water as for wine. Another was the addition of a 10 percent service charge to hotel bills while hotel employees still demanded tips, claiming that they saw nothing of the service charge.[32]

Within weeks the government had moved to counter these complaints by reducing or eliminating many of the charges.[33] A few months later, Adolph Ochs, the *Times* publisher, told a Paris audience that although American tourists' complaints about the French were now "steadily diminishing," the French could still do more to protect Americans from overcharging merchants. A number of Frenchmen agreed. One columnist said that the "arrogant visitors" of the postwar days, who had "come to France swollen with the [fortunes] realized at the expense of blood-soaked Europe," had been ruined by the Crash. The French should not confuse them with "the new generation of young Americans sincerely wishing to instruct themselves, open to comprehension, avid to know us and like us. . . . Let us not treat the newcomer like the miser treated the goose of the golden eggs. No overcharging."[34] The head of a large department store admitted that while it was certainly not true of his business, it was not unknown for shops in the luxury trade to have two prices, one for Americans and another for the French. He suggested that the national tourist office should publish a list of restaurants and shops to which tourists could go without fear of such practices.[35]

The government had already extracted a commitment from hotels not to charge more for rooms and meals than the prices they submitted to its official directory of hotels. This meant, said the *Washington Post*, that "the desk clerks will not be allowed to charge a guest according to their own judgement, often depending on whether the traveler's suitcase is of leather or pigskin, or whether he wears a diamond ring or a plain gold band."[36] In July 1931, after the government issued a special directory for tourists visiting the Colonial Exposition, *Collier's* magazine said that in the 1920s the way for a tourist to find a clean, comfortable, reasonable hotel room in France was "to get stung" until you finally found an honest place. This summer, it said, the government itself would find them that room. "You won't be gypped unless you insist upon it."[37]

To demonstrate that France was not more expensive than other European countries, the government sold coupons for all-expense fifteen-day tours for one hundred dollars.[38] Also, each year from 1930 to 1933, it treated large groups of American doctors and their wives to stays in French spas and resorts, in the hope of having them extol their healthful qualities to patients and friends upon their return.[39] In 1931 a group of American mayors were brought over for a three-week "gay tour" of Normandy and Paris, where they were feted by municipal officials and businessmen. The merry trip managed to overcome the sour note initially sounded by the teetotaling mayor of Los Angeles, who walked out of the welcoming banquet in Le Havre rather than toast to the president of France with champagne.[40]

Some Americans were impressed by the efforts to curb French rapacity. In July 1931 a number of tourists interviewed on their return to New York credited the office of tourism with having reduced prices there. A group of doctors said there was no evidence of overcharging in spas, and the American commissioner of labor reported that not only had the luxury tax been reduced, but that the national tourist office had also pressured hotels into reducing their rates. The prices of articles in stores were now plainly marked, he said, and there was only one price.[41]

But France's other efforts were more than matched by its European competitors. They, too, opened tourist offices in New York City and hired agents in other American cities.[42] Germany increased its advertising and had its railroads, hotels, and merchants band together to offer price reductions to tourists. Even the normally reticent English climbed on the bandwagon, mounting a publicity campaign whose slogan, "We must blow our own trumpet," was suggested by the popular Prince of Wales, the future King Edward VIII.[43]

The French were particularly upset over the apparent success of the Germans. In July 1932 a French newspaper columnist, lamenting the falloff in American tourism, said that the French had come to regard them as "succulent birds of passage . . . intended by Providence to be shot down while passing over France." Now they were flying higher and faster, passing over France and heading for Berlin.[44] When the Nazis took power in Germany in March 1933, they took out ads in the *Paris Herald* assuring American tourists: "The New Germany Welcomes You."[45]

— —

About two months later, in July 1933, the president of France opened the colossal new port facility at Cherbourg. Replete with the arms of New York City on its imposing classical Greek tower and a portrait of Ralph Waldo Emerson in its most honored position, it was intended to welcome American tourists in style, whisking them onto new Bugatti rail cars that would speed them to Paris in less than four hours.[46] Alas, there were only handfuls of tourists to whisk. Moreover, the United States had just gone off the gold standard, causing the dollar to fall by almost 40 percent, and many of those who did show up were distinctly parsimonious. That month the *New York Times* reported that none of the large Paris hotels were more than half full, that "the tourist centers of one-time 'gay Paree' are yawning emptily," and that "'to let' signs appear in display windows all along the rue de la Paix, the shopping street once so dear to the hearts of American women."[47]

The next month, faced with empty gambling casinos along the Riviera, the government finally allowed them to offer that American favorite, roulette. Still, Riviera casino earnings continued to plunge. Hotels there published fake guest lists to hide the fact that they were empty. Nice's most famous luxury hotels careened toward bankruptcy.[48]

Throughout the country, hotels continued to slash rates and eliminate the innumerable charges for "extras," such as soap, that had so annoyed Americans.[49] Rooms that were 125 francs a night in 1931 were down to 50 or 60 francs in 1934.[50] Paris's exclusive Hôtel Ritz, which had spent much of the 1920s shooing ordinary tourists away, sent Charles Ritz, son of the founder, to the United States to drum up business with the message "The Ritz is not so ritzy."[51] Some luxury restaurants revamped their menus to reduce their prices; those that did not became "ridiculously expensive" for most Americans, said the *New York Times*.[52]

These efforts hardly helped shake the common American perception that the French were a particularly mendacious and rapacious breed. "I don't like the French much," a Smith College junior wrote home in 1933. "They're too grasping, stubborn and narrowminded. And they don't think much of Americans either. They think we're a naive bunch of dumbbells. . . . They think we're all rich too. And they always give you the impression they are trying to get money out of you."[53] The writer Thomas Wolfe sounded a common theme when he wrote his brother that France was "one of the most comfortable and beautiful countries in the world," but he liked "the country much more than the people."[54] Moreover, the price cutting hardly kept pace with the falling value of the dollar and was certainly not enough to attract back the large middle- and upper-middle-class market that had emerged in the 1920s.[55]

The evaporation of the middle-class market was reflected on the North Atlantic. Most passenger lines abandoned "tourist third class," the cramped accommodations in the bowels of the ships that had been converted from "steerage" for poor immigrants into budget accommodation for the middle class and students.[56] The drop in upper-middle-class travel was reflected in plummeting bookings in the all-cabin-class (formerly second-class) ships that had been introduced in the 1920s to cater to them.[57] In May 1933 the United States Lines, which specialized in the middle-class market, retired its monster flagship, the *Leviathan*, because of a lack of bookings to France.[58] In Germany Hitler forced the country's two transatlantic shipping lines to merge into one. Mussolini did the same with the three Italian ones, and in 1934 the two major British lines, Cunard and White Star, joined together. Famous ships that just a few summers before had been jammed with middle- and upper-middle-class tourists were now sent to the scrap yard. The new Cunard White Star Line alone sent eight of them packing.[59]

Yet at the same time, new liners catering to the upper classes were sliding

Staircase and first-class salon on the SS *Paris*, the most popular French Line ship on the transatlantic crossing from the 1920s to the mid-1930s. © Museum of the City of New York, the Byron Collection (93.1.1.11985).

down the ways. The Italians launched two large new luxury liners, and the British began building two more, all aimed at the American market.[60] In May 1935 the French Line launched the sleek, predominantly first-class *Normandie*, the largest, fastest, and most luxurious liner in the world, for the New York–Cherbourg run.[61]

The construction of these monster liners owed a lot to the nations' competition for prestige. The Italian Line's *Rex* was originally to be called the *Dux*, in honor of Il Duce, Mussolini, who uncharacteristically demurred from accepting the honor. The French government subsidized construction of the *Normandie* mainly to wrest the transatlantic speed record back from the Germans, whose *Bremen* had captured it, while the British funded the *Queen Mary* to beat them both.[62] Yet the intense activity also indicated that upper-class tourism was not at all down-and-out. "They're going First

The immense first-class dining salon on the *Normandie*, which became the French Line flagship in 1935, with its famous glasswork by Lalique. © Museum of the City of New York, the Byron Collection (93.1.1.11875).

Class Again," said a Cunard White Star line advertisement in early 1934, "the trend back to First Class is growing!"[63]

The French Line certainly believed this and made first class on the *Normandie* unmatched in terms of elegance. The restaurant was three decks high, allowing formally attired passengers (first-class passengers "dressed" for dinner on all the lines) to make a grand entrance through twenty-foot-high bronze doors at the top level and sweep down a staircase into the football-field-length dining salon, which was lit by floor-to-ceiling illuminated-glass columns and fountains by Lalique. There they were presented with lunch and dinner menus that each offered over fifty choices, plus a large cold buffet of such dishes as foie gras, lobster mayonnaise, rib of beef, and saddle of lamb. An even grander staircase swept down from the ship's Grill to the Smoking Room and Grand Lounge, which featured twenty-foot-high tapestries and murals as well as hundreds of chairs upholstered in petit-point by Aubusson. The decor of every one of her 431 first-class staterooms was unique.[64]

— —

The decision to make the *Normandie* a predominantly first-class ship paid off, for the ship turned a profit from the day it was launched.[65] But the reason this luxury ship could do so well in such difficult economic times was that the Depression's impact on American travel overseas, like its toll back home, was unevenly distributed. Those who were the hardest hit by the Depression, industrial workers and farmers, had never been overseas tourists to begin with.[66] The affluent middle and upper-middle classes were much less prone to catastrophic loss of income, but they were swept by deep economic insecurity. Instead of expensive trips to Europe, they chose automobile touring in the United States and Canada for their holidays. The upper classes, though, were another matter, for they generally survived the Depression quite well. As the *New York Times* correspondent in Paris had predicted in November 1929, "those who know America and Americans best, remain persuaded that . . . rich Americans will remain rich and will travel."[67] Although the vagaries of their investment portfolios forced many of the upper-class expatriates, like the Murphys, to pack up and go home, a steady stream of still-wealthy upper-class tourists continued to travel to Europe, and especially France, to holiday in their usual locales.[68]

For them, the French connection stretched back to the mid-nineteenth century, when the desire to flee the latest crop of crass nouveaux riches led successive waves of upper-class Americans to flee to France, where life seemed more civilized. Friends and relatives from America would visit them regularly, spending months socializing at the spas, seaside resorts, races, and Paris soirées. This relentless pursuit of what Thorstein Veblen called "conspicuous leisure" helped distinguish them from the equally wealthy but more hardworking people climbing up the ladder beneath them. The playwright Elmer Rice captured this in his 1931 Broadway play, *Counsellor-at-Law*, which he wrote after a visit to Paris.[69] In it, the upper-class gentile wife of a wealthy Jewish lawyer of humble origins tries to break him from his workaholic habits and adopt an upper-class lifestyle by persuading him to take a trip to France with her. When a career crisis prevents his leaving, she sails nevertheless, on a French Line ship with a man from her own class, a leech with no gainful employment. On the voyage over, her luxurious cabin is always fully stocked with fine food, while her friend has fresh flowers delivered to it every day. Their pampered life of indolent leisure is brought into relief by references to how, as young boys, her husband and his Italian American law partner made the same transatlantic crossing with their immigrant parents in the miserable steerage accommodations below.

The persistence of leisure-class touring was chronicled faithfully in the Paris edition of the *New York Herald*, commonly called the *Paris Herald*. Since its founding in 1887 by the American expatriate socialite James Gordon Bennett Jr., it had slavishly reported the comings and goings of American "society" in France. It continued doing so into the 1930s, long after Bennett's death, turning out fawning reports of life in the resorts and spas to garner advertising revenue from their hotels. (A sign hung in its newsroom said, "IT NEVER RAINS IN NICE. THERE'S ALWAYS SNOW IN SWITZERLAND" and "ALL RESORT GEESE ARE SWANS.")[70] There, and in its short-lived competitor, the Paris edition of the *Chicago Tribune*, one reads of the Astors, Vanderbilts, Du Ponts, Goulds, Wideners, Drexels, Firestones, Dodges, and Morrows socializing at Paris's *Grande Semaine* of horse racing in June and peregrinating through the social seasons of seaside resorts such as Deauville, Le Touquet, and Biarritz. They were not workaholics. Stays of from three to five months were common, with at least a month or two in each of Paris and a resort or spa.[71] In June 1933, not long after the worst banking crisis in American history, which forced the government to close all the banks, the *Herald* reported that Thomas Lamont, the top partner in the JP Morgan Bank, whom many held responsible for the crisis, managed to slip away to France on the *Majestic* and book into the Ritz in Paris, just in time for the *Grande Semaine*. A few weeks later, Bernard Baruch, widely regarded as a financial genius for selling all his stocks, at an enormous profit, shortly before the Crash, also arrived at the Ritz, where he joined his wife before moving on to Vichy to take the cure.[72]

Typical of the more long-standing Francophiles was Sara Delano Roosevelt, the domineering, well-born mother of Franklin Delano Roosevelt, who had been visiting France regularly since 1867.[73] Although now in her late seventies and early eighties, she spent about four months of each summer in Paris, staying at the Hôtel George V, which had opened in 1929 designed specifically to attract the American carriage trade. In early May 1931, when she came down with pneumonia there, her son, then governor of New York, dropped everything and rushed over on the *Aquitania*, with his son Elliot, to visit her in the American Hospital in Neuilly. In April 1933 her sister, who had moved to Paris many years before, returned from her nephew's inauguration as president and announced that she had no intention of ever returning to the United States and would spend the rest of her days in Paris.[74]

Also typical of this class was Mary Peabody, a feisty member of Boston's Brahmin elite, who had been visiting France since she was a young woman in 1901. In September 1932, with her daughter, two of her daughter's friends, and fourteen pieces of luggage in tow, she boarded the ship to France in New York City and was delighted to find it full of acquaintances from Boston. Her diary lists many of the familiar Boston Brahmin names, including Theodore Sedgwick, whose ancestral namesake's diary of his trip to France in 1836 is in the same Boston archive that now holds hers.[75] On a subsequent trip the next June, she arrived in Paris alone. This time the falling dollar (for which, she wrote in her diary, she felt no responsibility, having voted Republican in November) led her to stay in a fine apartment on the Left Bank rather than in a luxury hotel. On her first morning there, as soon as she emerged from getting some cash from a bank in the Right Bank, she ran into an American acquaintance. Then, even before she made it to a luncheon date with another friend, she encountered ten other people she knew. The next day, her diary says, she and a friend visited the Glades, an American couple who had bought and restored "a lovely chateau, really very grand," just outside Paris. After lunching there with a number of other American visitors, they were driven in the Glades' limousine to Versailles, where they took the train to Paris, arriving in time to watch the legendary Fred Perry play in the French tennis championship matches at Auteuil (now Roland Garros). That night they saw American friends who had come up to see them from Pau, a southwestern town where the British and American horsy set congregated. From then on, her stay was a head-spinning round of teas, dinners, and visits with other leisure-class Americans. All told, during her two-week stay in Paris, she records meeting well over forty other Americans there, all undoubtedly upper class.[76]

Men were also major players in this kind of socializing. In October 1935 Joseph Grew—who, like President Roosevelt, was a graduate of the Groton School with an impeccable eastern establishment pedigree—came to Paris on a holiday from his post as American ambassador to Japan. His daily routine revolved around golfing and dining with people with such names as Kermit Roosevelt, "Kippy" Tuck, and "Bunny" Carter. Grew and his wife lunched twice at Carter's château in Senlis and dined at the Versailles mansion of Elsie Mendl, an American woman who had married a wealthy Englishman, Sir Charles Mendl. Some days later Grew noted in his diary: "Called on Lady Mendl at the Ritz; found her in bed surrounded by gigolos, looking rather chic and pretty. She must be about 70 though she owns to only 52 I believe. Her much younger brother was in my class at Groton when she was dancing on the stage as Elsie de Wolf."[77] Perhaps Grew had her in mind when, speaking to the American Club in Paris, he said, "Can you therefore wonder why I love to return to Paris, why every American loves to return to Paris . . . because of Paris herself, Paris the beautiful, Paris the immortal, Paris the aged in wisdom and experience, Paris the always young."[78]

Younger members of the social elite kept coming to France too. Some continued the upper-class tradition of taking long tours of Europe after college graduation, but not in groups of one hundred—that was for the middle classes. In 1932 William Harlan Hale, an obviously well-connected young man, spent the whole year after graduation traveling by auto through France and other parts of Europe with a friend and had the *Atlantic Monthly* publish his rather pretentious memoir of it.[79] In 1933 Franklin D. Roosevelt Jr. and seven of his upper-class friends did the college graduates one better. They came to Paris after graduating from high school—Groton, to be exact. It was not, of course, young Roosevelt's first trip to France. Like his father, he had been going there since he was very young. He would return four years later, on a honeymoon trip, after marrying one of the Du Ponts.[80]

On the other side of the upper-class coin were those who were in the upper echelon in wealth, but not social standing. For instance, Mildred Cox Howes and her husband, a wealthy couple from the prosperous Boston suburb of Brookline, traveled to France five times in the years from 1931 to 1938. Their crossings, on a number of different liners, were like most first-class passages—bridge and "horse races" every afternoon, followed by late-afternoon cocktails and "dressing for dinner."[81] However, when they arrived in Paris, unlike the social elite, they did no socializing, for they knew no one there. Instead, after checking into the Ritz, they would seek out the usual tourist sights—the Louvre, Notre-Dame, and Folies Bergère—and hire chauffeured limousines to take them to out-of-town sights such as the palaces in Versailles and Fontainebleau. In 1937 they arrived with Mildred's friend Idie, who had an elite American friend in Paris who put a car and chauffeur at their disposal. However, there were no invitations to dine with Idie's friend, and no doors were opened to the kind of circles in which Joseph Grew had just been circulating. Instead, they used the car and driver to once again visit Versailles and other sights, and to take them to dine in expensive restaurants.[82]

— —

The persistence of rich people's tourism was reflected in the steadily increasing number of tourists bringing their own automobiles, until by 1938 the transatlantic liners' holds were so crammed with cars that prudent travelers booked space for them six months in advance.[83] Many brought their own chauffeurs with them as well, but this did not always work out. In 1930 the Boston Brahmin Pauline Ames Plimpton wrote her mother from Paris that she had run into Mrs. Charles Sumner Bird, another woman of their set. "Poor old Mrs. Bird," she said, "she certainly has bitten off more than she can chew. Two granddaughters over here, one with dog, a tutor, a chauffeur who can't speak French—Mrs. Bird can't either—a car which bored the granddaughter, and then trying to find proper French families."[84] Hiring French chauffeurs and limousines could also be problematic.[85] Pauline Plimpton wrote her mother that her father-in-law was finding his ten-day visit to Paris "rather tedious" because their hired chauffeur did not speak English. "Mr. Plimpton . . . doesn't understand one word of French," she said rather condescendingly. "You should hear him try to say Bois."[86]

Those who drove their own cars could literally run into much more serious trouble. One cause of the problems was the most attractive thing about older French highways, the long rows of trees that line them. In May 1930 Mr. and Mrs. David Adler, two socially prominent Chicagoans, headed back to Paris in a light drizzle with her at the wheel after lunching in the cathedral town of Evreux. The car spun out on a slick part of the road and crashed into a tree, killing her. That August the car driven by the twenty-two-year-old son of the chairman of the board of the Remington Arms Company, a grandnephew of John D. Rockefeller Sr., was hurtling down the Bordeaux–Bayonne highway at high speed when it suddenly swerved from the road and hit a large oak tree with terrific force, instantly killing the driver and severely injuring his passenger, a young man from Kansas.[87] The French tourist bureau in New York City may not have been wise to entitle their press release encouraging Americans to take their cars to France "American Motorists Find French Highways Thrilling."[88]

— —

By the summer of 1933, although the Depression was still at its nadir, enough of the tony set had made it safely to their traditional watering holes to inspire optimism that the good old days had already returned. They rented large villas in seaside resorts such as Le Touquet, on the English Channel, and Biarritz, on the Atlantic, where they rode, golfed, played tennis, and visited the casinos with French Rothschilds, British aristocrats, and other fashionable international counterparts. At Deauville, down the coast from Le Touquet, casino receipts were up 44 percent over 1932, largely, it was said, because of the Americans.[89] A guidebook for less wealthy Americans (traveling with children, of all things) called high-season Deauville "unbelievably expensive—absurdly so. . . . No one ever seems to go to bed. All the famous names you've ever heard of—parading before your eyes. The most wonderful clothes and cars and jewels you've ever seen, and the most beautiful women." Of Biarritz, it said, "You thought you had seen all the fashionables in the world at Le Toquet and Deauville, but here is another crowd, no less wealthy, no less bored, no less cosmopolitan. . . . You'll gasp at the gowns and jewels."[90] In May 1933 an American stock brokerage firm confidently opened an office with a stock board in Aix-les-Bains, the spa in the foothills of the Alps long favored by wealthy Americans.[91]

But it was the Riviera that outshone the rest, particularly among the less stodgy set. Its reputation as a winter resort for the international upper class had developed during the previous century, when the winter sun was strong enough to spread good cheer, but not powerful enough to afflict one with an ugly tan, the mark of poor people who worked outdoors. In the 1920s, however, tanned skin became fashionable and the summer season gained popularity. The summer tours taken by young middle-class Americans now routinely included a week in what the *New York Times* in 1932 called this "paradise of luxury, splendor, gambling and other naughtiness."[92]

By then, the Depression had knocked out the underpinnings from this kind of middle-class touring, causing a severe setback for the hotel industry in Nice, the most popular stopover. The collapse of the British pound in 1931 was another blow, restricting the flow of British fleeing their gloomy winters. The take at the huge seaside casino that the American Frank Jay Gould opened in Nice in 1929 plunged by over 75 percent in four years. One-quarter of the city's first-class hotels, sixteen in all, closed. Most shocking, in 1936 and 1937 the three famed luxury hotels that reigned in Cimiez, in the hills overlooking the city—the Grand, the Majestic, and Queen Victoria's favorite, the Regina—shut their doors. A local newspaper called the neighborhood "Cimiez la Morte" (Cimiez the Dead). Down the coast in Menton, almost all of the first-class hotels, eighteen of them, closed.[93]

But the situation was not nearly as bad as it looked. What had happened was that upper-class Americans, along with the rest of the international set, now avoided Nice, which was engulfed in labor and political strife, and stayed away from Monte Carlo, which the *New York Times* called "too small and prim for the active generation of today." Menton, which had developed a dreary reputation as a place where old people went to die, also went out of fashion.[94] But, instead, each winter the elite rented villas in the hills overlooking other attractive towns along the coast. In Cannes they played golf, tennis, and polo during the day and congregated at night at the new Palm-Beach Casino, which, after it opened in 1929, became an international byword for upper-class socializing. By the winter of 1935, hoteliers and restaurateurs in other Riviera resort towns were also applauding the return of their "Old Guard" clientele. The next winter seemed even better, as dining rooms and casinos all along the coast filled up again.[95]

Meanwhile, the summer season maintained its newfound popularity among the upper class, despite an influx of campers and other un-chic vacationers after June 1936, when the leftist Popular Front government made fifteen-day paid holidays for workers mandatory.[96] The Prince of Wales gave Cannes a great boost by spending the summer of 1935 there, trailed by hundreds of journalists, photographers, and tourists.[97] Rose Kennedy, wife of Joseph Kennedy, the ambassador to Britain, spent all of the summer of 1938 on the Riviera, returning to London only in mid-September, after a stopover at the Ritz in Paris, where she habitually shopped for clothes.[98]

Some of the upper-crust Americans would take the luxury *Train Bleu*, the "train of paradise," from Paris to Cannes. Others would motor down; while still others would arrive directly from New York on the superb new Italian liners, the *Conte di Savoia* and the *Rex* (called the most romantic ship ever built), which stopped at Cannes and Villefranche on their way to Genoa.[99] Simon Guggenheim, the millionaire philanthropist and art collector, arrived in Cannes on the *Conte di Savoia* in June 1936, on the same day that the ex–Prince of Wales, now Edward VIII, the new king of England, announced that he would again take his summer holidays there.[100] That December Wallis Simpson, his American bride-to-be, sat in her rented villa in Cannes, with the world's press camped outside her door, waiting for him to announce his fateful decision to abandon the throne in order to marry her. Immediately after the broadcast, he flew to Cannes to join her. Later the

The sunny "veranda" of the *Rex* in the mid-1930s. Called "the most romantic ship ever built," the Italian liner took Americans directly from New York City to the Riviera. © Museum of the City of New York, the Byron Collection (93.1.1.13448).

management of the Palm-Beach Casino let it be known that the ex-king, now the Duke of Windsor, had orchestrated a dramatic meeting there with Winston Churchill, a regular at its tables, to publicly acknowledge his appreciation for Churchill's support during the abdication crisis.[101]

— —

France's special place in the hearts of the upper class was reflected in the money they gave to preserve its architectural heritage. Thomas Cochran, a wealthy New Yorker, funded the restoration of Napoléon's triumphal arch at the Carrousel, in front of the Louvre palace. Edward Tuck, who liked France so much he moved there permanently, helped restore Malmaison, Napoléon and Josephine's delightful château outside of Paris, as well as other monuments.[102] Others, such as Anne Morgan, daughter of the bank-

21

ing mogul J. Pierpont Morgan, and the social monarch Mrs. William K. Vanderbilt, helped rebuild the hundreds of towns in northern France that had been destroyed during World War I.[103]

By far the most prominent of these benefactors was John D. Rockefeller Jr., who in 1924 made rebuilding the French architectural treasures one of his pet projects. Thanks mainly to his contributions, the cathedral in Reims, a Gothic masterpiece that had been almost completely destroyed during the war, was painstakingly rebuilt and reconsecrated in 1931.[104] He also helped restore the Palace of Fontainebleau, outside of Paris, and built a hospital in Lyon. Well over half of the $3.5 million he spent in France by 1936 went to helping restore the Palace of Versailles. When he arrived there in June of that year, the president of France gave him the Legion of Honor and the Versailles city authorities renamed the huge square in front of the palace "place Rockefeller."[105]

— —

By 1937 upper-class tourism to France was more or less fully revived. Americans again dominated the guest lists of the Ritz and other luxury hotels.[106] The Hôtel Plaza Athénée, which had closed in 1934, had reopened and was renting expensive apartments to Americans. Fleets of limousines carried Americans to villas in Deauville and to take the cures in Vichy and Aix-les-Bains.[107] But Americans back home were hardly aware of their extravagances, for the upper class had learned to keep a low profile during hard times. Memories were still fresh of the outrage sparked by the extravagant costume party thrown in New York City by Bradley Martin in 1897, in the midst of a terrible industrial depression, when the press told of guests arriving at a mock court of Versailles in the Waldorf Hotel dressed in costumes costing upward of ten thousand dollars.

On the other hand, stories of luxury consumption went down well with the public if they involved celebrities, especially those in entertainment. During the 1920s celebrities had displaced the pre–World War I social elite (the kind of household names who had gone down on the *Titanic*) as the ones whose travels garnered media attention. A new breed of professional "public relations" men had arisen to take advantage of the explosive growth in newspapers, magazines, movies, and radio to help them bathe fully and continuously in the glow of publicity. In the 1930s newspapers and movie newsreels regularly featured pictures of beautifully dressed celebrities answering reporters' anodyne questions on the decks of sleek transatlantic liners.[108]

With stories of Depression hardship still appearing on the same pages, the old social elite were more than happy to cede the limelight to the stars. They could even look benignly on those of their celebrated fellow passengers whose behavior they regarded as rather crude. After meeting the Hollywood character actor Wallace Beery in the first-class lounge of the *Ile de France*, Mary Peabody wrote in her diary, "He and his beautiful chorus girl wife . . . were as common as could be and a strange and rather interesting product of American life—as they did very well and were likable. . . ."[109]

By the time the handsome film star Robert Taylor visited Paris in 1937, the celebrities' publicity departments were hard at work in France itself. His studio's Paris publicist gathered a group of reporters to accompany Taylor as he took "a night's leave from fame," starting with the can-can dancers in

Among the many celebrities who flocked to France in the 1930s was the high-living ex-mayor of New York City Jimmy Walker, shown leaving the town hall in Cannes after marrying showgirl Betty Compton there in 1933. Courtesy of the Library of Congress.

Montmartre and finishing with the traditional early morning onion soup at Les Halles, the all-night wholesale food market.[110] Clark Gable was taken to be photographed on the sidewalk terrace of the Dôme, the famed Montparnasse café.[111] In August 1937 the PR men at NBC Radio assembled reporters to meet the immensely popular radio comedian Jack Benny and his wife, who were passing through Paris on the way to Cannes. This allowed Benny to divulge to them that he was "having a great time."[112]

Other celebrities did not need PR men. In mid-July the colorful ex-mayor of New York City Jimmy Walker, an ex-songwriter and bon vivant who had been forced to resign under a cloud of corruption charges, married Broadway showgirl Betty Compton in a private ceremony in Cannes, where he had taken refuge from corruption investigators. After the mayor of Cannes offered his congratulations, in French, and Walker responded with, "What's he talking about?" the doors were thrown open to a horde of reporters and photographers. The bride smiled graciously, but the groom broke into an uncharacteristic scowl.[113] Five weeks later, though, in Paris, he and Compton emerged smiling from his suite in the George V and, explaining to the mob of reporters that he "had a yen for Paris," he led them to Harry's New York Bar, where he genially downed a number of drinks.[114]

The publicity surrounding celebrity visits to France inevitably portrayed France as a destination for pleasure, rather than cultural uplift. Never was it said that Walker, Benny, Taylor, or Beery ever set foot in the Louvre, Notre-Dame, or any other serious cultural site. They all seemed to be going to France only, as Benny said, to have "a great time." With the upper classes concentrating on socializing, it was left mainly to those middle-class travelers who could make it to France to keep the flames of cultural tourism flickering.

TWO

The Return of the Middle Classes

We . . . travel, not that we may broaden and enrich our minds, but that we may pleasantly forget we exist.

—ALDOUS HUXLEY, *Along the Road*

It was not at all clear at its outset that the Great Depression was indeed going to be the "Great" one. Indeed, it actually took about two years for its full impact to be felt in the middle-class travel market.[1] Clara Laughlin's Chicago-based travel agency, which specialized in European tours for upper-middle-class women, had its best year ever in 1930, and in 1931 she opened an office in Paris.[2]

Even some of the companies that aimed at the lower end of the middle-class market managed to survive. The writer Bergen Evans spent the summer of 1931 as an "assistant courier" for a company whose fast-paced, rock-bottom-priced tours of Europe "were not designed for the rich and certainly not for the idle." As they assembled in London to tour the Continent in special trains and caravans of buses, Evans was surprised that once "they realized that the eight hundred and sixty frenzied people milling about the boat train at the Liverpool Street station were part of the same hegira . . . they did not, one and all, turn and flee." When they reached Paris, over two hundred of them were sent to Cologne, leaving 640 to invade Munich, sweep through Switzerland and Austria, dash down through Italy to Naples, and rush back up through Nice, Marseille, and Avignon to Paris again, where they stopped, finally, for six days. Before then, they had rarely stayed in one place for more than a night. All told, nineteen of the thirty days between their departure from London and arrival in Paris were spent on trains or boats or buses. "Most of the clients," he recalled, "were not sure where they were, and some were not sure where they had been."[3]

By the gloomy summer of 1932, however, tours such as Evans's had practically disappeared. Clara Laughlin had to close her new office in Paris. The number of Americans visiting France continued to fall until 1934, when fewer than 100,000 Americans showed up—less than one-third the number who had come in 1929.[4] By then, France was in its own depression, and reports of violent clashes between mobs of leftists and rightists on the streets of Paris hardly helped its fortunes as a tourist destination.

French officials were particularly concerned over the disappearing middle-class tourists, who had been so numerous in the 1920s. In early 1935 a vigorous new high commissioner of tourism, Roland Marcel, set out to attract them back. He, too, regarded his countrymen's reputation for greed and chicanery as a major impediment to this and mounted another anti-gouging campaign. Hotels and restaurants were implored to abide by their published rates. Paris taxi drivers who overcharged tourists would have their licenses suspended. A "Trouble Bureau" was set up in Paris to handle tourist complaints, and local *syndicats d'initiative* (chambers of commerce) in the rest of the country were told to turn themselves into "a nation-wide complaint bureau" for tourists.[5] (Some eyebrows were raised when 60 percent of that year's complaints came from French people, but Americans ranked next, with over 20 percent.)[6]

American tourist traffic began to climb again in 1935 and 1936, but largely because the American economy was recovering.[7] In late September 1936, the new French left-wing government, the Popular Front, gave middle-class tourism a further boost by devaluing the franc by one-third.[8] It also tried to abolish tipping, substituting service charges on hotel and restaurant bills.[9] In 1937, when Paris hosted another International Exposition, the government again tried, with limited success, to force tourist hotels and restaurants to give up their highly priced ancient right to gouge exposition visitors.[10] (The exposition's official report lamented that France remained "the country of the unexpected supplements, of surprise taxes, of tips solicited a bit too visibly.")[11] Still, the number of American tourists kept rising. That summer the American Express office in Paris was swamped by Americans cashing traveler's checks, changing money, and making travel arrangements. Each day over a thousand people went there to see if they had mail.[12] By the end of the year, the number of American tourists was back up to 200,000, with most of the increase coming from the price-sensitive upper-middle class.[13]

— —

The long lines of them at the American Express wickets exemplified the contrast between their experience and that of the kind of upper-class personage discussed in the previous chapter. The upper class received their mail in the privacy of their banks' corresponding Paris branches, where they withdrew cash against the letters of credit they used when traveling abroad.[14] But the experiences had diverged from the outset, on the transatlantic crossing. While the upper classes mingled with celebrities in the magnificent salons and staterooms of the new luxury liners, many of the middle classes would sail on older all-second-class (now called cabin-class) liners where the wealthy and the celebrated were conspicuous by their absence.[15] After Mary Mahony, a Smith College junior, appraised the men aboard the French Line's dowdy *Lafayette*, she wrote her sister, "Really, I don't know when I've ever seen such a rum lot." She said the other young women in her group had stooped to "putting their hooks out" for someone who called himself the "Comte de la Falaise," under the false impression that he was the film star Gloria Swanson's husband.[16]

The often-underpowered cabin-class ships were also more prone to the pitching, yawing, and heaving that can make life at sea so miserable. By the end of that first day at sea, the Smith women's interest in celebrities had flagged, for practically all of them were seasick. "I felt like saying," wrote Mahony, "'Captain, captain, stop the ship, I want to get out and walk.'"[17] A few years earlier, soon after Howard Sharp, a New Jersey businessman, sailed to Europe with 111 other Rotarians on the United States Lines' aging all-second- and -third-class *America*, he wrote in his diary that he felt himself "slipping." He spent most of the next five days in his cabin, emerging mainly to catch some fresh air on the cold, windswept deck. Unable to keep any food down, he did not make it to the dining salon until the sixth evening, for the captain's dinner that traditionally marks the last night at sea.[18] In March 1938 the composer Glenway Wescott, sailing to France aboard the *President Harding*, tried describing the indescribable. "I've changed, changed, for I was seasick for almost two days," he wrote in his diary. "The pressure in the pit of the stomach, the vacuous belching, the hot and cold, the stupidity, the exhaustion."[19] That June a desperate thirty-seven-year-old woman from Ohio leaped overboard from the deck of a heaving transatlantic liner. After she was rescued by a lifeboat, she locked herself in her cabin, opened the porthole, and jumped into the water again, forcing the ship to again circle back to pick her up. "Mother's so sick," her fourteen-year-old daughter explained.[20]

Even when they sailed on the more luxurious liners, the middle-class passengers would be packed into second- and third-class cabins in the cramped and stuffy spaces in the interior of the ship or below sea level, with none of the fresh air or views of the horizon that help combat seasickness. In September 1935, when a Smith College group crossing in second class on the new *Normandie* had a group picture taken, one of them noted in her diary, "Many of us looked very sunk and of various shades of green."[21]

Shipboard experiences differed as well. On the luxury liners, second- and third-class passengers were so rigidly segregated from first-class ones that they never even saw each other. The Smith students were thrilled to hear that a number of movie stars were in first class on the *Normandie*, but, one of them wrote, there was "nary a chance of getting a look at them."[22] But at least the *Normandie* got them across the Atlantic in a mere four and a half days. The older, slower boats for the rest of the middle classes could take up to ten days. Their passengers would discover another downside of ocean travel: mind-bending boredom. The schoolteacher Jan Gelb spent much of her first full day at sea enthralled by the ocean. Relaxing on the upper deck, she wrote, "It is beautiful here, to watch the water, the foam and the spray. In late afternoons the water is a mild blue and the foam pale green and opalescent. But in the morning it's bright and piercing and the foam dazzling white." Two days later, though, while sitting in the same spot, she wrote, "This begins to bore me. The ocean is beautiful but one can't forever watch the ocean. I could enjoy teaching 50 kids their 'one ands' right this minute!"[23] After dinner there was little to do but watch a second-rate movie, play bridge in the lounge, or return to one's reading. British ships were said to be especially boring. A stupefying silence would descend upon them after dinner, and most people would turn in by 10:00 PM.[24]

Once in France, the middle classes also had to watch their expenses much more closely than the wealthy, particularly before the 1937 devaluation. From the moment they disembarked at Le Havre or Cherbourg and faced the crowd of blue-clad porters demanding what seemed to be outrageous sums for taking their luggage through customs onto the boat train, middle-class tourists were painfully aware of how different France now was from the 1920s. "The American tourist who lit his cigarette with a five-franc note and asked jocularly, 'How much is that in real money?' is no longer to be found in Paris," said the *New York Times* in October 1933.[25] Frugality was now the norm, and middle-class tourists were not ashamed to be seen with guidebooks such as *Through Europe on Two Dollars a Day* and *France on $50*.[26] They now tended to stay in Paris for only four or five days, instead of two or three weeks, and to search out inexpensive restaurants. Paris prices "are impossible," John Gutknecht, a Chicago municipal court judge, wrote in his diary in July 1934. He and his wife felt lucky to have found a small restaurant not far from American Express (with "no foreigners") where he had a "very good" meal of melon, roast beef, artichokes, tomatoes, bread, and wine for eleven francs (about seventy-five cents.) Unlike their middle-class predecessors of the 1920s, who went everywhere by cab, or the upper class, who had chauffeured cars, the Gutknechts got around by bus, tram, and subway.[27]

— —

The Gutknechts were fortunate in that most of their encounters with the French went smoothly, for avoiding unpleasant encounters with the French was a constant concern for middle-class visitors. Upper-class socialites could insulate themselves by plugging into the social networks that awaited them. The unconnected rich still had chauffeurs, fawning employees of luxury hotels, and other such servants to protect them. Middle-class tourists traveling independently had recourse to none of these. They faced the prospect of using their halting French to deal with rapacious taxi drivers, stone-faced bus drivers, and incomprehensible railroad agents—of asking directions from passersby who responded with quizzical shrugs and walked on. All of this was compounded by the widespread conviction that the French were cheating them at every turn.

The best way to avoid such situations was to employ the services of travel agencies, whose prepaid tours had been popular in the 1920s. Although the Depression practically eliminated the inexpensive all-inclusive group tours of the kind that Bergen Evans helped lead, Thomas Cook & Son and American Express survived by shifting their focus upward and providing prepaid tours for individual upper-middle-class travelers. Cook's clients would be met at Le Havre or Cherbourg by an agent who would shepherd them through customs and put them on the boat train to Paris. Another agent in Paris would put them in a cab to their hotel, while at the hotel yet another one would take care of the cab fare.[28] American Express had agents stationed at the major train stations who would give clients their coupons for hotels and meals and hire cabs to take them to their hotels.[29]

The agencies also arranged for trips and guides to places outside Paris. When some Smith College junior-year-abroad students decided to take their 1931 Christmas vacation in the South of France and Italy, American Express in Paris made their hotel reservations, arranged for private cars and guides to pick them up at each stop, and supplied them with a guide who accompanied them on the whole trip.[30] Even on tours involving second-class rail and second-class hotels, agents would accompany travelers between hotels and railway stations and arrange for guided tours, usually by private chauffeur, at every destination.[31] Unlike the imperious martinets who marched the large tour groups about, these individual guides were often personable and charming. The Frenchman who guided a group of Smith students through the Rhone valley in the South of France in September 1930 presented each of them with a picture of himself when they parted, asking them "never to forget the Rhone Valley, where the sky is always blue and every breath of air a caress."[32]

The diary of Colin Kay, a middle-aged businessman from suburban Larchmont, New York, who toured Europe alone in 1937, shows how helpful these travel agents could be, especially to tourists wary of French predators. His worst fears about French greed and mendacity were confirmed even before he arrived in France, when he went to the French consulate in London to get a visa. There, his diary says, "I found how dishonest some French people are and greedy too," when the visa clerks tried to overcharge him by two pence for his visa.[33] Things did not improve when he arrived in Calais on the steamer from Dover. He wrote, "I got a taxi to the railroad station (called Gare) and put my suit case in the taxi and as I reached for my hand bag a porter took it and put it in the taxi and I gave him a Frank [sic]. He held up two fingers and said two francs and I paid no attention to him and felt like saying something to him—Greedy type and plenty of them in France."[34]

Luckily for Kay, though, he had booked his tour of France with Cook's, who had a room waiting for him in the Hôtel Cosmos in Paris. When he pulled up in a taxi, someone from Cook's was there to tell him how much to pay the driver, "who seemed satisfied and tipped his hat to me." Cook's also told him exactly how much the hotel room would cost and how many days (five) he should stay in Paris. He was also very pleased with the modestly priced second-class hotel into which Cook's had booked him. He especially liked the fact that one of its two dining rooms was set aside for English speakers and that while the typical French breakfast of rolls and coffee was included in the room price, one could, as he did, pay a supplement and have ham or bacon and eggs too. Taking Cook's day tours was also, he said, "most enjoyable." On his first three days in Paris, he took their all-day tours of the city, Fontainebleau, and Versailles. The wisdom of doing so seemed confirmed on his last day there when he went, unescorted, to the International Exposition and found it "disappointing." When he checked out of the hotel, he was greatly relieved to see that tips were included in the credit slip Cook's provided to settle the bill.[35]

— —

Most middle-class visitors to France were first-timers who, soon after arriving in France, were confronted with some puzzling things for which neither American Express nor Cook's could prepare them. The most obvious one was the function of the bidets in their hotel rooms. "Oh what a mistake we made about the little bathtub for the feet or what not," Jan Gelb wrote in her diary of her and her mother's first encounter with one in their Paris hotel room.[36] Discussing "this delicate topic" in his budget guidebook to France, Sydney Clark said, somewhat obliquely, "To the French, a bidet is a real bathtub and any American who cannot learn to use it is merely stupid. . . . Any dictionary by merely translating the word bidet ('nag' or pony) gives virtually full directions for its use."[37] Eugene Fodor's 1936 guidebook was equally circumspect:

> There are a large number of new hotels in Paris where every room has a separate "cabinet de toilette" with a wash basin each for the upper and lower parts of the body and a separate W.C. Only the bath tub has been forgotten everywhere. On the other hand, the aforesaid vessel for the hygiene of the southern portion of the anatomy is all the more in evidence.[38]

Bergen Evans said that when word of what bidets were really for swept through his tour group, it "shocked them, and confirmed their darkest suspicions."[39]

Rarely mentioned, but equally disconcerting, especially for American women, were the public urinals—the famed pissoirs—on the sidewalks of French cities. In many places these consisted of little more than a sheet of iron, stretching from shoulders to knees, behind which men nonchalantly did their business. In Paris women tourists would be nonplussed to see men quickly step behind one of the small mushroom-shaped structures and then quickly emerge while still buttoning their flies.[40]

As Fodor implied, French standards of personal hygiene could also be unsettling. The first thing Marie Hulsag noticed when her ship docked in Le Havre in August 1930 was how "dirty" and "disheveled" the porters were. Then, in Paris she found that, like the porters, the taxi drivers were "dirty and bearded."[41] Americans were particularly sensitive on this score because during the 1920s and 1930s they were bombarded with advertisements for soap, toothpastes, and cosmetics that made them extremely conscious of personal cleanliness. Newspapers, magazines, and radio stations were awash in cartoons and stories of people whose romances or careers had been ruined by body odor or bad breath—the dreaded "B.O." or "halitosis." (Just in case they forgot, the *Paris Herald* carried large Listerine advertisements saying, "Did you bring HALITOSIS to Europe with you?")[42] To come from the land of the daily shower or bath, where underwear and socks were changed every day, to a country where these events occurred much less frequently (*Fodor's* said French hoteliers regarded the desire for a daily bath as "a crazy foreign foible") could be disconcerting, if not disgusting.[43] A group of Smith College women who arrived for a three-month stay with French families in Grenoble were shocked to learn that they would only be allowed to bathe twice a week. A resident American told them they would now be acquiring "French atmosphere."[44] Betty Wells, a Mount Holyoke student, told her family in Boston that she was greatly relieved that her landlady was "spicky neat" and "horribly disapproving of the dirty charac- teristics of her own race."[45] In 1936 Mary Cahill, another Smith junior, wrote home, "You can't appreciate American plumbing till you come to France. No hot water—the funniest toilets you've seen." She was especially outraged at the practice of hotels below the luxury level charging to use bathrooms. "It cost some of the girls 35 cents to take a bath in Paris," she wrote. "Joyce said it's a wonder they don't charge you a franc for every breath of French air."[46]

— —

As in the 1920s, Paris's reputation as the sensual capital of the Western world remained a major attraction to middle-class tourists. Until Prohibi- tion was repealed in 1933, the crossing provided many young middle-class tourists with their first tastes of something illicit in the United States, French wine and spirits. Jan Gelb first drank champagne on the French Line ship *De Grasse* and saved the cork as a souvenir of that fine moment.[47] Some reveled in drinking's legality. Two recent college graduates, William Harlan Hale and his friend, each ordered a bottle of *vin rouge* during their first meal ashore and, according to Hale, "suddenly [made] the astounding discovery that drinking has no connection with sin and morality."[48] Other young people felt the need to be apologetic to parents back home. A Smith College student wrote home from Paris in 1930, "All along the streets there are bars with tables in the sidewalk. If you get thirsty you sit down and have a drink. It is impossible to get a glass of water fit to drink. So we have given up water. We drink wine and beer with our meals. It was hard to get used to. At first I hated the white and red wine but now I almost like them."[49] When Frances Hurrey, a Mount Holyoke student, confessed to her mother that she had enjoyed wine with her meals in Paris restaurants, she received stern admonitions not to drink too much of it.[50] Betty Wells responded to her parents' similar warnings by assuring them that she was not "getting to be a depraved and drunken sotte." The wine glasses were small, she said, and the wine "doesn't even warm my gullet *much less* make me dizzy! . . . and don't you know that wine is indispensable because it is a regulator of constipa-

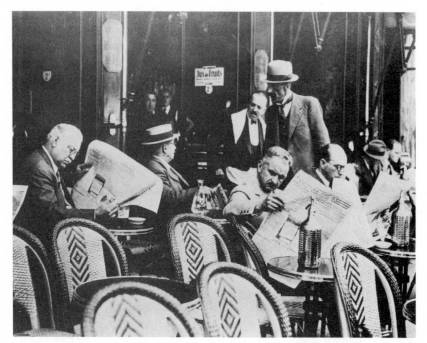

A sidewalk café in Paris with dour-looking Parisians in the early 1930s. Americans took great pleasure in drinking legally in outdoor terraces such as this, something that was very rare in the United States. Courtesy of the Library of Congress.

tion?" She had drunk a glass of champagne, she said, and it was not at all "insidious" and "potent." Moreover, one of the wines served at a dinner party was "the most beautiful thing I have ever tasted—a luscious dark amber, smooth, heavy, and every little sip glowed way down inside like mellow fire."[51]

Sex was also a major attraction. Searching for it in suitably nonthreatening circumstances, though, could be a problem. John Gutknecht and his wife were greatly disappointed when they ventured out to sample risqué Paris nightlife on their own. They intended to start off at the Folies Bergère, but when they emerged from a mediocre dinner at a restaurant near there, she was "disgusted" at a "pick-up couple" on the street and they left the neighborhood. They then took a cab down to the Champs-Elysées, where they saw plenty of sidewalk cafés, but none of the cabarets and dance halls they were looking for. The cabbie then took them up to Montmartre, but the place he suggested, the "Paris Follies," looked "too tough." They finally ended up in a regular café, reading the newspapers.[52]

Thanks to her well-developed powers of imagination, Helen Keller, the famous blind and deaf author and speaker, was more successful than the Gutknechts in plugging into sexual Paris. In a journal she kept during a visit there in January 1937, she described how, on a nighttime walk down the Champs-Elysées, she and her assistant, Polly Thompson, were excited to "pass three cocottes [prostitutes] awaiting their paramours." The next night, at Maxim's, the expensive restaurant that had been as renowned for the courtesans who congregated there as for its food, she was disappointed to find that "that sometimes gay, naughty café" had "mended its ways" and was "patronized by good Paris society."[53]

Most tourists searching for safe titillation would take one of the "Paris by Night" tours, which regained their popularity in the mid-1930s. The full tour would take tourists up to Montmartre, where the first stop would usually be the famed dance hall the Moulin Rouge. Its stage show had been replaced by movies, but visitors would be suitably shocked by its crowded dance floor, where young white Parisiennes could be seen paying black-skinned gigolos to dance with them, and could peer at the prostitutes who patrolled the halls around it. The next stop was around the corner at the decidedly more wicked-looking Bal Tabarin, to watch lusty young women expose their thighs and bottoms performing the "can-can." Then the tourist groups would move on to an "Apache" dance hall, where rough-looking patrons would fling their women around on the dance floor and stage prearranged fights, supposedly with rival suitors. The buses then took them across the river, to the Left Bank, where sexy women sang doleful songs for them in a basement cabaret and thinly veiled dancers performed for them at the "Arabian Mosque." Then it was across the river again to the Lido, on the Champs-Elysées, billed as "the world's most luxurious night club." The last stop would be Les Halles, for the traditional early morning onion soup.[54] By the summer of 1936, demand was so high that every evening American Express was filling fifteen busloads of tourists for a truncated version of the tour, where five dollars bought a visit to three of the nightclubs, two glasses of champagne, and one cup of Turkish coffee.[55]

American Express would also arrange tickets to the Folies Bergère or the Casino de Paris, the two big music halls whose elaborate lighting, scenery, costumes, and nudity *Fodor's* called "a dazzling Niagara of eroticism."[56] The Folies Bergère in particular, with its array of bare-breasted women, allowed tourists to feel they were seeing "naughty" things that were forbidden in the United States. Not everyone was impressed, or titillated. Colin Kay wrote in his diary:

About 20 nude women who only wore a sort of fig leaf danced very poorly and I was disgusted as they were a blasé lot and not one a good enough figure for an artist to want to pose for him. As far as I'm concerned I think the Folies are a grossly exaggerated show and I have seen sincere, cleaner shows in NY for 50 cents.[57]

Sydney Clark's guidebook wondered why "no single institution in Europe holds such imperial sway over the tourist imagination" when it was hardly more "undressed" than many failed New York revues.[58] Yet for many middle-class tourists, it seemed to provide a palatable blend of show business glitz and titillation. "Much nudism but loveliness of setting" reads the diary entry of twenty-five-year-old Jeanne Bird, who went there with her college professor husband in 1939.[59]

In fact, the Casino de Paris had replaced the Folies as Paris's favorite music hall, but its show, which emphasized song and dance more than exposed flesh, was not nearly as popular among foreigners.[60] Yet it, too, could shock. When young Nancy Reagan's father took her there, he was nonplussed when Josephine Baker, the African American star, took the stage and began performing topless. He rushed Nancy from the place at the first opportunity.[61] Others, who had not brought their young daughters, were more impressed. Howard Sharp, a single man from New Jersey, pronounced Baker's show "very spectacular."[62]

— —

We know little about American tourists patronizing Paris's many prostitutes, female and male. However, we do know that the city's historic reputation as a place where sex was for hire in an extraordinary number of guises remained intact. Female prostitution was legal if it took place in one of the roughly three hundred licensed *maisons de tolérance*, which ranged from dingy workingmen's dives to opulent mansions.[63] At the luxurious Chabanais, located (coincidentally) just around the corner from the Bibliothèque Nationale, women in frilly outfits lounged on plush settees amidst dim lights and a fin-de-siècle atmosphere. It proudly displayed the huge bathtub that forty years earlier had been reserved exclusively for the use of the portly Prince of Wales, who was a regular patron.[64] At La Maison des Nations, each room evoked a different country. The Italian one had opera piped in; the Japanese one had tatami mats and a large print of Mount Fuji. Railroad enthusiasts could use a facsimile sleeping-car compartment, where a train whistle sounded and scenes of the countryside rolled past the window. Those with voyeuristic tendencies could watch pornographic movies and live sex shows, while sadomasochists had access to a ready supply of whips and chains.[65] The Sphinx, which opened in 1935, displaced the Chabanais as the most popular *maison* for American visitors. It was said to be "a model of modernity, spotless and blazing with light, teeming with healthy girls." Its main problem was the likelihood of encountering other Americans one knew there.[66]

Thousands of unlicensed prostitutes also patrolled the bars, cafés, and, on the lowest level, the streets. Montmartre, of course, was full of them, but they were also common in the tonier Right Bank tourist zone. The diary of La Rue Brown, a single Boston man visiting Paris, records being approached by prostitutes in the bar of the Ritz and on the street by the U.S. embassy. Pimps sidled up to him on the nearby place de la Concorde, offering to show him "some very exciting things."[67] Women were not as well served in this respect. The dance halls where "gigolos" still plied their trade—officially they were just excellent dancers who one paid by the dance—were still around in the 1930s, but unlike the 1920s, there are few references to American women having liaisons with them. Helen Josephy and Mary Margaret McBride's 1929 guidebook, *Paris Is a Woman's Town*, which heartily recommended using their services, was never reprinted. Clara Laughlin's guidebooks to Paris and France, which were regarded as the "Bibles" of women tourists in the 1930s, did not mention them.[68]

Nor was there much that was extraordinary to attract homosexuals. France was much more tolerant than America of homosexuality but did not have enough of a reputation in this regard to specifically make it a gay men's destination. Although the Riviera was well known as a place where gays could feel comfortable with their sexuality, the Depression had forced many of the American and British writers and artists who had fostered that reputation to move on, some to less pricey Italy, most back home. Paris did maintain its long-standing reputation as a place that tolerated lesbianism more readily than anywhere else in the Western world. In the 1920s a lesbian social scene revolving around a number of hyperactive American women had developed on the Left Bank. This continued into the 1930s, but on a less visible level, as most of the women became more discreet about their sexual preferences. The wealthy heiress Natalie Barney still hosted lesbian gatherings at her town house on rue Jacob, but the elaborate theatricals she had staged there gave way to simpler gatherings where her "nymphs" read poetry and maxims. The most famous of the lesbian couples, Gertrude Stein and Alice B. Toklas, held court nearby, at their apartment on rue de Fleurus. They gained celebrity status in the United States after Stein published her *Autobiography of Alice B. Toklas* in 1933 and went on a sensational lecture tour there in 1934. However, they, too, abided by French norms, which demanded discretion in displaying what was still considered "deviancy." The expatriate American writer Djuna Barnes did rock this boat in 1936 by publishing *Nightwood*, an anguished novel that sought to correct the idyllic gloss put on lesbian love by Barney, who recommended it, among other things, as a cure for aging. (Barney did live to age ninety-six.) However, it was perhaps an indication of the paucity of lesbian tourism that few people bought this "cult guide to the homosexual underground nightworld of Paris."[69]

— —

One of Paris's oldest naughty attractions was "dirty pictures" and "dirty books." Often, male tourists at popular tourist spots would be approached by purveyors (eight of them patrolled the entrance to Notre-Dame Cathedral) carrying what looked like a stack of postcards. They would flip aside the photo of Notre-Dame on the top and reveal something like a painting of a satyr about to ravish a maiden, offering the hope of better things to come below. After a quick exchange of money, the tourist would slip the pile into his pocket, often to discover when got back to his hotel that he had purchased a pile of reproductions of similar classical works.[70] La Rue Brown's diary says that on the bustling place de la Concorde,

> two very dirty gentlemen with an air of great furtiveness offer me what they represent to be very naughty pictures for 10 f and when I finally offer 1 f (4 cents) to be rid of them they hastily accept. To their expressed horror (a cause de police) I open the packet to full public view and sure enough the crude sketches are pure enough to satisfy even Mr. Sumner.[71]

Even when they were "naughty," there was little concern among those in the moral enforcement business about tourists bringing pictures back home, for most were the kinds of faded photographs of plumpish naked women that were readily available in America. However, works of literature that the American authorities banned from entering the country on the grounds of obscenity were a different story. As is often the case, the controversy surrounding the obscenity rulings helped arouse interest in them, encouraging many tourists to smuggle them back to the States. In the 1920s the best known of these works was James Joyce's modernist novel *Ulysses*, which was published in Paris. In the 1930s the book of choice was D. H. Lawrence's *Lady Chatterley's Lover*, which describes some mutually satisfying sexual encounters between the lady and her gamekeeper and liberally employs four-letter words. It was privately printed in Florence, Italy, in 1928, and then turned out in a larger edition by a Paris publisher in 1929. The ink was hardly dry on that printing run when it was banned as obscene in both the United States and Great Britain. In August 1930, soon after arriving in Paris, Phoebe Adams looked at a copy that one of her Smith College classmates had bought and wrote in her diary that "one [look] was enough. How anyone can write such stuff I don't understand."[72] Nevertheless, for the next thirty years, as long as the bans lasted, thousands of copies of the work would be secreted away in the baggage of tourists returning from France.

Henry Miller's *Tropic of Cancer* was less well known but much more salacious. Published in Paris in 1934, this graphic evocation of the sex life of an American living among Paris's whores and low-lifes was far too racy for most middle-class Americans. Only after World War II would it find its way into the bottom of many tourists' suitcases. Even fewer tourists were ready for fare as raw as *House of Incest*, a fantasy of lesbian and other kinds of sex published two years later by one of Miller's lovers, Anaïs Nin, who subsequently moved to America.

— —

One thing of a sensual nature that is missing from most of the middle-class diaries and correspondence is a love for French food. During their five trips to France in the 1930s, the Howes ate regularly in Paris's finest restaurants, but although Mrs. Howes's diaries often record how much they enjoyed their decor and service, their food is not even mentioned once.[73] This is because French food had almost slipped from the map in America. Before World War I, when an appreciation for French food was a mark of elite status throughout much of the world, wealthy Americans had often used the trip to France as a kind of gastronomic training ground, from which they returned with more refined tastes. However, Prohibition sounded the death knell for French restaurants in America, who needed the healthy markups on alcohol sales to pay for their French chefs, large staffs, and expensive ingredients. By the time it was repealed in 1933, the French chefs were gone and there was little to entice them back. The few French restaurants that then opened in New York and a few other cities were noted much more for their snobbery than their food.[74]

Middle-class tourists in the 1930s were thus quite unfamiliar with French food and tended to approach it with considerable trepidation. Many had heard that French meat—the quality of which was all-important to Americans—was inferior to that in America. Worse, it was said that the

French used tasty sauces to disguise rancid meat and repulsive ingredients. The French "could take shoe leather and make it palatable," said a *Saturday Evening Post* article in 1931, adding that the meat in cheap restaurants often started out no better than that. Moreover, it warned, horse meat was widely appreciated and was a common ingredient in cheaper restaurants' stews.[75] Breakfasts were also problematic, for Americans still enjoyed eating hearty breakfasts, usually with some kind of meat. French breakfasts, which consisted merely of some breads and dark-roasted coffee, seemed hardly adequate to fuel a hard day of touring. Bergen Evans reported that when his tour group arrived in Paris and were served their first Continental breakfast, "their indignation was echoed from every table around them ... and it would have been impossible for them to have formed any opinion except that a Continental breakfast is a penurious barbarism condemned by all right-thinking people."[76]

— —

That Evans's group also stopped in the Riviera was a sign of how it was no longer the preserve of the upper class and celebrities. Howard Sharp, the Rotarian from New Jersey, passed through there in August 1931 with a group of Rotarians on a bus tour. After trying his hand at roulette during their one-hour stop in Monte Carlo, he remarked in his diary, "Cheap class of people there."[77] In the years that followed, although middle-class tour groups such as Evans's and Sharp's became more thin on the ground, some upper-middle-class people continued to find ways to holiday there. There is no mention of the "cheap class of people" in the diary of Clara Breed, a single, middle-aged, upper-middle-class woman from New York City who, in the twenty-eight weeks she spent in France in the winter and spring of 1936–37, embodied the old genteel nineteenth-century tradition of wintering in Nice. Each day she would leave the modest hotel where she took all of her meals and take long walks along the beautiful seaside walk, the promenade des Anglais. Sometimes she would then sit there for three hours, watching the passing parade. Two afternoons a week, she would relax at the municipal band's outdoor concerts. In the evenings there were American movies, some concerts, an occasional operetta, and, twice, the opera. She took bus excursions to picturesque surrounding towns such as Saint-Paul-de-Vence, visited various churches on Sundays to watch Mass, and on rainy days would paint and shop.[78]

On her way up to Paris in the spring, she stopped at the spa in Vichy for over a month, taking cures, massages, and seeing doctors for some recurring faintness. Again, she led the genteel life, going to concerts and, after four weeks, feeling well enough to have fillet of beef for lunch and play nine holes of golf. On May 30 she proceeded to Paris and immediately headed, not to the exclusive boutiques and couturiers that catered to the likes of Rose Kennedy, but to the giant department store Au Printemps.[79] When her feet began hurting her, rather than take a cab, she walked back to her hotel. The next day she tried once more, but again but her feet gave out and she ended up resting in the Tuileries Gardens. There is no mention at all in her diary of taking taxis to get around and certainly not of indulging in any of Paris's gastronomic delights. All she allowed herself was a stop at a café for a restorative crème de menthe.[80]

THREE

"Beautiful Beyond Belief": *Cultural Tourism Survives*

Before World War I, Americans traveling to France commonly believed that gaining a familiarity with European art, architecture, music, and drama was both morally and socially uplifting. By the 1930s, though, many middle-class American tourists in Europe, especially males, were dismissing this kind of search for high culture as something of interest only to social-climbing women. They defined human achievement in terms of industrial and commercial prowess, at which America excelled, and felt no need to slog through museums trying to decipher the Old Masters' allegorical paintings. In 1934 the *New York Times* reported that many American tourists in Paris now professed to having no interest in high culture. It quoted a typical man as saying, "I don't have the museum habit and I can't acquire it during the few days I have in Paris. Further, I scarcely know a fresco from a fireplug. Why should I tire myself out by trudging miles and miles through a museum, when I can have a much better time somewhere else?"[1] Nevertheless, the age-old search for cultural improvement was by no means over, especially in its traditional repository, the upper-middle class, many of whom still believed, as Cook's magazine for American tourists said, that exposing oneself to "the richer, deeper things Europe has to offer" was good for the soul, and that the tourist who did so would become "a rare and fine companion to himself."[2] For these Americans, France's unparalleled artistic and architectural heritage remained an exciting attraction.

Some went at it with daunting enthusiasm. Almost immediately after getting off the boat train in Paris on June 28, 1932, Cordie Culp, a New Jersey clergyman, and his wife took a bus tour of the city's major architectural monuments. By the end of the day, his diary says, he "had a fearful headache and did not get up until seven the next morning." Still, during the next two days, he and his wife managed to see almost every one of the city's great buildings. They also spent two mornings at the Louvre, toured Notre-Dame twice, and were stunned by the medieval Sainte-Chapelle, which he called "beautiful beyond belief." Evenings were spent walking to see less demanding sights, such as the Eiffel Tower. On their fourth and last day in Paris, they explored yet more of its architecture before taking an informative half-day tour of the World War I American battlefields about sixty miles outside of the city. But that was not all. Two months later, after traveling to the Holy Land, the couple arrived in Marseille. They did not even pause there to taste its famed bouillabaisse, for there was little in the raffish port city to interest the high-minded tourist. Instead, they took an exhausting twelve-hour train trip to Paris, where they plunged into yet another round of cultural touring, including repeat visits to Notre-Dame and the Louvre. On their final day, they toured the vast Palace of Versailles, where Culp observed, as his diary says, "After one sees the way these kings . . . spent money to satisfy every notion, foolish or otherwise, one can understand something of the French Revolution."[3]

The only thing Culp mentioned seeing at the Louvre was Hammurabi's Code, which he declared "certainly worth seeing." However, like practically every other American visitor there, he almost certainly sought out its Big Three masterpieces: the two classical statues, the Winged Victory and the Venus de Milo, and Leonardo da Vinci's painting *La Gioconda*, commonly called the *Mona Lisa*.[4] Most often, while tourists would be impressed by the first two, the *Mona Lisa* would disappoint, mainly because it is relatively small. Even Jan Gelb, who later became a professional artist, was "surprised at the small dimness, almost, of Mona Lisa."[5] Less confident people would blame themselves for not appreciating its genius. Dudley Ann Harmon, a Smith College student, wrote her father, "Somehow I didn't get any huge kick out of it." However, she said, "am going back soon to keep and keep looking at it until I discover why it's so wonderful. Maybe I don't know enough about art to really appreciate it, though I ought to, having taken history of art twice."[6]

The Louvre's reputation for holding the world's greatest collection of art made it the number one sight for foreign visitors to Paris in the 1930s.[7] However, some tourists also sought out the new museum devoted to the works of Auguste Rodin, who by the time of his death in 1917 was being acclaimed as the greatest sculptor of the age. There, the major sight was *The Thinker*, perhaps the most famous modern sculpture of the day. In January 1937 the museum closed an hour early so that Helen Keller could tour it and be accorded the unique privilege of being allowed to touch the sculptures. She said she was most impressed by the portrayal of the six *Burghers of Calais*, bound in ropes, who had surrendered themselves to the invading English so their city could be saved. In a remark prescient of events three and a half years' hence, she said, "It is a work sadder to touch than a grave, because it is a conquered city typified."[8]

Well-educated women continued to provide a good market for this kind of cultural tourism. In the 1920s Dorothy Marsh, a Smith College graduate, had pioneered all-women's tours of Europe that emphasized serious sight-seeing and cultural self-improvement. Initially, the Depression cut into her business seriously, but by the summer of 1937, she was running twenty-five tours. For early 1939 she proposed a daunting-sounding four-month tour, led by "Miss Lois Nicholas Beal . . . of an old Boston family," that would begin with a one-month stay in a Paris college, where the women would take classes in French conversation, history, and art. These would be punctuated by city sightseeing trips, day trips to Fontainebleau, Chartres, and Versailles, and, of course, a number of visits to the Louvre. After a similarly serious stay in Florence and heavy-duty sightseeing in Rome, they would stop for a week on the French Riviera before finishing in London, where the brochure promised, rather sternly, "Visits to museums with instruction: British Museum, National Gallery, the Tate Collection, etc."[9]

——

Of course, Miss Beal's kind of high-brow cultural touring was a minority taste, even for women with cultural improvement in mind. For the most part, such women stopped using the stern Baedeker guides, with their pedantic listings of must-see masterpieces of art and architecture, that were de rigueur for self-improvers before World War I. Instead, they used Clara Laughlin's popular guidebooks for women tourists in France, which said, "A thoroughly enjoyable low brow tour is worth more than a miserable high brow tour, but your travel need not be of either extreme."[10] Although firmly committed to cultural tourism, she downplayed the traditional emphasis on art and architecture, advising that those who did not go to art museums at home (and here she meant the vast majority of tourists) should not spend much time doing so in France.[11] "Don't suppose that an ardor for culture will seize you on European soil," she wrote. "It will develop, if you give it a chance—but it's no mushroom."[12] Instead, Laughlin gave her guidebooks a high-cultural gloss by filling them with the kind of history she thought women would like: tales of the exploits, often amorous, of the people associated with the places being described, stories she said, that showed the "romance and charm" of France.[13]

Cultural tourism also persisted, in a way, on the agendas of the large group tours that still occasionally swept through France. These tourists, too, expected to see famous works of art, even though most were not quite sure why. Bergen Evans said:

> Galleries were "done" with an immense sense of duty. The "Mona Lisa," the "Madonna of the Chair," and the "Last Supper" were recognized with pleasure. They learned to exclaim over perspective and were hardly to blame—considering the tedious iteration of the guides—for believing in that the eyes "following you around the room" was the supreme excellence of portraiture.

However, he said, most of the pictures "were meaningless to them" because of their ignorance of Christianity, history, and mythology.

> Now and then a particularly athletic rape of the Sabines or an unusually steatopygic [i.e., hefty around the buttocks] Venus could not be ignored and drew whispers from the younger and frowns from older members of the party. Rubens' heroic presentation of Diana of the Ephesians (in the Grand Gallery of the Louvre) provoked open indignation. Sixteen breasts on one woman was apparently thought to exceed the permissible limits of the artistic imagination.[14]

The Thomas Cook travel agency was somewhat more charitable toward Americans who derived little from these encounters with high culture. Its *American Traveler's Gazette* said that the American tourist expected to mix having a good time "with a certain amount of selective sightseeing . . . yet as he strolls through the Louvre trying to 'do' it in an hour, he wishes wistfully that he had taken time somehow from the business of making a living to have brushed up a bit on art appreciation." Alas, said Cook's, his lack of background in art, architecture, music ("Mozart? What did he compose?"), literature, and history meant that he encountered most of the sights of Europe in a state of dull incomprehension.[15]

— —

France did remain a magnet for more serious art lovers, especially those interested in modern art. Impressionist painting, which had put France in the forefront of modern art in the later nineteenth century, had more or less died with Claude Monet in 1926. However, the so-called "School of Paris" helped the city remain the world capital of modern art.[16] Although the economic crisis thinned the ranks of American artists lounging about the Montparnasse cafés, a goodly number of them managed to stay on. The diary of Elizabeth Foster Vytlacil tells of the "amusing conversations" she and

Terrace of the Dôme café in Montparnasse, a popular gathering place for American artists, writers, and tourists in the 1930s. © Bettman/CORBIS.

her artist husband had with American artists and their hangers-on at the Dôme, the most popular of the cafés, during their 1932 visit and of an exciting fight that broke out there between

> an Italian American named Stella who was not asked to exhibit [in a show of American artists in Paris] and a funny little Jew named Stillman who is exhibiting. Neither of them are good painters and they apparently pounded each other with sticks and cracked each others' heads and also the head of a young Frenchman who tried to interfere. Everybody shed a great deal of blood and they were all arrested.[17]

Even in the summer of 1934, the year when the number of American tourists and expats in France reached a low, the New York art gallery owner

Onya LaTour had no problem finding a host of friends in the art world at the Montparnasse cafés.[18] Among the district's habitués was Raymond Duncan, the "Hellenist" brother of the famous modern dancer Isadora Duncan, who strode about, clad in toga and sandals, recruiting visiting young American women to his Paris "colony," which he called "New Paris York," telling them it was "taxless, lawless, and without obligations."[19]

The Montparnasse cafés' interesting-looking patrons drew more conventional tourists, such as John Gutknecht, a young Chicago municipal judge, whose diary from the summer of 1934 tells of how he enjoyed a good meal at the Dôme and then just "sat around watching the crowd."[20] The next year, when Pablo Picasso and André Breton led an exodus of artists, writers, and intellectuals to the quieter cafés on the boulevard Saint-Germain, American visitors followed them there as well. One of their favorite ones, the Café des Deux Magots, soon developed a reputation among the French as a place for "well-to-do American ladies."[21]

Paris also continued to draw serious American art collectors.[22] According to the art historian John Russell, "The 1930s was in many ways a heyday of American modernism, but for glamour, prestige, and an intoxicating change of scene, American collectors almost without exception still preferred to go shopping in Paris."[23] More modest art enthusiasts also tried to come back from Paris with a painting or two. In the summer of 1939, Jeanne Bird, a twenty-five-year-old Mount Holyoke graduate on a first visit to Europe with her husband, a university professor, made the usual visit to the Louvre but then spent much of her time in private galleries, where she eventually bought two paintings, one of which she said was "in the cubist manner."[24]

— —

Student travel was hit very hard by the Depression. Most of the companies that in the 1920s had taken thousands of students through Europe in groups of 150 or more folded. However, other, less ambitious ones, such as the National Student Federation and Open Road, continued to organize tours.[25] By 1935 they and other companies were again loading fifty to eighty students into cheap steamship berths and taking them sightseeing in Europe, with Paris an essential stop.[26]

Most of the students probably went mainly to "have a good time." However, there were also more serious student visitors: young people who, as the dean of the American Cathedral in Paris said in 1932, came to France "to partake in its unparalleled culture."[27] The three-month summer school at the American Conservatory of Music in Fontainebleau continued to attract

ambitious applicants. Many were drawn there by the reputation of its director, the composer Nadia Boulanger, a musical genius who had taught many
of the new generation of famous American composers, including Aaron
Copland, Virgil Thomson, and George Gershwin.[28] Paris's art schools also
continued to attract serious American students, as did the regular courses at
the University of Paris—the Sorbonne. An indication that Francophilia was
becoming feminized might lie in the fact that about half of the more than
two thousand students arriving each year for serious study in Paris were
women, a much higher proportion than those pursuing postsecondary education in the United States.[29]

Student travel also received an impetus from the era's vibrant peace
movement. Peace advocates had begun promoting it during the 1920s in the
belief, said one optimist, that the student "is capable of understanding that
our foreign neighbors are just like us" and that "universal peace . . . will be
nearer fulfilment when this understanding is felt everywhere."[30] The rise of
bellicose fascism and Nazism in the 1930s seemed to make this idea even
more relevant. In the summer of 1935, the Students International Travel
Association of New York City planned to send five hundred American students touring Europe in twenty-five-person "bicycle brigades" that, with an
American teacher, a European teacher, and five European students, would
travel the countryside with the objective of "spreading tolerance, good will
and sympathetic understanding." One of the organizers, Professor Ben-
jamin Andrews of Columbia University Teachers College, said: "Here is no
desire to cram one's head full of museum pieces, ancient castles or art collections. . . . Our students cannot help but adopt a broader, more wholesome and more appreciative attitude towards other cultures when they
travel this way."[31] The same year, Teachers College tried to make a stay of at
least eight months abroad a requirement for its undergraduate teaching degree, saying that "intimate contacts with other phases of life and culture"
would make the students better teachers.[32] In the summer of 1938, it sent
160 students to England, France, and Scandinavia on trips for which they
received academic credit.[33]

— —

The students on junior-year-abroad programs were probably the best able
to benefit from France's cultural opportunities. The two original ones,
those of the University of Delaware and Smith College, had begun in 1923
and 1925, respectively. In both, students would arrive in late August and be
taken to a provincial city, where they would be lodged with a French family
and given orientation and language classes at the local university.[34] Then, in

late October, they would move to Paris, to stay with other French families and enroll in courses at the Sorbonne.

Like most young people their age, the students could careen between the juvenile and the high-minded. Twenty-year-old Dudley Harmon arrived in Paris, with her mother, in mid-July 1933, well over a month before the program began. Her initial diary entries read:

> July 17: Well, I'm in Paris. . . . The hotel is quite nice, as everyone speaks English. The staff is really wonderful—they do nothing but bow at us and be affable.

> July 18: Walked around with Mother. Paris is ~~awfully very~~ quite nice. Went around the Eiffel Tower—it's nice. Saw the Arc de Triomphe—that's nice too. But the rue de la Paix is not what it's cracked up to be—dinky, I thought.

> July 19: Went to Bricktop's [an American-style nightclub] tonite, with that American boy from the boat. No one but Americans there, so swell time.

> July 21: The [?] Americans from the boat showed up today. However, was simply furious because had wanted to see the Louvre, but they simply dragged me by the hair to some cafe where they literally forced me to stay all afternoon. Went riding in the Bois tonight. It's nice.[35]

Six months later she wrote from Paris that she was going to a concert conducted by "Ravel himself," adding, "I certainly realize I've wasted my cultural opportunities over here so far, but am going to quit wasting them."[36]

Others, such as Miriam Anderson, another Smith woman, had no worries about wasting their cultural opportunities. Soon after arriving in Paris, she visited the Louvre a number of times on her own. She wrote her mother, "I always have the greatest feeling of satisfaction after I've been to the Louvre, and every time I go I feel more at home and those wonderful pictures seem like old friends. That, I think, is really the test of a great picture—to be able to see it again and again and always find it beautiful."[37] Often, the students' year abroad would end with their parents joining them in Paris, where the now-sophisticated-sounding student would shepherd them through the cultural high spots before renting a car for a trip through provincial France that would really allow the students to show off their fluency in French.[38]

Paris was also an important stopover for left-wing touring. In 1929 Open Road, which had pioneered in "study tours" of the Soviet Union, began putting on two-month guided tours of Europe "to study socialism, fascism, and capitalism" for the pro-labor League for Industrial Democracy. It also ran an inexpensive, leftist-oriented six-week summer school in French studies in Grenoble. With the onset of the Depression, Paris became a popular jumping-off point for many leftists seeking to confirm Soviet claims that Communism was immune to its impact.[39] They could also make pilgrimages to the Montparnasse cafés, where exiled Bolsheviks were said to have plotted their revolution. When Onya LaTour, a Soviet enthusiast, arrived there in August 1934 on the way to the Soviet Union, she headed almost immediately to the run-down Hôtel Odessa. It was, she wrote in her diary, "the little hotel where Lenin and Stalin both have stayed and Marks [sic] and Engels have drunk on the little terrace beneath."[40]

— —

If one of the aims of cultural tourism is to enhance self-esteem, then the African Americans who visited France could also be seen as cultural tourists. The many thousands of African American servicemen stationed in France during World War I had returned home describing France as a land where they were treated as equals. During the 1920s a steady stream of African American writers, artists, clergymen, educators, and professional people visited there and confirmed this. By the end of the decade, the African American writer Claude McKay recalled:

> The cream of Harlem was in Paris. . . . There was an army of school teachers and nurses. There were Negro Communists going and returning from Russia. There were Negro students from London and Scotland and Berlin and the French universities. There were presidents and professors of the best Negro colleges. And there were painters and writers and poets. . . .[41]

They, and a steady stream of reports in the African American press, helped reinforce France's positive image among the folks back home. Joel Rogers, the Paris correspondent for a number of African American newspapers, wrote that the African American who traveled to Europe for the first time found himself "as bewildered as a lifer out on parole, or a canary tossed out its cage. No more bars to beat against. . . . In their place is a sense of freedom that is almost alarming."[42] In April 1931 he wrote of how Billy Pearce, an African American dance teacher, was welcomed into some of Paris's most exclusive venues, including "the stylish paddock" of Longchamps race track on Easter Monday, where he joined "the elite of the racing world, and the mannequins with the new spring styles."[43] This was something that was almost inconceivable in the United States of that time.

Although the African American middle class was very hard hit by the Depression, tourism from that source did not evaporate completely. The French continued to extend an enthusiastic welcome to choirs from black colleges singing Negro spirituals, something they had been doing since the late nineteenth century.[44] Some black writers and artists came on fellowships or, like the writer Countee Cullen, for short summer visits.[45] Many African American ministers, educators, and professional people still managed to find the means and the reasons to travel overseas.[46] In September 1933, about six months after Hitler took power in Germany, Adolph Hodge, an African American teacher from Brooklyn, New York, arrived in Paris leading a group of teachers and nurses who had just visited Italy and Germany. Hodge was pleased to report that "the German people were perfectly lovely to our group" and that every one they talked to was "as enthusiastic over Hitler as the Italians are over Mussolini."[47] In 1936, however, an apparently chastened Hodge had his tour group avoid the fascist countries and, instead, like a number of other African American tours, head for Scandinavia and the Soviet Union before coming to Paris.[48]

— —

Black American tourists in Paris found a fairly well-established community of African Americans. Although there was an American-style restaurant, the Chicago Inn, that featured an African American chef, most were in the entertainment business.[49] African American bands had been in the forefront of introducing jazz to France in the 1920s, when they became featured attractions in many of Paris's top nightspots. However, in the early 1930s, the authorities responded to the pressure of out-of-work French musicians by forcing clubs to hire as many French musicians as foreigners. Some clubs then hired two bands to alternate between jazz and tango music, which was sweeping Paris. In 1931 a Smith junior told her sister of how she "adored" going to Les Ambassadeurs with a young Frenchman: "The music is marvellous. A Russian tango orchestra [sic] and an American nigger band [sic] which changed off. . . . Henri got sentimental during the tangos and I during the jazz."[50]

Still, famous jazz clubs such as the Le Boeuf sur le Toit and Florence's folded left and right. In July 1933 Joel Rogers reported that the luxurious Zelli's, "once a little corner of Alabama in the heart of Paris, and the greatest place of its kind in Montmartre," was now "but a cheap nudist joint."[51]

A number of African American musicians managed to convince the American Aid Society in Paris, which had been set up in 1920 to repatriate destitute ex-doughboys, to pay their fares back to the States.[52] But many others stayed on, congregating in raffish Montmartre, trying to scratch out a hand-to-mouth existence in its few surviving clubs.[53] Better-off African American visitors were now dismayed to find the entertainers barely eking out an existence there, living in run-down hotels amidst the district's pimps and hookers. There were disturbing reports that some had taken to petty crime. In 1933 Carter Woodson lamented that although African Americans formed but a small proportion of the population of Paris, "it is a common thing to read of their committing crimes. This year a Negro jazz artist had to be connected with the worst murderer in the city in many years, Violette Nozierea."[54]

Luckily, the "Negro jazz artist" associated with the notorious Nozierea, who killed her parents for their money, had a French name, and most African Americans in Paris continued to receive good press. Duke Ellington and Louis Armstrong were mobbed by admirers when they arrived with their bands in 1933 and 1934, as was Ellington on a return trip in 1937. Other jazz greats, such as Coleman Hawkins and Benny Carter, were much better received in Paris than in America. Bricktop's nightclub, named after the carrot-colored hair of its African American owner, Ada Smith, managed to survive in various forms until late 1936, and Smith remained a popular hostess in other clubs until 1939. Although she welcomed black celebrities such as the ex–boxing champion Jack Johnson and actor/singer Paul Robeson effusively, her clubs were particularly famous for their white celebrity patrons, such as the songwriter Cole Porter and the Prince of Wales and his American consort, Wallis Simpson, later the Duke and Duchess of Windsor.[55]

The only other African American in Paris whose fame surpassed Bricktop's was Josephine Baker. Practically from the moment she arrived in 1925 as a nineteen-year-old dancer with the Revue nègre and danced the Charleston almost naked, the brown-skinned "Ebony Venus" from St. Louis embodied black sensuality and exoticism to the French. By 1930 she spoke French well enough to expand her act from dancing clad only in a string of bananas around her waist to include songs, patter, and sketches (she was an excellent mimic). One of her songs became a national hit, and she went on to appear in two French movies, including one with Jean Gabin, the country's reigning heartthrob.[56] The warmth of the French welcome for her was reciprocated, and she became an important figure in maintaining France's reputation among African Americans as a haven from racism. During her appearance at the Ziegfeld Follies of 1936 in New York City, she told reporters for the African American press that she was refused a room at a Midtown hotel. "That is enough for me," she said. "I nearly ran out of the hotel. Paris! I have lived there for years without experiencing such humiliation

The ex–heavyweight boxing champion Jack Johnson and his wife sightseeing in Paris in 1933. Like many other African Americans, Johnson—who was driven from the United States because of his refusal to abide by laws, written and unwritten, supporting segregation and inequality—found France to be a welcome haven from racism. Courtesy of the Library of Congress.

and without knowing how happy one is when he does not feel the weight of this horrible prejudice."[57]

— —

There was a perceptible lessening of tensions between black and white Americans in Paris during the 1930s. In the 1920s the sight of a black man walking into a Montmartre bar, especially with a white woman on his arm, had regularly enraged white Americans and led to numerous ugly incidents.[58] In the 1930s there were no reports of such incidents. Edgar Wiggins, who wrote a column on African Americans in Paris for a number of African American papers, credited this to the economic crisis. "In Europe," he said, "the dollar was once king, and this made the American the world's greatest strutter. Today the wind has been taken from him. Drunken Southerners who used to go to Zelli's and blow a few hundred, and even thousands of dollars a night on champagne and would throw empty champagne bottles at any black face that entered, save the musicians, are down on their uppers now."[59]

It may also have been that by the 1930s white American tourists were better prepared to confront, literally, France's greater tolerance for racial mixing. Tourists were now told to regard interracial couples as a French idiosyncrasy that, like eating snails and frog's legs, might be unacceptable in America but should not be quarreled with there. Among the fifty "snapshot memories of France" Sydney Clark listed in his guidebook to France is "a negro in a Paris café actually sitting with a negress. It simply 'isn't done.' Negroes have a tremendous vogue with white Parisiennes."[60] In February 1933 Elizabeth Foster Vytlacil wrote in her diary of meeting the expatriate African American writer Eric Waldron in terms similar to those one would use about meeting beings from another planet:

> He speaks like an American without a trace of a Negro accent. I think he speaks good French too. He dresses very conventionally and seems so very unlike a ~~negro~~ nigger as we think of them in America. That is a constant surprise as we look at his black face. . . . One is constantly impressed in Paris with the difference in manner of negroes—even American negroes here and at home. They have so much poise here and show neither any feeling of inferiority or deference. They are very popular in Paris as entertainers in all the smart night clubs and in the cheaper dance places too. And one sees them constantly with white girls—or white men with black girls. Waldron came last night with a Jewish girl who paints. . . . The attitude of the French seems to me so much better than the American attitude and I wonder if we will ever achieve this in America. That is be able to mix with them with no more feeling of constraint than if they were Italians or Germans. But there is always that horror of mixing the white blood and the black which the French really don't seem to feel.[61]

Nevertheless, the French would still tread lightly on white Americans' sensibilities on the race question. Dudley Harmon wrote home that a young French friend did not tell her his girlfriend was a woman of color because he feared Harmon would refuse to go to a party with her. After the party, Harmon wrote home about the incident, commenting, "They don't think about negroes going around with whites over here."[62] Clearly, for some white Americans, learning to accommodate themselves to interracial couples may have been the most culturally improving aspect of their trip to France.

FOUR

Watching the World Go By

Americans with money to travel have nothing else to travel with.

—MAUDE PALMER THAYER,

"The American Student Leaves the Reservation" (1937)

Sooner or later, most middle-class tourists ended up at the Café de la Paix, an attractive café/restaurant on the boulevard between the bustling place de l'Opéra and the American Express office. There, Clara Laughlin's guidebook told them, "everybody goes to sit on the sidewalk and watch the world go by."[1] If you sat there long enough, the saying went, sooner or later you would meet someone from back home.

Why, one might ask, would one come all that way wanting to look for people from back home? One reason, of course, is simply that most of us enjoy finding the familiar amidst the unfamiliar. However, it is also that Paris was one of those places where most Americans felt cut off from the natives, both by language and the natives' inclinations. Middle-class Americans learned some French in high school, but few had practice in speaking it or listening to it. Moreover, the French rarely traveled abroad, and Parisians in particular tended to have little empathy for travelers struggling to speak their language. Also, since Paris was regularly full of visitors, they had little curiosity about tourists and would rarely try to engage them. The writer Joseph Wood Krutch felt that the French regarded the tourist business as "a disagreeable necessity" and "would prefer never to see an American again if they knew how to get rid of him."[2]

One result of this was the development of a well-demarcated American tourist zone on the Right Bank of the Seine. This comfortable enclave of "English Spoken" signs stretched from Notre-Dame Cathedral on the east to the Arc de Triomphe on the west, and from the Seine north to the place de l'Opéra—an area of less than two square miles. It was here that the major sights were concentrated (although one did have to pop across the river to ascend the Eiffel Tower and see Napoléon's tomb). It was also where

Americans' favorite hotels and restaurants were located and where they did their shopping. Few of the French people they encountered in this quarter had any interest in them other than to profit from their presence. When a group of American tourists there began discussing what "queer people" the French were, one of them said she hadn't a clue as to what they were like. After several weeks in France, she said, "I haven't seen any Frenchmen except waiters and taxi drivers and shop clerks."[3] If tourists did meet a friendly Frenchman in a bar or café, he would often turn out to be a "confidence man," trying to prey on them.[4]

This absence of any meaningful contact with the French, along with the tourists' expectations of "having a good time," made them easy targets for critics of middle-class tourism. Throughout the nineteenth century, people higher on the social ladder had put down tourists from the class below them as crude nouveaux riches who were unable to appreciate the Old World's cultural heritage. Toward the end of the nineteenth century, when new upper-middle-class tourists began dedicating themselves seriously to cultural tourism, the upper class turned toward leisure tourism and derided those below them as feminized culture-vultures. When, in the 1920s, many middle-class tourists followed the upper class and opted for leisure tourism over cultural tourism, they were condemned for turning European tourism into an exercise in frivolity.

Thomas Craven rang two of the changes on this theme in an acerbic article in the April 1930 *Forum*, a magazine for serious upper-middle-class readers. One was that middle-class tourists demanded artificial, inauthentic experiences. Travel, he said, had originally been "an exploration of unknown or unfamiliar realities [that] leads unquestionably to the enrichment of the spirit and the collection of new forms of knowledge." To have everything so prearranged and comfortable "that one is scarcely conscious of a change of scene is to deny all that travel has to offer. . . . For those desirous of forming an intelligent conception of other cultures it is a fool's errand." Americans, he said, were now the "champions of the world" at this kind of frivolous touring. Their travel in Europe was just "an excursion into a more extended Coney Island." Tourists could not appreciate "the profounder humanities" behind the sights of Europe, "the ages of culture behind them," because they knew nothing of their history. "To the average tourist they are merely a succession of passing objects, a kaleidoscopic profusion. . . ." In the great galleries of art, the American tourist "rushes from picture to picture, gaping for a moment or two at works that were years in the making. As if masterpieces epitomizing the tendencies of an epoch could be apprehended at a single glance!"

Craven's other major criticism was that they were interested only in sensual pleasures. He wrote:

Cultured Americans are held in suspicion by their compatriots. The great majority travel because they are restless, homeless souls with a surplus in the bank; lacking any worthy purpose for life, they flock to the Old World for a wild time. . . . The Continental . . . offers them the more cultivated vices, and in Paris—where the tradition of wild and abandoned carnality must be maintained—he reserves special quarters for those Saturnalian relaxations which Americans demand the moment they set foot on French soil. . . . To the vast multitudes who march through Europe every year, travel is a prolonged debauch. . . . On their return . . . they compare notes on their orgies, those of wealth dwelling on the smarter imbecilities of the Riviera, the rank and file boasting of wonderful times in the cesspools of Paris.[5]

Although critiques such as Craven's were much more applicable to the decade that had just ended, they continued to reverberate in the more threadbare 1930s, and indeed for rest of the century. Student tourists were particularly easy targets. Maude Thayer wrote of spending the summer of 1936 trying to control a group of one hundred "privileged" young college students—"young unteachables and bleating chauvinists"—as they left a trail of wrecked hotel rooms across Europe. On the trains, they amused themselves by throwing empty orangeade bottles at passing telegraph poles. When one of the young women purloined a parked bicycle in the South of France and began riding it wildly through the traffic, their French guide told Thayer, "Don't be disturbed. People won't mind. They expect American students to act like wild Indians." For the most part, Thayer said, "when not bent on destruction, the young men seemed consumed by ennui, boredom, and bigotry." The young women, she thought, came mainly "to shop and flirt."[6]

Disdain for such superficiality was not just aimed at students in groups. As Thyra Edwards, the left-wing African American social worker and writer, sat in her cabin in the *Lafayette* on the last night of the return voyage from her 1934 tour to study workers' education in Europe, she found herself "keyed up and on edge . . . chain smoking again . . . and thinking black." Just then, an older man she had befriended returned from the upper reaches of the ship, where he had attended the traditional formal captain's dinner on the last night at sea. He was, she said,

amazed and amused at the innocent ignorance of the bejewelled girls with whom he had danced. Beauties who had spent 4 months in France, going each

Sunday to the American church, and had never spoken to a Frenchman, be-yond the maitre d'hotel, and thought the most impressive thing in all of France was a cute little cottage they saw in Normandy. Yes, they had heard something or other about the street riots in Paris, but they understood that it was just a part of the Communists' annoying program.[7]

Nor were African American tourists immune from criticism. In 1933 the African American historian Carter Woodson wrote of his mortification at seeing an African American tourist strolling down a boulevard in Paris "dressed in our typical gay style. His attire of loud colors went to the ex-treme, and above all he had his hair straightened and packed upon his head as if it had been dipped into tar and then ironed out around his empty poll [crown]." From the back, he said, "it resembled the gathered bob tail of a black horse." Woodson lamented that "when the average European sees an American black man, then, [he] wonders whether [he] is a jazz musician or a clown. The observer does not expect this man of color to know anything about art, philosophy, science or literature or to manifest an interest in those things. Instead, the European would ask the African-American to do the 'Charleston' or some other dance." The African American would com-ply, said Woodson, for he liked to "show off when he has nothing to exhibit but what excites derision and contempt among thinking people. It is sad in-deed to be a dunce and to have not knowledge at all of this handicap."

Woodson also condemned African American tourists in Europe for not being serious enough. He said, "Too many of us go there merely for the pleasure which the trip affords, and when we return we do not know any more than if we had not made the trip. We do not stay in one place long enough to become acquainted with any country and its serious minded people." Every year African American educators, businessmen, clergymen, and profes-sional people went to Europe and failed to establish any lasting connections with Europeans. "They come back talking about the interesting things which they saw and did not have time sufficiently to understand."[8]

— —

Other Americans were more concerned about the bad impression the tourists made on the French. Writing in the newspaper *Le Figaro*, the play-wright Sherwood Anderson pleaded with the French not to judge Ameri-cans by "that rich braggart you meet vacationing in Paris, throwing money out the windows."[9] The critic Gilbert Seldes lamented that two main themes dominated French criticisms of American tourists: that they were poorly mannered—particularly too loud—and traveled at a breakneck speed, getting false or only superficial impressions of the places they visited.[10]

But such concerns were rather misplaced, for, as would also be the case after World War II, French views of Americans reflected French politics as much as it did the objective reality of the United States and its tourists. In the 1920s French leaders were quite divided over the significance of the United States' emergence as the world's premier industrial power. Some "modernizers" saw it as the result of Americans' freedom from thralldom to the past and their willingness to experiment and take risks. However, those committed to older industrial forms saw it as the product of a culture of greed and a system of mass production that posed a grave threat to the French way of life. Practically all agreed, though, that American insistence that France repay the huge debts she ran up in the United States to purchase arms during the war was an unfair demand on a nation that had shed enormous amounts of blood in the common defense of freedom. It showed how "Uncle Shylock" was driven by nothing but greed and materialism.[11]

The Wall Street Crash and worldwide depression brought a paroxysm of criticism of the United States.[12] Intellectuals saw its consumer economy, based on mass production and the assembly line, as the harbinger of a dystopian mass society.[13] They called it "the country of standardization" and said it was a mechanized, depersonalized, mindlessly materialistic place, where respect for individual differences and higher cultural pursuits had disappeared.[14] France must protect itself from "the American cancer," said a booklet of that title in 1931. It was a way of life ruled only by the imperatives of mass production.[15] "Cocktails, jazz, and Charlie Chaplin may have conquered the world," Joseph Wood Krutch wrote in 1931, but to French intellectuals "and the semi-intellectuals who run the newspapers . . . America is a half-barbarous country whose inferior culture threatens the morally and intellectually superior civilization in Europe in general and France in particular."[16] As if to prove his point, one of the anti-American pamphlets said, "Out with the Yankees! Out with the people and their products, their methods and their lessons, their dances and their jazz! Let them take back their Fords and their chewing gum."[17] That year, when Le Figaro asked a number of intellectuals what they thought of "American civilization," the large majority, eighteen out of twenty-nine, attacked it for its materialism, puritanism, racism, and, in the case of some conservatives, for the inordinate power that women wielded there—a sign of the breakdown of the family. "America is detested—it's the fashion among the intelligentsia," said Paul Morand, one of the minority who had some good things to say about America.[18]

For a while, anti-Americanism was a handy tool across the political spectrum. The Right used the American example to defend small business and agriculture against the threat of extinction by large enterprises. It attacked Hollywood movies for luring young people into soulless, materialistic, and immoral lifestyles that undermined respect for culture and the family. A Smith junior said that her landlady in Grenoble thought that "all Americans smoke, eat no bread, drink milk, and get divorced, and the young girls lead absolutely free and unhampered existences."[19] Right-wing anti-Semites said America reflected the rootlessness, vulgarity, and obscene wealth of the Jews who wielded inordinate power there.[20] The Left, on the other hand, condemned the American system for enslaving workers to the insatiable demands of speeded-up assembly lines and efficiency experts, forcing them, as in Charlie Chaplin's movie *Modern Times*, to produce profits for rapacious employers at ever more frenetic speeds.

However, as the 1930s wore on and the French became, in Eugen Weber's words, "increasingly morose and ill at ease," these critiques became more muted.[21] The stories of mass unemployment and hardship in the United States took the edge off conservative condemnations of American materialism and consumerism. It was reported that smugness and optimism were no longer rampant, and Americans' new understanding of suffering was making them more reflective.[22] Warnings that America represented the triumph of mass politics faded as it became apparent that Mussolini and Hitler were the real masters of that game.[23] Moreover, as a fascist threat arose in France as well as in the rest of Europe, anti-fascists of various stripes now worried, not about America's power over them, but about the absence of American political involvement in Europe. In the mid-1930s, supporters of the leftist French Popular Front, including the Communists, began to nurse the hope that the New Deal reforms instituted under Franklin D. Roosevelt bespoke a natural affinity between the two movements and, hopefully, the two nations.[24] As a military showdown with Hitler began to loom ominously on the horizon, successive French governments tried to ensure that America, and Americans, would be on their side if a conflict broke out. Indeed, France's improbable war strategy involved banking on the massive defenses of the Maginot Line along its German frontier to hold off the Nazis long enough for the Americans to arrive and once again tip the scales to their side.[25]

The government thus set about encouraging American visits to France that would recollect the alliance of World War I, when the United States sent a huge army to France. The most obvious site for this kind of exercise was that conflict's battlefields, which formed a great arc from the east through the north of France. However, they were a rather hard sell. Most of the visible evidence of the war's incredible toll on the countryside—denuded forests, huge craters, hundreds of miles of trenches gouged into the earth—had disappeared soon after the war's end, replaced by bucolic-looking green fields. Returning veterans were inevitably disappointed at not being able to recognize where they had fought.[26] In 1931 a Smith College junior wrote home after touring the battlefields near Reims, "The war-time seemed hard to imagine then, in that still peaceful landscape, with a blue-bloused farmer driving his three slow horses across the next field."[27]

By then, the other main war tourist sights, the ghostly ruined towns such as Reims itself, had been reconstructed. The main remaining reminders were the countless cemeteries laid out near the battlefields, which were (and still are) a very moving sight. When, at her husband's urging, Eleanor Roosevelt took her two sons, fifteen-year-old Franklin Jr. and thirteen-year-old John, to tour the battlefields in the summer of 1929, they were singularly unable to comprehend her descriptions of the disfigured countryside, for it was now covered by grass. (She called it "the forgiveness of nature.") However, they *were* moved by the cemeteries, especially by the birth and death dates on the tombstones, and the realization that many of the dead were boys not much older than Franklin Jr.[28]

But this was not the kind of thing that Americans tourists looking for good times wanted to see. "I question whether you really do like the battle-fields," said Sydney Clark's guidebook. "I do not mean to minimize the immense significance of these sacred places, but somehow they do not fit into the brief cheerful holiday which is ours in France." Only the Catholic shrine at Lourdes, which he called "unquestionably the most depressing and pathetic spot in Europe," received a more discouraging write-up.[29] It is no surprise that less than 1 percent of the visitors to the battlefields in the 1930s were American.[30]

— —

There was one kind of visitor, though, with a special interest in the cemeteries and battlefields. In May 1930 the first of six thousand "Gold Star Mothers and Widows" arrived in Paris, their expenses paid for by the U.S. government. These mothers and wives of servicemen who were buried in France during the war were more like pilgrims, visiting a sacred place, than tourists. However, they generally came from less privileged backgrounds than the usual tourists, and it was inevitable that they would also regard the trips as once-in-a-lifetime opportunities for tourism as well. Upon arriving in Paris, each group would lay a wreath at the Tomb of the Unknown Soldier under the Arc de Triomphe and be taken to tea at the beautiful Laurent restaurant. There they would be welcomed by the American ambassador, French dignitaries, and General John Pershing, the wartime American commander in chief in France who moved to Paris in 1931 as head of the American Battle Monuments Commission. Then, over the next five days, they would be taken on sightseeing tours of Paris, which they often appreciated more than conventional tourists. An English-speaking guide at the Louvre wrote in her diary, "Spent some good moments on the American Mothers—the poor dear souls were grateful and some really sufficiently versed in the facts to enjoy the Louvre." After one tour, one of the women returned in the afternoon, asking for more information on the paintings. "She told how she had brought up nine children, and had always been poor, in Texas, and had always wanted to paint, and to see the great art of the world!"[31] The next week they would be split into smaller groups to visit the battlefields and the cemeteries where their sons and husbands now lay.[32]

Like the doughboys, the Gold Star Mothers were racially segregated. At first only whites were invited to France, but in 1933, after the number of white applicants began to dry up, the government reluctantly gave in to pressure from African American organizations and invited black mothers too.[33] Their trips were also rigidly segregated. They were sent over on more Spartan boats and stayed in lesser hotels than their white counterparts.[34] When they arrived, they were pointedly ignored by General Pershing, who had vigorously opposed having African American troops fight under his command and had detailed as many of them as he could to labor battalions, graveyard details, or the French army.[35] To help counter the snubs and second-class treatment, the African American musicians of Montmartre organized a band to entertain them.[36]

— —

By mid-1937 the growing German menace was spurring the French to do all they could to remind Americans of their successful wartime alliance. In 1927 the American Legion had held its convention in Paris, with decidedly mixed results, for their drunkenness and boorish behavior had hardly endeared them to the French. The French government had issued a polite invitation to hold its convention there again ten years hence, but in 1936 the Legion declared it would never again hold its convention outside the United States and selected New York City as the site for 1937. The French, recognizing the Legion's tremendous influence in American politics, then invited all the delegates to follow the New York convention with a six-day "pilgrimage" to France, at its expense.[37]

Initially, it was hoped that ten thousand members and their wives would take up the offer, but less than two thousand showed up. The French, nevertheless, pulled out all the stops. In August, shortly before their arrival, they provided an impressive array of dignitaries, headed by the president, to accompany Pershing as he presided over the unveiling of a series of eight large American war memorials. Speaker after speaker told of how, in Pershing's words, the two countries had always been bound together by "a common love of justice and liberty" and, as President Roosevelt said in a live radio broadcast to the first unveiling, that this tradition stretched back to France's aid in the American Revolution.[38] Then, when the Legion's "pilgrimage" arrived, the French hauled out their country's most honored war hero, the aged Marshal Pétain.[39] On October 5 the little old man, practically covered from head to toe in medals, presided over a huge banquet for the Legionnaires at the Invalides, the seventeenth-century veterans' home where Napoléon and other French military heroes are buried. The conservative newspaper *Le Matin* said that when he rose to speak, the cheers were so loud and long it seemed like they would never end.[40] Two days later he and Pershing went to Versailles for the unveiling of an equestrian statue of Pershing. With American Legionnaires and French veterans standing side by side in the rain in front of them, each extolled the other's armed forces' contributions to preserving "the eternal principles of liberty." They evoked, said *Le Matin*, "the story of a collaboration that can never be forgotten." (Three years later the term "collaboration," as well as "liberty," would take on a different connotation when Pétain became the head of the Nazi-supported Vichy government in southern France.)[41]

There was no hint from these French conservatives of the disgust they had previously expressed for how American ideas of liberty undermined the family and religion. Nor was there anything but praise from the Left. The Communists, who had excoriated the Legionnaires in 1927, were now part of the Popular Front government and were desperate to rally American support for a worldwide anti-Nazi alliance with the Soviet Union. Even though the Legion was notorious for its blood-curdling anti-communism, the Communists' newspaper, *L'Humanité*, was just as positive about the Legionnaires' visit as *Le Matin*.[42]

True to its word, the French government paid for the Legionnaires' six-day stays in Paris and arranged tours for them to Versailles, the châteaux of the Loire, and the battlefields.[43] Some isolationist American newspapers reported that the Legionnaires complained about the quality of their Paris accommodations, but the always-upbeat *Paris Herald* pictured them as enjoying a warm French welcome. It quoted them as saying such things as,

"We like the way we've been treated everywhere" and "French food is great." A New York City policeman is supposed to have said, "I've tried everything in France but snails . . . and I'm going to try them, because I've liked everything else," while a man from Baton Rouge, Louisiana, listed "the courtesy of the shopkeepers and taxi drivers" among "the outstanding points of the trip." (His wife added, "All there's left for me to do is that big museum, the Louvre, I guess. Do you know the address?")[44] A Georgian was so impressed by the French welcome that he wrote a letter of thanks to the French government.[45]

The French government also encouraged tourism by other presumed American opinion leaders, including what it called the "young intellectual elite."[46] In the summer of 1936, government officials put on a lavish reception in Paris's ornate Hôtel de Ville for a rather undistinguished group of one hundred touring American college students, few of whom seemed interested in anything besides each other.[47] Undeterred, in February 1937 it announced that it would pay for fifty American students visiting the upcoming Paris exposition to spend two weeks visiting the "recovered provinces" of Alsace and Lorraine, which Germany was again coveting.[48] The next month it announced that it would finance Anne Morgan's Museum of Franco-American Cooperation in Blérancourt to "pictorialize" all that Americans had done to help rebuild France since the Great War. Among those to be honored were John D. Rockefeller Jr., Andrew Carnegie, and the Morgan family.[49]

The problem was that, at least among white Americans, Francophilia was already concentrated in this rarified East Coast elite, who had a long-standing admiration for French style and culture.[50] Beneath that level, the usual uncomplimentary views of the French—that they were surly, unclean, and out to cheat Americans—continued to percolate. Most worrisome was the idea that Germans were preferable to the French. In 1933 two Mount Holyoke women who had been on the previous year's junior-year-abroad program in France passed through Paris on the way back from Austria and Germany and told a friend that although they spoke French well and had French friends, they "felt so much more at home and in sympathy with the Germans . . . above all [because of] the neatness and order."[51] In 1935 the writer Thomas Wolfe, who had spent some months in Paris in 1930, wrote his editor that Germans were "the cleanest, the kindest, the warmest hearted, and the most honorable people I have met in Europe."[52] The next year Margaret Goddard, who took her family on a tour of France and Germany after spending her junior year in France, wrote in her diary on her first night in Germany, "The German people are certainly different from the

French! Cheery and more than willing to help and to try to get what you want." (The family had gotten hopelessly lost looking for the hotel they had booked in Freiburg because its street name had been changed from Kaiser-strasse to Adolf Hitler Strasse.)[53] In 1938 alarming surveys showing little American enthusiasm for France in its disputes with Germany prompted the French government to bend over backward for touring American opinion leaders. The prime minister himself ordered local prefects to comply with an Antioch College professor's request that they arrange meetings with local French students for a group of students he had on a camping holiday in the French countryside.[54]

— —

That spring the French government had again promised tourists benefits such as discounts on trains and gasoline, but the looming crisis over German expansionism dampened the hoped-for summer boom.[55] Most Americans now looked to their own hemisphere in making travel plans.[56] Then, in late September, the situation worsened when Hitler threatened to invade Czechoslovakia if it did not give Germany the Sudetenland, a strategic province with a large German-speaking population. War seemed inevitable, for France and Britain had guaranteed Czechoslovakia's borders. The American embassy in Paris advised Americans who had "no compelling reason to prolong their sojourn here" to return to the United States.[57]

All the transatlantic liners were immediately booked solid, and during the next three days, seven liners, crammed far beyond their official limits, took over ten thousand Americans back from France and England. Thousands more descended upon the steamship lines' offices in Paris and London trying desperately to get tickets of any kind.[58] Forty Smith College juniors who had arrived in France just two weeks before were ordered by their college president to return immediately. Reluctantly, they boarded a rented bus in Dijon at 4:00 AM and made their way to the port of Le Havre.[59] When they arrived there on September 28, all the departing liners were fully booked. They stared at the cold, gray, windswept sea, crestfallen at the wreckage of their year in France. However, as one of them wrote her parents, on the morning of September 30, "the funny little [hotel] maid came dashing into our room with the breakfast trays. She literally danced all over the room, exclaiming, 'La paix est sauvée, la paix est sauvée!' [Peace is saved!]"[60] The French and British prime ministers, Edouard Daladier and Neville Chamberlain, had just emerged from a last-ditch conference at Munich with an agreement granting the most strategic part of the Sudetenland to Germany in return for Hitler making no further territorial demands.

Le Havre, France
Sept 1939

57-19A

Tourists being evacuated from Le Havre aboard an American ship as World War II was about to break out in early September 1939. Courtesy of the Library of Congress.

The Smithies then turned their trip to Normandy into a mini-holiday, while in Paris tourists rushed to the steamship offices to cancel their reservations.[61] By the time the smoke cleared, the year 1938 ended up as the decade's high-water mark for American tourism to France, although the 170,000 visitors still paled in comparison with the almost 300,000 who had visited in 1929.[62]

Munich, of course, failed to appease Hitler. Yet the American government was firmly committed to supporting rapprochement, rather than confrontation, with him and would not support the relatively few French politicians who wanted to confront him militarily.[63] By the time the 1939 summer tourist season began, the air was again full of forebodings of war. In March German troops had taken over the rest of Czechoslovakia. War production in France and Britain went into high gear as Hitler began making demands on Poland, whose frontiers they had guaranteed. However, other news distracted tourists from the increasing probability of war. Giant new passenger liners rolled down the ways and into the headlines. The new *Queen Mary* challenged the *Normandie* for the fastest crossing time. In early July another huge new Cunard liner, the *Mauretania*, arrived at Cherbourg on its maiden voyage, carrying twelve hundred passengers, including President Roosevelt's niece. The day before, the press had gathered at the Hôtel Meurice in Paris to hear the handsome movie star Cary Grant confirm that he would marry the beautiful blond actress Phyllis Brooks. After he returned from a two-week trip to the Riviera, he would meet her in Paris and they would sail together for America.[64]

By the time the briefly happy couple reached New York in mid-August, Hitler's willingness to go to war was readily apparent. Tourists again began cutting their vacations short. Then, on August 23, Germany and the Soviet Union stunned the world by signing a nonaggression pact. This seemed to pave the way for a German invasion of Poland that would inevitably provoke French and British declarations of war. The news "burst like a bombshell in our midst," said one of the upper-class American socialites enjoying the social season in Cannes.[65] Two days later the president's mother, Sara Delano Roosevelt, cut short her long annual vacation in Paris. When she sailed on the *Washington* from Le Havre with her son John and his wife, the ship was so crowded with fleeing tourists that she had to share a cabin with her grandson.[66]

Initially, a steamship line spokesman said the demand for bookings did not match the previous year's Munich crisis.[67] However, the next day the German and Italian transatlantic liners that normally stopped in France on their way to America now bypassed it, stranding Americans booked on them. In Paris merchants began to shutter their windows. Municipal workers turned Métro stations into makeshift bomb shelters and replaced the bulbs in streetlamps with small blue ones. True to form, though, what was now called the *Paris Herald Tribune* kept churning out upbeat reports from the resorts. The beach at Deauville was already "filled with a brilliant crowd of international socialites," it said, and now that the *Grande Semaine* of race meetings had started, there were even more arrivals. Although it admitted that there had been departures "because of the crisis," it went on to list an impressive array of barons, princes, duchesses, lords, and rich Europeans and Americans who remained there, including the actor Edward G. Robinson.[68]

But by then the British and Canadian steamship lines had canceled their voyages from Europe, and stranded American tourists were flooding into Paris, searching for a safe way home. Much of Paris looked deserted, as civilians fearing bombing fled the city, but the American embassy was mobbed. Hard-up students and tourists whose finances had dwindled at the end of their summer vacations were particularly distressed, because they had no money to pay for new tickets to replace the ones that were not being honored. On August 31 the pressure eased a bit as the *Manhattan* stuffed extra cots aboard and, after doing a quick turnaround in Le Havre, sailed for New York with eleven hundred passengers, including a large group of congressmen and the film star Norma Shearer, who had been vacationing in Cannes.[69]

The next day the Germans invaded Poland and the British and French declared war. Hundreds of the Americans still in the Riviera instinctively followed the Duke and Duchess of Windsor, who hastily packed their luggage and staff into a convoy of limousines and set off for Paris. However, Barbara Hutton, heiress to the Woolworth fortune, headed for Biarritz, where she quickly paid $500,000 to her latest estranged husband, a Danish count, for custody of their three-year-old son. She then took off for Italy with the boy and her staff in two Rolls-Royces and a caravan of other vehicles. After barreling down to Naples, near its boot, they boarded the *Conte di Savoia*, which was packed with fleeing Americans. Once aboard, they were startled to learn from her cousin that he and his mother, who had also fled Biarritz in a bevy of Rolls-Royces, had boarded the ship much earlier, in Genoa, not far from the French border. The frantic Hutton entourage had driven right by the ship on their way down to the other end of Italy.[70]

Back in Paris, the gathering crowds of Americans grew frantic upon hearing that the *Normandie* had canceled her next scheduled trip to New York. However, the U.S. government began chartering American ships to ease the pressure. They, and the Cunard liner *Andorra Star*, which sailed from Cherbourg, all made it to America safely. So did the relatively few passengers on the Pan American Airways Clipper "flying boats" that had begun flying once a week to America from Marseille and Lisbon that July.[71] However, the almost six hundred Americans who, along with hundreds of Canadians, took the Cunard liner *Athenia* from Britain were not so lucky. On September 3, it was torpedoed and sank in the North Atlantic, taking 128 lives, including those of twelve Americans.[72]

The government stepped up its program of chartering American-flag vessels, sending four small boats from the American coastal trade to Europe with huge American flags painted on their sides and decks.[73] This hardly satisfied the survivors of the *Athenia*. They berated the bearer of this news, John F. Kennedy, the son of the American ambassador to London, with shouts of "We want convoys!! You can't trust the Germans! Or the government!"[74] The American embassy in Paris set up a temporary consulate in Deauville, to help the socialites caught there at the end of the *Grande Semaine* find passage back to America.[75]

Then, the strangest thing began to happen, or, rather, not to happen. As the German army swept across Poland, the Western front remained quiet. Parisians, and many of the Americans who had heeded their embassy's advice to leave Paris, now drifted back and resumed their normal lives. There was still a strong demand for accommodations on the ships back home, but mainly for the cheaper berths. First-class accommodations on most of the ships were there for the asking. By the third week in September, the social page of the *Paris Herald Tribune*, which had been full of notices of upper-class American tourists and residents leaving for America, now began to carry stories of Americans staying on in Paris, Dinard, Cannes, and other resorts.[76] Peggy Guggenheim, the wealthy New York art collector, came to Paris and spent months acquiring a huge stock of modern paintings and sculpture at laughably low prices.[77] Most famously, Gertrude Stein and her companion Alice B. Toklas decided to stay on.

Wildly optimistic French government tourism officials, heartened by news that some Italians were trickling into the Riviera to gamble, began trying to attract patrons from other neutral countries there, as well as to the Alpine ski resorts.[78]

But even the most blinkered optimist could not hold out much hope for reviving tourism in Paris. Although the cafés were again lively during the day, each evening, with the blackout, an eerie silence settled over the city.[79] With nightlife practically extinguished, the remaining African American entertainers of Montmartre began finding their way back to America.[80] The best publicized of the African American returnees, Colonel Hubert Fauntleroy Julian, the "Black Eagle of Harlem," had hardly been there at all. On September 30, after only two weeks there as the war correspondent for the *Amsterdam News*, the New York African American newspaper, he announced in a shipboard interview that he was returning to New York with "a better idea." "France," he said, "has been known for its democratic attitude towards Negroes from time immemorial." So, he would put aside war reporting and instead concentrate on raising $1 million from African Americans to send to France 2,000 nurses, 200 surgeons, 50 pilots, and 10 hospital planes. All of the pilots would be African Americans.[81]

That same day the French Line, whose ships could no longer venture into the Atlantic for fear of German submarine attack, closed its office in Rockefeller Center and laid off its thirty American employees. A sign in the window read:

For centuries France has been universally loved and respected as a land of exquisite countryside and art treasures, of valuable cultural and agricultural resources. Today conditions prevent you from visiting her shores and enjoying the beauties of her magnificent heritage. May time leave this heritage unchanged.[82]

By then, of the estimated ten thousand American tourists in France when war was declared, only about five hundred remained.[83]

In January 1940 President Roosevelt proclaimed 1940 "Travel America Year," asking Americans to visit "the friendly nations of the Western Hemisphere."[84] This surely turned out to be one of his least necessary proclamations. In May 1940 the so-called "Phony War" came to an end. The Germans swept around the Maginot Line into Belgium, whose government quickly capitulated, and headed for northern France. By the first week of June, the British army was retreating to the Channel and Dunkirk, from where it would be evacuated to England while the Germans drove southward, toward Paris. When the government packed up and fled to Bordeaux, it was accompanied by 360 notables of the American community in Paris and a crowd of stranded tourists. On June 13 the German army rumbled into Paris. Nine days later the French government signed an armistice. Under its terms, the Germans would occupy the northern half of France and the entire west coast, while a new, pro-Nazi dictatorship, headed by the eighty-four-year-old Marshal Pétain, would govern the south. The Americans in Bordeaux made their way to Portugal, where the SS *Manhattan* was waiting to pick them up. Once aboard, they wired the State Department to have financial aid awaiting the 160 of them who were completely bereft of funds. Ironically, one of the men who did have money in his pocket was robbed of it almost as soon as he left the pier in New York.[85]

Early in the morning of Sunday, June 23, 1940, Paris received its most famous, or infamous, wartime visitor. Adolf Hitler made a whirlwind three-hour tour worthy of the most superficial day-tripper. He expressed his admiration for the Opéra, peered down at Napoléon's tomb in the Invalides, posed for pictures looking over the Seine at the Eiffel Tower, was unimpressed by the interior of the Panthéon, walked past the artists' cafés in Montparnasse, and was driven up to Montmartre. There, after taking in the magnificent view, he was (like many other artistic people) struck by how "appalling" was the Sacré-Coeur, the huge nineteenth-century church at its top. On the way back to Germany, after telling the architect Albert Speer, who accompanied him, "It was the dream of my life to see Paris," he stopped for photo opportunities at the cathedrals in Laon and Strasbourg.[86]

That day, the *New York Times Magazine* ran an article from Paris saying, "Few cities so completely meet the varied wants of man; few are so full of beauty, history and pleasure; few so take possession of both senses and imagination; probably none has quite the inexhaustible enchantment of Paris. . . . If this were a normal year, throngs of Americans would now be disembarking . . . to discover or rediscover Paris. But this June the only visitors are the young men from east of the Rhine, wearing greenish-grey uniforms and steel helmets and hand grenades."[87]

WAR AND REVIVAL

2

FIVE

Martial Visitors

In October 1940 the Vichy government made one of its more sensible decisions. Citing the almost complete absence of tourism due to gas rationing and its own restrictions on foreigners entering its territory, it abolished the office of high commissioner of tourism.[1] However, the prospects for tourism seemed quite different in the large part of northern France under German occupation. Within weeks of the takeover, the German authorities created an organization called Jeder einmal in Paris (Everyone in Paris Once) to offer all of its troops a holiday in Paris and began publishing guidebooks and pamphlets about Paris for them. The Louvre was reopened, as were the Palace of Versailles and other sights. Germans were allowed to ride free on the Métro.[2] On July 6 the Casino de Paris, where Josephine Baker had performed, reopened, with a sign on its stage door saying: "ENTRANCE PROHIBITED TO DOGS AND JEWS."[3] Soon the Folies Bergère was back in business, too, as were many of Paris's swank restaurants, serving an almost exclusively German clientele.[4] The Germans commandeered many of Paris's better hotels, including the Ritz, where the Royal Suite was set aside for Hitler's close associate Hermann Göring, the rotund air force chief who became Paris's highest-profile (and perhaps largest-profile) German visitor. A bon vivant and art lover, Göring, in between sumptuous meals at Maxim's and the Ritz, set about plundering the art and jewelry of France's Jews.[5]

German tourist literature portrayed France as "simultaneously exquisite and morally deficient," a characterization with which many Americans would have agreed.[6] Indeed, the French collapse of 1940 had reinforced American doubts about the French moral backbone and made cooperation with the French forces resisting the Germans problematic. The influential syndicated columnist Westbrook Pegler, for example, said the French defeat was the result of "the decay so thoughtlessly but accurately summed up in the drunken yelp of the tourist: 'So this is Paris! Where are the naked women?'" Prewar French society was thoroughly corrupt, he said: "Everybody 'grafted.' . . . Even in their biggest and best hotels the traveler had to check his possessions against pilferage and examine the bill with care. . . . Chiseling was a national custom."[7]

The U.S. government continued to deal with the collaborationist Vichy regime until early 1943 and worked to undermine General Charles de Gaulle and his Free French movement at practically every turn. Indeed, Roosevelt developed a visceral distaste for the man, regarding him as arrogant and pompous, and vowed that he would not "give de Gaulle a white horse on which he could ride into France and make himself master of a government there." When the Americans finally gave up on Vichy, they threw their support, not to de Gaulle, but to Admiral Darlan, a last-minute convert from Vichyism. Then, when he was assassinated, they backed another ex-Vichyite, General Giraud, who was widely regarded as featherbrained and inconsequential. Even after de Gaulle maneuvered Giraud out of the leadership of the Resistance movement, the Americans were reluctant to deal with him.

American policy was based in part on the misguided notion that de Gaulle was a stalking horse for the Communists, but it was also grounded in two perceptions about the French that had arisen in America in the interwar period. One was that the French were inveterate anti-Americans. Even though it was the right-wing Vichy regime that was officially anti-American (among other things, it condemned American popular culture, especially Hollywood and jazz, for undermining traditional family values), it was de Gaulle who was thought to be the most virulent of the anti-Americans.[8] The other idea was that not only were the French personally immoral, but that their entire political culture was complacent, self-indulgent, and morally bankrupt.[9] At his meeting with Stalin and Churchill in Tehran in November 1943, Roosevelt agreed with Stalin that the Vichy regime, which they both now thought nefarious, represented the "real" France. Roosevelt said that no Frenchman over the age of forty should be allowed to participate in postwar politics, as they were all corrupt.[10] He and his advisers planned to ignore de Gaulle and the Resistance after the planned invasion of France. The American army would occupy and run liberated France and set it on the road to becoming an open, honest society.[11]

Luckily for the American image in France, the plans to administer France directly, which would surely have propelled French anti-Americanism to astronomical levels, were shelved just before the June 1944 invasion of Normandy. The United States reluctantly recognized de Gaulle as head of a provisional government of France, and the American troops landed as liberators, not occupiers. When they broke out of Normandy in the late summer and pushed south toward Paris and west toward Germany, people lined the streets of the villages and towns to cheer them on, inviting them to share glasses of wine, scarce food, and, at times, their beds. For many of the GIs in the advance columns, it was, as a tank commander later recalled, "an emotional thrill to liberate a French town. After the fighting was over . . . the streets were suddenly filled with joyous crowds of people who appeared from nowhere. We were offered everything and anything they had in the way of food and drink."[12]

The first Americans to reach Paris were greeted by a tumultuous welcome. Captain Ben Welles said, "A physical wave of human emotion picked us up and carried us into the heart of Paris." As he leaned over, ankle-deep in flowers, to embrace a gray-haired women reaching up to kiss him, she said, "Thank God you're here. Paris will be Paris again." The French, said one sergeant, "made each of us feel like Lindbergh must have felt when he went up Broadway." By the time Major S. L. A. Marshall's jeep reached the Seine, there were sixty-seven bottles of champagne clanking around in it. That night Parisians swept the GIs into their arms, dancing, drinking, singing, and often making love with them. It was, said one private, "the greatest night the world had ever known . . . a glorious night of wine, women and song."[13] The lovemaking that night was so widespread that a Catholic group hastily ran off tracts addressed to Paris's young women saying, "In the gaiety of the Liberation do not throw away your innocence. Think of your future family."[14]

The reverberations of this "greatest night" would be felt for years to come. The stories of easy sex flashed through the military, reinforcing the World War I doughboys' stories of Frenchwomen being easy pickings. *Life* magazine, widely read at the front as well as at home, was a particularly enthusiastic purveyor of stories and pictures of Frenchwomen welcoming GIs into their arms.[15] The troops who followed would be disappointed to find that most Frenchwomen were not at all cut from this cloth.

The vanguard entering Paris also included a tourist, of a sort. The middle-aged writer Ernest Hemingway was officially a war correspondent for *Collier's* magazine but spent little time writing. He had donned a helmet to cover his thinning hair, strapped a pistol around his thickening belly, and attached himself to a Free French irregular unit outside the city. Later he liked to tell of his leading them straight to his favorite watering hole, the bar of the Hôtel Ritz, and liberating it from the Germans. According to him, when he arrived there with David Bruce, an upper-class American intelligence officer, and about seventy scruffy-looking French Resistance fighters, he found only one person there, an assistant manager, who recognized him and Bruce from before the war. When the employee asked what he could

Crowds welcoming Allied troops during the liberation of Paris on August 25, 1944. Frank L. Duberbvill / National Archives of Canada / PA130252.

get for them, Hemingway said he replied, "How about seventy-three dry martinis?" Hemingway immediately ensconced himself in the hotel, surrounded by a more than ample supply of Scotch whiskey, and spent much of the time holding court for crowds of army officers, journalists, and attractive women such as his fellow Ritz resident the actress Marlene Dietrich. In his seven months in Paris, he filed only two articles for *Collier's*.[16]

The next large group of Americans to pass through Paris did so under more unusual circumstances. On August 27 de Gaulle, fearing that Communist resistance groups might challenge his control of the city, asked General Dwight Eisenhower to send an American division into the city to demonstrate Allied support for him. Ike complied, and two days later the entire Twenty-ninth Infantry Division arrived, in full battle dress, at the eastern edge of the city. It promptly marched down the Champs-Elysées and then kept right on going out the other end of the city, arriving at the battlefront before the end of the day.[17]

Within weeks a horde of journalists, military functionaries, diplomats, and anyone else who could find the lamest of official reasons were pouring over from London to visit Paris. Like the Germans, the American army now requisitioned most of the city's luxury hotels for its officers. French wags were soon saying that SHAEF (Supreme Headquarters Allied Expeditionary Force) stood for "Société hôtellerie d'Américaines en France"— American Hotel Corporation in France.[18] One hotel, the Scribe, was set aside for journalists. After some weeks at the Ritz, Hemingway moved in there and quickly became a fixture at its bar. Officers with an interest in literature and art were soon making pilgrimages there, as well as to the apartments of Gertrude Stein and Pablo Picasso, who now lived around the corner from each other on the Left Bank.[19] Other officers discovered the *bonnes adresses*—the high-class whorehouses—that were even more welcoming to the new conquerors than they had been to the old. Luxury restaurants such as Maxim's and the Tour d'Argent, which were said to have been rather too solicitous to their predecessors in field gray, allowed senior Allied officers to dine free. Perfume companies showered them with gifts of

GIs marching through the place de la Concorde in full battle dress on August 29, 1944, in what was intended as a show of force to the French communists. Courtesy of the Library of Congress.

free perfume for their wives and girlfriends. Fine seafood restaurants such as the Mediterranée performed miracles on the black market to turn out fabulously fresh dishes for the new visitors.[20]

As combat troops began making their way back to Paris on two- or three-day "Rest and Recuperation" passes, many enlisted men were also able to bask in the post-Liberation glow. Ernie Ricci, a sergeant who set up a mess hall for American troops in a Paris hotel, recalled giving chewing gum to everyone and food to the children. "We were well liked, well looked upon, the heroes," he said. Both men and women, he thought, "liked our mentality—full of piss and vinegar. We were their heroes."[21] Simone de Beauvoir recalled, "The easy-going manner of the young Americans incarnated liberty itself."[22] Closer to the battlefront, the GIs continued to be welcomed as liberators. Joseph Gusfield recalls his unit being rushed through northern France that winter to help in the relief of the troops surrounded in Bastogne, in Belgium. Unable to leave their trucks for the twenty-four-hour ride, they were forced to urinate and defecate off the backs. When they did so on the main streets of villages where they were stopped, the villagers would gather around and cheer them.[23]

The GIs on leave in Paris quickly found their way to Montmartre, and the streetwalkers who congregated around place Pigalle at the foot of its hill. The writer John Phillips recalled Paris being engulfed by "a sea of cocksmen":

> We soldier chauvinists called it Pig Alley and GIs in filthy fatigues and muddy boots were hauled in from the front in six by six trucks and dumped loose on a forty-eight-hour pass. The whores gathered at the truck stops to select the evening's clients, removing the men's helmet liner, running fingers through his scalp to check for lice.[24]

Men in khaki uniforms now replaced those in gray in the audience at the Folies Bergère and other such shows. The U.S. Army took over the Olympia, the famed music hall theater, and sponsored nonstop entertainment by such stars as Fred Astaire. The Glenn Miller Orchestra stayed in Paris from December 1944 to October 1945, playing for American and French audiences despite the death of its leader, which was rumored to have occurred not, as officially reported, in an airplane crash, but in a Paris *maison close*.[25] Ricci recalled the dance halls being packed with carousing GIs. "We had a couple of bucks in our pockets. We used to spend our money until we were broke, and then wait for paydays to do it all over again."[26]

After the Germans were ousted from the Riviera in August 1944, the

GIs heeding the army's advice to take advantage of their free trip to Europe to do some sightseeing. Courtesy of the National Archives.

army turned it into the "United States Riviera Rest Area." The city of Nice was set aside for enlisted men. By the time the war ended in May 1945, some six thousand GIs a week were arriving there to spend ten-day leaves in some of its fanciest old hotels, where boys from Iowa and Nebraska basked in huge rooms overlooking the sea. Vehicles with loudspeakers rode back and forth on the promenade, announcing the free movies, jazz concerts, and nightclub shows that were laid on for them that evening. Traffic signs in English were erected everywhere, completing the feeling of being an occupied city.[27] The American Express office quickly reopened, offering tours in open-air sightseeing buses. These carefully skirted Monte Carlo, which, having provided too warm a welcome to German and Italian officers during the war, was declared off-limits to army personnel.[28]

Time magazine called Nice "GI Heaven," a place with "no saluting" signs where enlisted man could have "a millionaire's vacation for peanuts."[29] One heavenly aspect was that officers were nowhere to be seen, for they spent their leaves where the real millionaires had cavorted. Cannes was set aside for male officers and the Hôtel du Cap, a super-luxury hotel in nearby Cap d'Antibes, was the preserve of the highest-ranking officers. Juan-les-Pins, an exclusive resort between Cap d'Antibes and Cannes, was reserved for the Women's Army Corps and Red Cross nurses. Together, they all helped turn Cannes' Palm-Beach Casino into a giant American nightclub.[30]

Like the Germans, the War Department tried to prepare its troops for touring France. It distributed guidebooks to the south and north of France that said, "So far as your military duties permit, see as much as you can. You've got a great chance to do now, major expenses paid, what would cost you a lot of your own money after the war. Take advantage of it." The *Pocket Guide to Paris and the Cities of Northern France*, published in the summer of 1944, included advice on what to see in bombed-out Rouen, where Allied air raids had severely damaged the cathedral and leveled the medieval buildings and historic bridges along its riverfront, as well as in Cherbourg, whose port had also been practically obliterated.[31] In April 1945, as the war was ending, a GI who had slogged through many of these cities wrote home: "I came through Metz on the way up but did not see much of it. What I did see was blasted to pieces. That is the way with the army. . . ."[32]

As the liberated zone expanded, the booklets were merged into *A Pocket Guide to France*. It now advised visiting Nice, Cannes, and other liberated Mediterranean ports; however, since it was written before the liberation of Paris, which was expected to cause severe damage, it was unsure about what there would be to see there.[33]

The guide predicted a "rousing welcome" for the GIs, saying that their fathers and uncles who served in World War I would have told them, "Americans are popular in France." Yet, in fact, much of its advice was aimed at avoiding the many conflicts that had arisen during that war. It cautioned, for example, against sneering at French farmers as backward "hicks" because they did not use machinery. It also warned against getting drunk. "Like all wine-drinking people," it said, "the French do not drink to get drunk. Drunkenness is rare in France. . . . The only thing the French have never been able to say against the Nazi Army of Occupation was that it was a drunken army. Don't let them say it about the American army."[34]

During World War I, the American military authorities, particularly General Pershing, worried that venereal diseases were putting more American soldiers out of commission than the enemy. Yet by barring doughboys from the *maisons de tolérance,* where licensed prostitutes underwent regular health checks, they helped contribute to the spread of infection by unlicensed streetwalkers. The World War II American military authorities did not make the same mistake. However, the pamphlet warned that "no system of examination ever made a prostitute safe. Her health card means absolutely nothing." Either the "regular" or "irregular" (i.e., unlicensed) prostitutes "can present you with a nasty souvenir of Paris."[35] As for "gay Paree," it warned that

> the French have far less of a regular habit of pleasure than we Americans. Even before the Nazi occupation . . . a whole French family would spend less on pleasure in a month than you would spend on a weekend. The French reputation for gaiety was principally built on the civilized French way of doing things; by the French people's good taste; by their interest in quality, not quantity; and by the lively energy of their minds.[36]

It also said, "The French have a remarkable capacity for minding their own business. [They do not] sit in railway cars and tell their private affairs to a total stranger. They are observant; don't think they won't notice what you do. But they have little curiosity."[37]

The provisional French government also tried to smooth the way for GI tourists. It set up an agency on the avenue de l'Opéra to arrange sightseeing tours, get them tickets for the Folies Bergère, and provide them with addresses of restaurants.[38] The newly reestablished office of commissioner of tourism rushed out English-language guides to France, complete with apologies for the delay in rebuilding the 1.5 million homes destroyed during the war.[39] When some drunken GIs broke through the police lines during a major French army parade and were pushed around by his men, the prefect of police apologized and promised that henceforth they would not be "molested" by his force.[40]

— —

All of this did little to forestall the rapid end of the honeymoon. Initially, an estimated ten thousand GIs failed to return to their units from leaves in Paris. Although most soon found their way back, hundreds of others deserted and found that they could subsist in the city by selling cigarettes, gasoline, or a host of other supplies stolen from army bases. In the four months after the Normandy landing, some 15.5 million of the 17.5 million jerry cans that the U.S. Army used to deliver gasoline disappeared in

France: that is, more than 300 million liters of gas. Prostitutes became enthusiastic intermediaries in the booming black market. Long lines of GIs would wait patiently outside the officially sanctioned *maisons closes*, a carton of Lucky Strikes in hand or a jerry can of gasoline at their feet.[41]

The exchange of cigarettes or gasoline for sex or alcohol soon blossomed into a vast illicit traffic in all kinds of military goods. The deserters, who often acted as middlemen or armed protectors in the black-market trade, sometimes supplemented this income with that from muggings and armed robberies.[42] One gang of twelve deserters, led by an Eddie Bass, terrorized a small village in the north of France for almost a year, using it as a base from which, dressed as MPs, they robbed banks, pillaged storehouses and isolated farmsteads, and raided American bases. They would shoot cows and sheep in fields with their carbines and sell the carcasses on the Paris black market.[43]

The situation deteriorated further after the war in Europe ended in mid-April 1945. Preparations for the anticipated invasion of Japan now meant redirecting shipping and men to the Pacific, leaving over 4 million troops in Europe waiting impatiently to go home. A vast demobilization process began after Japan's defeat in August, but there was no way transport could be found for a quick exit from Europe. The army tried desperately to keep the troops occupied and to minimize conflicts with the French. Paris, Reims, Marseille, and some other cities were declared leave towns. Three large camps, through which over 500,000 soldiers would pass, were set up in the beautiful Champagne countryside outside of Reims, a city of about 100,000. Almost all of its recreational facilities were commandeered for their use—16 hotels, 34 apartments, 16 restaurants, 4 theaters, 4 dance halls, 4 campgrounds, 2 athletic stadiums, 2 gymnasiums, and a tennis court. Four Red Cross clubs and two officers' clubs were set up, along with a recreation center. Despite the reputation of the local bubbly beverage, they erected a Coca-Cola factory.[44] Le Havre was ringed by huge tent camps, each named after a brand of American cigarettes, where tens of thousands of GIs milled about waiting for ships to take them home. The military authorities there tried to diffuse the explosive tensions with the locals by organizing sports events between teams of GIs and local men. They invited locals to concerts in the camps given by such notable groups as the Duke Ellington and Glenn Miller orchestras. They gave out free clothing and cleaned up the town beach so that it could be opened for swimming.[45]

Other schemes were aimed at keeping GIs on leave from pouring into Paris. In November the Army Air Force began offering them the use of jeeps to take unescorted tours of Europe.[46] Perhaps the most ambitious effort to distract the troops was to bring over three hundred faculty from American colleges and universities to set up two universities, in France and England, as soon as the war ended. Not only would they occupy idle soldiers; they would also begin fulfilling the government's commitment to provide veterans with access to further education.[47] The army practically took over Biarritz, turning forty of its hotels and nearly one hundred of its villas into classrooms and dormitories. The ornate casino was converted into a library, and the spectacular palace of Napoléon III's Empress Eugénie, which had been turned into a luxury hotel, became the mess hall. By mid-August close to four thousand students were enrolled in each of the universities for two-month courses in such subjects as engineering, agriculture, fine arts, and the liberal arts. Years later Nathan Shoehalter, a lowly private from New Jersey, recalled, "It was wonderful. I was housed in a hotel [and] we had our meals at Empress Eugénie's palace. It was a huge hotel . . . absolutely spectacular." On weekends they were taken on overnight trips to Bordeaux, Lourdes, and other tourist attractions.[48]

The over ten thousand men who passed through Biarritz by the time it closed in March 1946 were called "the most contented GIs in Europe," but there was not much competition for that label in most of France. Only in Paris were there many signs of GIs having soldiers' proverbial good times, and even there, gloomy faces often prevailed. On any given day, up to sixty thousand American troops were there, about six thousand of them on three-day or five-day passes. By day, said Newsweek, they would wander about, "aimless, incurious, vaguely lonely."[49] Typical of them was Clarence Davis, a thirty-seven-year-old private from North Carolina who got a one-day pass to visit Paris in February 1945. He wrote his wife:

I used the subway but you can't see much from it and I did not know how to find places I wanted to see. And it seems none of the GIs I met knew either. There is not any use to ask any of these frogs anything for they will just chatter for about ten minutes and you do not know any more than you did before.[50]

After a later visit, he told her that the best thing about Paris was the fountain Coke at the Red Cross canteen.[51]

At night GIs would flock to Montmartre, especially to the bars, strip joints, and cabarets around "Pig-Alley."[52] There they would get drunk and maudlin listening to sexy chanteuses singing doleful songs, be conned into paying outrageous prices for champagne and cognac by cabarets' sultry entreneuses, or dance wildly with young Frenchwomen who claimed to be interested in learning how to jitterbug. "For many GIs," said Life magazine, "it adds up to an adolescent boy's dream of Paris come true, with some interesting grown-up overtones."[53]

— —

For many Parisians, though, the dream was more like a nightmare. Most disconcerting was the widespread public drunkenness and the violence that often accompanied it. In this respect, the most celebrated Americans seemed to be no better than the lowliest army privates. Stories circulated about how some officers who Hemingway entertained at the Ritz had vomited all over his paramour Mary Welsh's bathroom and that he had drunkenly beaten her when she complained of their oafish behavior. He was also said to have wrecked his own room's bathroom by shooting it up with a German machine pistol. Another story told of how the staff of the Hôtel George V had to call the gendarmes to break up a drunken chair-smashing brawl between a gang composed of Hemingway and his friends and those of the writer William Saroyan, whom he had insulted.[54]

In January and February 1945, when Parisians were polled about GI behavior, three-quarters had rated it as at least "generally good" while only a quarter pronounced it "rarely good" or "never good."[55] Within weeks, though, reports of growing resentment toward the GIs were pouring into the American embassy. In one instance, it was said, a crowd of Parisians stood about and cheered when a woman responded to the usual wolf whistles and offers of a pack of "Luckys" by taking one of the cigarettes and then grinding it underfoot.[56] By November 1945 it was clear that French dissatisfaction was very widespread. *Newsweek* reported that the French disliked being pushed off the streets by rowdy Americans and did not appreciate drunken soldiers' pranks, such as tossing French babies in the air or pulling loaves of bread from under housewives' arms. They resented the comments and passes the GIs made at women and "the totally false assumption they make that all young women can be had." Above all, though, they could not abide the drunkenness: the soldier "lunging in and out of subway stations, stores, and cafés, in broad daylight with a bottle sticking out of his pocket" who uncorks it and takes a long swig on the street. "They are amazed," it said, "at the glass- and bottle-throwing, window-breaking, brawls, knifings, and shootings that punctuate the nights of certain sections of their cities." Drunken GIs lay passed out practically everywhere, in bushes, Métro stations, and on sidewalks, until MPs came along and picked them up.[57]

Similar complaints resounded in the embarkation port of Marseille, where local women were outraged by GIs who would walk down the street asking every passing woman, "How much?"[58] On the Riviera, people who had initially welcomed the creation of the "Riviera Leave Zone" for its much-needed economic shot in the arm now had second thoughts, as prostitutes swarmed in from Marseille, Toulouse, and even Paris, and drunken, violent GIs prowled the streets bent on destruction. "The streets of Nice are not safe at night," said a local newspaper. At a protest meeting in May 1945, a physician pleaded with American authorities to rein in those soldiers "who forget that Nice is place of repose, not an extension of the field of battle."[59]

In Le Havre, residents complained of a steady stream of armed robberies, beatings, hit-and-runs, and pedestrians killed by vehicles driven by what they suspected were drunken GIs. Among the dead were a women's college teacher hit by a truck and a three-year-old girl run over by an amphibious vehicle. Night after night there were reports of brawls between GIs, often brandishing weapons, and locals, including a perplexing story about an Algerian passerby having been beaten to death by five or six African American soldiers.[60] Finally, in early November, the military admitted that the bars and cabarets of the port had become like the "Barbary Coast" and bowed to French demands that they be made off-limits to Americans. In addition, GIs on furlough would be able to visit other towns in the area only in groups led by an officer. The American military in Reims, responding to similar complaints, moved the curfew up from midnight to 11:00 PM and flooded the town with MPs, who, along with French police, tried reining in prostitutes. In a laughable attempt to provide an alternative to going to town, they mounted what was described as an "educational exhibit of photomurals" in one of the camps.[61]

Le Monde ascribed some of the conflicts between GIs and locals to GI frustration at not being able to get home. It called Le Havre "the port of bitter men" and quoted the American commander in Marseille as saying such problems were the inevitable result of having one group of men who did not want to be there thrust alongside another who did not want them there. In November the U.S. government hastily fitted out twelve large warships with extra bunks and hammocks to aid in the evacuation of Le Havre, but the problem continued to fester into the next year.[62]

In Paris, where regular reports of assaults, robberies, and occasional murders continued, French newspapers began turning on the liberators. In early November, *Resistance* carried a front-page editorial saying that Hollywood movies had led the French to believe that Americans were hardy, polite, chivalrous, and refined. It was hard to associate these images with the often-hostile soldiers they met every day. Parisians thought it much funnier to watch a Texan shoot up a saloon on the screen than to see it happen in a

Montmartre bar. *Combat*, another generally pro-American paper, estimated that GIs in the Paris region were responsible for thirty acts of violence each night.[63]

A few nights later, these perceptions were reinforced. On the night of November 10, as the provisional government was preparing to hand over power to a new National Assembly, gangs of uniformed GIs roamed through Paris, beating up passersby and stealing their wallets. They cut a broad swath from Montmartre through the elegant Passy district and then rampaged down the Champs-Elysées, where some of them broke into a hotel and forced the manager to hand over his cash box. *Le Monde* said that Frenchmen wondered if these men belonged to the same army of healthy young men who had liberated them last year.[64]

General Eisenhower warned GIs "whose standards of courtesy . . . had fallen below the level that Americans habitually observe at home" to begin minding their manners. But the Paris disturbances continued on and off through the next week. Several gangs of soldiers beat up pedestrians at the traffic circle around the Arc de Triomphe with revolver butts and made their way up to Montmartre. One group robbed a café before they were finally intercepted by French police, who managed to arrest only two of them and turn them over to MPs.[65] "We've always had cases of assault, battery, larceny, manslaughter, and murder," said the officer commanding the MPs in the Paris area. "What we have now is a general increase in disorders—drunkenness, petty robbery, assaults, and destruction of civilian property."[66]

The French police, on the other hand, assessed the situation much more seriously. Some years later, a retired French detective recalled:

> The American GIs, who displayed a brutality unknown in France, introduced an unheard of level of violence into the criminality of this country. They attacked banks, jeweler's shops, and did not hesitate to kill in cold blood to obtain their ends. . . . The number of criminals, big and little, who were part of this army was truly impressive. For some of them, murder was just an ordinary thing. Hardly a week passed without the discovery of a prostitute killed in a hotel, in Paris or the provinces. In Reims, where the Americans constructed a huge camp for the blacks, camp "San Francisco," the owners of the *établissements*, fearing brawls, closed up before nightfall. But the soldiers knocked down the doors with their trucks, forcing the *patrons* to serve them drinks and occupying themselves with the prostitutes who the pimps had brought in from the region for them. Violence erupted every night and more than one American was found drowned in the canal.[67]

For French newspaper readers, the image that now came to mind was that of the 1930s gangster movies. "PARIS MUST NOT BECOME CHICAGO" was how *Ce Soir*, the Communist mass-circulation paper, headlined a story saying that MPs had seized a large arsenal of weapons used by an American gang.[68] The French military governor of Paris told an Englishwoman at a British embassy dinner that the American servicemen were "barbarians, worse than the Russians. You cannot imagine, *chère madame*," he told her, "how appalling the situation is."[69]

Disappointment over America's failure to help France get back on her feet made matters worse. In a September 1944 poll, 67 percent of the French people who were asked which nation they expected to help them most to recover from the war responded the United States. In January 1945 only 24 percent thought so, while 25 percent thought it would be the Soviets. In June 1945, asked which country had disappointed their hopes most in the past year, 54 percent named the United States.[70]

— —

GIs' perceptions of the French deteriorated about as rapidly as those of the French toward them. By late 1944 and early 1945, the atmosphere resembled that of late 1918 and early 1919, when many doughboys also soured on the French. As in 1918, the first major American complaints were against French overcharging. Now this problem was exacerbated by the unrealistically low number of francs they received for their dollars on the official market. The exchange rate had been set by the French and Americans when the United States invaded North Africa in 1943 and was maintained unchanged, it was said, in order to prevent GIs from using strong dollars to buy up all the consumer goods in France. However, that reasoning cut little ice with GIs on leave who were charged a week's pay for a dinner.[71] Nor did the knowledge that French shops often had two prices—an American price and a lower French price—create many friends. In January 1945 the *New York Times* reported that thousands of letters were arriving daily in America complaining that the French were gouging the very GIs who drove the Germans from France. One of its correspondents warned, "If two million American boys come home with the idea that after doing so much to liberate France Frenchmen profiteered at their expense, we will have the same situation that followed the last war."[72]

The *New York Times* report set the French Ministry of Foreign Affairs to worrying that the "profound bitterness . . . reflected in [the GIs'] correspondence . . . will probably be echoed before long in the whole country and in Congress."[73] Yet the government's refusal to alter the exchange rate just fueled the bitterness. GIs forced to use the black market to get a decent rate for their dollars were often swindled by shady operators. The many French people who accosted them offering to buy everything from their uniforms to butter contributed to the idea that the French preferred to live off the black market and stolen goods rather than work for a living. In July 1945 a French-speaking U.S. Army officer who was a self-described "Francophile" told French government officials that the Americans thought the French were mercenary, lazy, poor workers, morally deficient, filthy, dishonest, and seething with anti-Americanism.[74] A *Newsweek* report from Paris that week said that, aside from the normal restlessness of troops wanting to go home, most of the GIs "now detest" France. They felt they were being swindled when they paid for things at the high official rate for the franc, only to be offered the same items for much less on the black market. Yet when they tried dealing on the black market, they were usually cheated as well. When they visited Paris and the other designated leave centers "for the sole purpose of having a good time," they ended up "in Montmartre or some other entertainment center" where "beneath the honky-tonk Bohemian color, float[ed] some of the worst elements of the French population—prostitutes and thieves." Paris's reputation was not enhanced when it was revealed that it was the chief source of venereal infection for troops in Europe.[75]

There now resurfaced the notion that the Germans were preferable to the French. *Newsweek* said, "[The GI] compares the mercenary, unsavory French streetwalker with the unprofessional, acquiescent German girl and, of course, prefers the fräulein." He compared the rubble still lying around battle-scarred French towns with the neat and tidy Bavarian hamlets he had seen and concluded that "the French are lazy and shiftless."[76] In June 1945 Horace Day, a GI whose battalion had been transferred from Germany to Paris, wrote in his diary that "most of the boys regret the good old days of living like conquerors among a supine people. They forget that these Germans would not be so cordial if they did not *have* to be. The French being a free people reserve the right to be rude to us if we behave like barbarians, which we sometimes do. Every French girl is not 'a two-bit broad.'"[77] He also noted that his comrades thought that the French were lazy, and he was incredulous that

> ninety per cent of the men in our battalion prefer the Germans to the French and their argument is that they are more civilized! I asked one of the men what he meant by that, and he said they had a higher standard of living and were cleaner. How ironical it is that we Americans consider a nation which has tol-

erated the most horrible savagery and oppression . . . the most civilized! Are we so materialistic that we can only judge a country's culture by its plumbing?[78]

Yet this was indeed the case. Julian Bach, a journalist who accompanied the army for two years while it slogged its way through the villages of France into Germany, reported that the GI arriving in Germany from France "smelled less manure in the countryside, and found more sidewalks in the cities. As the highest praise that most Americans feel like bestowing on anything foreign is 'It's Clean!' he was surprised and pleased with Germany's physical plant."[79]

Gertrude Stein was outraged at the many GIs she heard speak of their preference for the Germans and tried to tell them it was because the Germans obeyed and flattered them, while the French were independent and honest about their feelings toward them.[80] In January 1946 a letter writer to the *New York Times* who had just returned from two years in Europe tried to explain the preference for the Germans a little more realistically. The GI in Europe, he said, wanted only a "good deal," that is good food, good quarters, and women to do his bidding.

He has little respect for civilians, no interest in their affairs. If he doesn't understand their language, he jabbers and hoots at them, and they, knowing they must smile at their "conquerors" if they want to wangle extra blankets, clothing, or delicacies, are complaisant. In Germany, naturally, the GI gets the best deal. . . . The Germans yield because their main concern is for the physical well-being the Americans can furnish them. . . . In France the deal is different. The GI doesn't find the all-out bootlicking of Germany. He can't make France the plaything he heard it was from his dad and from the liberators of 1944.[81]

The army tried to combat the negative view of the French by distributing a clever pamphlet called *112 Gripes about the French* by the writer Leo Rosten, who was then stationed in Paris. It included such complaints and answers as

4. "The French don't bathe."

The French don't bathe often enough. They can't. They don't have real soap. They have had no soap worthy of the name since 1940. The Germans took the soap, for four years. That's a long time. The ration for a Frenchman today, four months after the war is over, is two cakes of poor ersatz soap per month—20 grams every two months. . . .

14. "Every time we go into a night club we get soaked by these Frenchmen."

Were you never soaked in a night club at home? . . . A GI comes out of a night club in the States and says, "A buck and a half for a Scotch and soda! That place is a clip joint!" The same GI comes out of night club in Paris and says, "Ninety francs for a shot of cognac! That's the French for you—they're all robbers!" . . .

25. "The French are gypping us."

Some Frenchmen have certainly gypped *some* Americans. We remember the times we were gypped. We forget the number of times we were not. How many times were you treated fairly, honestly? Were you never "gypped" back home—in towns near army camps? . . .

52. "You can drive all through Paris and never see anyone working."

It depends on where you drive and where you look. Incidentally, where did you get the gas and time to drive "all though Paris?" . . .

56. "French women are immoral."

Which French women? Most French girls before the war had far less freedom than our girls back home. A great many were not permitted to go out without a chaperone. France is dominantly Catholic in religion and in morals. The immoral French women are, of course, the easiest women for us to meet. That's why we meet so many of them.[82]

Although about 200,000 copies were distributed, the pamphlet could probably best be seen as testimony to the powerlessness of the written word. Surly troops continued to mill about French cities and towns well into 1946. In January of that year, with 1.5 million troops still in Europe, repatriation was slowed down. Ostensibly this was in order to ensure that enough remained to man the occupying armies, but it was also to send a signal to the Soviets, with whom relations were rapidly cooling. GIs in France joined in worldwide demonstrations calling for a speedup in the process, forming a "GI Liberating Committee" that marched through the streets of Paris.[83] The government responded to the protests and the threat of political repercussions at home by speeding up the pace of repatriation. By the end of July 1946, the last of the war veterans who wanted repatriation had returned to the States.

— —

By the time the last troop ship pulled out of Cherbourg harbor, the GI presence in France had made indelible marks on both the Americans and the

French. On the American side, it had a dual impact. On the one hand, particularly among the enlisted men, it had helped reinforce the stereotypes of the French that had flourished in the aftermath of World War I. "The general opinion all down the line," an American reporter said, "was that France was a tremendous brothel inhabited by 40 million hedonists who spent all their time eating, drinking, making love and in general having a hell of a good time."[84] Returning GIs once again regaled the folks back home with stories of how sexy, greedy, immoral, and perfidious were the French. GIs such as Clarence Davis, a middle-aged, not-very-well-educated mill worker from North Carolina, had already written from wartime and postwar France portraying a people who were "backward," hated work, were "disgusting . . . European negro lovers," and could not even produce good beer and wine.[85]

On the other hand, for many of the officers and the better-educated enlisted men, their time in France reinforced the historic stereotypes of France as a center of civilization and culture. The writer Irwin Shaw, who entered Paris as a private in the Signal Corps on Liberation Day, had dreamed of becoming a writer in Paris since he was an eleven-year-old boy reading French novels in Brooklyn. What he saw confirmed to him that Paris was a city where great writers flourished. He returned on a visit in 1951 and ended up spending much of the rest of his life there.[86] Some GIs fell so much under the spell of Paris's beauty that they did not even return to the States for demobilization. In April 1946 an American relief worker in Paris wrote home about the "youngsters who, when demobilized, wanted to stay longer to learn more about the place."

> I asked one young journalist the other day why he decided to stay on after he got out of the Army. "I was in the Place de la Concorde one evening at sunset, and when I looked from the Tuileries along the Champs-Elysées to the Arc de Triomphe, I simply could not leave all that beauty!"[87]

Other soldiers stayed on for less aesthetic reasons. One GI, who had made so much money on black-market dealings that he bought two hotels, stayed on after being demobilized to run the hotels. Another sized up French banks as easy pushovers and stayed on as a bank robber.[88] After the war ended, sergeant Ernie Ricci kept having the authorities extend his tour in Paris. Finally, when they would do so no longer, he obtained an American passport at the embassy and arranged to be demobilized there, rather than back home in Boston. In 1999, when asked why he had done this, he replied, "I was having too good a time." How was this good time defined? "Wine, women, and song," he replied. Despite the postwar shortage of electricity, he said, Paris was "the city of light and music. . . . Life was much gayer than it is now." If he had gone home, he said, he would have had to "settle down."[89]

— —

Among the French, the GI legacy was as varied as among the Americans. As we have seen, the GI presence revived the anti-American stereotypes that had flourished after World War I. Among these was the French Right's notions that Americans were uncultured, materialistic boors, who had no respect for morality or family values, and the Left's view that America was the fountainhead of dehumanizing capitalist imperialism. As in the aftermath of World War I, all were united by the feeling that the GIs were overbearing louts who had overstayed their welcome. In March 1946 the American government arranged a tour of France for a group of small-town American newspaper editors in the hope that it would build sympathy for the French and help head off a revival of isolationism in Middle America. Yet even they recognized that the American military presence had put off many of the French. The U.S. Army had inevitably "stayed too long," an Illinois editor wrote home. "The French do not say this in many words, but they thank God that the American occupation is over."[90]

By then, many of the French were also convinced that the Americans preferred the hated Germans to them. In part, this was the result of knowing what GIs now said among themselves. However, much of the bitterness had originated in the tough winter of 1944–45, when the French, facing severe food shortages, saw GIs, complying with the international rules of war, provide German prisoners-of-war with rations equivalent to their own. The sight of German POWs who were supposed to be working at reconstructing France sitting around munching on bananas, oranges, chocolate, and other delicacies the French had not seen for years could be infuriating, to say the least.[91] It is not surprising that one of the main reasons given by the 54 percent of French people who expressed great disappointment with the Americans in June 1945 was their insufficient toughness toward the Germans.[92]

— —

However, the military legacy was not all negative. Many French people in the towns liberated by the Americans nursed the joyous feelings of days of the Liberation for the rest of their lives. The impressive American war machine, and the outpouring of goods it brought to France, also stimulated admiration for Americans' efficiency and their ability to get things done. Many French people now thought the American system of mass production and consumption was producing a fruitful combination of liberty plus power.[93] The GIs' casual informality seemed to embody this freedom. Years later, when she saw some young GIs in France, Simone de Beauvoir recalled those days when America seemed to represent a new world, where youth and informality ruled the day. "America symbolized so many things!" she thought. "It had stimulated our youth."[94]

The GIs' aura of freedom and informality also spurred admiration for American popular culture, particularly among the young. French youngsters took to chewing gum, imitating GIs' casual style of dress when on leave, and listening to American popular music. French jazz buffs, though often shocked at the animosities that divided black and white troops, encountered enough American jazz lovers to reinforce their positive views of this aspect of American culture. Here, too, the impact was mainly on the young. In April 1946, when jazz aficionados circulated a petition calling on the government radio network to play more jazz, they pointedly said, "Jazz is the music of the young." For them, it symbolized a break with the older generation who had gotten France into such a pickle in 1939.[95] A French study of Le Havre concluded that, despite the tensions brought by the two years of American presence there, the people of the city learned to appreciate "swing" and "jive," as well as the "the famous 'negro spirituals,'" which they heard "during the black troops' religious ceremonies."[96] This undercurrent of appreciation for American popular culture, and its association with youth and modernity, would help deflate the jeremiads of the intellectuals who, over the next half-century, would regularly denounce its pernicious influence in France.

SIX

A Tattered Welcome Mat

As the war came to an end, many French businessmen and officials began hoping that American tourist dollars would help lift their prostrate country back on its feet. In July 1945 Emile Servan-Schreiber, editor of the business newspaper *Les Echos*, warned that if the French did not encourage American tourism, and instead followed those who wanted to "drape ourselves in our dignity and in our patched-up coat like Don Quixote," their country would remain in ruins, like a twentieth-century Pompeii. "The choice is clear," he said, "Miami or Pompeii? I vote Miami."[1]

This view found considerable support in the provisional government, which began using its meager resources to encourage dollar-bearing soldiers to spend their money on tourism.[2] Its first ventures were rather tentative. One of its first English-language brochures was reluctant to portray war-ravaged France as the land of joie de vivre. "One didn't want [the face of France] to look like those of other times, times of the bonheur de vivre," it said in Franglais. So, along with the usual pictures of beautiful attractions, there were two pages of photos of "murdered cities," such as Caen and Falaise, which were reduced to rubble in the Allied invasion, and the town of Oradour-sur-Glane, which the Germans systematically destroyed after executing its entire population in reprisal for suspected support for Resistance attacks.[3]

But there could be no ambivalence over the fact that France desperately needed American tourists' dollars, for the war had wrecked the French economy.[4] In late 1944 its industry was producing only 20 percent of what it had in 1939.[5] Although Paris escaped relatively unscathed, one-quarter of all the buildings in France had been destroyed. Hundreds of bridges had been knocked out by Allied bombing, and over half its train tracks were out of commission.[6] The Germans had also looted much of the railroads' rolling stock, leaving behind a ramshackle collection of dilapidated cars. Industry began to revive after Germany surrendered in May 1945, but agricultural production and the supply of consumer goods resumed only fitfully.

Inflation surged and black markets flourished. A severe housing shortage made things worse. On the Riviera, many of the grandest old hotels were converted into low- and middle-income housing. At Mediterranean beach resorts such as Juan-les-Pins, much of the sand—a not-too-plentiful commodity to begin with—had been carted away by the Germans to build defensive fortifications, which now had to be dismantled so that the sand could be returned to the beaches.[7]

It all hardly bode well for the tourist industry, and local chambers of commerce began fearing that it might never be revived.[8] In a poignant gesture, the gardeners' association of Cimiez, overlooking Nice, hoping to encourage the return of the Anglo trade, restored the head of Queen Victoria to the statue from which it had been severed during the war and mowed the grass in the little garden in which it stands.[9] During Easter 1946 desperate residents of Monaco, which had been off-limits to Allied military personnel, rushed to the streets to confirm rumors that the first car with foreign plates had arrived. A few weeks later, most of the small group of journalists and film producers who gathered in Cannes for the film festival the local authorities had just organized thought that it would be the last.[10]

However, officials in the new Fourth Republic could not afford the luxury of despair. Despite the instability of the governments that followed de Gaulle's retirement from politics, they began working vigorously to revive foreign tourism. A powerful former Resistance leader, Henri Ingrand, was made the commissioner of tourism, and he immediately embarked on a determined campaign to promote American tourism.[11] In April 1946 it was announced that tourists would be given ration cards allowing them to eat meals with quantities of meat, fats, sugar, and coffee far in excess of the French rations. They would not have to smoke the foul-tasting cigarettes of the government tobacco monopoly but could buy (somewhat less acrid) ones "of a kind usually reserved for export." They would also receive coupons for up to five hundred liters of gas for three months.[12]

The new newspaper Le Monde greeted this enthusiastically. It said that the dollar shortage had thrust tourism, which before the war had been regarded as an "extra" industry, into the first ranks of the nation's industries. Despite the terrible state of the country's hotels, the widespread ruins, and the persisting poverty, the basis for a good promotional campaign remained intact: "The prestige of Paris, the variety and beauty of our sights, the tenderness of our climate, the interest of our old buildings and museums, the liveliness of our resorts, and the virtues of our spas. No other nation can boast such attractions on its soil."[13]

Still, few tourists could look forward to a comfortable holiday there. The

An example of the tremendous problems France faced in trying to reconstruct her tourist industry after the war: the ruins of the railway station at Cherbourg, where many of the transatlantic liners arrived. Courtesy of the National Archives.

American press was full of reports that France was caught in a downward economic spiral and portrayed a country mired in gloom, doom, and short-ages during the exceptionally cold winter of 1946–47.[14] They were not off the mark. An American relief worker who had spent the winter in a Paris hotel wrote home: "Fuel, food and clothing are still difficult to get. . . . I've shivered or nearly so ever since I came." There were hardly any taxis and not only were basic food items in short supply, so were the utensils with which to eat them.[15]

French pleas for American aid for reconstructing their country also un-dercut the attempts to revive tourism, for they emphasized the hardship that reigned there. American opinion leaders were taken on tours showing them deprivation, rather than fine living.[16] The nationally syndicated newspaper columnist Drew Pearson was so struck by France's plight that in

1946 he organized a "Friendship Train" to tour America, collecting parcels for the hungry and destitute children in France and Italy. This snowballed into ten trains that crisscrossed the country in 1947 and 1948, collecting enough to fill two ships.[17] Efforts such as this, and those of the American Red Cross and American Aid to France, which raised $25 million to feed hungry French people, hardly contributed to reviving the old image of France as the home of joie de vivre.

If the government's hopes that American tourism would revive in the summer of 1946 were too optimistic, so, too, was its confidence that tourist facilities would be quickly rebuilt and refurbished. Many of the resort towns in Normandy were still surrounded by minefields; lovely old towns such as Saint-Malo, in Brittany, and Caen, in Normandy, were still practically flattened. The Riviera, which had been cleaned up to serve as the army leave zone, seemed to be in better shape, but this was mainly because of publicity surrounding the celebrities who began to trickle back. The Duke and Duchess of Windsor drove down there in April 1946 to reopen their villa and engage a staff of twenty-two servants.[18] The British writer and entertainer Noël Coward seemed to be everywhere, but most of the other celebrities were French ones who were little known in America. Things were even worse at Biarritz, where foreigners were conspicuous by their almost complete absence. Moreover, in both places, people who before the war had stayed for three months now stayed for three weeks; those who had stayed for three weeks now left after ten days. The only destination that really bounced back was Lourdes, which the Germans had closed to French pilgrims during the war because its location close to the Spanish border put it on the main escape route out of France.[19]

— —

The situation remained grim into the next year. The playwright Arthur Miller was shocked by what he saw when he arrived in Cherbourg in February 1947. His ship could not dock because the massive concrete piers were "brokenly tilted into the water." Passengers were taken ashore in small boats to "the gigantic nineteenth-century railroad station, whose stories-high, cathedral-like vaulted roof of glass panes, stretching several blocks, was totally smashed, an eyeless structure all that remained." Paris was hardly cheerier. Food and fuel were still in very short supply, and the city seemed enveloped in "a doomed and listless silence, few cars on the streets, occasional trucks running on wood-burning engines, old women on ancient bicycles." The staff in his hotel, the Pont-Royal, wore fraying clothes, and "a hungry-looking, garishly got-up young woman in black lace stocking with a fallen hem on her skirt was allowed to sit in the lobby all night for the convenience of the guests. . . . In the streets no man seemed to have a matching jacket and trousers, and many who looked like professionals wore mufflers to hide bare, shirtless chests."[20] That spring *Le Monde* criticized the government for publishing brochures extolling the beauties of the coastal resorts when in reality most of them had only partially repaired their extensive wartime damage. Furthermore, it said, while 300,000 Americans may have expressed an interest in visiting France, there were only 70,000 berths for them on the transatlantic liners.[21]

The reports of those Americans who did venture over there were hardly encouraging. The humorist S. J. Perelman could find little that was humorous in a *New Yorker* piece about his stay in Paris in the summer of 1947:

> The character exists, unquestionably, who managed to have a rip-roaring time in Paris in the summer of 1947, but who he is, where he did so, and how he found the inclination, I cannot imagine. . . . The food scarcity was acute, the cost of living was astronomical, and a pall of cynicism and futility hung over the inhabitants. . . . Everywhere you went, you sensed the apathy and bitterness of a people corroded by years of enemy occupation. . . . Montmartre was not half as iniquitous as Barnegat, New Jersey, and considerably less charged with glamour. . . . Food was a constant preoccupation and, with the majority of people we met, the sole topic of conversation; the American tourist like ourselves, who symbolized prosperity and whose dollars ruled the world economy, was popularly regarded as either a pigeon or a usurer.[22]

The only Americans who turned up in large numbers on the Riviera seemed to be in the latter category: GIs from the occupation forces in Germany who showed up loaded with American cigarettes and other luxury items they hoped to trade on the black market for a luxury vacation.[23]

To make matters worse, the American press was full of reports of the chaos caused by Communist unions, who in late 1947 began a wave of strikes that repeatedly tied up France's transport and other tourist-related industries. When Martha Churchill arrived in Cherbourg in September 1948 on the newly revived Smith College junior-year-in-France program, the first thing she encountered was a longshoremen's strike, which left her stewing on the ship waiting to disembark for many hours. After arriving in Paris, where stiff food rationing was still in force, she wrote home that "people here don't really get enough to eat and you can see it by looking at their faces which are wan and pasty looking."[24] It hardly added up to an enticing place to travel.

Still, the French government kept trying to attract American tourists. It let it be known that they would not be bothered by policemen enforcing the regulations against exchanging dollars on the black market. It abolished the need for tourist cards and encouraged the wealthier of them to bring their cars over by raising the gas ration for foreign-registered cars to six hundred liters for three months.[25] But instead of the freer-spending upper and upper-middle class, there was an onslaught of impecunious young people.

Many of them were creative types, intent on following in the footsteps of the famous exiles of the 1920s. They were lured, not by Paris's now rather asthmatic joie de vivre, but by the old notion that France was more welcoming to the creative, cultured person than materialistic America, where art and creativity were scorned. Norman Ruddington, an artist from New Haven, Connecticut, said, "When I came to Paris it felt like coming home. I could breathe. People asked me what I did. I said I was an artist. They said, 'Ah, an artist.' In America they said, 'How do you live?'"[26] Later, the artist Romare Bearden, who came for an eight-month stay, recalled being at the Dôme, on boulevard Montparnasse, when the aged Matisse walked by, supported by two young people. "A waiter hollered something like, 'He is passing by!'" said Bearden, "and all the waiters ran to the front of the café and started clapping." When Matisse realized the applause was for him, he smiled, walked over to the waiters, and started shaking hands with them. "Then," said Bearden, "all the people were reaching over to shake hands with him. I thought, 'Isn't this wonderful. They are not applauding a movie star, but a man who changed the way we saw life because he was a great painter.' After being in the States, Paris was a miracle because things like that could happen."[27]

The novelist Saul Bellow, who arrived there in 1947 on a Guggenheim fellowship, recalled that he had "decided not to let American business society make my life for me" and was determined to be "free from measures devised and applied by others." Paris, he thought, had something that was lacking in American life: "the capacity to enjoy intellectual pleasures as though they were sensual pleasures."[28] Art Buchwald remembered arriving in 1948 on a run-down ship "loaded with fresh-faced American students— budding Pulitzer Prize winners, eager painters, future geniuses of the arts and sciences . . . the stepchildren of Gertrude Stein, F. Scott Fitzgerald, Henry Miller, and Ezra Pound."[29] The aspiring writer William Demby arrived the same year, after having devoured magazine stories of the Paris exploits of Hemingway, Stein, Picasso, and the others. To him, Paris was a place where one could be a creative artist: where one could "waste time and dabble around with a notebook."[30]

The celebrated African American writer Richard Wright found confirmation for such notions almost as soon as he arrived on his first visit to France. After his ship docked at Le Havre in March 1946, he went from compartment to compartment on the boat train to Paris, talking to Americans and French. He soon became aware, he wrote, of the vast psychological gulf separating the two peoples. "I have discovered that the French know more about people and life, while the Americans know more about 'techniques.' America is a civilization, while France is a civilization and a culture."[31] Another African American writer, James Baldwin, a homosexual, was particularly attuned to Paris's reputation for personal freedom. He wrote, "Paris is, according to its legend, the city where everyone loses his head, and his morals, lives through at least one *histoire d'amour*, ceases, quite, to arrive anywhere on time, and thumbs his nose at the Puritans—the city, in brief, where all become drunken on the fine old air of freedom."[32]

Wright, who had written two highly acclaimed novels, came by invitation of the French government.[33] Gertrude Stein met him at the train station in Paris, along with a friend from the American embassy who brought two limousines, one for the Wrights and another for their baggage. The city of Paris and his French publishers held receptions for him where he was introduced to much of the French literary establishment.[34] Less successful young Americans, such as Baldwin, sailed in dormitory-style accommodations on slow ex-troopships and arrived with no one they knew to greet them.[35] Robert Gwathmey more or less summed up their shipboard experiences in a letter to a friend: "The trip across was long (9 days) and uneventful. I was fine on dramamine and there was a nun throwing up."[36]

Many, like Buchwald, were veterans taking advantage of the GI Bill of Rights. It provided money for tuition and seventy-five dollars a month in living expense for veterans enrolled in further education courses, whether at home or overseas. All one needed was proof of enrollment in almost any kind of educational establishment—it could be a university, an art school, or even a culinary college. Edward Ratcliffe, a middle-aged ex-army officer from Raleigh, North Carolina, decided to spend what he called "a cultural year" in Paris while retooling for a career as a reference librarian in Illinois. Although he enrolled in the Sorbonne's course in French civilization, difficulty with the language led him to pass up many of the lectures. Instead, he indulged in a veritable orgy of high-cultural activities. He wrote a friend, "The offerings in music, the ballet, and fine arts in general are so numerous that we go wild looking at the list of current events," and he frequently compared them favorably to what was on offer in New York City, where he had lived before the war.[37]

For many of these men, registration day was the last time they saw a classroom. Buchwald discovered that, for a small price, the woman who took attendance at his language school, the Alliance Française, would mark him present each day. A friend told him that if all the veterans who were enrolled there actually showed up for class, "they would need a soccer stadium to accommodate them."[38] Ernie Ricci, recalling the "good time" he and his friends had on the GI Bill, said GIs would enroll in the Alliance and then take off for the Riviera. Friends would pick up their checks for them at the embassy: "'He's sick,' they would say, while the guy was down in Cannes." Ricci and his friends would also go to Switzerland to cash their checks, taking advantage of a better exchange rate, and return to deal on the thriving black market outside the American Express office in Paris. "The American dollar was king," he recalled. "There was black-marketing galore."[39] Anton Rosenberg, a well-off veteran who was supposed to be taking art lessons, did not bother with such energetic pursuits. He refined the art of just hanging out and doing nothing to such a degree that he became the prototype of the laidback persona apotheosized as the cool "hipster" by Jack Kerouac, the "Beat Generation" writer who encountered him later in Paris.[40]

However, not all the veterans avoided classes. One of the first to arrive in France, Robert Owens, an African American from Berkeley, California, persisted through four years of piano training at the tough Ecole Normale de Musique.[41] The artist Robert Rauschenberg faithfully attended the classes at the venerable Académie Julien, where hundreds of American artists had studied since the turn of the century.[42] So many veterans attended the classes at the Cordon Bleu cooking school that it set up a separate course for Americans.[43] Studying there was in no way a free ride. Some classes for ex-GIs began at 7:00 AM, and much of their day would be spent chopping, slicing, mashing, and scalding themselves on the ancient stoves under the stern eyes of congenitally grumpy instructors.[44] In 1999 the cookbook author Julia Child recalled that even though fifty years had passed since she attended the school, she could not forget how bad-tempered was the owner and chief instructor, Elizabeth Brassart. "She really was nasty," said Child, "particularly towards Americans. The French thought we were a bunch of hillbillies."[45]

Some who avoided classes at the approved places where they were registered took instruction elsewhere. The sculptor and painter Robert Breer would only drop by the Académie Julien once a month, to fulfill the attendance requirement, but studied diligently with the brilliant sculptor Ossip Zadkine at an unapproved school.[46] The artist Romare Bearden enrolled in postgraduate work in philosophy at the Sorbonne because, he wrote home, "for one who doesn't want to be bothered with school that is the best deal."[47] But he worked doggedly at his art and soon became a very productive and highly regarded artist. So did many of those whose GI Bill stipends helped revive the American school for the arts at Fontainebleau. Its famed music composition instructor, Nadia Boulanger, now added later famous names such as John Cage and the jazz artist Donald Byrd to a list of students/disciples that already included Aaron Copland and Leonard Bernstein.

— —

Some of the young visitors spoke enough French to participate in the flourishing Left Bank intellectual scene, where Jean-Paul Sartre's exciting ideas about existentialism were once again thrusting France onto the cutting edge of intellectual life. Lionel Abel, an aspiring playwright and critic, spoke French well and developed a wide circle of French and foreign contacts, including Sartre, Albert Camus, and the artist Alberto Giacometti. To him, Paris was different from other large cities. "If you have no previous acquaintances in cities such as London and New York," he said, "you are going to spend a good deal of time alone. . . . But Paris tells everyone who enters it that he or she will meet other persons there. It is a city that must have been designed for meeting others; in Paris there will always be rendezvous."[48]

The writers Saul Bellow and Norman Mailer also mixed with some French intellectuals during their stays. After leaving the manuscript of his novel *The Naked and the Dead* with his New York publisher in October 1947, Mailer and his wife Bea sailed first class on the *Queen Elizabeth* to spend a year in France, living on his publisher's advance and the GI Bill. He enrolled in the Sorbonne's French civilization course, but soon dropped out. Bea, who also qualified for the GI Bill, completed the course, something that only eight of the more than two hundred other enrolled students did. Although Mailer's closest friends were mainly fellow Harvard grads, he knew enough French to befriend Jean Malaquais, a French-speaking left-wing Jewish immigrant from Poland who thenceforth had a profound influence on his politics. He had also imbibed some of Sartre's existentialism in New York and in Paris read Sartre's pieces in his magazine, *Les Temps Modernes*. However, when he went looking for Sartre in his hangout, the Café de Flore, he came up empty.[49]

Visitors who were not themselves writers or artists could also find the atmosphere stimulating. Cynthia Brants, a wealthy twenty-four-year-old graphic artist from Fort Worth, Texas, looked up her friend Shirley Jones in

Paris in November 1948 and wrote in her diary that she found her "completely taken up with . . . Paris in particular. She is having a whirl meeting the intellectual lights of France, seeing the sights, and generally enjoying the things which perceptive, observant Americans seem to find in Paris." Jones and "a lot of others," said Brants, thought that Paris had more to offer than America "in the way of artistic, intellectual and aesthetic freedom."[50]

—— ——

For most of the young visitors, though, difficulties with the French language inhibited all but the most superficial relationships with the French and their culture. Instead, the men often ended up growing beards, wearing berets, and trying to re-create the ribald lives their prewar predecessors had famously enjoyed in the cafés and nightclubs of the boulevard Montparnasse. Herbert Gentry, an aspiring art student from Harlem who came to Paris on the GI Bill in 1946, recalled:

> Everything was rationed. . . . But it didn't matter to us, because we were young, the city was exciting, the city was so beautiful. . . . We would sit at the Dôme. It was not only our café, it was our office. Wine was very cheap, but we still considered it expensive so we brought our own wine and we'd stay there and the waiters wouldn't bother us, so we would just hang out. It was the Americans who really made Montparnasse at that period. . . . [W]e gave the spirit to Montparnasse.[51]

A few years later, he gave more spirit to the neighborhood by opening a jazz club there.[52]

Although Gentry recalled that "the French opened up, I mean they really opened up to us," it was much more common for the Americans to find the French remote at best and at worst, as William Demby recalled, "awful."[53] The language barrier was often at the center of the problem. Romare Bearden wrote home:

> The Americans here are a little island to themselves. . . . I had said (as I suppose many others did) that I wanted to be among the French, but it is not very possible. The French students while not outwardly hostile to Americans are rather stand-offish. . . . It seems the soldiers behaved rather badly during the war, and the people feel [that Americans think] that any Frenchman can be bought . . . for a pack of cigarettes, or a bar of soap. [Also], many Americans here refuse to learn the language—so that intimate conversation is only possible with those French men who speak English.[54]

French waiters and other service personnel, whose patience with foreigners trying to speak French was notoriously limited, did not help. Demby, exasperated by the poor treatment he received when he tried to speak French, took to speaking to them very rapidly in English, "to destabilize them."[55]

A major preconception that was shattered on the rocks of experience was the popular idea, still rampant in the media, that Frenchwomen were sexier than others. (MGM advertised the 1949 film of Flaubert's *Madame Bovary*, a grim novel about a nineteenth-century small-town doctor's wife who has a disastrous extramarital affair, with the slogan "Whatever it is that French women have, Madame Bovary has more of it!")[56] Bearden wrote home that he and the other Americans were quickly disabused of the idea of Paris as "such a gay city [where] women will be breaking into doors— mad artists' balls take place all the time, etc." Instead, he found "everything closed at midnight." Even the prostitutes standing on street corners in Pigalle and the Champs-Elysées were "off the streets by 12." "Very few Americans," he said, "are intimate with the average French girl—they go out with other Americans or girls from the Scandinavian countries."[57] Demby recalled that African American men went out with so many Scandinavians that they adopted "Scans" as the generic term for white women. There was no thought of marriage resulting from these encounters, he said. "Everybody was in Europe for casual relationships. It was assumed you were going back."[58]

The few men who managed to establish relationships with Frenchwomen often discovered, to their surprise, how straitlaced they could be. A veteran of the Pacific war who enrolled in the Sorbonne told an American woman living in Paris, "I don't know what those European vets were talking about. After listening to their stories about Paris I find myself over here wound up in a romance with a French girl whose family is so austere I'm not even allowed to take her out. It seems we haven't been properly introduced or something. We made a deal with a French boy. He takes her out and they meet me in a café. She has to be 'home by twelve.'"[59]

It seems to have been mainly veterans with no artistic or intellectual ambitions such as Ricci who, flush with money from the black market, managed to overcome their fractured French and establish lasting liaisons with Frenchwomen. Ironically, much of their income derived from French government attempts to encourage tourism, especially the extra gas coupons offered to visitors. Ricci and his friends would buy decrepit old cars, register them for the distinctive red tourists' license plates, and get coupons entitling them to two hundred liters of gas a month. They would then abandon the cars and sell the coupons to the French, who could only get twenty-five liters, on the black market. At one stage, he recalled, he had four old wrecks registered in his name sitting around—he was not quite sure where—and was collecting coupons for eight hundred liters a month.[60]

———

The other Americans who began to reemerge in France in 1947 and 1948 were the upper class and celebrities. While the young Americans in the Left Bank cafés were inspired by the old idea that only in France could Americans feel free, on the Right Bank the equally old idea that France was the beacon of style and civilization was being nurtured by its traditional custodians, the East Coast social elite. When France fell to the Germans, wealthy socialites such as Anne Morgan, who had helped rebuild shattered French villages after World War I, had sprung into action. Fresh from their successful efforts in support of the fascist Franco regime in Spain, they enlisted fellow socialites in drives to aid the French people. Their fund-raising balls, with themes such as "A Night in Cannes" and "A Day in Cannes," helped preserve France's image as the epicenter of the civilized life.[61] Although there were early divisions between those who supported Pétain and those who leaned toward de Gaulle, in 1944 they all united to help people in the places destroyed during the Allied invasion.[62] Their major fund-raising organization, Relief for France, was headquartered in the Madison Avenue mansion of the blue-blooded Whitelaw Reid family, whose properties included the *New York Herald Tribune* and *Paris Herald Tribune*. There, as the war neared its end, ex-debutantes would assemble once a week to make bandages, sew pajamas, and sort out old clothes to be sent to France.[63]

In the Reids' social set, there was no question that France still reigned supreme in art and fashion. In May 1946 the charity staged a fund-raising fashion show for seven hundred select guests that featured haute couture and jewelry from Paris's top designers. Vincent Impelliteri, a Democratic-machine politician from lower Manhattan who had just become New York's mayor, could not hide his befuddlement at the proceedings. "I don't know why," he said, "but we Americans still look to France for the latest in art and the latest in fashion."[64] In November 1946 a campaign to raise over $2 million for France was kicked off in the Reid mansion with the auctioning, for $125,000, of a Renoir painting donated by Consuelo Vanderbilt, whose social status was astronomic.[65] That evening three hundred of New York's most socially prominent citizens attended a gala dinner for the cause aboard the French Line *Ile de France*, which was just ending her service as a troopship. There, Secretary of Commerce Averell Harriman, himself one of the wealthiest, most socially prominent men in the land, said that America's interest in France's recovery lay not just in economics, but also in France's culture. The American tourists who visited France in prewar years, he said, went to visit "not a statistic, but a culture and a rich tradition expressed in a vital and interesting people."[66]

— —

Until mid-1947 the trip to France was still fraught with too many deprivations in terms of creature comforts to revive the old glamour of first-class transatlantic travel. The first American civilian ship did not return to France on a passenger run until November 1946, and she still looked more like a troopship than a luxury liner. In May 1947 there were still only nine passenger liners back on the transatlantic route, all overcrowded and overcharging.[67]

In France the tourist office lamented that although the country could now accommodate 300,000 American tourists, the transportation shortage would likely limit the number to 60,000.[68] Its spokesman in America painted a picture of a country ready to welcome Americans in comfort. He said that all the mines had been cleared from around Deauville, and "contrary to what a lot of Americans believe, the French are deeply appreciative of what Americans did in the war and they speak of it all the time." Many streets in Normandy, he said, were marked with the names of American soldiers and the battlefields were being protected from commercialization.[69] However, an article in *Harper's* magazine that same month was much more pessimistic. It warned that Americans who had neither wealth, a sense of adventure, nor "an intimate knowledge of the country (including, preferably, some acquaintance with its language)" should not try to brave the inconveniences caused by shortages of food, accommodation, and transportation.[70] In the end, few Americans took the tours to the Normandy beachheads and battlefields that summer, and tourism by GIs stationed in Austria and Germany dropped by over half.[71] Ultimately, only seventy thousand Americans came to France that year, a mere thirty thousand of whom were tourists.[72]

Yet there was a very good omen for the future, for prominent among those who did show up were the socialites and celebrities who would play a major role in restoring France's reputation as a glamorous destination. Some began arriving by air. Government-owned Air France had joined Trans World Airlines in offering flights from New York to Paris in the summer of 1946 on converted wartime transport planes. On October 7, 1947, though, it started weekly "sleeper plane" service to Paris aboard a Lockheed Constellation, the "World's Most Beautiful Airliner," for a very steep $495 each way. Advertised as "the Ultimate in Luxury Speed Travel," its interior was designed by Raymond Loewy, America's top designer. After taking off from New York, the eighteen passengers would be treated to champagne and caviar before sitting down, at tables set with china and silver, to a sumptuous multicourse meal, accompanied by fine wine and followed by coffee and cognac. They would retire to bed in comfortable curtained-off upper and lower berths that were twice as wide as the ones in the Pullman railroad cars that they resembled. Breakfast was served in bed.[73]

That summer Air France chalked up another first, "the first aerial pilgrimage on record": a trip to Lourdes for twenty-two Pittsburghers led by Father James Cox, a well-known radio priest.[74] Six months earlier, however, TWA had embarked on the real harbinger of things to come: it reduced the legroom between the rows of its Constellations and increased the number of seats from twenty-six to thirty-two.[75]

Despite the beginning of the space squeeze, transatlantic air travel was still prohibitively expensive for the vast majority of Americans. A regular round-trip New York–Paris ticket still cost $630, at a time when an income of about $3,000 made a family middle class. Nor was the flight anywhere near as speedy and comfortable as the airlines claimed. The Constellations cut the flying time from twenty-one hours to about sixteen hours, but they still had to make white-knuckle landings for refueling at Gander, Newfoundland, and Shannon, Ireland.[76] Pan American Airways' DC-4s were even worse. They were much slower, and because their cabins were not pressurized, they could not fly above turbulent weather, making airsickness common. They boasted of having "sleeperettes," but these were just reclining seats with curtains around them.[77] On both planes, sleep did not come easily amidst the noise of the howling piston engines and the regular plunges into "air pockets." Prodigious amounts of alcohol were the common sleeping aid, but the lengthy flight meant that hangovers would set in even before landing.[78]

The noise and turbulence were particularly disconcerting because long-distance air travel was still a new and fearful experience for most people. Betsey Schaefer muttered "stiff upper lip" to herself as she boarded the flying boat for the second flight on the short-lived prewar route from Marseille to New York. As she looked at the photographers taking pictures, she thought that the pictures would probably be used under the heading "among the lost were . . ."[79] Widely publicized wartime air crashes that took the lives of celebrities such as the beautiful Hollywood star Carole Lombard and the band leader Glenn Miller did little to quiet such fears.[80] The airlines took out newspaper advertisements that emphasized their safety, but these were undermined by reports in the same papers of crashes that took the lives of well-known personages such as the great French boxer Marcel Cerdan. The plane carrying him from Paris to New York for a title fight (and to his lover the singer Edith Piaf) went down over the North Atlantic in mid-1949.

As a result, many of the upper class who did not have pressing commitments still preferred the luxury, security, and social life aboard the great steamships. For celebrities, there was the additional advantage of the publicity garnered in the traditional shipboard interviews in New York Harbor. Their presence aboard was also a tourist attraction. In 1948 Stuart Murray's *Traveler's Guide to France* said tourists on the transatlantic liners would find themselves among "the great, the near great, and the internationally important." They would watch the latest Hollywood films and then might be seated beside the stars of these very films in the dining salon.[81] As in prewar days, one of the first things ordinary passengers did on boarding a ship was to look over the passenger list to see which celebrated names they might hope to see during the crossing.[82]

Unfortunately for the French, there was little chance of this happening on the ships of the government-owned French Line, for two-thirds of its fleet lay at the bottom of various harbors. The *Normandie* had burned and sunk in New York Harbor during the war; the *Paris* lay rusting in shallow water in Le Havre harbor. They began refitting the fast German luxury liner *Europa*, which the Americans gave them after seizing it and using it as a troopship during the war, but it broke from its moorings in Le Havre harbor during a storm, struck the sunken *Paris*, and settled into the shallow waters beside it.[83] So, they had to stand by while the Dutch, with the *Nieuw Amsterdam*, and the British Cunard Line, with its two celebrated *Queens*, grabbed the lion's share of the luxury trade.[84] Their only competitor, the smaller, lumbering old *De Grasse*, which reentered service in the fall of 1947, was no match for them, despite a profusion of potted palms, gilded mirrors, silk-lined staterooms, and delectable seven-course dinners.[85]

Still, no matter what the ship, the old pleasures of crossing on first class remained. Normally, the ships left New York at noon, meaning that from 9:00 to 11:00 one could entertain friends aboard, tour the ship with them, and retire to one's cabin, to toast a bon voyage with champagne, amidst baskets of fruit, boxes of books, flowers, and other presents. (One of the most appreciated gifts was a credit at the ship's bar.)[86] At 11:00 the ship's horn would sound a massive blast, signaling that it was time for the visitors to weave their way down the gangplank to the jetty, where they would wave heartily as the ship slowly pulled away.[87] Once under way, first-class passengers would unpack and change into casual clothes for their first forays onto the decks, where they would cuddle up on their assigned chairs and wait for the solicitous crew to bring tea, bouillon, and sandwiches. They would then go below to change into formal wear—still practically mandatory—for cocktails and dinner. The more important of them would be invited to cocktails with the captain. The most important would dine at his table. Others would settle for the other officers. The meals would be lavish, with an emphasis on filet mignon in various guises, climaxed by the gala "Farewell Dinner."[88]

— —

When they arrived in France, the socialites and celebrities experienced a much different Paris than the young Americans scrounging around the Left Bank. They checked into fine Right Bank hotels such as the Crillon, next door to the U.S. embassy, which was favored by the politically well connected. The rich and famous tended to prefer the more modern George V (known as "an American hotel in Europe"), the Plaza Athénée, and the Meurice, which had been spruced up after being damaged by fusillades of machine-gun bullets directed at German soldiers holed up there during the Liberation.[89] The Ritz was a bit more problematic. Although it had been more than satisfactory for the German High Command and for the famous fashion designer Coco Chanel, who passed much of the war there with her German lover, many pampered Americans found its once-modern turn-of-the-century bathrooms (it was the first hotel to have bathrooms en suite) too antiquated.[90] Still, it normally had a six-month waiting list.[91]

Their activities also differed markedly from those of the young Americans drinking cheap wine in down-at-heel Left Bank cafés and hotel rooms. The diary of Cynthia Brants, a wealthy young artist from a well-established family in Fort Worth, Texas, who, along with her friend Palmer, stayed for a number of months on the Right Bank, tells of how they and other women in their social set regularly lunched at the Ritz and went out with American or foreign businessmen, professionals, or exiled aristocrats for roast duck dinners at the Tour d'Argent and champagne-soaked evenings at expensive nightclubs. She became so well known in one club, Casanova, that whenever she entered, the conductor of the orchestra would yell, "Hey Texas," and the fifteen Gypsy violinists would break into "Deep in the Heart of Texas" or "San Antonio Rose."[92] She tells of going to a small party in a luxury Right Bank hotel room in November 1948 with two young British doctors. There they drank "several quarts of champagne" with their host and Pat, a pretty twenty-year-old college dropout from New York who passed her time partying in Paris, London, and New York. Pat, Brants wrote, spent much of the time "disappearing through one or the other doors with one or the other boys."[93]

Still, the idea that, in Brants's words, "so many Americans feel that at last they can be free here" seems to have been as current among young people of Brants's class as it was across the river on the Left Bank. This she attributed to their being "far away from home and away from those who expect something different from them than they would like to give." However, she also thought, "the Frenchman's attribute of minding his own business and not being as ambitious as we are generally helps the liberated American in his belief that in France he is free."[94]

— —

By then, the prewar social elite and a host of new celebrities were back in France in force. Among the trailblazers were the Duke and Duchess of Windsor. They had originally arrived (with 134 pieces of luggage) on the boat train at Paris's Gare du Nord in late 1946. However, Paris apparently lacked something during that grim winter, and they soon returned (with 155 pieces of luggage) to New York and Palm Beach. The next summer, though, they were back (traveling lightly, with only 85 bags) to spend the season in Paris and the Riviera.[95] By late August the *Paris Herald Tribune* was cooing, "The roster of celebrities toasting their toes in the Riviera sunshine reads like pre-war." These included Barbara Hutton and Doris Duke, two heiresses who now competed for the titles of richest and/or unhappiest woman on earth ("one with a new prince and one without"); Elsa Maxwell, a droll raconteuse famous for giving parties for famous people; William Paley, owner of the Columbia Broadcasting System and one of the bedrocks of New York society; Henry Cabot Lodge Jr., a Boston Brahmin and future senator and vice presidential candidate; the Hollywood star Ray Milland; and, of course, the Duke and Duchess of Windsor.[96] Jessie Donahue, Barbara Hutton's aunt, single-handedly provided a substantial boost to the French economy by arriving, as she did in subsequent summers, with $300,000 in cash to gamble away in Biarritz and Monte Carlo. She helped furnish the Windsors' Riviera villa and picked up the bills for many of the Duchess's shopping forays to French clothing merchants and jewelers. Each summer she would take them out for several weeks on a yacht she would charter in the Riviera.[97]

Perhaps the most celebrated tourist of the summer of 1947 was Virginia Hill. While she was visiting Paris, her companion, the famed gangster "Bugsy" Siegel, who had practically created Las Vegas as a gambling resort, was killed by a blast of rifle fire through the window of her Beverly Hills home. The Beverly Hills police chief warned that two "hit men" were now on their way to Paris to do her in too. She quickly checked out of her suite in Paris's fashionable Hôtel Westminster but soon reappeared in a luxury hotel in Beaulieu, on the Riviera. From there she called the newspapers to denounce them for saying that Siegel, "a perfect gentleman," had been involved in narcotics and challenged the two hit men to "come ahead. They'll find me here."[98] (They never did.)

— —

One important element in quickly restoring France as a destination for elite Americans was the reestablishment of Paris's role as the arbiter of women's fashion. This rebirth was capped in 1947 when, at the annual spring showings of the Paris couturiers, Christian Dior, a previously obscure designer, exploded into the world's headlines with his "New Look."

Paris's women's clothes designers had been trendsetters for the international upper classes since before the Revolution of 1789. In the late nineteenth and early twentieth centuries, fashionable upper- and upper-middle-class women would return from Paris with trunks bulging with made-to-measure dresses, handbags, gloves, jewelry, and other "accessories." During the 1920s the strong dollar made many of these things positive bargains, and even middle-class women would return laden with them from trips to Paris.[99] In 1930, however, as the dollar sank and the franc rose, comparable products became more expensive in Paris than New York, and Paris shopkeepers began bleating in pain as upper-middle-class American women virtually stopped buying.[100] The situation worsened after 1931, when the United States slapped steep tariffs on most imported goods. But for elite American fashion plates such as Rose Fitzgerald Kennedy and Wallis Simpson, the regular trips to the famed couturiers' biennial fashion shows in Paris were still de rigueur, and the American press continued to describe their creations as the mandate for future fashion. "Those who have feminine figures are going to be the lucky ones this Winter," said a typical *New York Times* report from Paris in September 1937. "The great have spoken in Paris. At all costs one must have curves."[101]

The war, however, hit the French high-fashion industry hard. A number of houses closed, and those that remained open struggled with shortages of both materials and wealthy clients. In 1945 and 1946, when it was virtually impossible for American women to come to Paris for the showings, the French government helped the couturiers by sending their products over to New York City, to be shown at upper-class fund-raising events for French charities. Only in the spring of 1947 were there enough American women and fashion reporters back in the salons for the showings to regain their prewar prominence.

It is hard today, when the sources of women's fashion are so diverse, to imagine the impact of the "New Look." (It came by its label when an American fashion editor at the sensational first showing exclaimed to Dior, "Your dresses have such a *new look!*")[102] Featuring flared dresses with tight waists and longer hemlines than before, it was said to be a "feminine" and "romantic" repudiation of the previous years of hardship and privation.[103] "We are saved," Mary Patten, an American who attended the first show, wrote to a friend in New York. "Becoming clothes are back, gone the stern padded shoulders, *in* are soft rounded shoulders without padding, nipped in waists, wide, wide skirts about four inches below the knee."[104] In America, *Life* magazine immediately devoted six full pages to it.[105] The unwritten message was again, "Paris has spoken; the rest will follow": France was again dictating fashion and style.

The American Wallis Simpson, the Duchess of Windsor, played an active role in maintaining Paris's role as the center of high fashion. Annually voted the world's best-dressed woman, she was regularly photographed at the major showings, along with celebrities such as the wealthy playboy Ali Khan and his soon-to-be bride Rita Hayworth, widely regarded as the most beautiful actress in Hollywood.[106] Visits to the fashion houses again became obligatory for the upper crust. Those in the forefront would attend the spring and fall showings. Others would simply go at any time to have dresses made.

These elite patrons knew there was more to a couturier's appeal than the mere design of the clothes. Knockoffs back in America could achieve much the same look, but the similarities were superficial: they could not duplicate the impressive craftsmanship of the French shops.[107] Cynthia Brants had been skeptical about fashion and had initially resisted going to a couturier that a family friend in America had recommended. However, when she went there, she was immensely impressed at how they fitted her for a reduced-price model's dress that was altered to her more ample dimensions. Then she watched while her friend Palmer was fitted for a made-to-order dress at another house. She was so impressed by the dressmakers' skills that she wrote in her diary, "The complicated cutting is amazing. Having now been to two big couturiers' houses I can understand what all the fuss over French dresses is all about. It is the first time I have ever felt a keen interest in clothes. . . . This is really a worthwhile pastime as it is done in Paris. Clothes *can* make the woman, something I have heretofore had no reason to believe."[108] By early 1949, when she wrote this, prominent women were heading again not just to the Paris couturiers, but to other favored prewar destinations such as Deauville and the Riviera as well. Not coincidentally, many Americans below them on the social ladder were now preparing to make the trip to France as well.

SEVEN

Searching for Sartre

On July 27, 1949, the French Line's newly refitted *Ile de France* sailed into New York Harbor on its first postwar passenger crossing. Billed as "your gayest entrée to France" and hailed as "a symbol of the renaissance of France," her extra-large first-class section boasted "brilliant salons, exquisite decor, and superb meals created by masters of French cuisine."[1] She was, the travel writer Horace Sutton recalled, "probably the best French restaurant in the world. Her dining salon sparkled with the old élan. . . . Crêpes suzettes broke out like brush fires in the first-class dining salon, and the caviar thumped onto chilled plates in huge pearl-gray globs."[2] As the Movietone News cameras rolled, a female model in what was described as a "brief, French-style bathing suit" climbed the gangplank to be the first to greet the liner.[3] The message seemed clear: not only was the French Line back in the luxury transatlantic trade; France itself was back as American tourists' favorite overseas destination, offering them its delightful mix of elegance, gaiety, and naughtiness.

A major devaluation of the franc at the end of January 1948, which ultimately more than tripled the value of the dollar, had helped spur the comeback.[4] Suddenly, Americans found that Paris's shops were again full of bargains.[5] Susan Patten told a friend that for the Americans cashing traveler's checks at the bank the next day, it was "like Christmas morning, with strangers beaming at each other."[6] The American press now reported that it was cheaper to travel in France than in America.[7] *Time* magazine said that room and board in a luxury hotel in Biarritz was only eight dollars a day and that slightly less fashionable places were going for two to four dollars a day.[8] Within a week of the devaluation, bookings on the French Line's *De Grasse* doubled.[9]

The Marshall Plan, which began that spring, spurred the revival. The multibillion-dollar five-year American aid program was aimed at rebuilding the Western European countries as a bulwark against Soviet Communism and as a market for American goods. France, whose powerful Communist

A French Line ad promising that "your heart and your spirits lighten the moment you cross a French Line gangplank" and "your mood is caught up and carried along with the vivacious, fun-loving spirit of the French." Courtesy of Ad*Access, Rare Book, Manuscripts and Special Collections Library, Duke University.

Party lurked at the threshold of power, was to be the centerpiece of this effort. Paris was made the headquarters of the Economic Cooperation Administration (ECA), which ran the plan, and some three thousand Americans were sent over in the spring of 1948 to run it. Many of them were graduates of elite eastern colleges and universities—from the same circles where traveling to France was much appreciated. The economic advisers included many business executives who were used to dining out on ample expense accounts. The chief of mission was David Bruce, the connoisseur of French food and wine who had accompanied Hemingway in the "liberation" of the Ritz hotel. Needless to say, many of the staff became appreciative patrons of the country's finer restaurants. "When it comes to food," said one of them, the French "wrote the original book."[10]

Complementing them were operatives of the newly created Central Intelligence Agency, whose new recruits, also mainly from the Ivy League, were later described in an internal report as "young, enthusiastic fellows possessed of great funds" sent to meddle in other countries' affairs.[11] There was also a host of embassy political officers, military intelligence operatives, and American trade unionists secretly subsidized by the CIA who enjoyed having reasons to wine and dine their way around town.[12] Soon, the *Herald Tribune* had Art Buchwald stop covering nightclubs and devote himself wholly to writing about restaurants.[13] Norman Mailer blamed the ensuing rising prices on "Marshall Plan imperialism." "All the fucking Americans are here," he wrote a friend.[14]

Joining this influx of high-living Americans into Paris were the well-publicized international social set. Elsa Maxwell, a short, chubby, loquacious woman who wrote a society column for a New York paper, returned to Paris, which she had visited regularly during the 1930s, and began hosting celebrity-packed parties dressed as Napoléon, Sancho Panza, or in a children's sailor outfit that emphasized her turkeylike legs. At a party in which guests were asked to wear the costume "least or most becoming" to them, she wore a tight black lace "vamp" dress.[15] (A rival party giver, the svelte Englishwoman Lady Diana Cooper, said bitterly that she "burst on the scene like a stink bomb . . . with her appalling French and revolting appearance.")[16] The renowned "playboy" Ali Khan and the beautiful movie actress Rita Hayworth shuttled through a sea of flashbulbs between the Paris fashion shows and the Riviera villa owned by his immensely wealthy father, the Aga Khan, who was famous for the annual ritual whereby he was given his weight in precious jewels by his Islamic sect's followers.[17] Their wedding in Vallauris, a small town next to Cannes, attracted over a hundred reporters to

Spectators surrounding the actress Rita Hayworth and her husband Prince Ali Khan after their May 1949 wedding in the Riviera town of Vallauris, an event that helped restore the Riviera's sybaritic image. © Bettman/CORBIS.

the dingy town hall where French law said the ceremony had to take place. The guests included the artists Pablo Picasso and Maurice Utrillo, as well as the fearsome Hollywood gossip columnist Louella Parsons. That the mayor who performed the ceremony was a Communist railway worker made for even better copy.[18] The press then followed the happy couple north, to Deauville, where they were going to do the summer "season."[19] The next day the Aga Khan and his wife, a former Miss France, made more headlines when they were held up at gunpoint on the road outside of Cannes and relieved of $850,000 worth of jewelry.[20]

Louella Parsons moved on to Paris, where she attended a lavish dinner celebrating Maxim's "birthday."[21] At the coastal resorts in Normandy and the Côte d'Azur, the glitterati's nightlife revolved around the casinos, which featured bars, dancing, theater, concerts, and movies along with the usual gaming tables. Formal evening dress was mandated in the inner gambling rooms and at the gala dinner dances, where two stylish orchestras would alternate, along with a tasteful floor show.[22]

In the spring of 1949, however, the Monte Carlo casino was bleeding. British government currency restrictions were eating into its traditional British clientele. American high rollers were flocking to the more fashionable Palm-Beach Casino in nearby Cannes or the new gambling palaces in far-off Las Vegas. Desperate to recapture them, Monte Carlo sent croupiers over to America to learn how to run craps tables, which Europeans had hitherto disdained. When the tables opened that summer, some big shooters did come. The cigar-chomping Hollywood mogul Darryl Zanuck, surrounded by aspiring starlets, could be counted on to stay at the tables until 4:00 AM. In July 1949, when he finally married his longtime mistress, the actress Jennifer Jones, in Genoa, they immediately sailed on a luxury yacht to the Riviera, so he could spend their honeymoon shooting craps.[23]

The move into craps was a mixed blessing for Monte Carlo. Europeans at the other games, who gambled in dead silence, were put off by the whooping and hollering of the Americans as they rolled the dice. Many of them fled to the Palm-Beach Casino, where Americans such as Zanuck's stocky competitor, Jack Warner, who owned a villa in nearby Antibes, played the traditional European games in a less raucous fashion. Hollywood stars would shuttle between the two casinos, accompanying wealthy suitors such as the Greek ship owner Aristotle Onassis, who later tried to buy the Monte Carlo gaming operation. Soon the harbors of both Monaco and Cannes were studded with their luxurious monster yachts.[24]

More sedate upper-class Americans also returned to France. In April 1949 ex-governor of New York Herbert Lehman, a major art collector who was the heir to a huge banking fortune, arrived with his wife at the Meurice. He told the press that he had been staying there off and on since 1894, when his family brought him to Paris at age sixteen. He planned to visit a number of private galleries before looking in on the Louvre and the exhibition of Impressionist pictures that had been moved from the Louvre to the Jeu de Paume, the historic indoor tennis court in the Tuileries Gardens. He brought with him a list of favorite restaurants and was looking forward to the race meeting at Auteuil, a traditional gathering ground for old wealth and titles.[25] The socially prominent embassy attaché William Patten and his wife would entertain visiting American socialites such as the Vincent Astors and the William Paleys in their château in horsy Chantilly, outside of Paris. The Paleys would then move on to Paris, into "their" suite in the Ritz, a stone's throw from the top couturiers patronized by "Babe" Paley, who later became famous for uttering the immortal words, "You can never be too rich, or too thin."[26]

— —

The Marshall Plan officials worked assiduously to promote tourism to France by publicizing these rich and famous people's visits to France. But they and the French officials saw them mainly as bait for the lesser orders. Indeed, soon after the war ended, the French decided that the major economic benefits of American tourism would accrue not from Americans swilling champagne at Maxim's or playing baccarat at the Palm-Beach Casino, but from what Commissioner of Tourism Henri Lagrand called "the great middle class from America, which has not hitherto traveled to foreign countries."[27] In 1948 they saw statistics showing that the middle class was the main beneficiary of America's new prosperity as confirming the wisdom of this policy.[28]

Marshall Plan officials enthusiastically supported the campaign for middle-class American tourism. France had initially been told that "thanks to the favorable light in which it is viewed by Americans," it would receive the lion's share of the funding.[29] Yet Americans were frustrated by the seemingly antiquated French economy. A distressingly high proportion of the population were small farmers, and most of France's industries were too small scale and inefficient to compete in export markets. French businessmen seemed crippled by a resistance to innovation that was endemic in the entire country.[30] There seemed to be little, aside from champagne and haute couture, that France could produce that could earn her the dollars to buy American products and repay the Marshall Plan loans. Even if there were, these imports would likely meet fierce opposition from domestic American producers of similar goods.[31] Dollars earned from tourism, though, would face none of these obstacles and could be used to buy American-made goods. Developing tourism to France from the "dollar area" thus became "objective number one" of the Marshall Plan, which counted on its providing one-third of France's dollar receipts.[32]

In 1948 the ECA set as a goal having half a million American tourists visit Europe annually by 1952.[33] It adopted a plan to eliminate the shortage of steamships on the North Atlantic, encourage off-season tourism, organize low-cost tours, and cut the red tape that snarled border crossings.[34] It financed an advertising campaign by the newly created European Travel Commission to lure American tourists to Europe.[35] It paid the cost of the French refloating the *Europa* and refitting it as the *Liberté*, one of the largest and fastest liners on the North Atlantic run.[36] It offered low-interest loans to rebuild and modernize hotels and other tourist facilities and guaranteed American companies who used them that they could repatriate their profits freely.[37]

The French government joined in with other inducements for the

American middle class. Despite continuing electricity shortages, the government arranged for the great sights of Paris such as Notre-Dame and the place de la Concorde to be floodlit at night.[38] It tried to control the price gouging that middle-class tourists found so reprehensible. When the French minister responsible for tourism returned from a visit to the United States in April 1948, he said that there would be a "massive arrival of currency bearers" whose main problem was going to be prices. Hoteliers and restaurateurs should stick to their set prices, he warned, and there should be "no more '*menus surprises*,' which surprise the customer so disagreeably." Nor should they try to extract higher prices by offering only fixed menus with a large number of courses. In America people ate only three courses: entrée, meat course, and dessert. Finally, he warned shopkeepers not to stock up on luxury goods. Middle-class Americans were "essentially democratic" and interested mainly in bargains.[39]

Yet the path was still not smooth. Infuriating exchange controls and visa requirements remained on the books.[40] Henri Lagrand said Americans still received a poor "welcome," especially from "the man on the street."[41] Worse, though, was that although tourism picked up in the summer of 1948, most of the tourists were not the newly prosperous middle-aged ones that the French and American officials were counting on. Instead, they were astonished at the wave of young people that now arrived, squeezed into steamships' third-class (now called "tourist-class") cabins or on the two troopships that had been turned into "student ships." In mid-August they reported that "a mob of young men and women between 20 and 25 have rushed the travel agencies to get passage. It is absolutely impossible to get return space in that class." First-class accommodation, on the other hand, could be had for the asking.[42]

There was good reason for their disappointment, for the young people hardly left much in the way of dollars in France. Soon after landing, many of them learned to exploit their right to buy gas coupons. A monthly supply sold on the black market could bring in about forty-five dollars, almost enough in itself to live modestly in the Latin Quarter, where one could find a perfectly adequate room for less than one dollar a night. By summer's end, the French press, disappointed at their penny-pinching ways, were mocking their checked "cowboy shirts," blue jeans, and moccasins, and deriding them as "tourists without banknotes."[43] Nor were the numbers much to boast about. Although more Americans—120,000—visited France that year than in the previous postwar years, this was still nowhere the 300,000 who had visited in 1929.[44] Indeed, despite the ECA's great push, only about

200,000 Americans traveled to all of the Marshall Plan nations in 1948, and many of them were immigrants visiting their homelands.[45]

The next summer, however, brought a breakthrough. From everywhere came reports of packed ships and planes. In late August it was announced that to all intents and purposes there were no eastward passages available, by either mode, until early October. It was estimated that by September 1 the number of Americans visiting France had already passed the 200,000 mark, and the year's total might well approach 250,000.[46] The number of Americans visiting the Riviera was double that of the previous year.[47] All of this was despite the fact that inflation in France had rapidly undercut the previous year's bargain prices.[48]

French tourist officials now took ECA advice, and funding, to encourage American visits in the off-season. Their "Fall Is Fine in France" promotion was complemented by a European Travel Commission campaign, aimed at older tourists, for cultural tourism.[49] In October 1949 Janet Flanner reported that tourists in Paris were not complaining about rising hotel rates. "The only outcry right now is of frustrated travelers who can't squeeze in anywhere, regardless of what they are willing to pay." It was difficult to believe, she wrote, that this was only one decade after the "war season of 1939."[50] The next year, when the final figures were tallied, the ECA tourism promoters proudly noted that the 235,000 Americans who visited France in 1949 had spent $65 million there, more than the value of all the goods France exported to the United States that year.[51]

— —

One of the most powerful attractions, especially for younger Americans, was Paris's Left Bank, which had resumed its historic role as a center of bohemian life. This derived in large part from the flowering of existentialism. The ideas of Jean-Paul Sartre, its major French exponent, either befuddled most Americans who tried to understand them or struck them as too pessimistic. After seeing Sartre's play *State of Siege*, in Paris in January 1949, Martha Churchill, a Smith College junior, wrote home that it reflected "a war psychology of the absurdity of life which is very depressing, but which is nonetheless very prevalent over here. . . . It would have gone over like a lead balloon in the U.S."[52] However, Sartre did have a palpable impact on more bohemian Americans. A 1946 Broadway production of his play *No Exit*, directed by John Huston, had made some of his ideas familiar in New York City, as did a 1947 paperback by William Barrett called *What Is Existentialism?* Speaking tours in those years, mainly of American colleges, by him and his partner, Simone de Beauvoir, helped familiarize many academics and students with their ideas.[53]

The simplified version of existentialism circulating in America appealed mainly to young people who did not share the prevailing faith in bourgeois business culture and their country's moral superiority in the cold war. Life was "absurd," it said, and had no purpose in the conventional sense, but one had freedom, and one had to act—to make choices—to affirm this freedom and therefore one's humanity. Exactly how one was to act—what choices one should make—was often unclear, but what was clear was that existentialists did not take their cues from business civilization and the values of the middle class. This was symbolized in their dress, which rejected bourgeois styles in favor of simple outfits of black turtleneck sweaters and trousers for men and women, and what de Beauvoir, who herself shunned such clothes, called "ballerina shoes" for women.[54] By October 1948 there were so many American devotees in Paris that Edward Ratcliffe told a friend it was difficult to get tickets to Sartre's latest play because "there are enough stupid Americans around here to continue the vogue, as the groups in New York play him up."[55]

In America the movement's association with France and its emphasis on personal freedom meant that it was inevitably associated with sexual license—what was then called "free love." That Sartre and his followers were headquartered in Saint-Germain-des-Prés, alongside the Latin Quarter, solidified this image. The historic student district had been a mecca for Americans searching for casual sex since the 1830s.[56] The young Americans arriving in Paris in 1948 almost inevitably gravitated there, turning it, said Janet Flanner, into "a campus for the American collegiate set." Martha Churchill's first impression of the district in September 1948 was that "a lot of the men have long beards, berets, and a generally arty look. Everyone is shabbily dressed but very gay."[57] At the end of the next summer, Ollie Stewart reported in his column in the Baltimore and Philadelphia African American newspapers that young white Americans experienced an exhilarating sense of freedom on the Left Bank. They mixed freely with and slept with young colored people, he said.

> They let their hair down in everything they do. The young men blossom out in beards and goatees six weeks after they get off the boat, and go around town in sandals without socks. . . . They live with girls openly, and when they get broke they lose all modesty and demand that the girls take care of them. A lot of girls deliberately refrain from combing their hair for days to acquire a sophisticated look. They go to cafes wearing a bra and blue denim pants, rolled up the knees.

They drink pernod and call for absinthe—and get sick after a few sips. They will show you a vaccination mark on the hip, or an operation scar just any old place, at the drop of a hint. They're free for the first time.[58]

Many of them packed into the Café de Flore, where Jean-Paul Sartre and his partner, Simone de Beauvoir, the "High Priestess of Existentialism," were said to spend much of their day, and filled the terrace of its neighbor-

The Café des Deux Magots and Café de Flore, which tourists would scour in the hopes of catching sight of Jean-Paul Sartre and Simone de Beauvoir, celebrated apostles of existentialism. Courtesy of Roger-Viollet.

ing café, Deux Magots, where de Beauvoir would spend her mornings. The Flore, said Flanner, became "a drugstore for pretty upstate girls in unbecoming blue denim pants and their Middle Western dates, most of whom are growing hasty Beaux-Arts beards."[59] The *Herald Tribune* said the Deux Magots was "filled with bearded, bereted Americans trying to look like Frenchmen and zooty, gum-chewing Frenchmen trying to look like Americans."[60] After visiting the cafés, an unimpressed Edward Ratcliffe described "Existentialist Man" as "terrifically long-haired, sloppily and dirtily clad, invariably with a beard and that look in the eye of vapid detachment."[61]

Much to the young people's chagrin, the Left Bank cafés also became a regular stop for more conventionally dressed American tourists. In July 1949 *Time* ran a series of cartoons of American tourists in Paris including one of Sartre at the Flore with the caption: "Headquarters: the famed Flore, successor to the Dôme of the Hemingwayward '20's, where customers drink and sometimes think. Center rear (raised hand): Jean-Paul Sartre himself."[62] A French journalist explained to his bemused countrymen that tourists could not return to America without having seen Sartre, the Eiffel Tower, and the Folies Bergère.[63] A French wag said Saint-Germain-des-Prés was now "the Cathedral of Sartre."[64] Rather bizarrely, in early 1949 the Communists, who had recently turned on Sartre, warned American tourists that the English-language entertainment guide that told them they could see "the chief attraction of Paris, France—Jean Paul Sartre . . . the terrible rebel," in the Flore was guilty of misleading advertising, for he had been "tame for a long time."[65]

The real misconception, though, was that Sartre was still at the Flore. By then, he and his cronies had long since fled to the basement bar of the Hôtel Pont-Royal, a rather elegant place not far away. Then, Flanner said, by the time "the tourist intelligentsia" finally caught on and followed them there, they found it "full only of themselves."[66]

— —

But Sartre was by no means the only Left Bank sight on the American tourist beat. In the evening they would search out what the diary of Louis Bishop, the forty-nine-year-old Long Island cardiologist, called "some left bank crazy existentialist places."[67] These *caves* (cellars) were usually dark basement cafés where the young black-clad French jitterbugged to bebop, the latest American jazz trend. The most popular of these, the Vieux Colombier, became a frequent stop for visiting Hollywood stars and claimed the distinction of having left the pampered tobacco fortune heiress Doris Duke cooling her heels, waiting for a table, for all of fifteen minutes.[68]

However, most tourists were more than satisfied with the revived "Paris by Night" tours, which added Left Bank *caves* to their itineraries. A French journalist told of a couple from New York who thought one of the places they visited on such a tour must be one of the most fashionable places in the city. In fact, he said, it was one of those fake-historic *caves*, with "*oubliettes*" (deep holes into which medieval miscreants were supposedly tossed and forgotten), trapdoors, and false secret walls into which only foreigners and hicks from the provinces ventured. Nothing, he said, sounded more beautiful to the tourists than songs such as "Auprès de ma blonde" (the French counterpart to "I've Been Working on the Railroad").[69]

Some of the nightspots attracted boisterous crowds of homosexual Americans, reveling in their freedom from the constraints of their homeland. The favorite haunt of James Donahue, the flamboyantly gay Woolworth fortune heir who back in New York was a pillar of the Catholic Church, was Le Boeuf sur le Toit, which one regular called "the city's number one chic queer nightclub." One night, when Donahue was there in drag, he consulted with the lady fortune-teller who occupied a table in the rear. When she failed to recognize that he was a man, he got up on the table, pulled up his skirt, and displayed his private parts to her and the rest of the clientele.[70]

Sometimes gay Americans became so rowdy, and so demonstrative in their public displays of affection for each other, that offended Parisians called for police intervention. Even though homosexuality was legal in France, the police would round them up, put them in paddy wagons, and take them to the station, where officers would ask whether they were "inverts," duly record the answer, and then release them, in the usually vain hope that they henceforth would be more discreet in their behavior. With the Communist press delighting in denouncing what they called "The Scandal of the Latin Quarter," an angry André Gide, the anti-Communist homosexual who won the Nobel Prize for Literature in 1947, presented a visiting American with a copy of one of his books advocating a more restrained kind of homosexuality. Waving a finger in the young man's face, the old writer said, "*Je ne suis pas tapette, Monsieur, je suis pédéraste.*" ("I am not a fag, Sir, I am a homosexual.")[71] Americans were also embarrassed by the gay men's behavior. Shortly after he arrived in Paris, Saul Bellow lamented to a friend that "America's chief export to Europe has been its homosexuals."[72]

— —

When it came to art, many of the new upper-middle-class tourists seemed satisfied with the usual quick tour of the Louvre, where one was led to the aforementioned Big Three: the Venus de Milo, Winged Victory, and the *Mona Lisa*. This would be followed by a quick trot down the immense Long Gallery, whose huge array of historic paintings would usually confirm their prejudices concerning how tiresome old pictures could be, and a quick exit out the small door on the floor below to the waiting bus.

However, there were also tourists who were very impressed by it and the other public museums. "We went to the Louvre, we went to the Musée Moderne, we went to every museum in Paris," said Herbert Gentry, who found the experience overwhelming.[73] Minna Citron wrote home in July 1947 that a huge van Gogh show at the Orangerie and the Bibliothèque Nationale was "beautifully installed" and that the "pièce de résistance" was removing the Impressionist works from the Louvre and hanging them in the Jeu de Paume.[74] Romare Bearden wrote of the "amazing job of presentation" at an exhibition of Yugoslav frescoes at the Museum of National Monuments, whose curators had fitted perfect copies of the frescoes into reconstructions of the Serbian monasteries. "I came out of the museum perspiring and shaking," he wrote to a friend back home, "and had to take two cognacs in an effort to collect myself. . . . After this the Louvre, the Cluny, the Museum of Oriental Art, the Bibliothèque Nationale with Rembrandt drawings, the Museum of Man with African sculpture." It all inspired his own creativity, he said.[75] Cynthia Brants, the painter from Texas, was excited to see all the people in the Louvre. "The vista down the long gallery," she wrote in her diary, "with its spectators, copyists, and guards looks like a 19th century engraving of the interior of the Louvre. . . . The atmosphere is busy, in contrast to our empty, quiet and rather lifeless museum galleries at home."[76]

Other artists were inspired by France's creative past. Robert Gwathmey thought the stained-glass windows of Chartres were "the finest visual expression ever." He saw the hand of great Impressionists and Post-Impressionists practically everywhere. At the old Circus Medrano, he told his dealer, "one sees Seurat, Degas, Lautrec, etc. Renoir and Manet at the Opéra; Courbet, Renoir, Manet, Seurat at the Bois, etc. One step into the countryside and there is a Sisley, a Monet, a Pissarro, after every blink. Even with the exotic references of Matisse and Picasso, the distilled work comes out of France. Their still lifes and those of Braque are seen in the raw in every local house one enters."[77] Bearden wrote that before setting to work, "I look out of my [hotel] window and see a convent founded in 1620—the building next to it where Victor Hugo wrote 'Les Miserables'—next to it the little school which Pasteur attended in his youth. After this, a nice stroll in the Luxembourg Gardens and I'm ready."[78]

American art lovers also sought out the works of new artists, such as Bernard Buffet and Jean Dubuffet, who were said to be taking Paris by storm, and tried to track down the artistic old guard, some of whom were now congregating in the beautiful light of the Côte d'Azur. Marc Chagall returned to work in Nice after spending the war in the United States. Although increasingly crippled by arthritis, Henri Matisse managed to finish painting the lovely chapel in Vence in 1951. Pablo Picasso now spent much of his time in Villauris, reveling in what a visitor called "a riot of publicity." He welcomed a steady stream of visitors to his studio and delighted in taking his children to the beach, where he pretended not to notice the tourists who surrounded him, taking photos of his doodles in the sand.[79] Actually meeting the aging artist could be a riveting experience. The composer Ned Rorem wrote in his diary of Picasso tapping the shoulder of a companion while leaving a Riviera movie theater: "We turned: it was Picasso. Those jet bullet eyes both burned into my brain and absorbed me into his forever. I was so carbonized I forgot their glib exchange."[80] It is no wonder that when Romare Bearden visited Picasso in his Villauris studio in 1950, people stopped by to see the master all day long: "It was like going to see the Eiffel Tower."[81] One night at a party, as they were surrounded by a crowd of admirers, Picasso turned to the celebrated artist/writer Jean Cocteau, who was painting a chapel in Menton, and said, "You, me, and the Aga Khan could sure fill a room."[82]

— —

One attraction that was not particularly high on the new upper-middle-class tourist agenda was French food. The Left Bank bohemians appreciated the *boulangeries*, cheese shops, and vendors of cheap wine, as well as the inexpensive student cafés, but many of the wealthier tourists were more apprehensive about French food. They might enjoy looking in on the little bistros with paper tablecloths and a pitcher of Beaujolais on the table but rarely ventured in themselves. The old fears of people raised on plain Anglo-American fare that French sauces camouflaged putrid ingredients persisted. These were reflected in a song in the 1949 Broadway show *Miss Liberty*, whose lyrics, by Irving Berlin, said that while the Frenchman's food "was very plain, the fancy sauces with ptomaine are only for Americans."[83]

A number of new restaurants, such as Le Hamburger and the Pam-Pam, which specialized in Le Chicken Hash, tried catering to these fears. The only one that had any long-term legs was Leroy Haynes's "soul food" restaurant in Montmartre. Haynes, an African American ex-GI with a master's degree in sociology, opened it in 1949, serving southern-fried chicken, greens, and other "down home" favorites. Publicity about such celebrated customers as Louis Armstrong soon attracted a growing white clientele, including celebrities such as the sex-kitten actress Brigitte Bardot, who ate one forkful of chitterlings and lots of lemon meringue pie, and the Hollywood superstars Elizabeth Taylor and Richard Burton, who celebrated her birthday in 1967 by washing down their fried chicken with quarts of Jack Daniel's sour mash whiskey.[84]

Some hotels, such as the Plaza Athénée, realized that their American guests could not handle leisurely multicourse French lunches and installed American-style snack bars. The Café de la Paix turned its back on café tradition, which demands that breakfast consist only of coffee and bread or croissants, and began serving American-style bacon-and-eggs breakfasts—albeit not until 10:00 AM.[85] But the vast majority of French restaurateurs refused to adjust to American tastes. Demands to be served ice water during meals, something many French thought bad for the digestion, were flatly refused. "They say," reported Ollie Stewart in 1950, "that if Americans don't know better than to drink water with meals, it's just too bad. The restaurant has a reputation to maintain."[86] Predictably, the Café de la Paix was the only major restaurant to give in and began plunking down a pitcher of ice-cold water on American diners' tables as soon as their orders were taken.[87]

Americans were much less demanding when it came to the food that accompanied the water. Stanley Karnow, a *Time* magazine correspondent in Paris, was severely disappointed when what looked like a juicy opportunity for top-notch expense account dining melted away. The Joint Distribution Committee, which helped Jewish refugees settle in Israel, regularly assigned him to take wealthy Jewish donors around Paris during their stopovers on the way to and from the new state. He would take them to super-luxe restaurants such as Maxim's, the Tour d'Argent, and Ledoyen, expecting that he could dine on fine haute cuisine. "Regrettably to me," he later wrote, "their tastes tended to be modest. They would shun the *spécialités de la maison* and instead order a prosaic *filet de sole* or *côte de veau* and, if any, one glass of wine. Under the circumstances, I could not decently savor a marvelous *pièce de résistance* and had to choose something just as banal."[88] Other wealthy visitors had even more modest tastes. The travel writer Horace Sutton told of an American man who sat down in the elegant dining room of an ultra-fashionable Paris hotel, looked through the gigantic menu, shook his head, and asked for ham and eggs. "Presently," he said,

> after the French custom, there appeared in the doorway leading from the kitchen a procession of waiters and assistants pushing before them a great sil-

ver tureen mounted on wheels. Blue flames from a mobile fire played on the underside. The busboy drew back the sliding cover of the tureen with a flourish, a waiter extracted a plate, which was taken by the headwaiter and placed before our man. He looked down at the eggs, which were shirred [lightly scrambled], also after the French fashion, took a forkful in his mouth, and turned to a compatriot sitting nearby. "These people can't make a fried egg worth a 'goddam,'" he said.[89]

The gap between such well-heeled first-time tourists' suspicions of dining in France and the enthusiasm with which well-traveled upper-class *bec fins* such as David Bruce and Herbert Lehman tucked into their foie gras and *canard pressé* at the Tour d'Argent could be immense. Indeed, when he became ambassador, poor Bruce had to field many complaints from the former kind of tourists, who were outraged at seeing the French, who were thought to be living off American taxpayers' handouts, eating expensive meals at outposts of *la grande cuisine*.[90]

Between these poles lay well-off people, like the Long Island cardiologist Louis Bishop, who could afford the fine dining but were constricted by relatively conservative tastes. Although, like Lehman, he, too, had visited Paris more than once before the war, he did not arrive with a list of old favorite restaurants in mind. Instead, his diary says, he and his wife "did not know any restaurants so we had no idea where to eat." They went to the old American hangout, Harry's Bar, where the bartender recommended "an excellent little restaurant" around the corner called L'Opéra. There they had "a delicious Steak Chateaubriand," a grilled fillet of beef with sautéed potatoes, and a bit of sauce on the side that was a common item in expensive American restaurants. They liked the steak so much that they returned again, for more, a week later. Otherwise, when left to their own devices, they favored the snack bar at the Plaza Athénée for lunch, the Ritz for tea, and the Café de la Paix, then renowned for tailoring its food to American tastes, for dinner.[91]

— —

Despite the heartening revival, by the end of 1949 the great age of mass middle-class tourism still showed few signs of arriving. French and American officials had grounded their hopes in the fact that the number of American families defined as middle class had risen from 16 percent of the total in 1941 to 50 percent in 1947. But it only took an annual income of between $3,000 and $5,000 for a family to be defined as middle class, while it cost about $900 just for a tourist-class ticket on a transatlantic liner. Since the average cost of the basic one-and-a-half-month visit to Europe was $1,400, only those living on well over $5,000 could even conceive of taking a trip to Europe. Moreover, although by 1950 the number of families living on over $5,000 did number 9 million, where would they find the time? The average middle-class annual holiday lasted only two to three weeks, not much more time than it took to get to Europe and back by sea.[92] Clearly, for the most part, those with the time and money to travel to Europe would have to be at the upper reaches of what Americans called the upper-middle class. In 1951, when the New York ad man in charge of the British Travel Service account in America tried to decide who to target, he concluded, "Aim for the near-upper market. . . . Let's be sure our prospects can meet the tariff." Their advertising campaigns thus relied on *Life* magazine, because it had a high proportion of readers with a college education, and the *New Yorker*, because of its high-income readership.[93]

EIGHT

"Coca-Colonization" and Its Discontents

*The people of those foreign countries are very ignorant. They looked curiously at
the costumes we had brought from the wilds of America. They observed that we
talked loudly at the table sometimes. . . . In Paris they just simply opened their
eyes and stared when we spoke to them in French. We never did succeed in making
those idiots understand their own language.*

— MARK TWAIN, *Innocents Abroad* (1869)

In 1949 some observers said they noticed a new attitude among American
tourists in Europe. They were, said American news magazines, much more
political than ever before: more "serious" than their prewar counterparts
and "more interested in world affairs."[1] Cornelius Vanderbilt Whitney, the
American undersecretary of commerce, said that, unlike the wealthy tourists of prewar years, these new tourists were "serious-minded professional
people, shopkeepers, and small business men" who wanted "to study modern Europe, its political institutions and its economy."[2] Marshall Plan officials hoped tourists inspired by this new kind of "purposeful travel" would
return from Europe sympathetic to the Plan and to the American-led "Atlantic Community."[3] But this view of American tourists in France was as
evanescent as the sun on a December day in Paris. Even as it was being pro-
pounded, it was being blotted out by much more negative views of the tourists that were the by-product of an extraordinary wave of anti-Americanism
sweeping France.

In mid-1947 France's powerful Communist Party, responding to the re-
frigerating cold war, had mounted a fierce anti-American campaign, and
American tourists presented readily available targets. *L'Humanité* portrayed
them as uncultured cowboys—"young lords from Oklahoma"—who were
bent on turning France into an amusement park. They packed Paris's bars
and expensive restaurants, it said, trying to "forget the mediocrity of their
American existence."[4] The Communist weekly *Samedi-Soir* harped on the
"scandalous" behavior of homosexual American tourists while the magazine

Action vilified "the pederasts of the American intelligentsia" on the Left Bank. One of them, *Action* huffed, had made "undisguised propositions" to a cavalry colonel in civilian clothes, "even though he was accompanied by his charming wife."[5] More curious, given their claims to represent working-class values, were the Communists' criticisms of the tourists' failures to conform to bourgeois French notions of taste and propriety. *Samedi-Soir* condemned their lack of appreciation for French fine cuisine, waxing indignant over reports that they asked for ketchup with their *canard pressé*—a specialty of luxury restaurants.[6] The Soviet newspaper *Izvestia* condemned them for slouching in Paris cafés with their feet on the table, looking over passing women "like a horse dealer looks over horses."[7] Moscow Radio interviewed a Polish writer who bemoaned the "junk" culture brought over by the "endless stream of American tourists [rushing] headlong to France for a good time."[8]

The campaign also labeled almost every other sign of the American presence in France as a nefarious one. A slew of American films appearing on French screens provided them with plenty of ammunition, especially since the government had been forced to drop its restrictive quota on American films to get a U.S. loan in 1946. Critics derided most of them as banal "B" grade Westerns, violent gangster films, simple-minded comedies, or blatant advertisements for America.[9] The leftists also condemned the influx of low-brow American comic books and the launching of a French-language edition of the *Reader's Digest*, which, although denounced as crude propaganda for the "American Way of Life," promptly became the highest-circulation magazine in France.[10] In 1949 the party rallied the nation against Coca-Cola's plans to establish bottling plants in France, calling the drink a major threat to the French way of life. Recalling the old German national anthem, "Deutschland über Alles" (Germany over all), it said, "One will soon be able to say 'Coca-Cola over all.'" It charged that the American intelligence services, the State Department, the Chase Bank, and their French allies wanted to impose the addictive beverage on France "along with American spies."[11]

Much to the dismay of American diplomats, the attacks on Hollywood, comic books, the *Reader's Digest*, and the "*Coca-Colonisation*" of France resonated far beyond the Communists and their followers. The anti-Coke campaign even had considerable business support, especially from producers of fruit juices and wine, who claimed the beverage was addictive and perhaps poisonous. Thanks in part to them, the French National Assembly passed a resolution authorizing the government to ban it if (hopefully) it proved "noxious."[12] Non-Communist social critics called it a symbol of a relaxed, leisure-oriented American lifestyle that had no place in France.

Even Catholic publications, in France and the United States, attacked it for contributing to the American "economic colonization" of France.[13] Although Coca-Cola vehemently denied such charges, its president did little to defuse them when he proudly proclaimed that at the bottom of each Coke bottle one found "the essence of capitalism"; nor did the American newspaper that picked up this theme and defended Coke's expansion into France on the grounds that "you can't spread the doctrines of Marx where the people drink Coca-Cola."[14]

Similarly, the attacks on Hollywood's incursions also drew support from across the political spectrum. Rightists picked up where they had left off in their prewar attacks on Hollywood movies' glorification of materialism, gangsterism, and eroticism. The non-Communist Left charged that they dragged down the level of French culture. In mid-1946 Jean-Paul Sartre, who said he supported the Soviet Union as the lesser of two evils in its conflict with the United States, cited Hollywood movies (and canned fruit) in his accusation that America was exporting its debased culture to France.[15] The coeditor of his magazine, Raymond Aron, split from Sartre and sided with the United States, but justified this on grounds that were even less flattering to American culture. He said he supported America as the lesser, not just of two evils, but of "two abominations." The Gaullist intellectual André Malraux, who had often condemned America's soulless, materialistic civilization, reluctantly agreed that Europe had to side with the United States in defending "Atlantic civilization" against the Soviets. However, he pointed out that the Americans had contributed only "technical knowledge," rather than anything of cultural value, to that civilization.[16] The future Nobel Prize–winning writer Albert Camus rejected both Stalinism and Gaullism, yet he, too, had nothing positive to say about the culture of American capitalism.[17] It seemed that, wherever they stood on the political spectrum, the intellectuals' almost unanimous refrain was that the United States was the country of "mass produced goods, mass produced culture, and mass produced feelings."[18] To them, a French writer later said, "the United States was not a country, but a sin."[19]

To Americans, one of the most disturbing aspects of the anti-American critique was that it was not confined to intellectuals. By 1950 it was flourishing among politicians on the Left (the Communist Party and the "neutralist" socialists) and the Right (the Gaullists and the right-wing colonialists).[20] Most worrisome were reports that the French "man-on-the-street" also subscribed to it. One of the most significant conclusions of an in-depth poll of French attitudes in late 1952 was that fears of American economic and political domination crossed all class and political lines.[21] That year the

American sociologist Arnold Rose returned from a year in France and reported that the common view was that America was

> a giant, physically healthy and full of energy, but crude, reactionary, and without a soul. This creature—whose "instincts" . . . are directed solely toward the accumulation of wealth, physical labor at a destroying speed, and simple amusements like drinking Coca-Cola and whiskey, and viewing banal films and comic strips—is of course incapable of understanding the finer aspects of life like good food, love, leisure, intellectual conversation, and the arts.[22]

To Americans concerned about rectifying these negative images, American tourists seemed to be part of the problem, not its solution. Most of those now arriving in France seemed to exemplify, not the "serious-minded" new investigative tourists that *Time* magazine hailed, but exactly the kind of cultural nincompoops that America was said to be producing. Their ignorance of France's language and history was usually manifest; their lack of interest in high culture was assumed. Some French people even complained that they were incapable of appreciating the beauties of Paris.[23] Even those with an interest in encouraging American tourism had low opinions of the tourists' cultural level. One French hotelier advised his colleagues to avoid talking about complicated subjects such as literature, music, and art with American clients. Instead, it was best to stick to the movies and to ask them about their hometowns. He suggested they convert their hotels' libraries to bars, since "boredom is, with lack of hygiene, a great enemy of the American who wants, above all, 'to have fun.'"[24]

One French writer saw tourists' disgust with escargots as a reflection of their superficial culture and ignorance of French history.[25] Indeed, to many, this apparent inability to appreciate French food and wine was the most reprehensible quality of all. Horror stories circulated about the group of Americans who, after trying some rare Vosne-Romanée, one of the greatest of Burgundy wines, ordered Coca-Cola to wash it down.[26] "The French," said a French historian, "expecting to win all hearts with the excellence of their food, were staggered to find that it didn't suit the tastes of these tiresome visitors at all."[27]

Rather than defend the tourists, pro-American Frenchmen tried to explain them away as atypical. In August 1950 Henri Peyre wrote in *Le Monde* that there were Americans who were cultured and who knew about France, its art, and its literature. Unfortunately, he said, "the face which America shows us most openly is not always its truest and loveliest one. The soldiers, and especially the tourists who America sends us, are excellent Americans, but they are hardly representative of American intellectuality, culture, or idealism." He said that a French person traveling abroad often looks for stimulation from the arts of the countries he visits and prepares for his trips by reading up on them. The American tourist, on the other hand, was "frequently a newly-rich businessman [or] a bored woman from the sticks" who did not.[28]

Even such feeble attempts to defend America's cultural level seemed to cut little ice among the French. Many non-Communist papers and journals echoed the Communist calls to resist the "new occupiers" of France.[29] In late 1950 an American embassy analyst reported to Washington that it had become "chic" in higher French circles to "gripe" about "the American occupation of France." He ascribed *Le Monde*'s support for French neutrality to French fears of being swamped by inferior American culture. He said that its director, Hubert Beuve-Méry, was

> resentful of his country's dependence on the U.S., and contemptuous of what he imagines to be the American scale of values. He once told the writer of this dispatch that, in his view, the United States is like a great glacier, slowly but relentlessly crawling down the mountainside, absorbing and crushing everything in the path and spearheaded by . . . Coca-Cola and Reader's Digest.[30]

Tourists who behaved like occupiers added to the embassy's problems. Indeed, some of them, like their obnoxious predecessors of the 1920s, seemed to enjoy flouting America's wealth as proof of their superiority over the French. Ernie Ricci, one of the GIs who stayed on, recalled that in 1949 and 1950 tourists began "flashing it around" and "belittling the French." They would also walk around "flashing big wads of dollars" and then, when hooked by pickpockets, would complain, "The French are thieves. The French are this and that."[31]

Another source of French disgust was that, despite the strength of the dollar, tourists continued to complain about French price gouging.[32] Over half the "causes of friction" listed in a report on American tourists in France in the summer of 1949 concerned perceptions that they were being overcharged.[33] Among the most common complaints in a 1951 survey of returning American tourists was the old notion that there were two prices, one for the French, another for Americans.[34] So persistent were these grumblings that in September 1953 the advertising executive David Ogilvy, whose company promoted travel to Britain in America, told his staff that he had read and heard so much about American tourists "complaining louder and louder about the excessive prices they are charged in France" that he thought they should mount a campaign saying that "Britain is not a clip joint."[35]

Ambassador David Bruce and other embassy officials were horrified by the tourists' insensitivity and ignorance. Even visitors from their own families were an embarrassment. "The town is full of tourists," Janet Flanner wrote her friend. "Mother of one chap in the embassy ruined his reputation the other night by saying of the Louvre, 'Well, I declare, it's just the biggest bank building I ever did see.'"[36] Letitia Baldrige, an embassy employee, wrote her friend Nancy Mitford that "Americans in Europe do create harm and ill-will" and were "careless, complaining, spoiled people."[37] *Look* magazine called its report on how American tourists were regarded in Europe "Mr. American—the World Thinks He's a Spoiled Sugar Daddy." Its Paris correspondent said, "The same man who is . . . a hard-headed businessman in London arrives in Paris full of preconceptions about the city and determined to relax." He comes "to see the girlie shows and try the cognac," and makes a fool of himself in Parisians' eyes. "To the average Frenchman," he said, "the American remains the man in the seersucker suit trailing an immense camera and flinging thousand-franc notes around him like autumn leaves."[38]

The tourists' image would have been easier to defend had they just worn white seersucker suits. But their propensity to dress in casual clothes in places where the French dressed more formally was an added embarrassment. "Nothing grieves me more," said the author of the chapter on France in Fodor's *Woman's Guide to Europe*, "than the sight of a pretty American gal trudging about Paris in a pair of slacks. What can you say to a Frenchman who asks incredulously, 'Do all American girls chew gum and wear *pantalons?*'"[39] "You should have seen them in the Ritz as I did this morning," the English writer Nancy Mitford wrote Evelyn Waugh that August from Paris, "all dressed up in beach clothes."[40] An American woman arriving in Nice in the summer of 1952 was disappointed to see that "even on the glamorous Promenade des Anglais," whose hotels were full of Americans, "swarms of people are constantly parading the streets in shorts or bathing suits, which they wear throughout the day and evening."[41]

Yet, in fact, dressing down was not yet the American norm, for most tourists were still upper and upper-middle class and were not as comfortable with dressing casually in public as they would later be. This was still a time, after all, when first-class steamship passengers dressed formally for dinner and airlines banned men without ties from their first-class cabins. Many heeded Pan Am's advice to tourists in Paris to "wear your newest, smartest clothes. . . . Dinner jacket [i.e., tuxedo] is a necessity for a man."[42] In 1951

Lee Bouvier, a young American woman from an upper-class American family, traveling in France and Italy with her sister Jacqueline, the future wife of John F. Kennedy, wrote their mother, "I know you are right about us representing our country and that we should never do anything that would call attention to us and make people shocked at Americans. We DO sew on all our buttons and wear gloves and never go out in big cities except in what we would wear to church in Newport on Sundays."[43] The photos taken by Dorothy and La Rue Brown, a well-connected older couple from Massachusetts, on their European tour in the summer of 1959 invariably show them, and the retired schoolteacher from North Carolina who accompanied them, standing in front of Europe's most famous sights with him in jacket and tie and the women in dresses and hats. The only concession to informality is in a photo of him in Pompeii, in July, standing in what her diary calls blistering heat, in white shirt and bow tie, but without his jacket.[44]

But even properly dressed American tourists were open to derision. Ollie Stewart cited as typical a middle-aged Frenchwoman who said, "What I find distressing is the way elderly American women dress. They show up in Paris wearing red dresses, sometimes even green in the most violent shades. They seem to have no sense of color whatever. And the hats they wear look absolutely terrible, as a rule. It seems to me that American women must go out of their way to dress in the most unbecoming clothes they can find." As for the men, Stewart warned them, "Remember that the necktie that got you compliments in New York can get you laughed at in Paris."[45] Indeed, the satirical cartoons of American tourists usually had the men wearing ties, but "noisy" ones.[46]

— —

Ambassador Bruce and his wife tried to show that the tourists were not representative of American taste by inviting French opinion makers to gala parties with fashionably dressed Americans and fine French food and wine. The American government poured money into a number of efforts designed to show Europeans that America did produce high culture worthy of consideration. By 1949 the Paris embassy had twenty-nine cultural affairs officers turning out newsletters, loaning out documentary films, and arranging expositions, concerts, and talks by American artists, musicians, and scholars. The American Cultural Center in Paris became a beehive of high-cultural activities. Three American-subsidized libraries encouraged Parisians to appreciate American literature and others were established in seven provincial cities.[47] In the spring of 1954, the embassy helped stage a large American Arts Festival in Paris. That year Congress rushed through an "emergency" appropriation of $5 million to pay for such activities, which continued well into the 1960s.[48]

Yet these high-toned efforts failed to confront the charges that the thousands of ordinary, untalented Americans coming to Europe as tourists represented an invasion of American "junk" culture. In France the ECA tried to deflect these with a tongue-in-cheek pamphlet, illustrated with cartoon images of amiable cigar-chomping American tourists, that began, "*Aux Armes Citoyens!*" It said that yes, one could see the invaders, particularly in the summer, "going about the country in motorized columns (generally of Cook's buses) pitilessly machine-gunning our monuments with shots of Kodak. You will also notice that he is armed to the teeth, with cigars." The cartoon shows fearful chefs and waiters waiting, armed, outside of their hotels, but the tourist passes them by, leaving a cloud of hundred-dollar bills and traveler's checks.[49]

To combat the widespread notion that the Americans were so rich that their complaints about price gouging bespoke miserliness and greed, the ECA hired the French journalist Georges Ravon to explain in another pamphlet that there was no truth to the idea that America produced millionaires on a kind of assembly line, like automobiles or phonographs. He said that most of the Americans who visited France were hardworking people who traveled to France for relaxation. They came to discover "the sweetness of life," which was impossible to find in their frenetic country. France, they thought, was a country where one had the time to live.[50] In another ECA pamphlet, a Frenchman tried to dissuade hoteliers and restaurateurs from overcharging Americans. The typical tourist, he said, probably earned from $300 to $700 a month and had taken two years to save the $1,000 cost of a trip to France. "He in no way wishes to be thought of as the Golden Calf," he said, and was particularly annoyed at being overcharged. "Nothing bothers him more than being told a room rents for 1200 francs and discovering, upon checking out, that with taxes and other charges, the actual rate is 2000 francs." Also, the tourists might love French cuisine and call it "the best in the world," but this did not mean that they should be handed the menu "with the piteous condescension one would accord to a Huron Indian projected from a still-unexplored region to the paradise of civilization." The most important thing to bear in mind, though, was that although Americans love discovering France's old buildings, their love of old things stops at the toilet. "To make them happy, give them old stones, but good plumbing. *Plumbing* is one of the key words of American tourism. Eighty-five percent of American tourists return from France saying they were enchanted by their stay, but lamenting the mediocrity of our plumbing. . . . Give them good toilets that flush well and you will make for happy tourists."[51]

Some French officials thought the problems could not be solved that easily. When the French embassy in Washington asked its consuls in America to report on returning tourists' complaints about France, their man in Los Angeles sent in a scathing assessment of the tourists themselves. Most of the "unjustified critiques," he said, came from the less affluent tourists who "most often make a bad impression on the French." Although he conceded that some of them returned "filled with wonder for our cultural riches," others went to France "with the same spirit with which they visit Mexico." In their search for pleasure, they broke laws and flouted morality in ways that would land them in jail back home. He called for reinstating visa requirements and allowing only higher-income Americans to visit France.[52]

— —

Some Americans tried to solve the problem by teaching the tourists to behave better. From all sides came pleas to regard themselves as "unofficial ambassadors of good-will for America."[53] The European Travel Commission promoted American travel to Europe with the slogan "Understanding through Travel Is the Passport to Peace."[54] American Express handed out pamphlets warning tourists that "everywhere the tourist is creating an impression" and advising them on proper behavior. It also hired Emily Post, author of America's best-selling etiquette book, to make a TV film giving "pointers" on tourist etiquette abroad.[55]

Many of these admonitions echoed the old notion, popularized by Mark Twain, that American tourists were basically openhearted, well-meaning people whose ignorance of foreign languages and customs led them to inadvertently step on native toes. The *New York Times Magazine* ran "A Primer on Etiquette for Innocents Abroad," by its Paris editor and his wife. They warned against making comments in English on the assumption that those around you do not understand it, strolling into Paris restaurants before 7:00 PM, when the staff usually eats, remarking to Frenchmen that Frenchwomen do not know how to dress, and ostentatiously wiping the silver at the Tour d'Argent with one's napkin after being seated. Above all, they said, "RELAX."[56]

In 1952 the American government began distributing booklets entitled "What Should I Know When I Travel Abroad?" that interspersed practical advice with warnings against using demeaning terms like "Frenchies" and "natives."[57] Such efforts picked up in 1953, after President Eisenhower, who was a firm believer in tourism as a force for "international understanding," took office.[58] The government distributed another booklet, illustrated by the popular cartoonist Al Capp, urging tourists to behave well so that ordinary foreigners would support America in the cold war. New passports now came with warnings, signed by Eisenhower, to refrain from obnoxious behavior while abroad. Major airports and ocean liner terminals carried posters admonishing tourists to be on their best behavior in foreign countries.[59] "Don't Be an 'Ugly American,'" warned Frances Knight, head of the Passport Office, in a 1960 article in *Parade* magazine. "Each tourist season," she said, "produces a crop of unpleasant incidents created by the brash, the thoughtless, the bad-mannered." Among her litany of the most common complaints about American tourists were that they plastered their luggage with devalued foreign currency and talked loudly all through the opera. Most annoying to Europeans, she said, was "the matter of dress": Americans wore shorts in cathedrals and other inappropriate places. They were excluded from restaurants because they appeared in shorts or the women wore slacks and the men did not wear ties or jackets. Anti-Americanism was also caused by "bad manners in buses, trains, planes and ships," she said. Europeans were "both baffled and angered" by Americans defying no-smoking signs. "They also dislike loud arguments, complaints, boisterousness, shouted demands for service." She ended with "the most obvious offenses: getting drunk, engaging in street brawls, leaving a trail of bad checks and unpaid bills, and dabbling in black markets." Among her "tips for tourists" were "Don't throw your dollars around. . . . Don't sneer at somebody else's money. . . . Don't go around boasting, 'I only speak American.'" "A boast about how much better things are at home," she warned, "only causes resentment."[60] All in all, it was hardly a pretty picture of American tourists abroad.

Others suggestions for behavior modification were equally hard-hitting. In May 1950 the travel editor of the *Saturday Review*, Horace Sutton, wrote that Parisians were already "shuddering" at the prospect of another summer influx of American tourists, for "far too many" of them wasted their time in bars and other such hangouts. "These ambassadors of ours behave like barbarians," he said, "shouldering the natives out of the center of their cities every summer." He suggested that "a few million spent by the Government for schools to teach Americans how to behave while abroad, as well as the rudiments of foreign languages, would be an excellent investment."[61] Six months later he complained that too many travelers to Europe were not at all interested in really exploring Europe and told of a tour operator who said he had given up on trying to get them to leave their hotel lobbies and go into the towns in the evening. "You know," the operator said, "when we would go to Marseille I used to take some of the folks down to the fish houses along the harbor. I'd say to a lady from Dubuque, 'Why don't you try the bouillabaisse, it's famous in this part of the country?' And she would ask, 'What's bouillabaisse?' I'd explain it was a stew made from all kinds of shell fish and vegetables served in a soup bowl. 'Thank you very much,' she would tell me, 'I think I'd like a nice bowl of tomato soup.'"[62]

— —

Government officials tried to repair the damage the tourists were thought to inflict on the American image by arranging for French journalists and intellectuals to visit America to see for themselves what it was like. However, the results were disappointing, to say the least. A Swiss researcher who surveyed the books and articles they wrote on their return concluded that what they discovered was "an America smug in its power and naive in its materialism . . . a mass civilization, highly mechanized and rationalized, in which there was no place for the development of personality." The intellectuals saw "materialism, lack of culture. These Americans who seem so satisfied with themselves are really overgrown children whose optimism can be explained by their ignorance of the deeper sense of life. They do not feel that *inquiétude* (disquiet) which the French consider the true stimulant of an intellectual life."[63]

Most distressing to American policy makers, though, were indications that many tourists returned from Europe skeptical of the need for American aid there. A 1949 survey by Marshall Plan officials revealed that more of them were critical of aid to Europe than positive about it. The Marshall Plan was "making many people lazy," opined one. Others were put off by the signs of high living they saw there. "We noted luxury spending and gambling at high stakes in the Riviera by French and Italian people," said one. Another said, "In France I have seen more diamonds, furs, luxury yachts and expensive cars than I have ever seen at home. To give aid to the poor people of France when the wealthy of France are able to do so is a fraud and a betrayal of the U.S. taxpayer."[64] In 1951 a congressman from Montana entered into the *Congressional Record* a letter from a constituent complaining that a tour guide had admitted that Europeans were sucking Americans "like a big juicy orange," and that a Paris taxi driver had blamed "American warmongers" for the cold war. The congressman's most original complaint, though, was that by his calculations only three of the five hundred hotels in Lourdes were run by men. This showed, he said, that the French would be weak and unreliable allies in the event of war.[65]

——

Widespread anxiety over anti-Americanism helped make guided group tours look attractive to upscale people who would normally have shunned them.[66] In 1949 and 1950, American Express, Cook's, and other travel companies began promoting "luxury" group travel to the wealthy travelers who still formed the bulk of tourists to Europe. Given the sorry state of the continental railroads, much of this had to be by bus, a seemingly downscale form of travel that at first aroused considerable skepticism among well-off Americans. Rita Hamer, a Frenchwoman whose agency pioneered the field, recalled flying to Los Angeles to promote her forty-day luxury tours and explain "how twenty to thirty people could travel well in a coach."[67] She had little difficulty making her case. In the first place, the tours spared the tourists the planning problems caused by their ignorance of geography. "The Americans knew little about the geography of Europe," she said, "and had no idea how long it took to get from one city to another." They also needed guides, she said, because in each city they had no idea how to get from one place to another.[68] The guides, and the fact that the important expenses were prepaid, also calmed fears of being "clipped." There were no worries about extra charges on hotel bills, what to tip the concierge, and no need for haggling with porters and cabdrivers. The fact that the luxury buses were also air-conditioned was also reassuring, even though it was rarely needed in France.[69]

That such tours were conducted entirely in English was also a major attraction. Indeed, it is difficult to exaggerate how important this was, particularly for travel in France. Although most upper-middle-class Americans had taken some French in high school, few could understand it when spoken at a normal pace. (One study found that whereas American women spoke at about 175 syllables a minute and males at 150 per minute, French people of both genders raced along at about 350.)[70] As for speaking it, even those who had taken French in college had difficulty making themselves understood in their first weeks in France. Smith College junior-year-abroad students, who were French majors, would commonly find their first attempts to speak French greeted with "*Je ne comprends rien de tout*" (I don't understand anything).[71] Quick language courses and pocket dictionaries were of little use. A guidebook called *France on Your Own*, which promised to free one from dependence on tour groups by providing "An Easy Way to Learn 'Enough' French," was called useless by the *Herald Tribune*. Its weird transliteration of French pronunciation told tourists wanting a hotel room with a bath to ask the desk clerk "*zhuh day-zeer' ewn shambr a-vek' baing*" (*Je désire une chambre avec bain*).[72] It is no wonder that many of the tourists who traveled on their own felt adrift in a sea of incomprehension. They would gravitate to the American Express office in Paris, said an American reporter, mainly "to feel at home by talking to someone who speaks English!"[73]

The conducted tours also took care of the vexing problem of food. For Hamer, the tourists' ignorance on this score was a kind of blessing: "They knew nothing about restaurants," she said, so "they went where you told them."[74] Sometimes, though, restaurateurs misjudged group tourists' tastes. A Frenchman accompanying an American Express tour to Versailles described the red bus unloading its clientele in front of a small restaurant: "Everyone is delighted by the tree-shaded terrace, but when the set menu arrives a shiver runs through the group: there are escargots on it. One knew that the depraved French were capable of eating such things as rabbit and frog, but snails. . . . Everyone, to get back on track, orders rosé wine. It is such a convenient wine: it goes with everything."[75]

Bathroom and toilet facilities that hardly met American standards were another problem. It was for this reason, said Hamer, that the only part of provincial France where her luxury bus tours could stop overnight was the Riviera.[76] The tours also shielded tourists from the dreaded proximity to offensive-smelling Frenchmen. In his 1953 travel guide, Temple Fielding warned, "Considering that they have more than 100 spas, more than 300 bathing beaches, countless Turkish or Scandinavian baths, and ladies' hygienic devices in every bathroom, by our standards many French citizens in the middle or lower brackets show a puzzling lack of affinity for water."[77]

Finally, group tours had a particular appeal to women. Dorothy Marsh called women the "easiest to sell" on group tours, and it is easy to understand why.[78] For women traveling alone, they solved the vexing problem of what to do at dinner and in the evening. They also protected them from being accosted by European men who assumed foreign women alone were inviting sexual encounters. France was no worse than most other countries on this score, but also no better. The area around the place Saint-Michel on the Left Bank was (and still is) particularly rife with creepy men, often foreign-born themselves, sidling up to foreign women trying with a notable lack of success to pick them up. After staying alone near there for two weeks in 1956, Sylvia Plath wrote in her diary that she was "too sick of small dark sleazy men at [her] elbow to venture out for dinner."[79] The travel writer Rachelle Girson recalled sharing a second-class compartment on the Paris–Marseille train with three ribald workmen who, "taking literally my 'Je ne comprend pas français' . . . howled with laughter as they joshed me from Paris to Marseille with prurient suggestions, which I comprehended too well." "On the whole," she concluded, "I prefer entraining first class. One is accosted by more refined men."[80]

It is no surprise, then, to read in Louis Bishop's diary that when he, his wife, and a male friend boarded the bus for a luxury tour of eastern France and western Germany in 1950, he discovered that, aside from him and his friend, all the other passengers were American women.[81] What is more surprising is that despite its high cost and higher-end clientele, the tour hardly spared the tourists the grueling schedules for which such tours were already famous. Each day the diary begins with "Get up early . . ." and tells of the bus plunging on through France and Germany, stopping only for the briefest look at famous sights.[82]

Of course, none of these entries mentions any but the most perfunctory encounters with local people.[83] Although in interviews Americans would rank meeting the natives high among their expectations from foreign travel, in practice they would usually bond with each other and ignore the natives. Evenings spent in hotel lobbies talking about home were often the most interesting and enjoyable moments of the tours. In June 1958 two black women from Chicago returned to Paris from a bus tour through France to Spain and told Ollie Stewart that the highlight of the tour was talking about the race situation with the white Americans on the tour.[84]

The tourists' propensity to bond with other Americans may not have been all that unfortunate, especially in the case of France. Hamer recalled that, outside of the Riviera, most local people in the provinces in France did not speak English and "were no good with foreigners."[85] Only in the tourist-dependent Riviera could Americans count on a warm welcome, especially in Nice, where even the Communists looked favorably on them.[86] The city that had once been a synonym for aristocratic elegance was now struggling though hard touristic times. Each summer, thanks in large part to the French law giving all workers four or five weeks of holidays, it was engulfed by hordes of low-spending campers and other tight-fisted vacationers.[87] One disappointed tourist wrote in her diary in 1952 that Nice was "tawdry . . . a Coney Island atmosphere, with cheap hotels, stores, and dance halls [and] countless little souvenir shops."[88] Only a small part of it— a little park and a few flamboyant hotels such as the Negresco on the palm-lined, seaside promenade des Anglais—still reflected its former glory. It was here that the luxury tour groups deposited wealthy Americans into the welcoming arms of grateful hotel-keepers.

— —

As the French and other European railway systems revived, higher-end clients began forsaking the motor coach tours for what American Express called "Foreign Independent Tours." As in the 1930s, these gave tourists a feeling of independence while effectively minimizing contact with French people unconnected with the tourist industries. Tourists would arrive in Le Havre or Cherbourg with a neatly typed itinerary and a book of prepaid coupons for every service they would need including sales taxes and tip. A tourist agency representative would guide them through customs and put them on a train to Paris, where another agent—American Express and Cook's now had them permanently stationed in the major railroad terminals—would take them to their hotel. The next morning a limousine or small tour bus would show up and take them on a city tour. After a day or two of such touring, an escort would arrive early in the morning and take them to the train station, where they would be put on a train to the next city, where they would again be met by an agent, taken to their hotel, called upon the next morning for a city tour, and so on.[89] The trips usually ended back in Paris, where the tourists would be escorted to the Gare du Nord and put on the boat train. American Express boasted of the time that a wealthy woman from Houston arrived at the boat train and shrieked that she had lost sixty thousand dollars' worth of jewels. "Don't worry, lady," her Amex escort said. "You take the train and we'll find the jewels." He then returned to her hotel room, where he found them under her pillow, and sent them by messenger to the ship in time for the sailing. For this kind of cosseting, clients paid a premium of about 25 percent over the retail cost of the hotel rooms and other services.[90]

— —

Of the many complaints the French voiced about tourists, the absence of meaningful contact with them surely ranked last. Few of them—especially Parisians—seemed at all interested in meeting tourists. "Unlucky indeed, as well as rare," James Baldwin wrote from Paris in 1954, "is the traveler who thirsts to know the lives of the people—the people don't want him in their lives. Neither does the Parisian exhibit the faintest personal interest, or curiosity, concerning the life, or habits, of any stranger."[91] This basic indifference was probably reflected in the surprising results of a poll taken for the magazine *Realités* in the summer of 1953, which indicated that the French were not nearly as anti-American as practically everyone thought they were. When asked whether they liked or disliked Americans, a majority—61 percent—said they liked them. Conversely, only 24 percent expressed anxiety or apprehension, 15 percent irritation, and a mere 8 percent antipathy toward Americans. Even among the working class, where Communist influence was strong, 46 percent said they liked them while only 16 percent felt antipathy, 9 percent said they disliked them, and 3 percent hated them. As for the much-discussed "u.s. go home" signs, only 13 percent of the entire sample approved of them. Forty percent disapproved, 26 percent were indifferent, and the rest said they had not even noticed them.[92]

Still, the prospect of traveling in a country where almost half the people express apprehension, irritation, or antipathy toward you is not exactly a pleasant one. Furthermore, the American press tended to exaggerate the extent of anti-Americanism revealed by such polls.[93] Nor was the fealty of 25 percent of the electorate to the stridently anti-American Communist party reassuring. "Like it or not," said Temple Fielding, "the American tourist of 1953 is despised by thousands of Frenchmen and Frenchwomen. . . . The strong communist element (by single party, the majority) does its utmost to keep the 'Yankee Capitalist' and 'Wall Street Baron' (ordinary Americans like us) from feeling at ease in France." He told of friends from New York whose three-year-old Chevrolet was broken into, sandpapered(!), and had an obscenity carved on it while parked on the Champs-Elysées.[94]

Other tourists returned with less harrowing but nevertheless unpleasant stories of being harassed for doing what seemed to be the most innocuous things. High on the list was merchants scolding them for touching items for sale, especially food. "Self-service" was still unheard of in French commerce, and "Ne touchez-pas!"—"Don't touch!"—seemed to ring constantly in tourists' ears. Sylvia Plath, who spoke French well, wrote in her diary of how, standing in front of an impatient gray-haired lady, she asked an "oily" stall owner in the Left Bank rue de Buci market for a kilo of red peaches. He responded that everyone asked for the red ones and proceeded to quickly fill her bag with green ones. She wrote:

> I looked in the bag while his back was turned to take the money; I found a solid rock-hard green peach; I put it back and took a red one. The man turned just as the hostile little woman made a rattling noise of furious warning to him, like a snake about to strike. One is not allowed to choose, the man raged, grabbing the bag back and rudely dumping the hard green peaches on the counter. We fumed, sick at the outrage, meanness and utter illogic.[95]

Art Buchwald's humorous column from Paris suddenly became less funny when he contrasted the warm reception American shoppers received in Rome and London with the rudeness and sneers that greeted them in Paris.[96] It is no wonder that, as another American correspondent in Paris said in 1957, "many tourists still come over here tremblingly, expecting to be insulted, robbed, and snubbed at every turn."[97] After spending some time observing American tourists in Paris, the novelist John Steinbeck wrote of how sad it was that most of them had prepared assiduously for the trip, trying to learn some of the language, unpacking old history books, and saving for the grand tour that they hope will assure them of "their cultural status." Yet when they arrived, he said, "they find themselves scorned, and they suspect they are being cheated. . . . They find themselves huddling together fearful of raised brows of headwaiters, the superior smiles of guides. Local people who have not in their lives been fifty kilometers from their villages look down on tourists. Prices go up when they appear. They become lonesome and some of them grow angry."[98]

— —

Only one kind of American visitor seemed immune from French disapproval and criticism: African Americans. The African American network telling the folks back home that France was practically racism-free was reestablished soon after the war. In June 1946 Edward Wiggins, an African American journalist who had been interned in France during the war, convinced the Associated Negro Press wire service to begin carrying his weekly "Pigalle Talk" column from Paris by telling its director, "Paris is not just another city." There was plenty of interest in it both among "the old gang that constituted Paris' pre-war American Negro Colony, now back home, and by the thousands of our GIs and WACs" who had just been there.[99] Ollie Stewart, justifying a similar column for the Philadelphia and Baltimore African American newspapers, wrote, "Traditionally . . . Brownskin Joe loved Pigalle more than Beale Street because he could enjoy freedom in Pigalle. He could eat and dance and sleep with any woman who liked him. Over and over you have heard how he can do a hundred things in Paris he could never do in the USA. It is true. He can."[100]

Similar messages came from elsewhere. Josephine Baker survived the war and quickly reestablished herself as a popular French music hall star. In 1948, on her first visit to the United States since her disastrous 1936 trip, she told students at the all-black Fisk University in Tennessee that if they wished to experience life without prejudice, they should visit France or

North Africa.[101] Richard Wright played a major role in reinforcing these views. On his first visit to France, in 1946, he told of encountering a black GI with a pretty blond Frenchwoman at a Paris street celebration of the first anniversary of V-E Day on May 8. When the GI told him that he intended to marry her and return to St. Louis with her, Wright was aghast, thinking that this would mean certain death. He asked the GI if he remembered what the racial situation was like in St. Louis, and the GI did not seem to know what he was talking about. Wright marveled, he wrote, at how two years in a land of racial liberty could lead one to forget such things.[102] When Wright returned to New York the next February, he told the press he had not encountered "one iota of racial feeling in France."[103]

Later that year Wright settled permanently in Paris, saying that leaving the United States was like feeling a corpse slipping off his back.[104] In 1951 he wrote in the National Association for the Advancement of Colored People's magazine that France was "a land of refuge" for American Negroes.[105] Wright then proceeded to infuriate officials at the embassy, the FBI, and CIA by joining with anti-American French intellectuals and issuing such pronouncements as "there is more freedom in one square block of Paris than in all of the United States."[106] When he died in 1960 of mysterious causes, many suspected that he had been assassinated by American government operatives.[107]

In many respects, James Baldwin was quite a contrast to Wright. When the short, homely, dark-skinned, barely published writer arrived in Paris in 1948, he quickly joined the acolytes at the feet of the tall, handsome, fair-skinned, and very successful Wright as he held court in the Café Tournon or in his spacious apartment on the aptly named rue Monsieur-le-Prince.[108] Baldwin then committed a kind of parricide by publishing a piece in an English-language Paris magazine attacking Wright's major novel, *Native Son*, as an unrealistic portrayal of the way African Americans coped with racism.[109] Yet Baldwin never disagreed with Wright's constant reiteration that France provided African Americans with a welcome refuge from racism.

Countless other African Americans took up this theme. In 1950, when Duke Ellington's large jazz band finished its Paris concert dates, the musicians were so enthralled at being welcomed on an equal basis that none of them wanted to return home.[110] William Demby, an African American who had served in the army in Europe during the war, said he returned to Paris in the early 1950s because "I could be myself if I went to Europe. I would not have to be a colored person; I would not have to go through certain daily humiliations."[111] Romare Bearden wrote a friend that it was not easy for

Americans to be accepted by the French because they "[are] rather reserved by nature and do not as a rule like Americans. However, the boys of color are much better received."[112]

"Better received" often meant tolerant of interracial sex. Demby recalled that in Paris he "found many black Americans . . . who were interested in having casual sexual relationships with white women. That was the big thing. When I went to Paris everyone was talking about 'Scans,' . . . young Scandinavian women who were also coming to Paris to find this freedom. For them freedom meant the young black men who were around these cafés in Saint-Germain."[113] African Americans reveling in the contrast with the United States were not immune to exaggeration. Ollie Stewart reported in 1949 that "American whites experience a greater sense of freedom when they come to Europe than colored!" and told of how he and his friends had been actively pursued by "frantic" white women looking for sex.[114] Later, as middle-class American tourism picked up, holidaying schoolteachers became prime consorts, along with other women looking for romance in Europe.[115] The African American writer Chester Himes said that when he arrived in Paris in April 1953 for what he thought would be a one-month stay (he ended up living there for the rest of his life), he found his Left Bank hotel (ironically called the Scandinavie) "filled with homosexuals and a large number of young American girls who wished to cram a life time of sexual escapades into the short time they would have before they had to return home and marry." His friend Richard Wright told him, "Chester, when it gets warm these American girls go down the street, flinging open their arms, and cry, 'Take me! Take me! I'm young and good in bed.'" Himes later recalled that "all of us vocal blacks" would gather at the Café Tournon each night "to choose our white woman for each night, and the white women gathered about us and waited our selection."[116]

But France also offered other kinds of freedom to African Americans. Until the mid-1960s, African American patrons were excluded from practically all first-class hotels and restaurants in the American South and had difficulty getting accommodation and service in many of those in the rest of the country. Traveling in France meant freedom from such humiliations. In March 1950 an African American couple from Baltimore arrived in Paris and told Ollie Stewart that "Nice was full of sunshine. Just like Florida—only we could go any place we wanted, and you can't do that in Florida."[117] In 1958 the pianist Hazel Scott, recently divorced from Harlem's Congressman Adam Clayton Powell, went to France on a three-week vacation and ended up staying for three years. France, she told readers of the African American magazine *Ebony*, gave her "a much needed rest . . . from racial tension. . . . You can live anywhere you want if you've got the money to live. You can go anywhere if you've got the money to go and whomever you marry or date is your business."[118] Quincy Jones, a successful composer and arranger for popular music stars, moved to the Riviera in the late 1950s and quickly befriended his neighbor Pablo Picasso. Later he would become pals with the future mayor of Paris and president of France, Jacques Chirac.[119] Ollie Stewart delighted in listing African Americans checking into "swank" Paris hotels such as the Royal Monceau. (He also reported on another kind of freedom, that unmarried couples did not have to pretend they were married to check in. "The French aren't interested in your morals," he said.)[120] In 1962 the black writer Lerone Bennett Jr. wrote in *Ebony* of how he and a group of African Americans on a twenty-two-day tour of European cities, including Paris and Nice, experienced a "complete absence of racial discrimination." This, he said, made the tour "a pure delight. . . . We lived in the best hotels and ate in the finest restaurants. So far as we could tell, no public door was closed to us."[121]

One of the things that contributed to African Americans' positive reception in France was the extraordinary popularity of jazz there. In America the great white "swing" bands that had brought it into the mainstream had broken up after the war, and jazz steadily became marginalized. "Bebop," which arose to replace swing, was a more difficult style and was identified with drug problems such as those that plagued its greatest practitioner, Charlie "Bird" Parker. In France, however, an organization called Le Hot Club, which had been publishing jazz magazines and organizing concerts since the mid-1930s, helped jazz survive Vichy suspicion and emerge in the postwar years as a symbol of the new, young avant-garde. For these young fans, jazz's American origins gave it a modern cachet while its association with blacks freed it from the taint of American imperialism. Even Sartre gave it his blessing, although his personal tastes ran more to Beethoven than bebop. As a result, African American musicians began returning almost immediately after the war, playing for discerning French audiences in Left Bank *caves*.[122] In 1949 top African American jazz artists such as Parker, Louis Armstrong, Miles Davis, Lester Young, and Dizzy Gillespie began touring France, playing to enthusiastic audiences. Large crowds in provincial cities like Rouen, Claremont-Ferrand, and Nancy welcomed the likes of Lionel Hampton and Thelonious Monk. Davis, who was introduced to Sartre and Picasso during his 1949 trip, marveled at what he called "the freedom of being in France and being treated like a human being."[123] Sidney Bechet, an older, tremendously talented tenor sax player, liked it so much that after the

Louis Armstrong on tour in France, autographing a fan's head with a drawing of a trumpet. Courtesy of the Library of Congress.

Paris jazz festival in 1949, he decided to stay there for the rest of his life and became one of the most highly acclaimed stars in France.[124] A number of others, such as the drummer Kenny Clarke, also found the atmosphere so welcoming that they, too, settled permanently in France.[125]

In 1956 the town of Cannes began following its June film festival with a July jazz festival, featuring such performers as Dizzy Gillespie and Ella Fitzgerald.[126] African American jazz artists frequently played to sold-out houses in large Paris auditoriums. In November 1958 the Modern Jazz Quartet, accompanied by Miles Davis, Lester Young, and Bud Powell, packed the Salle Pleyel, the Paris equivalent of Carnegie Hall.[127] James Baldwin said that African Americans became so associated with jazz that friendly French people would open conversations with them with "Jouez-vous la trompette?" ("Do you play the trumpet?")[128] Even Hollywood got into the act. In the 1961 movie *Paris Blues*, Sidney Poitier plays an African American jazz musician who has stayed in Paris for five years. He falls for an African American tourist, played by Diahann Carroll, who urges him to return to America to help "the Cause," but he tells her that he loves Paris because of the absence of racism. "You sit down for lunch and don't get clubbed for it. You look back over the ocean and say, 'Who needs it?' . . . Here nobody calls me Eddie Coke, Negro musician. It's just Eddie Coke."[129] Three years later *Newsweek* quoted a real musician, the saxophonist Sonny Criss, as saying, "Look, in the United States, I'm just another nigger. Here in Paris, I'm ME."[130]

NINE

"What Country Has So Much to Offer?"

At the end of the 1953 summer tourist season, *Business Week* reported that "a distressingly large number of American travelers found themselves uncomfortable, if not actually unwelcome, in such tourist havens as France and Italy." The natives were "often unfriendly and often downright anti-American," and there were "AMERICAN GO HOME" signs everywhere. In France, it said, the prevailing attitude toward Americans seemed to be "widespread dislike."[1] The thirteen hundred American tourists who filled in a Swiss questionnaire listed France and Sweden as the two most unfriendly countries in Europe.[2] Yet throughout much of the 1950s, when pollsters asked Americans which countries they would most like to visit, France regularly came out on top.[3] More important, American tourists continued to vote with their feet, as France remained unchallenged as their most popular overseas destination.[4]

Why, despite the regular reports of French hostility, did France remain such an American favorite? One reason was the continuing power of the romantic idea of France as a magical, civilized land where joie de vivre still reigned. As a 1954 travel guide said:

> Going abroad means, to many people, *going to Paris — to France.* . . . The aura of adventure and romance that these magic words conjure up is not undeserved, for what country has so much to offer? The unrestricted and yet never tiring gaiety of the life, the beauty of world-famous sights, the variety of entertainment, the marvelous cuisine—all make France the country to visit.[5]

The journalist Joseph Barry began his 1952 book about Paris, "Ever since we learned to read, we have dreamed a dream and called it Paris."[6] "Paris is a city with a gleam in her eye," said the *Herald Tribune*'s Art Buchwald in 1951. "It's no wonder everyone goes home happy—and broke."[7] A slew of magazine articles revived its 1920s image as a charming place where harried

Americans could escape the pressures of their frenetic business civilization by relaxing and enjoying themselves.[8]

Much of the media attention involved celebrities enjoying and extolling France. In the spring of 1951, when the French concocted a 2,000th birthday party for Paris, Frank Sinatra and Milton Berle hosted television shows offering tributes. Al Capp, creator of the *L'il Abner* comic strip, which boasted 60 million readers, made a well-publicized trip to Paris to search for locales for his lunkheaded hillbilly hero to visit, with Art Buchwald acting as his guide to the seamier side of Montmartre.[9] Other celebrities burnished its image as a destination for sightseeing and relaxation. In 1951 Margaret Truman, the president's daughter, was credited with causing a boom in transatlantic travel by announcing that she was going to take an auto tour of Europe that summer.[10] When she arrived in Paris, photographers crowded around to photograph her in front of the Eiffel Tower and on the terrace of Café de la Paix.[11] Five years later, when her now-retired father visited Paris, he was pictured enjoying himself on the same café terrace, greeting admirers of all nationalities.[12]

Press flashbulbs also popped for the junketing politicians who managed to fit Paris into their investigations of American government activities.[13] The most notorious of them were Roy Cohn and G. David Schine, two young assistants to the Red-hunting Senator Joseph McCarthy. They visited Paris in April 1953 as part of a luxury tour of European cities in search of "subversives" on U.S. embassies' staffs and books by "controversial persons" in their libraries.[14] Although a horde of reporters followed them around Paris, none reported that when they discovered that the two enormous suites the embassy reserved for them at the Crillon were not adjoining, they moved to the George V, where, in only thirty-six hours, they managed to run up an enormous tab on the embassy account.[15] Among the other junketeers was a millionaire contributor to the Republican Party who arrived in 1957 to investigate the United States Information Service. After telling the agency's Paris chief that he had "done" the Louvre in twenty minutes, he said, "Why should we have to approach the French on what is called a cultural basis? Everybody knows we are cultured."[16]

Many junketeers expected to meet the local celebrities. Ben Bradlee recalled spending much of his time as a *Newsweek* correspondent there in the 1950s catering to visiting "big shots" wanting this "to prove to their friends that they were big shots." The magazine's editor-in-chief and his wife would visit Paris each year and expect to be taken to the homes of the Duke and Duchess of Windsor and of Charles de Gaulle, who was then living in

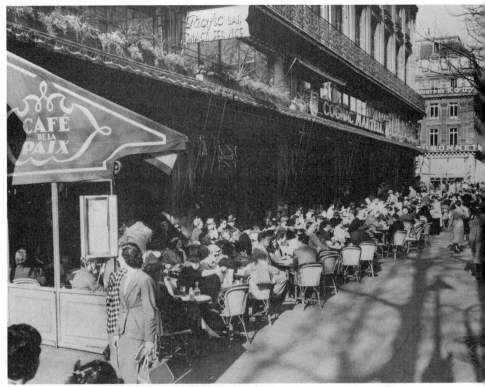

Sidewalk terrace of the Café de la Paix, a favorite gathering spot for Americans hoping to spot someone from home. Photograph by Albert Malioua (1955). © Bettman/CORBIS.

the small village of Colombey-les-Deux-Eglises. He would also expect the president of France to come for drinks at his suite in the Ritz.[17]

The tourist industries scrambled to profit from the luxury trade that followed on the heels of the celebrities and socialites flocking to France. New transatlantic liners catering mainly to the first-class trade slid down the ways. In July 1952 the United States Lines launched the *United States*, a sleek superliner with patriotic red, white, and blue stacks that finally thrust America into the forefront of luxury ocean travel.[18] Much to the delight of first-class passengers, the Windsors often graced it with their patronage. One man's journal of a crossing on it has as its high points watching them eating, playing cards, and, most thrilling: "Ran plum into the Duke of Windsor. Both of us coming around corner and met—bang."[19] The next year the Italians launched the splendid *Andrea Doria*, an ill-fated beauty doomed to sink three years later in a collision in the North Atlantic with another liner, the Swedish *Stockholm*.

The airlines kept pace in the scramble for well-heeled travelers. In April 1951 Air France doubled the frequency of its premium transatlantic luxury service, which offered seven-course champagne dinners and limited its seating to thirty-two passengers.[20] The next year it introduced a luxury extra-fare service offering spacious "sky lounge" seats or, for an even heftier surcharge, full-length beds in double-decked berths.[21] Pan Am countered with larger all-first-class Boeing "Stratocruisers" that, in addition to sleeping berths, featured a cocktail lounge in a deck below, linked to the main cabin by a circular stairway. While Air France prided itself on its meals, Pan Am's service was more in tune with American tastes in drinking.[22] After the evening takeoff from New York, passengers would adjourn to the cocktail lounge for a few drinks. They would then climb to the upper deck for a seven-course dinner with drinks (it was common for Americans to drink whiskey or martinis with meals), after which they would again head down to the lounge for more drinks. Meanwhile the attendants would pull down the overhead sleeping berths and prepare the reclining chairs for the passengers' well-lubricated attempts to fall asleep in the noisy main cabin.[23]

New guidebooks to France and Europe targeted these upper-echelon travelers. Fodor's *Woman's Guide to Europe* was full of information about "society" in Paris. It was written as if the reader expected to be invited to Elsa Maxwell's parties and to tea with the Windsors.[24] Temple Fielding's new guidebook, which quickly became the most popular one among Americans, dealt mainly with what the *Herald Tribune* called the "swank" side of Europe and was "beamed primarily at the gold-plated Cadillac trade."[25] (One of his complaints about Air France was that it served sevruga caviar, rather than the pricier beluga, in first class.)[26] He said the reader he had in mind was "the banker in the small town who is a big shot, has security and respect in his community, and to whom Europe is a jungle."[27]

When they reached France, many of the financially well-padded would head for the Hôtel Ritz, which, although fraying at the edges, continued to symbolize the ultimate in French luxury. Indeed, during the 1950s Americans made up half of its clientele. (When renovations could be put off no longer, the owner toured the United States to find out what Americans wanted, concluding that they were happy with traditional decor but wanted American plumbing.) In Anita Loos's best-selling novel, *Gentlemen Prefer Blondes*, which was turned into a hit Broadway play and movie, the not-very-bright heroine, Lorelei, loves only two things, diamonds and the Ritz. She is particularly fond of the Ritz bar, where, she says, a girl could see "all the important French people in Paris . . . the Dolly sisters and Pearl White and Maybelle Gilman Corey and Mrs. Nash."[28] The actress Audrey Hepburn got to like the Ritz so much while making the movie *Love in the Afternoon* there in 1956 that she practically made it her second home. The George V also remained popular with wealthy Americans. In 1954 the movie and television star Groucho Marx told Art Buchwald that he hadn't met many Europeans since he arrived. "I'm staying at the Hotel George V," he said, "and if you're caught speaking French they call the police and ask you to leave."[29]

The press also paid a lot of attention to American celebrities mingling at the Chantilly and Deauville race tracks with what Buchwald called "the horse-loving, pigeon-shooting set," but outside of Paris it was the Riviera that shone brightest in the media limelight.[30] The public relations man of Cannes's Palm-Beach Casino told the press that one night there, "by greatest accident," one could have encountered "three emperors, four kings, and a dozen princes, including the Prince of Wales."[31] These remnants of Europe's fading aristocracy were joined by a new crowd of tycoons, such as Greek ship owners Aristotle Onassis and Stavros Niarchos—what Buchwald called "the yacht-loving, waiter-slapping set."[32]

Hollywood and Broadway celebrities also flocked there. When Elizabeth Taylor debarked from a huge yacht in Cannes, one of her bodyguards whispered to the waiting limousine driver to wait for her baggage. "OK," said the driver, "I've got a big trunk." "No, no," said her aide, "I mean wait for the van, she has fifty to sixty suitcases."[33] After they struck it rich with their Broadway musical *My Fair Lady*, the songwriters Alan Jay Lerner and Frederick Loewe took a well-publicized trip to Paris, where they bought two matching Rolls-Royces and drove them down to Cannes. Loewe became such a fixture at the Palm-Beach Casino that Lerner would cable him directly at its chemin de fer tables.[34] In the neighboring town of Vallauris, Pablo Picasso, a genius at self-promotion, would welcome American celebrities to his studio and, while photographers snapped away, allow them to try their hand at his potter's wheel.[35] Famous Hollywood personages also began showing up at the May film festival at Cannes, which had finally caught the public eye thanks in large part to the bikini-clad "starlets" who pranced along its beach for photographers, artfully allowing their tops to drop.[36]

But the limelight never shone brighter on the Côte d'Azur than in 1955, when the reigning princess of Hollywood, the beautiful, cool-eyed, blond actress Grace Kelly, took up with Prince Rainier, the suave (albeit somewhat portly) ruler of Monaco. Her father was a self-made millionaire from humble Irish American origins, so the match had enough fairy-tale elements in it to enchant both starstruck and royalty-struck Americans. The story of their first encounter also embodied many a tourist's dream: They had met when, taking a break from the Cannes publicity machine, she had visited Monaco, not to play at the casino, but to wander alone through its oceano-graphic museum. There, it was said, a chance encounter with the prince had rapidly kindled the flames of love.

For Rainier, the encounter came not a moment too soon. Monaco had never really recovered as a tourist destination after the war, when it still bore the taint of having been rather too accommodating to the German and Ital-ian military. When the chic crowd abandoned its old competitor, Nice, they moved down the coast in the other direction, toward Cannes. American vis-itors were now mainly day-trippers, curious to see the steps in front of the casino where despairing losers were reputed to shoot themselves and the balustrade from which they were said to fling themselves onto the train tracks below. These were hardly the kind of tourists who were going drop a bundle at its tables.[37] Even worse were those who merely looked at the casino from buses that detoured through there on the standard European tour circuit, which gave them only one day to get from Cannes to San Remo, Italy.[38] As a result, the casino had been losing money since 1951, and in 1955 Monaco's biggest bank went broke.[39]

However, the prince now played the Grace Kelly card astutely. He re-ceived enormous press coverage when he went to Philadelphia to formally ask Kelly's father for permission to marry.[40] The media covered the wed-ding arrangements in minute detail, and the wedding itself, held in Monaco in April 1956, was mobbed. "There were 1700 reporters there," Peter Stone, a CBS reporter, recalled, "more than covered D-Day!"[41] When Americans saw photos and newsreels of the wedding, with the prince in a gold-epauletted uniform, Kelly, looking absolutely radiant in a gorgeous gown, kneeling and praying, and the honor guard looking as if they had stepped out of a Viennese operetta, it was hard to separate the stuff of Hol-lywood dreams from reality. The excitement even continued after the wed-ding, when it was discovered that during the event, some of the Riviera's most talented break-in artists had heisted valuable jewels from the lodgings of the princess's mother and a bridesmaid, and had removed a Rembrandt and a Rubens from the villas of some of the guests.[42] Ironically, Kelly had just costarred with Cary Grant in the Alfred Hitchcock movie *To Catch a Thief*, in which Grant played a brilliant cat burglar who had retired to the Riviera and was a suspect in a number of jewel robberies there.

But this was just the opening act, for although Kelly retired from the

Grace Kelly's fairy tale–sounding wedding to Prince Rainier of Monaco, which helped bring glitter back to the entire Riviera. Courtesy of the Library of Congress.

movies, she did not retreat from the public eye. She and her husband now actively cultivated the tourist trade. In April 1957 the prince confessed to a group of visiting American travel writers that the casino had not been doing well. However, he said, that was fine with him, for they now wanted to make their money from tourism: "We don't want to live off the people who lose their money."[43]

Henceforth, thanks to Kelly, they did not have to. To millions of Americans, Monaco was no longer famous mainly for suicides. It was now the idyllic little land ruled over by a beautiful American princess and her prince from their castle by the sea. The church in which the marriage took place now became a major tourist sight, as did the apartment building named the Schuylkill, after the river in Philadelphia where Kelly's father, a champion sculler, used to row.[44] The principality was soon running firmly in the black, and Rainier was easily able to fend off Aristotle Onassis's attempt to take over the casino. Onassis took the rebuff gracefully, and let his huge yacht, a refitted Canadian navy warship, remain semipermanently moored in its harbor, where it also became a popular tourist sight.[45] Kelly remained so important to the local tourist economy that when she died in a car accident there in 1982, a *New York Times* reporter seriously doubted that the place would survive her death.[46]

— —

To Catch a Thief was filmed entirely on the Riviera, for there were significant tax savings for Hollywood studios shooting movies abroad. However, France, and especially Paris, had become a popular locale for Hollywood movies even before then, when they were shot in Hollywood. Most of them repeated the mantras calling Paris the world's most beautiful and romantic city: that—as Sidney Poitier tells the tourist Diahann Carroll in *Paris Blues*, when she is shocked by all the couples necking in public—"It's the City of Love."

In the brilliant 1951 musical *An American in Paris*, which features Gene Kelly and Leslie Caron dancing to George Gershwin's music, Kelly plays Jerry Mulligan, an ex-GI who stayed in Paris after the war to try his hand as an artist. Although it was shot on a Hollywood soundstage, like many subsequent films it opens with the camera panning over the city's beauty spots accompanied by a voice-over. In this case, it is Kelly's voice, saying, "For a painter, the mecca for inspiration is Paris. No wonder so many artists have come here for inspiration. If you can't find it here, you can't find it anywhere."

Jerry lives in poverty on the Left Bank with lighthearted, friendly French neighbors. He says, "When I'm depressed I need wine and women," and his landlady replies, "That should be no problem; you're in Paris." When he meets Lisa, the beautiful young Frenchwoman played by Leslie Caron, they have evening encounters in one of Paris's most romantic spots—on the quays along the Seine. When Lisa says, "Paris has a way of making people forget," Jerry replies, "No. Paris is too real and too beautiful. It never lets you forget anything. It reaches in and opens you wide, and you stay that way."

Six years later Gene Kelly returned to a Hollywood soundstage that was again decked out like Paris, this time with Mitzi Gaynor, another great dancer, in the musical *Les Girls*. It begins by establishing that Paris is the world's gayest city, with a voice-over saying, "Everything about Paris was exciting." Then, to show how despondent Gene Kelly's character was, the voice-over says that he wasn't interested in all the beautiful women around him, even though "it was Paris; it was spring."

The curious notion that Paris is especially romantic in April owes much to the 1932 song "April in Paris" and the 1952 movie of that name. The movie, which was also made on a Hollywood soundstage, using rather blurry canned shots of Paris, did not do well at the box office, but the haunting rendition of the title song by its star, Doris Day, became a hit record. Along with Frank Sinatra's equally famous version, it led millions of Americans to dream of spending April in Paris, even though it is often gray and sodden that month. Even Miles Davis, who knew Paris well, bought into the idea. Describing his love affair with the French singer Juliette Greco, when neither of them spoke the other's language, he said, "You have to go on feelings. It was April in Paris. Yeah, and I was in love."[47]

The Last Time I Saw Paris (1954) is another movie whose title song outshines the movie itself. The most memorable things about the movie—which is based on a depressing F. Scott Fitzgerald story about drunkenness and ruined relationships—are Elizabeth Taylor's beauty and the song's first words, "The last time I saw Paris, her heart was young and gay." Songs such as this, and "I Love Paris," which proclaims a love for Paris, not just in the springtime, but in "every season of the year," surely did more to promote tourism to France than any French Tourist Bureau campaign.

Equally effective were films that, despite the constrictions of Hollywood's puritanical Production Code, evoked the age-old associations of Paris with nonconjugal sex. *Moulin Rouge* (1952) stars José Ferrer as the stunted artist Henri de Toulouse-Lautrec living among the prostitutes and entertainers of Belle Epoque Montmartre. Aside from making Toulouse-Lautrec a household name in America, it helped revive the fortunes of the moribund Montmartre music hall of the title's name by attracting droves of American tourists there to see the "can-can" dances highlighted in the movie. Paris is also the city of illicit love in director Billy Wilder's *Love in the Afternoon* (1957). In it, the aging Gary Cooper plays an American entrepreneur who falls in love with a much younger Frenchwoman, played by the twenty-eight-year-old Audrey Hepburn, looking nineteen. Made on location in Paris, mainly at the Ritz, it begins with the usual beautiful shots of the city and a voice-over saying that Paris is known for two things: "its cuisine and love—more specifically, making love." It then cuts to shots of various locales in the city, in all of which people are kissing. Early in the film, Hepburn overhears her private detective father, played by the French music hall star Maurice Chevalier, tell a client that his unfaithful wife is in Gary Cooper's suite in the Ritz. When Hepburn overhears the jealous husband say he is going over there to kill them, she calls the police and asks them to warn the couple. However, the police officer responds by saying that Paris has 220,000 hotel rooms, and on any given night similar scenes are taking place in 40,000 of them. If he were to warn them all, he says, he would have

to send the entire police force, the fire department, the sanitation department, and the Boy Scouts, "in their short pants."

Lerner and Loewe's lavish musical *Gigi* (1958) is also a reminder of how
much freer France was supposed to be with regard to sex. Set in 1900 Paris,
it has Leslie Caron in the title role, playing a young girl being trained as a
courtesan by her grandmother, the gravel-voiced Hermione Gingold, and
the grandmother's sister, both of whom were themselves kept women. It
begins with the naive teenaged Caron singing, "I don't understand the
Parisians, making love every time they get the chance. . . . Working every
night at romance." Much of the humor plays on French nonchalance about
infidelity ("Bad table manners, Gigi, have broken up more households than
infidelity," says the great-aunt), and it is full of exchanges about extramarital
affairs between Gingold, Maurice Chevalier, and Louis Jordan, the man-
about-town romantic lead.

Paris was also supposed to free American women from conventional
constraints. In *Paris Blues*, when Diahann Carroll has doubts about whether
she and her fellow-tourist friend, Joanne Woodward, should go to a jazz
club unaccompanied, Woodward replies, "This is Paris; anything goes."
However, perhaps the most effective advertisement for how a trip to France
could remake a woman was *Sabrina* (1954). It, too, features Audrey Hepburn and a man much older than she, in this case Humphrey Bogart, who
plays the workaholic head of a vast business empire. She is the chauffeur's
daughter on his family's large Long Island estate and at the outset is infatu-
ated with Bogart's feckless younger brother, William Holden. She is sent off
to a two-year cooking course in Paris, where she is befriended by an old
French baron who teaches her about fashion, horse racing, and other elite
pursuits. As "La Vie en Rose" plays in the background, she writes her father,
"I have learned how to live. . . . And I shall never run away from life, and
love." She says that when she arrives back, she will be "the most sophisticated woman" in the Glen Cove train station. In another letter, written by
an open window on a beautiful Paris evening, she tells him, "Paris is for
changing your outlook, for opening the windows and letting in 'La Vie en
Rose.'"

As she predicted, when she returns Hepburn/Sabrina has been completely transformed. Her ponytail has been replaced by a chic short French
hairdo, her makeup is perfect, her clothes are ultra-fashionable, she speaks
French with ease, and she refers often to French good taste. Holden, who
initially does not even recognize her, instantly falls for her. However, Bogart is determined that, for business reasons, Holden should marry someone

else. So, to head off Holden, he begins courting her himself, and she responds to his overtures. She suggests he travel to Paris to break with his nose-to-the-grindstone ways and get in touch with life's pleasures. He tells her that he was once in Paris, but only briefly. "Paris is for lovers," he says, "perhaps that's why I only stayed there thirty-five minutes." She responds, "Paris will make a new person of you, I guarantee it." Ultimately, he buys two steamship tickets for them but does not intend to use his. Finally, though, at the very last minute, he does, and they sail off together on the aptly named *Liberté*, once again reaffirming some of Paris's gender-specific promises: For American women, it is the place whose style, culture, and sophistication can turn one into an attractive new woman. For men, it is where one can break from the tyrannical demands of the work-obsessed life and enjoy life's sensual pleasures.

— —

The sexual overtones of France's image in the movies reflected sex's continuing importance as a draw for American tourists, particularly when public culture in the United States was still in one of its most prim and proper phases. It was a time, after all, when merely dabbing oneself with the contents of the cobalt blue perfume bottles labeled "Evening in Paris" was the last word in high school girls' seductiveness.[48] In 1952 Art Buchwald said that the legend that Paris is one of the world's most sinful cities had been passed on from generation to generation and "almost everyone who comes to Paris has a twinkle in his eye."[49] Although he added, "Unfortunately as the legend gets stronger, the sin gets weaker," there was still plenty to titillate visiting Americans. Temple Fielding's guidebook said there were nightclubs "practically on every corner [offering] literally every form of entertainment, legal and illegal, known to humanity. You have your choice of a $75 dinner, a rumba, a sophisticated bar, a 50—count 'em—50-leg show, a prostitute, a gigolo, an 'exhibition,' a glass of beer, a team of acrobats, or a Mickey Finn [a knockout drink]".[50]

The most popular of these entertainments were shows featuring practically naked women. Eleven of these places advertised regularly in the *Paris Herald Tribune*, but for much of the 1950s, the Lido, conveniently located right on the Champs-Elysées, was the hands-down American favorite.[51] There, tourists would sit down to a three-course dinner with a half-bottle of champagne and watch a Las Vegas–style show featuring spectacular lighting, onstage water fountains and pools, and talented cabaret acts, including such popular American artists as Danny Kaye and Lena Horne. It was most

The end of an act at the Folies Bergère, 1955. © Bettman/CORBIS.

famous, though, for the beauty of its statuesque women, clad only in G-strings and rhinestone tiaras, who posed on pedestals, under fountains, in mirrored swimming pools, or suspended from the ceiling.[52]

Buchwald's claim that "the sin was getting weaker" was correct in that the typical tourist experience was probably becoming less naughty. But this was not only because, as he said, France was changing. (He mainly had in mind the 1946 law that closed the *maisons de tolérance*.)[53] It was also because the tourists themselves were changing, with married women increasingly coming to the fore. In the early 1950s, 40 percent of American visitors to France were women. By the late 1950s, they were a majority and "housewife" was the largest single category on passport applications.[54] Their important role in deciding on holiday entertainment was reflected in the American response to the raunchy Parisian "striptease" shows, which, unlike the casino shows, featured women doing "bumps and grinds," and other erotic movements. Although trendy Parisians flocked to such shows, American tourists—people of more or less the same class—stayed away from them in droves, mainly because they were thought to be unsuitable for American women. Not only were they too erotic, but in the States striptease was associated with all-male audiences in seedy burlesque houses. In Paris only the Crazy Horse Saloon, which featured cowgirl strippers along with the cowboys and Indians in its floor show, drew any Americans.[55]

On the other hand, by sticking with practically immobile bare-breasted beauties who did hardly anything erotic, the Lido, which advertised itself as providing "family entertainment," and its equally high-toned rival, the Casino de Paris, were able to titillate both American women and men without crossing the boundaries of what was considered acceptable public sexiness among upper-middle-class American women.[56] Sixty-three-year-old Dorothy Brown, a political activist from Boston, insisted that a woman friend accompany her and her husband to what the husband's diary called "the usual opulent and considerably naked show" at the Casino de Paris because, unlike Brown, the friend had never seen one of these shows.[57] When Louis Bishop and his wife, who were now also in their early sixties, returned to Paris in 1963, they immersed themselves in its nightlife, which he described in his diary as "the best in the world," including the "excellent" show at the Casino de Paris.[58]

American women even felt comfortable at these shows when not accompanied by men. A 1950 cartoon in the *New York Times* was not off the mark. It showed two older American women tourists in Paris, with one saying to the other: "I want to take in l'Opera, Notre Dame and something naughty."[59] *Mademoiselle* recommended that its single young American women readers take a "Paris by Night" tour that included "your choice of the Moulin Rouge in Montmartre or the Lido—possibly the most spectacular and elaborate floor show in the world."[60] In July 1959 two well-off African American married women touring Europe without their husbands told the reporter Ollie Stewart that they wanted to extend their stays in Paris because they had so enjoyed "seeing Josephine Baker, the Lido, and picking up a few Paris gowns."[61]

Nightclub shows featuring homosexual males, usually in drag, were another form of titillation that was acceptable to "respectable" American women, although this was admittedly a minority taste. Janet Flanner wrote her (female) lover in the States that after a dinner with the actor Paul Newman ("a smart alec") and his ("sweet") wife, Joanne Woodward, she "got dragged to some amazingly dull fairy nightclub show. Third time I've seen it. Always dull and I got to bed at two."[62] Other nightlife experiences skirted closer to the borderline of middle-class respectability. Ollie Stewart told of two visiting American men who told a friend that they and their wives wanted to see something "spicy." He took them, said Stewart, "to one of the quiet houses where freak attractions between women and women, or men and women, are put on. This time it was a colored woman and a white woman putting on a show—and the Americans smacked their lips so much over what they saw they paid twice and had the whole thing done over again."[63]

For whites, dancing with black people, something that rarely occurred in America, could also feel deliciously risqué. Stewart said:

Night clubs run by colored, or clubs featuring colored entertainers, can always depend upon getting a fair percentage of white Americans who come to Paris. The men, who dance like jumping jacks, get a terrific kick out of grabbing a colored girl and hopping about the floor. The women usually giggle when a colored man asks them for a dance, but end up rubbing their girdles all over him and panting.[64]

But contacts with Paris's seamier side could also be disconcerting, or even distressing. During their stay in Paris in September 1950, Louis Bishop and his wife both enjoyed a relatively wholesome night at the Lido. Later in the week, though, a friend took them to dinner and then up to Pigalle, which was full of pimps, touts, and streetwalkers, to see the much sexier show at the Bal Tabarin. When they got back to their hotel, Bishop wrote cryptically in his diary, "The whole trip has been an interesting thing from the standpoint of showing our pitiful ignorance in so many respects." Some nights later, after returning to their hotel from the Folies Bergère, they had a brush with the problems that might befall tourists who strayed from their conjugal fold. Dr. Bishop had to console the wife of an American man who had left her in the hotel, gone off into the night alone, and disappeared. Not until the next morning did the wanderer return, claiming he had been given a "Mickey Finn" that had knocked him unconscious until the morning. "That just shows," Bishop wrote, "what can happen to a man alone in Paris."[65]

There were also more mundane reasons for sticking to the famous nightspots, including language. In the mid-1950s, visiting Americans would often tell Art Buchwald they did not want to go "where the tourists go." Yet when he would take them to the kinds of cabarets the French went to, featuring poets, political sketches, and French drinking songs, they would tell him, as did a visiting editor from New York, "This is lousy. They all speak French. Let's get out of here."[66]

— —

The introductory chapter of Fodor's *Woman's Guide to Europe* (1954) says, "If one concedes that, to most women, shopping is one of the world's most rewarding amusements and pastimes, there is no happier hunting ground."[67] In France this meant mainly women's wear. Even after 1954, when Dior's new bosom-abolishing "Flat Look" fell flat, as it were, magazines and newsreels continued to report breathlessly on the latest styles in what was the universally acknowledged capital of women's fashion.[68] "P-A-R-I-S usually spells one thing to women—FASHION," said the *Philadelphia Tribune* in 1958, as it reported how the African American singer Frances Burnett had detoured over to Paris after an engagement in London to pick up "several original designs by Europe's top couturiers."[69] Many tourists were excited to discover that it was easy for them to attend the shows at the forty-odd high-fashion houses.[70] Stewart told readers of the *Philadelphia African-American* that all they had to do was to contact someone who knew how to get an invitation, such as him or a concierge, "and when the show is over, you just get up and walk out, and nobody will high-pressure you into buying a solitary thing."[71]

The hit 1953 movie *Gentlemen Prefer Blondes* culminates with Marilyn Monroe and Jane Russell going on joyous shopping binges in Paris's most luxurious shops. Fodor's *Woman's Guide*'s chapter on France is devoted almost entirely to shopping in Paris. It lists fifty-four perfume shops, telling which of their scents are best for blonds or brunettes, which are best for evenings, and which are "exquisitely feminine," "sensual," "sombre," and "elegant."[72] Pan American Airways' guide was particularly high on France's "wonderful" made-to-measure girdles.[73]

Art, on the other hand, played a much-reduced role than in prewar women's guides. The Fodor's guide squeezed the arts, sights, and restaurants into a small-type section at the end, along with the addresses of banks and railroad stations. It listed only four of Paris's many art museums (the Louvre was excluded) and gave the impression that art's main function in France was social—that artists were invited to "salons, those artful meetings of politician and writer, diplomat and artist, still to be found in Paris."[74] In the same guide's chapter on "How to Be a Lady," the Paris-based writer Naomi Barry said bluntly, "A large percentage of young women who make the 'grand tour,' although ostensibly out to see the world's masterpieces of art, are actually in quest of a Prince Charming."[75] And, indeed, in the chapter on France, the real fulfillment of the woman tourist's dream seems to come when French romance enters her life:

> Suddenly it happens. There's a man in your life, and a Frenchman at that. You've been trudging about Paris, becoming grimmer and grimmer, with every twinkle of the Eiffel Tower's red beacon. You think you can't stand it alone another minute, this city of Abelard and Heloise, Mimi and Rodolfo, not to speak of their contemporaries who swoon and sway on every park bench. Once again, this evening, your favorite waiter has whisked an imaginary crumb from your chair, saying, as he seats you, "*Madame est toute seule?*" ("Madame is all alone?") You want to say. "Yes, damn it."
>
> But this kind of thing cannot go on forever in Paris, and suddenly here is a very presentable male popping up at your elbow, offering you a light, or indicating that you've just dropped your pearl necklace. You can be pretty sure he's appeared because you've actually let fall a smile. It doesn't matter if you have a face everybody—or just your mother—loves. A Frenchman's heart goes *trottinant* at the sight of what he calls *une visage sympathique*. He definitely loves American charm, and he finds your faltering school-girl grammar enchanting.[76]

—–

Women who did not connect with the Frenchman sitting at the table next to them could at least enjoy the food, for during the 1950s French food began to regain some of its status in upper-middle-class America. It had taken quite a beating in America during the Depression and war, when it was associated with unseemly extravagance and ration busting. Indeed, by war's end, America was practically a classless society when it came to food tastes. Postwar prosperity reinforced this, as elite foods such as beefsteak and chicken became affordable to most Americans. Celebrities and the elite members of "café society" frequented places known for their exclusivity, not their food. The Stork Club in New York was best known for its hamburger; the kitchen at Hollywood's Romanoff's, ruled over by a phony "prince" of that name, produced mediocre food that recalled his Ohio birthplace more than anything in Europe. With food tastes so irrelevant as indicators of status, it is no wonder that acquiring a taste for French food remained quite unimportant to most upwardly aspiring tourists.[77]

On the other hand, a small coterie of the upper class had preserved an appreciation for French food during those difficult times. In October 1941 the French restaurant industry in America had received a major shot in the arm when Henri Soulé, who had run the restaurant at the French pavilion at the recently closed World's Fair, persuaded ten of his staff to remain with him in New York, where he opened Le Pavillon. This elegant restaurant on Manhattan's swank East Side featured fine French haute cuisine amidst a profusion of fresh-cut flowers, gleaming silver, and sparkling crystal. The Vanderbilts, Astors, Cabots, Rockefellers, and Burdens flocked there, demonstrating that an appreciation for French food had not died out among the East Coast social elite.

Soulé manifested the snobbery so often associated with those who, like him, rose from humble origins to rub elbows with the elite, and cultivated this idea that an appreciation for French cuisine was a mark of exquisite taste and refinement. He let it be known that he was unimpressed by mere wealth: that for him, only good taste, manners, and breeding counted.[78] By the early 1950s, a number of people who had worked under Soulé had spun off and started expensive French restaurants of their own, trying to use him as their model. As a result, New York City was soon plagued with a generation of French restaurant workers whose specialty was the snub: the back permanently turned on the midwesterners patiently waiting for a table at the bar; the barely disguised sneer with which they reached for an unfashionable tie for men who were ignorant enough to show up without "proper dress"; the impatient glances over the shoulder when the young couple celebrating a special occasion asked them to explain the intricacies of the French menu. No restaurant was complete without a conspicuous "Siberia" for such lesser mortals. Julia Child, who spent her career trying to demystify French food, thought they actually enjoyed such cruel snobbery.[79]

During the 1950s such shenanigans contributed to untold numbers of first-time visitors arriving in France assuming that, as in the States, fine French restaurants were mainly venues for their humiliation. However, among the social elite, this kind of snobbery helped perpetuate the idea that a taste for French food was a sign of distinction. At the Long Island estate of the New York society czar William Paley, a Soulé regular, food was an "endless source of discussion" as the broadcasting magnate regaled his guests with stories of his culinary adventures in France.[80] In the summer of 1951, when seventeen-year-old Lee Bouvier wrote her upper-class mother, an incurable snob, to assure her that the European tour she and her sister Jacqueline were taking was paying cultural dividends, she made sure to say, "I adore French food."[81]

Gourmet magazine, which was founded in 1941 on the principle that French food was "probably the greatest national cuisine the world has ever known," had kept the embers of French cookery smoldering for a small but devoted upper-middle-class readership during the war and fanned them vigorously in the years that followed.[82] Throughout the 1950s its flagship recipes remained mainly French.[83] It also gushed over the pleasures of traveling to France and gave practical advice on going there. In 1949 it began regularly reviewing—or rather, extolling—restaurants in France. That March it also began a series of articles on "Epicurean Tours" of the French provinces, combining highlights of food and sightseeing, that ran for the next twenty-nine issues. This was followed, in 1954, by a monthly column on food and shopping in Paris.[84]

Thanks in part to such efforts, Francophilic attitudes toward food began to drift down into the upper-middle class. However, it was mainly women, particularly of the kind who were concerned about fine taste in clothes and furniture, who were most affected. In 1951 the women's magazine *House Beautiful* said that women "striving for gourmet status" should take a "gastronomic tour of France," which had "the finest, most fully developed, most sophisticated cuisine the world has ever known." It recommended renting a car and searching out restaurants with stars in the red Michelin guide, whose intricacies it explained. Even a short trip was "entirely feasible," it said, for "two great meals a day for two weeks" still added up to "28 gourmet experiences."[85]

The article did not mention the usual 1950s women's magazine motivation for learning about food: pleasing one's husband and family. Instead, it emphasized the pleasure to be derived by women themselves learning how to enjoy eating. A 1955 *Vogue* piece took a similar tack. It told of what "V.I.P.'s" such as Christian Dior, Laurence Olivier, André Malraux, and Alec Guinness ate at famous Paris restaurants such as Maxim's, Lasserre, and Le Grand Véfour. It was accompanied by recipes calling for ingredients like "Essence of Truffle" and complicated methods such as boning chickens that were more designed to enable readers to appreciate French restaurant food than to encourage emulation at home.[86] By 1958 *Vogue* was assuming that its readers were familiar enough with France's most famous restaurants to encourage some reverse snobbery. It published a piece on "6 Secret Paris Bistros" patronized by French tradesmen and shopkeepers. These included one "in a rather dingy blind alley" near Montmartre that had only five tables, and another small one in the distant 15th arrondissement, a district where, "as far as tourists are concerned, there is absolutely nothing of interest."[87]

Although most of this interest in gastronomic France was restricted to the eastern social elite and some upper-middle-class women, there were also some Francophilic gourmets scattered among the rest of the upper-middle class. Dr. Aubrey Maynard, the African American head of surgery at Harlem Hospital in New York City, made frequent trips to France, where dining out was his major priority. In September 1958 he bowled over Ollie Stewart with his fluency in French and knowledge of Paris restaurants. "I'm not particularly fond of Maxim's, but I highly recommend Laurent and Lasserre," he told Stewart, who probably could not even afford to check his coat at these deluxe places. "The food in both is good, and the service is impeccable. There are however, so many excellent restaurants in Paris that you don't ever have to worry about a good meal."[88]

— —

France's image in 1950s America was also bolstered by a new generation of creative Americans who found their way there. Many of the American artists who, like "Jerry Mulligan," had come there on the GI Bill remained after their benefits ran out. In 1950 Romare Bearden wrote a friend, "Paris is still very wonderful. . . . The place is full of phonies and the current crop of artists is not very interesting, but this is a good place to work."[89] Phonies or not, they constituted a thriving community that often gathered to debate new ideas and organize shows.[90] The American artist Man Ray, who had lived there before the war and returned there in 1951, wrote a friend that it was "just like the old days." "There are lots of exhibitions . . . and there is a continual exchange of ideas."[91]

But it was the revival of France's reputation as a hothouse for American writers that attracted the most visitors to Paris, especially among the young. One of the writers recalled, "Hundreds of Americans came over 'looking for Hemingway.' . . . They frequented Fitzgerald's haunts . . . and tried to write like Papa."[92] The novelist James Jones said, "It was thrilling as hell to come over in the Fifties and find the Closerie des Lilas [café] just the way Hemingway had described it. Even some of the waiters were the same."[93] Jones and Irwin Shaw, who had both written best-selling World War II novels, moved into spacious Paris apartments where they hosted endless parties for visiting Americans.[94]

The literary set and their hangers-on frequented many of the same Left Bank cafés that had been the haunts of the 1920s expatriates. The writer

Terry Southern recalled, "Oh it was a terrific scene. Because the cafés were such great places to hang out, they were so open, you could smoke hash at the tables, if you were fairly discreet. . . . So we would fall out there at one of the cafés, about four in the afternoon, sip Pernod until dinner, then afterwards go to a jazz club."[95]

The Left Bank became a kind of twin city to New York's Greenwich Village, and "hip" people such as Southern (who in the 1960s was known as "the hippest person in America") shuttled back and forth at will, often on cheap freighters. "It was a period," said Southern, "when The Village and St-Germain-des-Prés were sort of interchangeable. Once in a while you'd find yourself homesick, for one place or another, but it was okay, because both were good places to arrive at."[96]

Americans in Paris started literary magazines to publish the new generation of writers gravitating there. Magazines such as *Zero*, *Points*, and *New-Story* came and went, but not before they had published some fine work by the likes of Ray Bradbury, James Baldwin, and Mordecai Richler.[97] In the few years that *Merlin*, founded in 1952, existed, it published work by the future literary star Samuel Beckett, as well as Henry Miller, Jean Genet, and Jean-Paul Sartre.[98] Its more successful rival, the *Paris Review*, was founded one afternoon the same year by a group of fun-loving recent Ivy League graduates giggling uncontrollably while they ate hashish cookies.[99] Over the next few decades, it would publish an extraordinary amount of fine work by gifted young writers such as William Styron and Terry Southern.

Gay Talese, one of the participants in their high jinks, said that although they were mainly from wealthy established families, they "delighted in posing as paupers" to distinguish themselves from the mainstream American tourists.[100] However, the *Paris Review* did attract its own kind of tourists. The editorial board's sociability was legendary, centering as it did around the wealthy, well-bred founding editor George Plimpton, for whom life, it has been said, was a literary party. As a result, a steady stream of young people, mainly female, came to Paris for a few weeks or months to hang around its office volunteering to do some work for it.[101] They included Frances FitzGerald and Colin Wilson, who would later achieve great success as writers, as well as Jane Fonda, who left behind a sculpture she made for the office before going in a different direction.[102] Outside the office, they hung out at the nearby Café Tournon, which was also the watering hole of many of the African American writers, such as Richard Wright, James Baldwin, and Chester Himes, who were helping make the 1950s "the Golden Age of African American Literature in Paris."[103]

For most tourists, though, the best known American writer in Paris was Henry Miller, who in fact had not returned there after the war. Soon after the Liberation, Maurice Girodias, the son of Miller's original publisher, began feeding GIs' appetite for what was considered pornography by reprinting the two *Tropics*, along with other works. He soon found a ready market among the American tourists, who were arriving in increasing numbers. A piece in the *New York Herald Tribune* told of a schoolteacher returning by ship from Europe at the end of the summer of 1949:

> Our friend noticed a boy and girl reading a copy of *Jane Eyre*. The next morning she saw half a dozen other young people engrossed, oddly enough, in the same work. As a teacher, our friend was highly pleased. But on the last day of the crossing, she happened to find a copy of *Jane Eyre* on a deck chair and picked it up. . . . Inside were Henry Miller's twin volumes, neatly packaged by a Paris publisher.[104]

The publisher was Girodias, who the next year claimed to have sold forty thousand copies of each of the *Tropics* since the war. He subsequently published some fine English-language novels—works such as Samuel Beckett's *Watt*, Vladimir Nabokov's *Lolita*, and J. P. Donleavy's *The Ginger Man*. However, the tourists, he said, would not buy works such as these. "They were only interested in porno." They snapped up what he called "DB's" (dirty books) turned out by Terry Southern and a stable of hard-up American writers in Paris.[105] Alex Trocchi, the editor of *Merlin*, kept his struggling journal afloat by writing pornographic novels for Girodias under a number of names.[106]

In 1959 Girodias also published William S. Burroughs's novel *Naked Lunch*, one of the most noteworthy products of the "Beat Generation." The "Beats" had first made waves in San Francisco, in 1956, when Allen Ginsberg's poem *Howl*, published by the poet Lawrence Ferlinghetti, was seized for obscenity. Ginsberg and his friends soon moved on, first back to Greenwich Village, where they had started out, and then, in 1958, to Paris. There, along with a number of other impecunious American writers, artists, and musicians, they stayed in a smelly, run-down old Latin Quarter hotel that was soon labeled "The Beat Hotel."[107]

For the Beats, Paris's attractions were the traditional bohemian ones: it was cheap, tolerant of the substances they enjoyed abusing, and indifferent to their sexual proclivities—in their case, homosexuality (and, in Burroughs's case, a kind of rampant pansexuality). Above all, though, there was

France's long tradition of welcoming literary and artistic rebels. "They were living," says Barry Miles, "in a Paris of dreams—a fantasy of James Joyce and his 'Ulysses,' Sylvia Beach and Ezra Pound."[108] "I'd walk the Left Bank streets," Ginsberg later recalled, "thinking that Apollinaire or Rimbaud or Baudelaire had walked down these same streets. . . . You can't escape the past in Paris, and yet what's so wonderful about it is that the past and present intermingle so intangibly it doesn't seem a burden."[109] So he and Burroughs sought out and paid a respectful visit to the modernist poet Louis-Ferdinand Céline, even though he was a vicious anti-Semite who had collaborated with Vichy.[110] Their encounter with avant-garde artist Marcel Duchamp was less sedate. The friend at whose apartment the meeting took place recalled that they and their fellow Beat Gregory Corso were so drunk when they arrived that they could barely stand. "The first thing goddam Allen does," said the friend, "he gets down on his knees and starts kissing Duchamp's knees. Thinking he was doing something Surrealistic." All three Beats then crawled after the nonplussed artist on their knees, until Corso found a pair of scissors in the kitchen and cut off Duchamp's tie.[111]

Young white people were not the only ones intent on transforming themselves in France. William Demby, an African American ex-GI who had just graduated from college, arrived in Paris with a wardrobe of high-quality English gentleman's style clothes he bought in Canada while working as a waiter on a Great Lakes passenger steamer. He wanted, he said, to be a part of the world of the gentleman writer, sitting elegantly dressed in a café with his notebook, recording thoughts of he-wasn't-sure-what. "Paris," said Demby, "was a place where not just black Americans but almost everyone was living some kind of fantasy." They were all "reshaping their identity in a new context. . . . Everybody was role playing. . . . There was no feeling you had to congregate with other black people. Everything was open. It was as if you could now choose your destiny."[112]

— —

On the surface, the thousands of students who came to France on their junior year abroad in the 1950s were also quite a contrast to the bohemians of the Left Bank.[113] They were mainly (about two-thirds) female, and generally well-dressed and well-groomed. They lived under the watchful eyes of the French families with whom they boarded or the Americans who supervised them in Reid Hall, the Left Bank mansion that was a dormitory and social center for women students. However, it was very difficult to insulate them from the other young Americans imbibing the Latin Quarter atmosphere. Two very conventional American professors who investigated junior-year-in-Europe programs in 1958 reported:

> In Paris there is a group of American students who try to outdo themselves in sneering at the United States and in practicing what they consider "advanced" standards of behavior. They can be seen at various spots in the Latin Quarter. . . . Like our local beatniks they wear dirty blue jeans and sloppy, loose-fitting sweaters. The men begin by growing Lincolnesque beards or close-cropped goatees. From beards they may graduate to dope, and pass on through other stages of degeneration. Some go completely to pieces and end sleeping on the sidewalks; others pull themselves together and go home to be psychoanalyzed; many simply grow up and become reasonably normal adults.[114]

Although most students did not become so enmeshed in the Left Bank bohemian scene as to require psychoanalysis, few were unaffected by it. The Sorbonne, where they took many of their classes, was in the heart of the Latin Quarter, and Reid Hall was not far from the Montparnasse artists' cafés and the Saint-Germain nightspots. Moreover, despite some restrictions, Reid Hall residents and the students living with French families had infinitely more freedom in Paris than they did back in their college dormitories in America, where the strict regime of in loco parentis still reigned. Like the bohemians, they saw exercising this new freedom as in itself a form of self-improvement—in this case, something that expressed their maturity—and expected that experiencing France would expand and improve them.

The delightful thing about this variant of the idea that travel broadens was that one did not really have to do much to derive its benefits. A perceptive Frenchwoman observed of the students in 1950, "They have come here in search of neither science nor 'culture,' as we French understand it, but for the atmosphere of France. . . . It is in strolling about that they breathe it best."[115] Soon after arriving in France, Anne Rittershofer, a Smith student, wrote to her parents of sitting on the tree-lined cours Mirabeau, Aix-en-Provence's main boulevard, sipping (she said) pineapple juice and eating little cakes: "It was fascinating being there—looking at everyone pass by— Every day something new. There is nothing like travel to make one retain one's wonder and enthusiasm—I think these two qualities are part of LIFE. When they go—poof! No life. No zeal."[116]

A week later Rittershofer wrote home of how a serendipitous travel experience had broadened her appreciation of art. During a tour of the Arles, the ancient town southwest of Aix, she and her group were standing in a square when

> who should we see on the iron grille balcony leaning over in the sunshine but the man of the century—PABLO PICASSO!!!!!!! Holy Mary! Dressed in rose chemise, black jacket and yellow trousers, he was a picture of abstraction himself. His face was WONDERFUL! Intelligence: my heavens *and* warmhearted affection too. . . . Cotton Ayres, one of the girls, went up to the balcony and showed him her dress. It was made of material which he had designed and you should have seen his face light up! We saw him again later—What a man! Rather short, almost bald, white hair like a monk, yet very much alive. It was as exciting as seeing Eisenhower at West Point—Another memory to cherish—to have been so close to such a great man—to see the radiance in his face—his art now opens up to me.[117]

Informal "broadening" such as this, rather than the intellectual development derived from formal coursework, came to be the main justification for the study-abroad programs. The Paris director of the Council on Student Travel said, "The first objective of sending students abroad should be to open them up, to get them out of their limited environment and into a situation where they can meet new stimuli and new people."[118] Tracy Quayle, an ex–Smith College junior in France, agreed. The best instruction, she said, came in the evening, at the Latin Quarter cafés, where they would talk for hours about everything with French and foreign students. It was this, she said, that "broadened our opinions and reactions."[119] Anne Rittershofer thought that six months in France had prepared her for the rest of her life. She wrote home from Paris, "I know essentially what I am going to do with my life. I am now merely enriching my personal experience—developing a sense of judgement and a critical thinking mind which I hope will aid me in becoming an excellent loving wife, a good mama, and an active participant in the community."[120]

In typical 1950s fashion, the study-abroad programs also emphasized the psychological benefits of their programs: how adjusting to a foreign culture meant discovering one's inner resources of self-reliance and independence.[121] "Plunged into a strange environment," said one program director, "a person is impelled to try to adjust, to attempt new things, to strive for independence."[122] Some of the junior-year-in-France organizers even argued that it was "psychologically maturing" to be thrust into an environment where people did not like Americans: to study in a country like France, "where the people consider their culture infinitely superior to our own."[123]

Many students agreed. Tracy Quayle wrote, "The real significance of the stay in France is the discovery of ourselves, of our reactions to different and often difficult situations."[124]

It was understandable that the academics downplayed the intellectual benefits of study in France, for the fact was that, aside from improving the students' French, the programs were quite weak on that score. The weakest link in the chain was its central one, the Sorbonne's Cours de civilisation française. It never got over having been created by the university just to earn dollars from veterans looking for an easy GI Bill–funded course in Paris.[125] It was taught, said an American professor there, "by the rejects of the French educational system." Students complained it was no more demanding than an American high school—a damning indictment, indeed, during that heyday of academic credit for courses in "life skills" and driver education. One young woman claimed to have passed a course in philosophy there without ever attending a lecture and having read only one small book. Her grade was eighteen out of twenty, the French equivalent of an A+. Yet having students enroll in the Sorbonne's regular courses was not a viable alternative, for they were usually too advanced for the American juniors.[126] "The Smith girls," said one of their French professors, "are about the educational level of the last year of the *lycée* [French high school]. When they arrive in Paris they all want to go to the Sorbonne. At mid-year they all want to get out of the Sorbonne."[127]

Smith College dealt with the problem by offering an increasing number of its own courses at Reid Hall, for its students and others. A number of state universities such as Michigan and Wisconsin that banded together to offer a junior-year-abroad program in Aix-en-Provence imported American faculty to teach courses such as American history and political science. This, however, raised the question of whether the American students chatting with each other in the cafés on the cours Mirabeau were getting anything from the experience that they would not have had back in Ann Arbor or Madison.

Not surprisingly, 1950s-style confidence in empirical social scientific research led some academics to try to test whether these study-abroad experiences were indeed broadening or psychologically beneficial. Since almost any kind of experience can be called broadening, the researchers defined it as developing a tolerance for differences among people. On this score, the results were problematic. One study found that upon their return the students were hardly more tolerant of religious and racial diversity or more "internationalist" than those who had stayed behind.[128] As for the psychological benefits such as independence and self-reliance, another study indicated that there was little difference between those who had studied abroad and those who had stayed at home.[129]

Yet despite the results of the tests, the professors involved in the programs were certain that they had a positive impact on the students' mindsets: that, as the director of the Smith program said, "the biggest impact . . . is on the personality of the students."[130] Moreover, whether this was actually the case or not, most of the students *felt* that their stay in France had made them broader and more mature people. As a result, as they aged, these privileged young people would help keep alive the old belief that visiting France could be a personally transforming experience.

TEN

"Bandwagons Work like Magic in Tourism"

In the late 1950s and early 1960s, observers began accusing American tourists of being overly concerned with status. American tourists in Paris thought "their cultural status would never be assured until they have traveled," said the writer John Steinbeck.[1] In 1959, after combing through various market research studies, an advertising executive concluded that travel to Europe was especially popular among the college-educated because they were from a milieu where traveling to Europe gave them social status.[2] A 1960 *New York Times* editorial called on tourists returning from abroad to stop trying to one-up each other regarding their travels. "This status-versus-status game will soon begin to bore all participants," it said.[3] Two years later the advertising executive David Ogilvy told a meeting of European tourist officials that their advertising "must help the [American] reader to rationalize the cost of her journey by selling cultural and status overtones."[4] A subsequent summary of surveys concluded, "Travel is associated with status." Americans regarded frequent travelers as wealthy, well-informed, and "interesting to talk to."[5]

This propensity to see the drive for social status as the force behind Americans' behavior was, of course, as old as the country itself. However, two factors helped bring it to the fore in the mid-1950s. First, postwar prosperity produced a wave of new entrants into the middle and upper-middle classes who were searching for ways of behaving that were appropriate to their new economic status. Second, thanks to the era's triumphant consumer culture, these new ways of behaving were inevitably defined in terms of what one consumed.

Social scientists had been studying the links between consumption and class—or, as they later called it, social status—since at least the 1890s, when Thorstein Veblen came out with his acerbic analysis of the importance of "conspicuous consumption" in the lives of the very rich. In the 1920s the sociologists Robert and Helen Lynd made much of it in their brilliant dissection of class differences in Muncie, Indiana.[6] However, it was not until the

1950s that marketers really cottoned on to it, as they saw masses of upwardly mobile middle-class Americans trying to use their higher incomes to raise their social status.[7] Two best-selling books by Vance Packard on how advertisers played on this helped the term "status symbol" enter the lexicon to describe something one acquired to gain social status.[8] Although the term usually referred to a physical object, such as a car, it could also apply to behavior—what marketers liked to call "the thing to do."

High on this list was travel. David Ogilvy told the aforementioned Europeans: "Patterns of foreign travel are peculiarly subject to fashion. Your advertisements should put your country on the map as the place where 'everybody' is going. Bandwagons work like magic in tourism."[9] In 1956 Ollie Stewart wrote disapprovingly of the African American woman tourist who told him that she had come to Paris "because everyone else is doing it." Yet that same year, the *Philadelphia Afro-American* shifted his column on the comings and goings of African American tourists in Paris to the social page, which chronicled the activities of the status-conscious black bourgeoisie.[10]

What was it that gave European tourism its social status? As the above quotes would indicate, much of it derived from culture. Stewart, for example, said it was the cultural benefits of a European tour that differentiated it from other well-known "status symbols." The majority of tourists he met in Paris were there for the "broadening aspect of travel." Teachers, businessmen, and students "use their vacations to sop up a little culture here and there."[11] *Ebony* magazine said that it was this link to cultural self-improvement that made overseas travel "an acceptable status symbol."[12] Various surveys confirmed this. They indicated that while Americans thought domestic tourism was primarily for pleasure, they associated travel to Europe with both "interest in culture" and "enjoyment." In a 1957 survey, American tourists in Europe ranked sightseeing first among their objectives, "meeting the people" second, visiting museums and historical monuments third, and (rather implausibly) attending festivals, the theater, and musical events fourth.[13] In 1961 an Ogilvy & Mather researcher reported that it was the cultural dimension that made Americans feel that the European trip was "'the thing to do,' something that could be boasted about to friends." Advertising, he said, should "strike a balance between the two major themes of *enjoyment and culture*," and "the *prestige* of foreign travel should be implied."[14]

But what kind of culture did these tourists value? In 1950 *Life* magazine produced a chart that, although intended as tongue-in-cheek, is of some help. It divided Americans into the conventional "high-brows," who were regarded as a small, ineffectual, and effete intellectual elite; and "low-brows," who were attracted to essentially mindless, undemanding pursuits. However, instead of simply placing "middle-brows" in between, it divided them into "upper-middle-brows" and "lower-middle-brows," a distinction that can be quite useful for our purposes.[15]

In the first place, *Life*'s list of "upper-middle-brow" tastes provides clues as to the kind of cultural veneer the upper-middle-class tourists of the late 1940s and early 1950s hoped to burnish in Europe. It said that these were people who wanted to be known as comfortable with high culture, but without being labeled "high-brow." The men favored Brooks Brothers suits for business wear and tweed jackets for casual occasions. They liked theater, "solid non-fiction, the better novels, quality magazines, Maillol sculpture, and recordings of symphonies, concerts, and operas." Once in France, such people would put in some effort at appreciating its architectural and artistic treasures. John Steinbeck wrote in the mid-1950s:

> They have come to see and learn and to carry away impressions of the greatness and the beauty of Europe. For ten in the Place Pigalle there are a thousand in Notre Dame. For every one looking for a peep show or a circus, many hundreds with their guide books in their hands stare upwards at the glass of the Sainte-Chapelle. The Louvre draws crowds of quiet people, humble in their approach and earnest in their appreciation. . . . Perhaps they do not know the esoteric language of the art critic but they do come away enriched.[16]

As the 1950s progressed, however, many people with "lower-middle-brow" tastes prospered and rose into the upper-middle-income groups. In *Life*'s 1950 spreadsheet, the men in this stratum wore the "splashy neckties . . . sport shirts and colored slacks" that made American tourists the subjects of so much lampooning in Europe. Their tastes in entertainment ran to Hollywood musicals rather than theater, and they preferred "front yard sculpture" (implying plaster pink flamingos and black-faced jockeys) to Maillol. Their taste in records ran to the crooner Perry Como, light operettas, and orchestral music of the kind that would that would later be called "easy listening." Whereas "high-brows" preferred "a glass of an 'adequate little' red wine" and "upper-middle-brows" liked dry martinis, "lower-middle brows" were bourbon-and-ginger-ale folks.[17]

These Perry Como fans also wanted the trip to Europe to pay cultural dividends, but for them cultural improvement would come, not from slogging through the Louvre or dozing through operas, but from gazing upon famous sights. The most common answer given by a cross-section of Americans who were asked why they might want to travel to Europe involved cultural improvement, but by this they meant mainly "seeing sights."[18] Captain James Wilbanks, an army dentist stationed in Germany who set off with his wife on their first tour of European cities in 1955, typified this kind of comprehensive rapid-fire tourism. The couple told Ollie Stewart proudly that they "did [Paris] from end to end in three days flat [and] didn't miss a single big landmark." They had recorded them all on their camera and would be able to relive the experience at their leisure when they returned from the trip.[19] Rita Hamer recalled that the tourists in her upscale group tours wanted only to see the most famous sights: "In Paris, the Eiffel Tower." The Louvre, on the other hand, "was a hard sell."[20]

In 1956 the American travel agents' journal pointedly reported that a tour agency that polled clients returning from one of its European tours found that the only complaint was that a talkative guide kept them for too long in the Louvre.[21] Most tours solved this problem by making the obligatory stop in the Louvre as short as possible. Art Buchwald later recalled how, in 1953, during a visit to the Louvre, he and his friend Peter Stone were impressed that "the only things people wanted to see were the Venus de Milo, the Mona Lisa, and the Winged Victory. The rest of the stuff was all junk!" So, inspired by the recent success of the English runner Roger Bannister in breaking through the four-minute mile barrier, they decided Stone would try for the "six-minute Louvre"—the time it would take to see the three masterpieces and make it into a taxi waiting at the exit. While Buchwald stood at the taxi with a stopwatch, Stone raced by the three masterpieces in five minutes and thirty-three seconds.[22] By the late 1950s, American tour group operators were approaching that record, commonly allotting only half an hour to the Louvre. This often meant chopping the Winged Victory from the itineraries. "Just the *Mona Lisa* and the *Venus of Milo*," one promised.[23]

By the early 1960s, Americans in France had become very much identified with this kind of lower-middle-brow tourism. In 1961 David Ogilvy's brother in England wrote that he was puzzled by David's references to American tourists in Europe being part of the "upper crust." "That is not the impression people over here get of American tourists," he said. "Most of them seem to me very ordinary people with not very much higher education, no marked interest in the aesthetic side of life."[24] What he failed to realize, though, was that one no longer needed a "marked interest in the aesthetic side of life" to return from Europe feeling culturally enriched. As Captain Wilbanks and his wife knew, sightseeing alone allowed one to return thinking that the trip had made one a "broader" person: someone who had "seen the world." This is probably why the most common answer tourists gave to a tour group driver's question of why they took so many pictures of famous sights was "to prove that I was here."[25]

— —

In the 1950s and early 1960s, the number of these people with upper-middle-class incomes and lower-middle-brow tastes touring Europe increased exponentially. At first, they came by ship, taking advantage of the price competition induced by the steep rise in the number of steamships on the North Atlantic run.[26] So many of them began sailing in first class that it began to lose some of its luster. In the 1957 movie *An Affair to Remember,* Cary Grant and Deborah Kerr play two strangers who have a romance on a liner sailing from Italy and France to New York. They are in first class, with spacious cabins, elegant salons, swanky bars, and a beautiful dining room and dance hall. The other first-class passengers, however, are a distinctly lower-middle-browed lot, whom they try desperately to avoid. Most of these nosy, intrusive, unstylish, and uncultured shipmates are older, well-off businessmen and their dowdy wives. At one stage, Grant tells Kerr he was initially attracted to her because she was the only good-looking woman on the ship.

But it was expanding air service that ultimately had the most leveling effect on travel. When tourist class began in 1952, fare reductions of 30 percent spurred a 35 percent increase in traffic.[27] Fares dropped again in 1956, and the cheapest airfare fell to below the cost of first-class accommodation on a steamship. This contributed to a doubling in the number of Americans visiting France from 1950 to 1956, to close to half a million.[28] French tourist officials now calculated that a European vacation was affordable for a New York City bricklayer and that it was within the time constraints of the 15 million Americans who had three weeks of vacation with pay. But this was overoptimistic, to say the least, and the large majority of the tourists remained people from the upper- and upper-middle-income levels.[29] In 1957, when only 5 percent of families had an income of over $10,000, the average American tourist's European trip cost over $2,000 and lasted forty-seven days.[30] The cheapest New York–Paris airline "tourist" fares that year were still $558 return, while fares from the West Coast to Paris were $756.[31] In 1959 half of all visitors to Europe (about one-quarter to one-third of whom were immigrants returning to visit their families) were from the wealthiest 6.6 percent of the population—people with annual incomes of over $10,000.[32] Indeed, Americans associated the European tour so closely with high income that Ollie Stewart reported from Paris that almost every week another African American would tell him that on the boat or plane coming over, or on a tour, or in a fine restaurant, "some white American wants to know how they can afford to be traveling in Europe."[33]

It was not until 1958, with the introduction of transatlantic jet service, that the name of the game really began to change. Passengers initially saw the benefits of jets in terms of reducing the amount of time one spent confined in the metal tubes. After her first jet flight from Paris to New York in the spring of 1959, Natalia Murray wrote Janet Flanner, "The jet journey back was sleepless. . . . The air was bumpy too. Some people were a little airsick as well, as the plane rolled. It shook and shrieked so as we revved up for the take off I thought we were going to blow up! But the trip was really fine because brief. . . . It took seven hours and a quarter, but what is that? NOTHING, NOTHING."[34]

To the airlines, though, the most important thing about the new planes was that they carried over twice as many passengers as propeller planes, flew half again as fast, and needed much less time off for servicing. This meant an unprecedented surge in capacity. Faced with the prospect of a sea of empty seats, they were forced to tap into a wider market. Pan Am's president Juan Trippe said the added capacity on the New York–Paris route meant many more Americans would now be able to travel as "unofficial ambassadors" to Europe and "add to international understanding." However, he also knew that reduced fares would be needed to draw them into the yawning empty seats. For the next ten years, Pan Am took the lead in pushing the international airline cartel to offer inducements such as fifteen-day "excursion fares" that were designed to lower prices for tourists while continuing to extract the highest possible fares from business travelers, who had little choice of where and when to travel. By 1959 the airlines were carrying over 1.5 million passengers across the Atlantic, almost twice as many as the ships. The number of Americans visiting France soared from 535,000 in 1958 to 793,000 in 1960.[35]

Despite the hopes of people such as Trippe that jets would finally inaugurate the much-anticipated new "mass market" for overseas tourism, the first jet-age tourists were anything but representative of the masses. Instead, they were overwhelmingly well-off and middle-aged.[36] The Americans most likely to travel overseas, one analysis of early 1960s travel concluded, had incomes over fifteen thousand dollars, were married with no children under eighteen, and had already been overseas.[37] However, the proportion of first-time visitors to Europe—the category into which most of our newly rich lower-middle-brow tourists fell—had also been increasing steadily. Although they were still mainly from the big cities of the eastern seaboard,

An African American tour group in front of Notre-Dame Cathedral in 1954. Courtesy of Roger-Viollet.

more were now coming from cities farther west, especially Chicago and Los Angeles.[38] In the later 1950s, the Rotary, Boy Scouts, and various professional groups began holding their international conventions in France.[39] Travel agents organized long summer European tours for college fraternities.[40] African American travel agencies arranged for hundreds of first-time African American visitors from organizations such as the National Council of Negro Women, the National Beauty Culturists League, and various adult fraternities to be shepherded through the great capitals of Europe.[41] By 1960 first-timers comprised over half of all tourists to Europe.[42] At the Ritz bar, the champagne cocktails of the upper class made way for the martinis, Manhattans, and whiskeys-and-ginger-ale of the American nouveaux riches.[43]

A striking feature of many of the new tourists was not just their lack of interest in high culture and history, but their abject ignorance of the surroundings in which they found themselves. Some were just not interested. Mary Hulsizer, an older woman from St. Louis who loved France, wrote in her dairy that at her hotel in Nice she "talked with an American man from Columbus, Ohio, who said, except for Copenhagen, he had not seen anything that interested him! And he and his wife had been motoring over here for several months."[44] "Too many Americans," said the *New York Times* bureau chief in Paris, "come to France knowing nothing of its language, history or current problems, and do nothing to repair their ignorance while they are here."[45] A *New York Times Magazine* article in 1959 said the typical American tourist landed in Europe without knowing the language, how to catch a taxi, how much to give the porter, "or where the gents' room is, or whether he can trust the sinister-appearing character who offers him money at an illegal rate."[46] Another *New York Times Magazine* piece, commenting on American tourists' difficulties in getting around in Paris, said, "At heart, Americans would like to believe there is no abroad, a faith that expresses itself in the conviction that literally every human being speaks English. When the truth dawns on them, they are genuinely surprised."[47] One reason Temple Fielding's guide for Americans traveling to Europe became the best-selling one of the 1950s and 1960s was that he listed only restaurants where the staff spoke English.[48]

Perhaps it was these insecure newcomers who helped revive the American reputation, dating back to the 1920s, for being the loudest of all tourists.[49] In 1957 the Paris-based correspondent Joseph Wechsler observed:

> Well-balanced citizens arrive on the eastern shores of the Atlantic in a confused state of mind, a mixture of inferiority and superiority complexes. They hide their bewilderment by hotel porters, taxi drivers, ticket-scalpers, arrogant headwaiters behind the strength of their vocal chords. Everybody talks a little louder than back home, finding comfort in the English language. . . . Americans who wouldn't double-park their cars in their home town throw their weight around in European hotel lobbies.[50]

The writer Cornelia Otis Skinner complained that boorish American tourists disturbed the tranquil calm of her charming little Paris hotel with rude demands bellowed in "hog-summoning tones."[51] The "stereotyped complaints" of the French, said a Paris correspondent of the *New York Times*, were "about the American tourist's funny clothing and the decibel level of his voice in public." A charitable Parisienne said, "I think many of them feel lost and far from home and in reaction they tend to talk too loudly and complain about the absence of familiar things."[52]

A less kindly view would be that they were reflecting their sense of superiority over the French. Stanley Karnow recalled that the reporting of *Time's* Paris bureau, where he worked, "tended to treat the French with contempt, condescension, derision, or, at best, amusement." He said, "After a while, I began to feel, a *Time* subscriber might conclude that, by and large, France was a degenerate nation of gourmets, adulterers, leftist intellectuals and volatile politicians who could not prevent their governments from collapsing every few months."[53]

— —

Until the early 1960s, despite the official rhetoric about attracting less affluent Americans, much of the French tourist industry remained mesmerized by the very wealthiest ones.[54] So was American Express. Despite its president's effusions about the democratization of tourism, it kept concentrating on individual tours for the high-end market, even though it began losing money on these labor-intensive ventures. Only in 1963, after its market research showed that its clients, who were mainly wealthy males over forty earning over $10,000 a year, were a shrinking minority of European tourists, did it decide to go after those in the $7,000 to $10,000 bracket. To attract these people, who its researchers said were "less demanding," it decided to "enter aggressively the growing market for moderate-priced, motorcoach tours of Europe."[55]

But here American Express was playing catch-up, for other tour operators had already turned this into a very big business. Dorothy Marsh, whose company specialized in tours for women, was typical of many of the tour operators who organized escorted tours for the growing middle-class market during the 1950s. By the mid-1950s, she was offering a summer tour that lasted fifty-four days and cost only $1,516.[56] Eighteen of these days were spent crossing back and forth on a slow liner. However, the thirty-six days ashore tried to make up for this by providing first-time tourists with at least a glimpse of a panoply of famous Western European sights. Alternating between train and bus, the tour went from the north of Scotland to the south of Italy at a breakneck pace, rarely spending more than one night in a place. The longest stay was four days in Paris, where the schedule was packed with sightseeing tours.[57]

Once again, as they had been since Thomas Cook began them about one hundred years before, such packaged tours were derided for their frenzied pace. A *New York Times Magazine* article quoted one American woman saying to another outside of the American Express office in Paris, "We're going to see St. Paul's Cathedral today, aren't we?" "No darling," her companion was said to have replied, "that's tomorrow. Today, we're seeing the Duomo."[58] One of its writers called a bus tour he took "a goose step parade through an imaginary Europe that isn't there any more. . . . The rules are

A well-dressed tour group from New York City boarding a luxury tour bus in Paris, 1963.
Courtesy of Roger-Viollet.

strict. Do not linger." The only places the tourist did not have to hurry, he
said, were in the stores where the guides received their 10 percent commission on the tourists' purchases.[59] The French newspaper *Combat* said that
the American tourist "follows the path traced for him by the guide or tourist
agency. He makes no effort to mingle with the people he is visiting and still
less to learn their language."[60]

Many of these group tourists returned home satisfied with their experiences. Ollie Stewart, who often advised against such tours, had to admit that
he heard of only one of the seventy-six members of an African American fra-
ternal organization who arrived in Paris in two huge buses who was dissatis-
fied. "All the rest said it was 'terrific,'" he reported.[61] However, the tourists

were by no means the uncritical sheep satirized by the critics. Dorothy Marsh said that the first question prospective clients asked when shown the brochures was, "This tour seems so fast, would I have time to browse around?"[62] When Stewart spoke in December 1959 with a group of thirty-one African American beauticians on a one-month tour of Europe, a number of them complained about having only three days in Paris. Several said that "they would have preferred fewer countries and more time to get to know the people. . . . They never had time enough to get to know the money used by the various countries."[63] Other group tourists complained to him about their tour operators not meeting them at train stations, foul-ups in hotel reservations, and operators giving them money to buy their own meals rather than, as promised, taking them to restaurants.[64]

Clients were by no means reticent about sharing these concerns with their tour guides. There were enough complaints at Marsh Tours that in November 1964 tour guides were brought together for a long discussion on how to handle them. Some guides said they handled complaints about the pace by pointing out that the company did offer slower tours, which the complainant had chosen not to take. Others told grumblers that it was only such "super-planning" that allowed them to see as much as they were seeing. As for the frequent protests over the quality of hotels, the suggested response was to say that "anyone who had traveled in the United States would have little to complain of when it came to European hotels." Guides were also told to point out to clients who complained about hotel rooms without bathrooms en suite that "Marsh Tours is First Class, and has never used the word Deluxe."[65]

Whether on package tours or not, tourists continued the tradition of griping about being overcharged by French hoteliers, merchants, and restaurateurs. Each fall the American consulate in Paris would conduct a major "clean-up operation" to deal with the numerous complaints of summer tourists, now back in the States, regarding such things.[66] Grumbling about French food also persisted. It was, after all, a time when food neophobia—fear of new foods—still reigned supreme in America, and "He'll eat *anything*" was said with disgust rather than admiration. Historic fears that French sauces camouflaged inferior meat were hardly stilled by the widespread knowledge that, thanks to wartime shortages, eating horsemeat had regained much of its popularity among the French. In the South of France, garlic continued to jolt Anglo-Saxon nostrils and taste buds. A teen-aged boy reported in disgust, "Train's packed with French sailors. Some are singing, some drinking, and they've all been eating garlic!"[67] The long

French lunch also continued to raise hackles. A *New York Times* reporter said tourists "waxed indignant" and were "reduced to fury" by the unavailability of "a quick soda-fountain snack."[68]

Although tour operators tried to protect their clients from such culinary surprises by prearranging all three daily meals, there was no way of ensuring that French cooks were aware of the Americans' many food phobias. Madame Hamer recalled that when, in the early 1960s, her American tour groups first began stopping in the French provinces, the question "What do they eat?" was a constant problem. When, at a welcoming banquet, a fifty-voice choir that had just arrived in Europe was served fish with the heads on, the fish all went back to the kitchen untouched.[69] A 1962 article in the *New York Times Magazine* said, "Unlike other tourists, the American considers eating a necessary function, not a pleasure. The restaurant is the only place where he stubbornly refuses to relax. He would give all of French cuisine for a ham sandwich, and he is quite capable of asking for one, even in Maxim's."[70] Ben Bradlee recalled that when *Newsweek*'s general editor visited Paris, "at lunch, even in the very best restaurants, he wanted hamburger, or scrambled eggs."[71]

This unease over French food was so prevalent that even the British, whose food was almost universally reviled, tried to profit from it. In 1954 the Englishman David Ogilvy had his Madison Avenue ad agency mount an American campaign for the British Travel Authority extolling British roast beef. His staff were very dubious about this, he said, since they themselves regarded British cooking "as so inferior to French cookery" that they thought it best not to mention food at all. Ogilvy, however, knew his tourists better than they did. Although he regarded himself as "a gastronomic snob, and what's worse a French gastronomic snob," he said that he had "met a surprising number of returning Americans who honestly prefer English cooking to Continental [i.e., French] cuisine." So, over the next few years, the agency ran what Ogilvy called "good food ads," making sure, he said, to "avoid the 'gourmet' touch, sticking to rather simple 'good food' and eschewing everything Frenchified." In 1957 he told his copywriters to be sure to mention that the British "know how to cook food without smothering it in rich, complicated, foreign sauces," and to say that "English menus are not written in French, so you know what you're ordering."[72]

Finally, revulsion over French standards of personal hygiene remained a nagging problem. In early 1963 Ogilvy's agency did a market research survey among Americans deemed likely to be interested in traveling to Europe. One set of questions sought to elicit their view of the British and French by having them check off various characteristics that came to mind regarding each of them. Whereas "clean" ranked in the top ten of positive things about the British, it was the characteristic for which the French received their lowest marks.[73] The survey gave the French

Highest Marks For	Lowest Marks For
1. Interesting	1. Clean
2. Picturesque	2. Prosperous
3. Attractive	3. Moral
4. Not stuffy (not pompous)	4. Generous
5. Sophisticated	5. Efficient
6. Intelligent	6. Straightforward
7. Cultured	7. Pro-American
8. Cheerful	8. Modern
9. Educated	9. Honest[74]

It will be noted that the French received the highest marks mainly for the beauty of their country, not for their personal characteristics, while the summary of their lowest marks reads like a caricature of the powerful negative stereotypes that had persisted since World War I: they were poor, dirty, immoral, miserly, inefficient, devious, anti-American, old-fashioned, and crooked. It is no wonder that, in 1964, tour group leaders for Marsh Tours called France "probably the most difficult country of all" to explain to Americans.[75]

On the other hand, French people who dealt with American tourists also faced difficulties. French tourist officials in America thought they had to cope with an extremely "spoiled" clientele.[76] In 1962 a French hotel magazine advised hoteliers and restaurateurs that most American tourists were older people who were fearful and difficult to satisfy. They were "always ready to complain" and wanted to be protected from anything adventurous or unexpected, whether it be the food or the bathroom plumbing. Hotel and restaurant employees needed a great deal of patience in dealing with them, it said, and should try to explain matters to them no matter how "nonsensical" their complaints might seem.[77] Art Buchwald said that many Frenchmen would like Americans better if they were quieter and did not complain so much.[78]

— —

But politics was also causing difficulties. By the mid-1950s, the steady erosion of the French empire was having a growing impact back home. The army's defeat by the Communist insurgents in Vietnam in 1954 had led to a humiliating withdrawal from Indochina. A succession of weak coalition governments in Paris were unable to control a massive insurgency that erupted in Algeria, France's oldest colony in North Africa. Finally, General Charles de Gaulle was called back to lead the nation. In May 1958 a national referendum approved the creation of a Fifth Republic, with a constitution granting the presidency, to which he was quickly elected, much greater powers than heretofore. But the Algerian situation continued to deteriorate. In 1960 terrorist attacks spread to the streets of Paris, and the French security forces stepped up their strong-arm tactics against suspected supporters of the insurgency. Hundreds of North Africans were rounded up for interrogation, which in France did not involve niceties such as habeas corpus and Miranda warnings.[79] This climaxed in early 1961 with the suppression of a pro-independence demonstration in which the security services surreptitiously killed close to 250 mainly Algerian demonstrators, many of whose bodies were dumped into the swift-flowing Seine.[80]

The first Americans to feel the impact of this turn of events were African Americans, for the repressive tactics had led to a virtual reign of terror for brown-skinned people on the streets of Paris. Heavily armed police repeatedly stopped brown-skinned people to check their papers and harass them. A Canadian friend told me of being stopped while walking on a quiet side street with a brown-skinned man. She watched in terror as the police asked for his papers, frisked him, and then told him to "beat it," firing shots in the air from their submachine guns as he ran down the street. For William Demby, the Algerian War exploded the myth of French tolerance for blacks. For a brown-skinned person, he said, visiting France in the early 1960s became a very disturbing experience. There was a "nasty atmosphere of harassment." Americans read the magazine supplements about the glories of Paris, he said, but in reality "the people there were awful."[81] For Richard Wright, James Baldwin, and other African American expatriates, the Algerian War forced painful reassessments of their optimistic views of French attitudes toward people of color.[82]

Some white visitors were also put off by the tense atmosphere, but they tended to be politically engaged and French-speaking. On a 1962 visit, Lionel Abel sensed a pervasive fear of violence by right-wing terrorist groups opposed to independence for Algeria. He was told that Sartre's apartment had been bombed and that he was in hiding.[83] But William Demby was disgusted by most tourists' apparent obliviousness to all of this. The "café tourists," he said, did not see the real Paris; they avoided "the real world."[84] So, too, it seemed, did the increasing number of African Americans who stopped in Paris for a week or so on their visits to newly independent nations in sub-Saharan Africa.[85] But even those tourists who were bothered by the police presence found it mattered little to their enjoyment of the city. In April 1960 Charles Boggs, a white American artist, wrote a friend in the States, "France is becoming a police state, and that is not exaggerating." "Still," he continued, "Paris is wonderful."[86]

This attitude mirrored the positive view of de Gaulle then current in America as someone who rid France of its laughable political system and prevented a Communist and Socialist takeover. In 1961 he was widely applauded when he forsook the French settlers in Algeria and moved toward granting Algeria independence, something it achieved in 1962. Temple Fielding, whose travel guide had consistently lambasted French inefficiency and poor treatment of American tourists, now did a complete about-face. "The de Gaulle renaissance was so dramatic and so sweeping that it had to be seen to be believed," he wrote in late 1963. Among other things, he praised de Gaulle's tough stand against tax evasion, French officials' spiffy new uniforms, and the sandblasting of public buildings, all of which contributed to the "restoration of French patriotism and pride" and "the new climate in French dignity and self-respect."[87]

— —

Initially, de Gaulle's return also caused little concern among another major group of Americans in France: servicemen and their families. The creation of the North Atlantic Treaty Organization in 1949 had led to the American commitment to station 400,000 troops in Western Europe to defend against a possible Soviet invasion. The bulk of these troops were to be stationed in Germany, and in late 1951 the Americans began establishing a string of about sixty bases stretching across France.[88] The town of Villefranche, near Nice on the Riviera, became the home port of the U.S. Navy's large Sixth Fleet, which patrolled the Mediterranean. NATO headquarters were set up by the first supreme commander, General Dwight Eisenhower, in Saint-Germain-en-Laye and Fontainebleau, two towns outside of Paris. By 1958 there were over fifty thousand American servicemen and thirty thousand of their wives and children in France, interacting with the French in varying degrees.[89]

There were tensions from the outset. The first units had arrived at the height of the French Communists' anti-American campaign, providing visible evidence for their charges that France was becoming an American colony. For two months, in 1951, L'Humanité ran a daily feature, with contributions from different towns, entitled "The American Occupation in France."[90] Simone de Beauvoir said that seeing two GIs enter a Loire valley hotel in 1952 made her think that France was again being occupied, this time by the Americans. "Seven years earlier," she wrote, "we had adored them, these peaceful looking soldiers in their khaki uniforms: they had been our freedom. . . . Now these same uniforms were a symbol of our dependency and a mortal threat."[91] When fights broke out in Paris between white GIs and African American civilians crossing what in America was called the color line, Richard Wright warned that the troops were importing American racism to France. "With the advent of each new GI on French soil," he wrote in 1951, "the U.S. Negro feels that his immunity from American racism is that much less secure."[92]

The Defense Department tried to ensure that the servicemen's behavior did not play into these critics' hands. It rushed out a guidebook for GIs in France that said that many French people had a bad impression of Americans because of "the bad conduct of which too many servicemen were guilty during and after World War II and the equally bad impressions made too frequently by some American tourists." It warned those "fortunate enough to get to Paris" that the French wanted them "to admire it for its beauty, its quaintness, and for its historical tradition, and not just for the night spots." It was not a "leave town," and Parisians resented Allied soldiers who used it "as a place to cut loose in."[93] As for sex, it said,

> France has been done an injustice in much that has been written and sung about "Mademoiselle." Many of these ideas grew out of the abnormal conditions of World War One and its aftermath. They do not reflect normal French life. France is not a frivolous nation where sly winks and coy pats are accepted forms of address. . . . You're going to be disappointed if you have the idea that you'll find a nation of pretty girls with you on their mind.[94]

Like the 1944 guide, from which much of it was reprinted, it also warned that the French, like all wine-drinking nations, don't drink to get drunk. "They despise drunkenness," it said. "Don't let them say the American army is a drunken army." Finally, it cautioned servicemen against flaunting their relative wealth and said, "Remember that handling another country's money as if it were so much paper breeds contempt and that thoughtless spending sends prices skyrocketing."[95]

The last admonition was hardly necessary, for during the 1950s French inflation steadily undermined the servicemen's dollars' buying power. This helped reinforce their conviction that the troops stationed in Germany, where inflation was low, were much better off. Moreover, the troops in Germany were housed in comfortable dwellings on bases with extensive shopping and entertainment facilities while French and American red tape kept delaying the construction of adequate housing in France. In 1953 almost half of the troops in France shivered in rudimentary barracks with primitive toilet facilities. Officers and noncommissioned officers who had to rent scarce accommodations in small French towns near the bases complained about paying exorbitant rents for inferior housing with primitive plumbing.[96] As for other amenities, one noncommissioned officer said bitterly, "We had better entertainment facilities in Korea."[97]

In August 1953 *Le Monde* sent a reporter to check on reports that the American troops in France were living in terrible conditions and suffering from very low morale. The first American he came across at the large U.S. Army base at the port of La Rochelle hardly seemed to bear this out. He was an army dentist, a captain, whom the reporter encountered drinking crème de menthe on ice and socializing with locals in a café. The dentist told him that he would hop in his car every day at 5:00 PM, as soon as he finished work, and come to the café to meet with French friends. He would play some cards and then dine on "steak frites" (thin beefsteak and French fries) washed down with some Beaujolais. "I consider myself on vacation," the officer said, "and during these holidays I try to 'live à la française.'" The next day the reporter met the base public relations officer, a colonel, in the town's main parking lot, where the officer's Jaguar and the few small French cars were practically lost amidst a sea of servicemen's large Chevrolets. He was then taken to the base travel agency, which arranged tours of France for soldiers on leave, and was told they could take affordable tours of Europe by hitching free rides on military aircraft.[98]

At his next stop, however, the reporter saw what he concluded was a more typical scene. He arrived in the southwestern town of Châteauroux at about midnight to find what had been a famously boring little town ablaze with lights. It was now the center of a series of sixteen bases in southwestern France with thirteen thousand men, only thirty-five hundred of whom were with wives and children. The bars were full of men in uniform chugalugging bottles of bubbly wine and talking to women with startling décolletage. MPs walked menacingly along the streets, clubs handy at their side, each pair accompanied by a French gendarme.[99]

The *New York Times* had reported that it was "said" (by whom it did not say) that after the initial shock had worn off, most of the servicemen's dependents in France were "enjoying their experience in a foreign land"— that the wives were learning French, making friends with French neighbors, and "enjoying their experience in a foreign land."[100] The *Le Monde* reporter drew a much different picture. The vast majority of Americans had little to do with the French, he said, and few of the French would have anything to do with the Americans. "For the mass of the population," he said, "Franco-American relations are practically non-existent."[101] An ex-reporter now serving in the air force told him that most of the servicemen complained constantly and detested the service, Europe, and Europeans. There was a minority, he said, who would like to "adopt French manners and morals," but they were continually rebuffed in their "search for friendship and affection," and developed a "complex" over being "disliked."[102]

American military authorities adopted a dual strategy for avoiding friction with local French people. On the one hand, they tried to minimize contact with locals by re-creating, as much as possible, the American way of life on their bases. In Châteauroux, for example, in 1953 they constructed a 600-bed hospital, two big mess halls to feed and entertain two thousand men, and a large theater. Then came a huge officers' mess, a high school with rooms for boarders, and buildings housing bowling alleys, an NCOs' mess, a large PX, a laundry, civilians' mess, an auto shop, and a prison. By 1958 the base was a complete city unto itself, with housing complexes, stores, chapels, sports fields, and even a golf course. When the base could no longer accommodate everyone, housing that was equally isolated from the French was built elsewhere. Five three-story apartment houses were built for enlisted men, along with a primary school, in a green field outside of town. A self-contained American-style suburb was constructed for officers and their families on the other side of town. Few Americans shopped in town, for the base sold practically everything, at much reduced prices.[103] At Phalsbourg, in Lorraine, the air force first built a number of luxuriously outfitted clubs designed to keep the men from wandering into town—an officers' club, NCOs' club, enlisted men's club, rod and gun club, and a golf club, each with their own bars and food.[104] There was also an immense first-class golf course, a large supermarket, and a PX the size of a department store, all of which caused small-town French jaws to drop. (A French account said that French workers on the base were particularly amazed at how these places "gleamed with meticulous cleanliness.")[105]

Yet at the same time as they were isolating the Americans, the military authorities also tried to break down the barriers between them and the locals. After the base at Châteauroux was up and running in 1952, sixty officers, led by a general, began taking a course in French at the local high school. American bands and troops marched on Bastille Day, Armistice Day, and at other patriotic ceremonies. Local employees were honored as employee of the month and so on. Fund-raising campaigns were mounted for the local orphanage and other worthy causes. Every May, on Armed

Forces Day, the public was invited to tour the base and see various displays. (One local woman still recalls how impressed she was by the air conditioners and jukeboxes, things she saw for the first time on a visit to the base.)[106] At Phalsbourg families were invited to mess halls for Thanksgiving and Christmas dinners. At Christmastime the base sent carolers to sing for ten nights by a Christmas tree the town had set up for them in the main square.[107] The Châteauroux authorities also tried to encourage local tourism with articles in the base newspaper extolling various sights in the area.

But most of the well-meaning gestures came to naught. The Châteauroux officers soon gave up on the French course, and the vast majority of the servicemen made no attempt to learn French. A local newspaper reported that they said, "It's not worth the effort because the 'Frogs' all speak English."[108] In 1961 the same idea, and the same phrase, was said to be still current there.[109] The dearth of airmen who spoke French made the regular "open houses" held on the base puzzling affairs for French visitors, who complained that the airmen mumbled explanations of the displays to them in incomprehensible English. The base paper's attempts to promote local tourism merely provided fodder for the local Communist newspaper, which jumped on faux pas such as the one that suggested visiting the nearby home of the nineteenth-century writer George Sand, yet described her as ugly, obscene, and a writer of negligible talent.[110]

What put off most local residents, though, was the servicemen's scandalous behavior off the base.[111] A subsequent French study of Châteauroux noted that the problem with such self-enclosed situations—where the servicemen's work, family, neighborhood, and social lives were all conflated— was that the only place to escape their intense social pressures was in the French part of town. The town thus became a kind of "anti-base," where good behavior could be replaced by bad behavior, social cohesion could be discarded in favor of conflict, and order replaced by disorder. This was putting it mildly. Each day at five o'clock, and especially on weekends, men would descend on the twenty-odd bars in town that catered to them.[112] The French were simply astounded by their drunkenness. To Colette Brossard, who began working in one of the town's hotels in 1954, it seemed that their objective was to get as drunk as possible as quickly as possible. At the hotel's bar, she recalled, "they drank until they dropped, and then the MPs would be called to cart them away."[113] A local newspaper, describing the scene in one bar, said that "at 9.00 pm 250 'Ricks' are in the room; at 10.00 pm, 200 are perfectly drunk. At 11.00 pm, everyone is under the table. . . . The first stage over, these gentlemen then begin fighting like fishwives." Others would take to the streets, apparently bent on random destruction. Brawls, often interracial, would break out all over the place, bringing MPs charging in, brandishing their pistols, and laying about with their nightsticks.[114]

A massive influx of prostitutes did little to assuage Châteauroux residents' fears that order had broken down.[115] Some, accompanied by their pimps, arrived as soon as the base opened in 1951 and stayed on. Others would take the trains down from Paris on weekends, particularly on payday. Peasant girls arrived from the countryside, little cloth bags in hand, to try to set themselves up in the trade, and some local women took advantage of the opportunities to supplement their incomes.[116] Brossard remembered that the main drinking establishment for officers was a boîte with prostitutes in the rooms upstairs.[117] One consequence of this bawdy scene was that the servicemen adopted exactly the attitude toward Frenchwomen that the armed forces guidebook had warned against. They would commonly assume that all Frenchwomen were for sale and would proposition, grope, chase, attack, and sometimes rape passing women.[118]

As if this weren't disturbing enough, drunken servicemen behind the wheels of vehicles led to soaring accident rates. "You have to watch out for them all day long," said one Châteauroux local, "for they're often three sheets to the wind . . . once they arrive in France they drink very little Coca-Cola."[119] In Phalsbourg, as well, despite all the efforts to keep them on base, drunken airmen regularly caused mayhem and havoc on the public roads.[120]

Few of them were driving to see the sights. Colette Brossard, who subsequently made a career in the hotel industry, recalled that the local authorities' attempts to promote tourism in the area around Châteauroux fell flat. They handed out maps and information on driving a beautiful tourist route nearby, but the Americans showed no interest at all. Indeed, she remembered them having no interest in anything about France. Of the many people, bachelors and married couples, who stayed in her hotel waiting for housing to open up, she recalled only one person, an airman's wife, who did.[121] In 1966, when the base was set to close, a local woman expressed similar sentiments. Commenting to a reporter on the American refusal to learn French, she said:

> They don't want to learn anything at all, not how to drink wine, not even to eat as we do. And then some of them complain that in fifteen years not one person in Châteauroux has invited them to dinner. How can we ask them to dinner? They never have onion soup, steak à la madeira; and if at the end of the dinner, you offer cognac they ask for soda pop!

The journalist said that the only French things on the base were the electricity and sewers. "All the rest—conditioned, frozen, cellophaned and boxed—comes from the States. Even the bread. . . ."[122]

This lack of interest in learning about Europe was by no means confined to Châteauroux, or France. Allen Broussard, who subsequently became a California Supreme Court justice, thought that he was one of the few GIs stationed in Western Europe in the mid-1950s who did some reading about it and traveled extensively there. "A lot of the younger draftees and enlisted personnel missed a lot of opportunities that existed over there," he said.[123]

Again, though, there were many exceptions to these generalizations. A study of servicemen's expenditures in France found that they spent 7 percent of their income—a not insignificant amount—on tourism.[124] Indeed, in 1954 the French government estimated that the servicemen on leave and their dependents made up one in four or five of the Americans touring France.[125] Moreover, many of them spent weekends in places in the southwest and east not normally frequented by American tourists, who rarely strayed from Paris and the Riviera.[126] Some servicemen stationed in the bases near Paris took full of advantage of their proximity to the City of Light to enjoy its food, sights, and atmosphere.[127] A gay friend of the author's who served in the U.S. Navy in Villefranche in the late 1950s told of close relationships developing between navy men and Frenchmen of similar inclinations ashore. He also credited the trips he took while on leave with encouraging him to go on to graduate school in art history. Bob Allen, a communications officer on one of the ships stationed there, was completely enthralled by the area's beauty. He traveled to Paris and Geneva on leave with friends and befriended Frenchwomen all over the Riviera. He wrote home that French girls were "glad to be with an American, especially in southern France where the war decimated the male population." On a postcard home he wrote, "I'm in 7th Heaven a million times over. . . . Oh, I'm so happy I could scream. It's too much!"[128] Nevertheless, as Broussard said, such servicemen were exceptional. Throughout the 1950s and into the 1960s, Americans concerned about their country's image in France continued to bemoan the negative impact of both the tourists and the servicemen there.[129] At the same time, many of the servicemen, especially the enlisted men, returned to America reinforcing the negative stereotypes of the French that had previously been planted by the doughboys and cultivated by the GIs of the immediate postwar years.

3

ELEVEN

The Worms Turn: 1962–72

In June 1961 thirty-one-year-old Jacqueline Bouvier returned in triumph to Paris, accompanying her husband, the recently inaugurated president John F. Kennedy, on his first official visit to Europe. She now put her familiarity with France to the most exquisite use. She dazzled the French with her style, her beauty, and, most impressive to them, her ability to speak French. She stroked her hosts' *amour-propre* by genuflecting to French supremacy in fashion: First, she had a French hairdresser transform her hairstyle. Then, at the formal welcoming dinner in Versailles' gilded Hall of Mirrors, instead of wearing the American-designed gown she was slated to wear, she appeared in a sensational number by Givenchy of Paris. Later, President Kennedy introduced himself to the smitten Paris press corps as "the man who accompanied Jacqueline Kennedy to Paris."[1] Two years later, in his travel guide to Europe, Temple Fielding credited her with being "the most charming catalyst in our rejuvenated bonds with *la belle France*," as a result of which the next year's welcome for American tourists "should be the most pleasant since World War II."[2]

But beauty and fashion count for little in power politics, and Kennedy's wife's triumph only served to camouflage a steady deterioration in political relations between the United States and France. President de Gaulle never forgot the humiliations inflicted upon him by the Allies during the war and was determined to free his country from subservience to American power. Although previous French governments had begun developing nuclear weapons, they had also welcomed the protection of the so-called American nuclear shield and had placed their NATO forces under American command. Now, much to the Americans' consternation, de Gaulle began creating an independent French nuclear force, arguing that it would ensure France's being treated as an equal by the Americans. By the time Kennedy was assassinated in November 1963, relations between the two powers were already rocky. They worsened considerably under his successor, Lyndon Johnson, who was not at all amenable to granting equal status to second-rate powers. De Gaulle in return thumbed his nose at Johnson by cozying up to American pariahs. He visited Fidel Castro in Cuba and extended a warm welcome to the Soviet leadership in Paris. He had France formally recognize the Communist government in China and criticized the deepening American involvement in Vietnam.[3] In June, recalling how he was excluded from the 1944 invasion of Normandy, he conspicuously absented himself when American, British, and Canadian dignitaries gathered there on the twentieth anniversary of the landing.[4] Then, with his own nuclear strike force finally in hand, he began withdrawing French forces from the American-dominated NATO command. In 1966 he made the break complete, asking that the Americans leave all of their bases in France. The last of them closed down in April 1967.

Yet, simultaneously, de Gaulle's government was working hard to attract American tourists. Ironically, this was in part a result of the Americanization of the French economy. The Marshall Plan had encouraged French businessmen to adopt American management techniques and use advertising to create mass markets.[5] By the late 1950s, the country noted for backward-looking peasants and penny-pinching small shopkeepers was boasting of technologically advanced industries turning out mass-produced consumer goods for a growing consumer market. The white-collar middle class expanded rapidly and small farmers left the land in droves. The flood of affordable consumer goods and a generous social welfare system helped provide a palpable rise in the standard of living of the working class.[6]

Much of this economic revolution had been spurred by an informal fraternity of young bureaucrats who had been rigorously trained in economics and administration at the new Ecole Nationale d'Administration. While Fourth Republic politicians played musical chairs in the cabinet, these young men had seized control of the higher reaches of the civil service and quietly set about modernizing French government and industry along efficient, technology-friendly lines. When de Gaulle came to power in 1958, he gave these young "technocrats" an even freer hand. To him, there was nothing wrong with France adopting American business techniques to help free itself from American economic domination.[7]

Many of the bureaucrats, such as the future president Georges Pompidou, were impressed by how foreign tourism had helped France's postwar recovery. They were determined that France should now modernize its tourist industries to profit from the new age of mass tourism that the jet age was expected to bring. In 1960 the proud de Gaulle presided over the launching of the beautiful new liner *France*, the impressive successor to the *Normandie*, but his cry of "Vive le *France*, vive la France" had hardly stopped echoing through the shipyard when Air France, the government-owned airline, began rendering the new ship obsolete by putting new American-made jets on the transatlantic run.[8]

The age of cheap jet travel did not arrive quickly or smoothly. The International Air Transport Association (IATA), which the airlines used to fix transatlantic fares, was wracked by conflicts over how to maintain high fares for locked-in business travelers while courting the tourist trade with lower prices. In the early 1960s, they began offering off-season "excursion fares" for as little as $369 round-trip between New York and Paris. They also gave steep discounts on regular season fares to members of organizations who traveled as a group—so-called "affinity groups." Fraternities, business groups, and alumni organizations were able to arrange two-week European tours after their American conventions or even to hold the meetings in Europe. Among the latter were a number of African American organizations, which were now freed from having to choose between meeting in dingy black hotels in the legally segregated South or being rebuffed by white hotels in the informally segregated North.[9]

Then, travel agents began assembling affinity groups of people who had nothing in common except a willingness to fly over and back in the same plane, and the airlines began grudgingly easing other restrictions on pricing.[10] By the end of the decade, two-week tours including airfare and hotel for less than four hundred dollars were making the trip to Europe affordable for a whole new stratum of middle-class Americans. In 1970 the airlines carried over 8 million transatlantic passengers, while only 252,000 crossed by sea.[11] The jets' speed and extended range also made for easier access to Europe by people who did not live near the East Coast, from where a disproportionate number of tourists to Europe had always come. By the mid-1970s, California was not far behind New York in the number of travelers heading for Europe.[12]

— —

The impressive increase in the number of American tourists able to travel to Europe, plus the fact that they were the most free spending of the foreign visitors in France, made them the prime targets for the French modernizers.[13] In 1959 the French government hired Doyle, Dayne, Bernbach, the most creative firm on Madison Avenue, as its American advertising agency. Its first ads warmed Gaullist hearts by portraying France as a modernizing country that was still full of Old World delights. One of them, showing the spa at Aix-les-Bains, said that Roman soldiers had "once eased their aches and pains (hence the city's name?) here. It's still a very good idea. Especially after a hard workout at the local discothèque."[14] British tourist officials now demanded that Ogilvy & Mather put more "fun" into the ads for their country, which Ogilvy admitted looked "stale" compared to the "first-rate" ones for France.[15]

The technocrats also tried to bring France's aging hotels up to American standards. In 1960, responding to reports that it was the offensive plumbing and lack of rooms with en suite toilets that were keeping American tourists from staying overnight anywhere but in Paris or the Riviera, the government began providing low-interest loans for hotels to upgrade themselves. In 1964 it issued new norms for classifying hotels that forced many of them to either modernize or close.[16] American and British hotel companies bought and renovated older hotels, adding new bathrooms and laying off staff, whose old-fashioned personalized service was thought to make the new middle-class American tourists feel uncomfortable.[17]

Still, the hotel situation continued to look retrograde, even on the luxury level. After seventy-two-year-old Gladys Pratt and her husband checked into Paris's upscale Hôtel de France et Choiseul in early May 1964, she wrote in her diary, "The hotel dates back to 1800, and the suite they allowed us to occupy the first night looked it."[18] The government, noting that not one new hotel had been built in Paris since before the war, now encouraged the construction of modern American-style hotels there. In 1966 it applauded the opening of the new Paris Hilton, which, unusually for France, featured large rooms with double beds, American plumbing, and air-conditioning. It had a steak house with waitresses dressed like cowgirls and, most welcome to tourists and businessmen, an American-style coffee shop for cooked breakfasts and quick lunches. Yet despite the government's efforts and subsidies, the French hotel industry seemed stuck very much in the past. By the summer of 1968, only 20 percent of France's hotel rooms had the en suite toilets that most Americans demanded for even entry-level accommodations.[19]

— —

French officialdom thus spent the 1960s watching in frustration as the rate of growth in American tourism to their country lagged behind its chief European rivals, especially Spain and Italy. In 1961 they responded to the so-called "crisis" in the tourist industry by appointing a new tourist chief, Jean Sainteny, who thought that much of the problem lay in the French reputation as sourpusses. He therefore launched the first of many campaigns to encourage them to be friendly to tourists. Doyle, Dayne, Bernbach backed this up with an ad showing a map of France with a smile engraved into it and bearing the large caption: "There's a big smile on the face of France!" The smaller print said, "If you haven't been in France for the past few years, you are in for some tremendous surprises. France has become young and strong again. Her people happy. . . . And in Paris—lighthearted, witty Paris—you find the gaiety of a people who are vital again, leading *again*."[20]

But the problem involved much more than the dearth of smiling French faces. More important were the persisting French views that American tourists were ripe for plucking. In November 1962 the prime minister's office took over direct responsibility for tourism and tried to eliminate much of the chiseling that infuriated American tourists.[21] It ordered restaurants and cabarets to inform tourists in advance of their policies regarding tipping. Those that added a service charge had to display it prominently on the menu. In those that did not, the amount of tips was to be left up to the customer and not, as was often the case, to the initiative of waiters. Dubious "extras," such as the hated "cover charge" for bread and table linen, were now to be included in the quoted price of fixed-price meals. Menus had to be displayed prominently outside each restaurant and nightspot, *and* they had to be the same ones used inside. The government also offered to pay 10 percent of the cost of refurbishing the toilets in modestly priced "tourist-category" restaurants.[22]

Alas, these measures accomplished little. In August 1963 a French reporter dressed himself in American-style clothes, put on sunglasses, slung a tourist's camera around his neck, and, affecting a midwestern twang, set off with an American woman posing as his wife to see how Parisians treated American tourists. At practically every turn, he met people who cheated him, insulted him, and demanded exorbitant tips. His peregrination turned into a veritable calvary of insolent waiters, scowling policemen, and people foisting unwanted champagne upon him. A taxi driver who refused to take him to Versailles slammed the door on his hand. The concierge of a historic Marais building whose picture he was taking jumped in front of his camera and demanded payment. More than thirty times in three days, he wrote, he endured "shabby and unpleasant" treatment, making him feel like a "pigeon" or "a cow to be milked." It was no wonder, he concluded, that tourists were flocking to Italy rather than France.[23]

Making matters worse was that those who did come to France spent less time there. *Time* magazine said they used Paris "as a touch-down point from which to go on to other European countries where the prices were fairer and the courtesy greater."[24] In September 1964, as the summer tourist season drew to a close, *Newsweek* gleefully reported, in a piece entitled "The Worm Turns," that occupancy rates in Paris hotels were down 15 percent and that the Riviera season had been called a "disaster." The reason, it said, was that "the foreign worm has turned. Exasperated by overpriced squalor in overcrowded hotels, by poor service and incomparable insolence from servants," more and more tourists were avoiding France. It gave as a typical example:

> The scene: a sidewalk café near the Champs-Elysées. A girl, obviously foreign, even more obviously American, asks for a *croque-monsieur* (grilled ham-and-cheese sandwich). Ten minutes later, the surly waiter produces one charred piece of toast covered with a stringy slice of ham. When the girl complains that it isn't what she ordered, he snarls: "Yes, it is." Asked for a napkin, he picks up a dirty one and drops it into the girl's lap. His 15 percent tip, of course, is already added to the bill, and when the girl complains to the owner, he shrugs: "*Qu'est-ce qu'on peut faire, alors?*"—What can you do?

Newsweek went on to tell of the Riviera hotel that not only charged a Texan for parking a nonexistent car but also, when he inquired why the cost of his room had risen overnight from twenty to thirty dollars, told him brusquely that it was because of a "price stabilization plan." "Such tales of shamelessness are endless among tourists who visit France these days," it said. "They range from the American painter who ordered a filet of sole in a Normandy restaurant and was charged double the menu price because the waiter decided the portion was large enough for two people, to an elderly lady who refused to pay 30 francs for a cab fare that registered 11.50 francs. The cabbie grabbed a 100-franc note from her hand and roared away."[25] Temple Fielding now added a warning to his guide's section on Paris nightclubs, saying:

> But let's never forget, for one minute here, that some of the most cold-blooded, ruthless poachers of the evening world have set you up as their top-priority target. You're nothing more than a big, fat, ripe American chump who will drink any rotgut with the "champagne" label, applaud any tired old bag *sans* her usually necessary brassière, and pay a triple King's Ransom for the "privilege."[26]

The economic repercussions of the crisis were exacerbated by changes in French vacation habits. Historically, they had stayed in France for their annual holidays. Now, large numbers of them were taking advantage of the strong franc and vacationing outside of France, especially in Spain and Italy.

The large tourist trade imbalance with the United States was now the only thing keeping the nation's tourist account in surplus. A parliamentary committee investigating the problem reported in 1964 that the poor state of French hotels remained the most important and "most delicate" concern, but "the welcome" was also a problem. The tourist industry merited the criticisms leveled at it on that score, it said, and "the behavior of a large number of our compatriots towards foreigners is not what it should be."[27]

The result was yet another campaign to have the French be nice to Americans. The National Campaign of Welcome and Friendliness stationed attractive young English-speaking women at information booths in airports and railroad stations. They were also put in post offices frequented by tourists. The glum postal workers behind the wickets were to be "inculcated with notions of applied psychology in order to make them understand the importance of a good welcome." In April 1965 hostesses began welcoming female tourists landing at Paris's Orly Airport, the main entry point for Americans, with a rose and a small flask of perfume. Every ten-thousandth one received a high-fashion sweater and each hundred-thousandth one was fitted for a dress by Chanel, Dior, Lanvin, or other *haut-couturiers*. Customs inspectors were told not to act like "agents of repression," and the police were told not to tow away tourists' cars. Tourists were given a book of *chèques-sourire* (smile-checks) to hand out as rewards for cheerful service. At the end of the tourist season, there would be huge television extravaganza to climax this "45 million smiles contest" where the fifty French workers with the most checks would be awarded a car, a holiday in Tahiti, or other such prizes.[28]

Some tourist officials were skeptical of these campaigns. "Parisians are born complainers," said one; "they don't even like each other, let alone tourists. The smile of a café waiter is more fleeting than a rose."[29] Nor were all Americans impressed. After being welcomed to France at Orly Airport by the secretary of tourism himself, a Los Angeles businessman said he doubted the campaign would change the French. However, he added, "it's nice to know they know they've been rude."[30] Yet the government persisted. In the summer of 1966, the tourism commission encouraged local chambers of commerce to organize "invite a foreigner for coffee" campaigns, where families would search out tourists in hotels and invite them home for coffee or tea.[31]

But the French reputation for surliness was too well established among Americans to be dissipated so easily. In 1968 a French study of foreign tourism said that one reason Americans had now become the worst tippers in Paris's expensive restaurants and nightclubs was that they were put off by the staffs' lack of courtesy (*"manque de amabilité"*).[32] A sign of the campaigns' limited effectiveness came that summer, when the first two restaurants opened on the *autoroutes*, the new high-speed expressways. A French schoolteacher reported hearing the manager of one of them berate a waitress for spending too much time trying to understand what some German customers wanted. Then, when an English-speaking couple asked where the toilet was, "he practically refused to tell them." He then turned to one of his new staff and said that these foreigners could "go stuff it."[33] The introductions to guidebooks to France now routinely included denials that the French were as rude and rapacious as Americans thought them to be. One said that perhaps the authors had always been well treated in France because their "love of France and the French people shows, perhaps it radiates from us and brings out the best in those we meet." Another suggested that tourists who arrived thinking that "they don't like us" and that "service is sullen and grasping" should "wipe the chip from their shoulders" and check what charges were legal before blowing up. They should "lean on those three pillars of good relations called *S'il vous plaît, Pardon,* and *Merci.*"[34]

— —

Ultimately, though, the Gaullists' "Be nice to Americans" campaigns ran into the stone wall of the general himself. It proved impossible to convince most Americans that his manifest anti-Americanism did not reflect the feelings of his co-citizens. Before World War II, American tourists were little concerned that their dollars might help shore up governments they did not like. But the cold war and the emerging age of mass tourism stimulated the idea that unfriendly regimes could be weakened by depriving them of American tourist dollars. In 1961 the government began prohibiting American tourist travel to Cuba, hoping that this would bring the Castro regime to its knees. Now, thanks to de Gaulle, France became the object of these kinds of pressures.

Matters came to a head in 1967. As the deadline for getting American troops out of France approached, there was an outpouring of stories in the American media portraying de Gaulle as incorrigibly anti-American. *Newsweek* headlined its story about fewer Americans visiting France that summer than the previous year "Gaullism Empties Bistros." "Almost without exception," it said, "France's restaurateurs, hotel men and shopkeepers blame de Gaulle's policies for the downturn." It quoted a Paris bartender as saying, "It's the politics of our cher general."[35] Carol Denis, an American woman who that year married a Frenchman and settled in Paris, recalled that her father refused to visit her there because "he had no use for de Gaulle."[36]

To make matters worse, de Gaulle shifted France, which had very close military ties with Israel, to a pro-Arab position in the Middle East. When war broke out there in October 1967, he declared an embargo on arms shipments to Israel. Although Israel still emerged successful, enraged American Jews condemned de Gaulle as anti-Semitic and called for boycotts of travel to France. A group of leading New York dress designers, "incensed by de Gaulle's anti-Semitism," planned a boycott of French couture and fabrics.[37] Sales of a dartboard with de Gaulle's picture soared.[38] None of this seemed to faze de Gaulle. In January 1969 he ordered a halt in French sales of new jet fighters to Israel and of replacement parts for the many French jets its air force already had. The American Jewish Congress, responding to what it called an "avalanche" of letters, announced it was canceling all trips to France and all flights on Air France.[39]

More worrisome to the French were American government attempts to discourage tourism to France. Its campaigns to encourage travel abroad to help its allies earn dollars had petered out in the late 1950s. In the early 1960s, with the balance of payments tilting in the wrong direction and the dollar weakening, it began mounting "See America First" campaigns.[40] In 1967, with the costs of the war in Vietnam and the welfare state mounting and the balance-of-payments deficit ballooning, it acted more forcefully to discourage foreign travel. France became a particular target after de Gaulle's government started exchanging its surplus dollars for the bars of gold bullion in U.S. government vaults that were thought to support the value of the dollar. Senator George Smathers of Florida declared that Americans "would not enrich de Gaulle's coffers" while he tried to corner the world's supply of gold and introduced a bill that would slap a head tax of $250 on Americans visiting France.[41] William Fulbright, the chairman of the Senate foreign relations committee, urged tourists to avoid Paris. Red-white-and-blue cards appeared saying, "DON'T GO TO EUROPE. See America First. But, If You Must Go Abroad, AVOID FRANCE, and Other USA Enemies."[42] On New Year's Day, 1968, President Lyndon Johnson asked Americans to limit "non-essential" foreign travel for two years and called on Congress to levy head taxes on Americans leaving the country and lower the limits on their duty-free purchases abroad. France was understood to be a major target.[43]

The press now reported that many Americans were canceling flights on Air France and voyages on the *France* and were omitting France entirely from their European travel itineraries.[44] *Le Monde* worried that Johnson's proposals "would surely deprive France of a large part of its richest, if not its most numerous tourists."[45] However, Congress could not be persuaded that de Gaulle's foreign policies were offensive enough to infringe on Americans' inherent right to go anywhere (in the non-Communist world) they wished and to shop where they wanted.[46] *Le Monde* reported with some relief that people in the American tourist industry assured it that, for the majority of travelers, "the principle of individual liberty" would prevail.[47] Yet, ominously, between January 1 and May 1968, the Paris Hilton received twenty-two thousand cancellations.[48]

———

Meanwhile, one of French tourism's historic mainstays, the idea that tourists would be improved by exposure to the high culture of the Old World, was steadily eroding. Indeed, arbiters of high culture had begun questioning Europe's historic role in civilizing touring Americans soon after the war ended.[49] Most dispiriting was watching Paris's reign as the capital of modern art come to end, for the years from 1937 to 1957 were, as Robert Hughes has said, "precisely the time when the queen city began, like some Venice of modernism, to slide into debility."[50] The School of Paris had been shattered by the war, and although there was much talk of reviving it after peace came, few of the younger French artists, or the foreigners who returned to the city, gained the international stature of the older generation.[51] Moreover, the Nazi occupation had destroyed the infrastructure of art dealers and collectors, many of them Jewish, who created and sustained the market for modern art.[52]

Some Americans were struck by Paris's artistic decline soon after the war. Cynthia Brants, a graphic artist from Texas, found the Musée d'Art Moderne's 1948 Autumn Salon—a showcase for modern French artists—deeply disappointing. The artists seemed to her to be mainly poor imitations of Picasso, Monet, and Bonnard. "We'd seen these pictures a thousand times over," she wrote in her diary. "I saw about four [good] pictures out of the entire exhibition which must have numbered 3 or 4 hundred."[53] The next February, stopping off in Paris again, she saw an exhibition of works by Bernard Buffet, "Paris's new 21-year-old genius who has been causing quite a stir." She was disappointed to find his works "empty . . . surely a boring sight."[54] That fall the artist Robert Gwathmey wrote his dealer in the States that even those rare works in the 1949 Autumn Salon that rose above the surrounding "mediocrity" were "not up to American standards." "French art has slipped," he said, "rather like the stunning beauty, overtaken by age and fallen victim of every beauty hint. A facade of perfume and cosmetics. . . . An old bag."[55]

French critics were of little help in bailing out the sinking ship, for they were mired either in Stalinist reverence for muscular social realism or in fealty to older forms of modernism. In America, on the other hand, critics, the media, and even the government began promoting the so-called New York school of abstract painting as the new direction for contemporary art, calling it the embodiment of American freedom of expression. In the early 1950s, an American artist visiting Paris wrote the "abstract expressionist" Jackson Pollock that "of the live painters still working in Europe (the well-known ones and figuring that Matisse is ½ dead) it seems to me that very little if any of their stuff is in a class with yours."[56] On her first visit to Paris in 1956, Pollock's wife, Lee Krasner, wrote him that the Louvre was "so overwhelming—beyond belief." However, the modern painting she saw in the Left Bank galleries was "unbelievably bad."[57]

By then, Paris's thriving community of American artists was dwindling. *Time* magazine, which, along with *Life*, relentlessly touted New York as the new capital of modern art, gleefully reported that disappointment with Paris was driving them home. It said that Lawrence Calcagno, one of the community's leaders, was moving back because he thought Paris was washed up as an art center and quoted him as saying, "In another hundred years [Paris] will be just another dead museum city."[58] Calcagno was infuriated by the piece, for he had told the reporter that he was returning for other reasons. However, nine years later, an artist friend visiting Paris wrote him confirming the wisdom of his move. "It's a great town for the old masters," the friend said, "but there doesn't seem to be much else doing."[59] Romare Bearden, who had been forced to leave Paris by financial difficulties in 1951, ended up coming to similar conclusions. On a return visit in 1960, he wrote a friend, "In going round the galleries I was appalled. Really bad stuff. . . . Nobody is trying anything new. . . . New York, at this time in history, is far more alive."[60]

The artist Larry Rivers summed up the change by saying, "Paris in 1950 was still an 'up' atmosphere. There was an enthusiasm for the whole scene, but after that . . . it shifted to New York . . . because of the painting. Nothing was happening there, and more was happening in New York; there was more money, and more interest. . . . The center changed; it was going the other way."[61] The final blow came in 1964, when Robert Rauschenberg, the American artist who opened the door to the new "pop art" movement, won first prize at the prestigious Venice Biennale show. Few would now challenge the boast of the head of the American delegation to the show that the world had now recognized that the center of modern art had shifted from Paris to New York.[62]

— —

France also more or less ceased being a magnet for those with a literary bent. By 1960 most of the young writers who had congregated in Paris had returned home. In 1963 one of them, Gay Talese, wrote that the "Tall Young Men" who in the 1950s had enjoyed the endless parties and the writing in Paris had now moved their parties, and the *Paris Review* office, to George Plimpton's apartment on New York's East Side. "Paris," he said, "is no longer the scene."[63]

American interest in French writers also declined. Saul Bellow thought this was due to the weakening of "the conviction that . . . the answers to life's great questions lay in Europe and its literature." Paris no longer inspired young Americans interested in the arts, literature, and ideas. "A huge force has lost its power over the imagination. This force began to weaken in the fifties and by the sixties it was entirely gone."[64] The writer and literary critic Edmund Wilson, who spent the winter of 1963 in Paris, wrote in his diary that the city "had now fallen back onto the map of a much flatter world, in which Washington and Boston and New York were centers at least as active as Paris; in which France and England seem comparatively supine, while the United States was energetic and aggressive. Paris is now almost a provincial city."[65] The year before, when the writer Lionel Abel returned to Paris after a ten-year absence, he found the city "emptier." It was no longer "a center of spiritual interest" or the "cultural capital" of the twentieth century.[66]

— —

Of course, most middle-class American tourists were hardly aficionados of modern art or avant-garde French literature, let alone French philosophy. To them, abstract art was something that was discussed mainly in regard to the popular question of whether young children, or chimpanzees, could have produced similar works. The words "French literature" were associated as much with "dirty books" as with Rimbaud or Cocteau. That the artistic flagships of high-cultural modernism were now anchored in New York meant little to them. Indeed, high culture itself meant little to them, even for the many lower-middle-brows who now found themselves in the upper-middle class.

At first glance this would seem to be rather curious, for in the past, newcomers trying to rise into higher American social circles would feel pressured to adopt at least some of the high-cultural tastes of those who had already ensconced there. However, by the second half of the twentieth century, these pressures were weakening. Movies, radio, consumer society, and the popular culture they promoted had been steadily burying class, regional, and other distinctions. By 1960 the tremendous leveling power of television, reaching 90 percent of American homes, had weighed in. Dominated by three major networks catering to the same mass audience with practically identical programming, it blurred the remaining distinctions between the "brow levels" even further.[67]

The triumph of a kind of mass culture that made few demands on the intellect helped marginalize an appreciation for high culture as a sign of distinction in America. Fine art, classical music, difficult literature, and other demanding art forms became the terrains of the remnants of the old social elites, some of the very rich who aspired to join them, and small coteries on college campuses. For the upper-middle-class Americans who had formerly been the ones most intent on improving their cultural standing, there was now little to be gained in terms of distinction by hacking their way down that trail. As a result, fewer American tourists now felt the old need to return from Europe as more "cultivated" people. A 1962 article on American tourists in Paris in the *New York Times Magazine* said, "Culture is a problem. . . . Let us admit it: of all tourists, the American is the one best preserved from the effects of culture . . . the one who makes the least attempt to hide or cure his ignorance."[68]

High culture's fall from grace was reflected in the best-selling guidebooks of the 1950s and 1960s. As we have seen, Clara Laughlin's *If You're Going to . . .* guides were popular in the prewar years because they abandoned the ponderous historical, architectural, and art historical details of guides such as Baedeker in favor of a chatty style that personalized history, art, and architecture. Now, the new favorites, Temple Fielding's *Travel Guide to Europe* and Arthur Frommer's *Europe on $5 a Day* dispensed with the cultural information almost completely. Although Fielding's was directed at the well-heeled and Frommer at the budget tourist, both concentrated almost wholly on practical advice on hotels, restaurants, and tipping.[69] Fielding said that there were only two kinds of guidebooks when he came out with his in 1946:

the Baedeker class which measured the monuments and counted the stained glass windows and the . . . Clara Laughlin class which extolled the picturesque native dancers and the sunsets over Ben Gay castle. But sightseeing was not my motivation. At each stop, which would be the decent hotels? Which would have bedbugs? Where could I find the best food and how could I avoid the tourist traps? Which nightclubs would show the most? How much should I tip?[70]

Similarly, Frommer's advice on what to see and do tended to be limited to how to see the famous sights cheaply. His main cultural thrust was to promise tourists that by staying in the inexpensive places his book recommended, they would experience the "real" Europe and get to meet Europeans. ("Never ask for a private bath with your hotel room," he advised. "Few Europeans regard a bath or shower as a daily necessity.") The problem, of course, was that a listing in Frommer's book almost inevitably made the places American hangouts.[71]

— —

The popular culture of the 1960s also reflected France's eclipse as a destination where one's life might be transformed. There were no more hit songs like "April in Paris" and "The Last Time I Saw Paris" to make one want to stroll along the Seine with a loved one. Rock 'n' roll, folk, and country music were firmly rooted in the American landscape. Rock music extolled drug trips rather than ocean ones. The movies stopped fueling Sabrina-like dreams of finding oneself, or the right person, on a holiday in France. The 1963 comedy *Irma la Douce*, which featured Jack Lemmon as an air-headed French cop and Shirley MacLaine as a lighthearted prostitute, was probably the last movie to portray the old stereotypes of Parisian gaiety and sexuality in the kind of amiable manner that would encourage tourism. The *Pink Panther* and *A Shot in the Dark*, both of which came out the next year, were a rather different kettle of fish. With Peter Sellers starring as the bumbling French policeman Inspector Clouseau, they ridiculed the French reputation for joie de vivre and sexuality. *A Shot in the Dark* opens with the usual shots of Paris's beauty and a soulful Edith Piaf–style song on the soundtrack.[72] However, it soon becomes apparent that this is a spoof of the notion of romantic France. It cuts to Herbert Lom, playing Clouseau's boss, speaking endearingly on the telephone to "my love." "I'll bring the cheese and Beaujolais. See you soon, my dear," he says as he hangs up. Then comes a buzz from his secretary, and "Your wife is on the line." The infidelity theme then becomes the source of a series of running gags throughout the ribald and thoroughly unromantic movie, until in the end it seems that everyone is having an affair with everyone else, but with ridiculous and disastrous consequences, particularly for Clouseau. The movie's success led to four more

Pink Panther movies, whose unflattering portrayals of France as populated by accident-prone bumblers and cuckolds were hardly the stuff to fuel traditional tourist reveries.

Nor was there much to attract tourists in the French "New Wave" films of the 1960s. Turned out by brilliant young directors such as François Truffaut and Jean-Luc Godard, they were often bleak black-and-white portrayals of life in contemporary France. One of the few color productions, Godard's *Weekend*, featured what had to be the longest, most infuriating traffic jam in movie history. At the end of the decade, Hollywood producers returned to France to make parts of *The French Connection* (1971). However, although there are a few attractive color shots of the Mediterranean coast, the movie's most memorable French characters are not lighthearted bon vivants like Maurice Chevalier but vicious drug smugglers.[73] Even France's reputation as a source for "dirty" books, postcards, and pictures was eroded, as de Gaulle's puritanical wife, Yvonne, forced the old man to ban and censor all sorts of erotic literature, films, and pictures.[74]

— —

What, then, were the new tourists of the 1960s looking for in France? Surveys indicated that American tourists to Europe wanted above all to see famous sights.[75] This included some high-cultural objects, but only those that were famous. A 1962 *New York Times Magazine* article, citing the *Oxford English Dictionary* definition of tourism as travel for pleasure or culture, said, "Translated into Paris terms [the American tourist] diet reads: Mona Lisa and Lido, Versailles and the Folies-Bergère. . . . Their culture is, at best, skin deep, the result of a box-office hit or best-seller."[76] In other words, the cultural component of the trip reflected mass culture's infatuation with celebrity: the *Mona Lisa* was on the list because it was a celebrity among art works—it was famous for being famous.

In June 1964 a disgusted Janet Flanner, the *New Yorker*'s longtime Paris correspondent, wrote her friend that her hotel now took in American tours:

> Amurricans who have never been to Yurrup before, of an appalling type for the most part, who yap like poodles, sit in the halls all day and on their paid-in-advance tour do two things—go to the Folies Bergère or some substitute and to the Lido. Maybe they have an hour in the Louvre, but I doubt it.[77]

But Flanner was being rather unfair, for the new kind of jet-age tourism hardly allowed for sufficient time to do much more than see Paris's famous sights and push on to the next famous place. Although the jets helped make trips to Europe affordable for a much broader segment of the middle class, most tourists still had only two or three weeks for vacations.[78] Also, most were first-time visitors, who were not at all sure whether this would not be a once-in-a-lifetime opportunity and were naturally intent on seeing as much of Europe as possible. One study showed that in 1948 most American tourists to Europe visited just three countries. By 1967–68, even though their average stay was half as long, more than half a dozen was the norm. Many would arrive by air and, thanks to improved highways, be taken on fourteen- or twenty-one-day organized tours whose frenetic pace could be little short of stupefying.[79]

Unescorted tourists naturally felt superior to such poor souls, especially after the nightmarish portrayal of a whirlwind bus tour of Europe in the zany movie *If It's Tuesday, This Must Be Belgium* (1969). However, a variety of travel discount plans also encouraged them not to tarry for long in one place. Under the system of Eurail passes, introduced in 1959 for sale exclusively to Americans, the national rail systems of thirteen countries offered unlimited first-class travel at flat rates for one, two, or three months on over 120,000 kilometers of their track.[80] It was a real bargain—as long as one kept moving. The longer one lingered in Paris, Rome, or Oslo, the less one saved. Then, in the mid-1960s, the airlines introduced a system of "optional stops," which allowed tourists to make as many stops as one wished in three weeks in Europe as long as one did not backtrack. One woman recalled buying a TWA return ticket from New York to Rome and going eastbound via Lisbon, Madrid, Barcelona, Nice, and Genoa, and returning to New York from Rome via Florence, Milan, Geneva, Paris, London, and Shannon. It was, she admitted, "a trip of which I have the blurriest recollection."[81]

It is no surprise, then, that most middle-class American visitors to Paris in the 1960s stayed only from two to four nights.[82] Taking into account the time spent checking into and out of hotels, transfers to and from train stations and airports (let alone "jet lag"), even four nights in Paris would translate into only three full days there, which would normally be taken up by a bus tour of the city's sights, a day trip to Versailles, and a day of shopping. Even for the small minority interested in high culture, there was hardly time for the Louvre or the Jeu de Paume. Yet most were satisfied with this, for their main object was just the highlights, just the celebrities. Most of the American tourists questioned at Paris's most popular tourist attractions in 1970 said they were happy with their visit, for their main objective was to see the world-famous sights.[83]

— —

By 1968, then, France, which began the decade in first place in the European competition for American tourists, was falling behind on a number of counts. The number of American tourists it welcomed each year had risen, to about 700,000, but not nearly as rapidly as other countries. Both Great Britain and Italy were now outdrawing it.[84] In 1961 a Gallup Poll had ranked France first among the European countries Americans would most like to visit. A 1968 poll ranked it fifth.[85] A French reporter said that one of the most worrisome things was that the richest Americans were deserting France, leaving a much larger proportion of the tourists from the more penny-pinching classes.[86]

The French blamed themselves—or, rather, other Frenchmen—for the problem. Surveys done in 1967 and 1968 showed there was widespread awareness of how crucial foreign tourism was to the economy and much concern over it falling off. Most blamed the problem on the hotels—their high prices and "lack of comfort." As for the much-discussed "welcome," while few people in tourist-dependent regions such as the Loire valley and the south thought it a problem in their areas, Parisians were very critical of their fellow Parisians.[87] Non-Parisians heartily agreed. A 1970 survey found that French tourists from the provinces were much more critical of the "indifferent" or even "disagreeable" welcome they received in Paris than Americans and other foreigners.[88]

By then, tourism to France had suffered two double blows. First, in early 1968, archrival Britain devalued the pound, making it a real bargain in comparison. Then, in May of that year, a huge wave of strikes, sit-ins, and demonstrations brought much of France to a grinding halt. It began with students occupying their overcrowded, underfunded universities, demanding a raft of changes ranging from the reasonable to the impossible. ("Be realistic, demand the impossible" was a favorite slogan.) When, inspired by romantic visions of nineteenth-century revolutionaries, they set up barricades in the streets of the Latin Quarter, tough, truncheon-wielding squads of riot police, the fearsome semi-military CRS (Compagnies Républicaines de Sécurité), descended on them, intent on bludgeoning them back into the real world. As tear gas wafted through the city center, the movement spread to secondary school students and workers—white and blue collar. Striking transportation workers brought the Métro, buses, train systems, and airlines to a halt. Orly Airport, the main gateway, was closed, and air traffic control over all of France was shut down, as were the seaports. Thousands of tourists were stranded, with no way to get out of France or back to the United States.[89]

Hundreds of American tourists made their way to the American Express office in Paris, where, their bags and pockets bulging with baguettes, sausages, and cheese, they camped out in the lobby, pleading for repatriation. "They looked like a bunch of Polish peasants," said the manager, somewhat condescendingly. Buses were chartered to take them to safety in Belgium, Luxembourg, or the Channel ports.[90] On the Riviera, Americans and other wealthy foreigners, fearful that revolution was on its way, paid outrageous fares for taxis to take them to Milan, Zurich, or anywhere else outside the explosive country.[91] Thousands of Americans planning to visit Europe quickly changed their plans to avoid France.[92] "What we are seeing," said the head of the American Society of Travel Agents, is "the final withdrawal of those few who want to go to France. The French attitude towards the dollar made most of them stay away. Now this trouble has put the icing on the cake."[93] The only Americans now visible on the streets of Paris were some young leftists eager to join in the revolutionary games.[94]

Finally, at the end of May, after disappearing for a day to ensure he had military support, de Gaulle went on TV to denounce the disruptions and to call for new elections for the legislature. A massive crowd assembled in Paris to support him, and the strikes began to crumble. The elections early that July resulted in a convincing victory for the Gaullist and other conservative opponents of the May movement. With the country back on the Gaullist rails, in mid-July millions of French departed for their usual four- or five-week vacations.

Still, American tourists remained leery of France, and especially Paris. "From the tourist point of view," the *New York Times* reported in late June, "Paris looks like a ghost town." Thomas Cook & Son's Paris office said that 75 percent of its bookings for July and August had been canceled, mainly by Americans. The government tried to revive the tourist trade by having the railways and French Line cut fares for foreigners by 20 percent. In mid-August the minister in charge of tourism announced that after the "accident" of "the events of May–June," the tourist season was again back on course.[95] Few Americans were reassured. Even in October, the artist Jack Levine arrived in Paris expecting to find a city still in turmoil. When he expressed surprise that the only signs of the chaos were graffiti-filled walls, he was told to expect "new uprisings" now that the students were back at school.[96] In the end, American tourism dropped 25 percent from the previous year, the greatest one-year drop ever.[97]

But by then the backlash against the May movement was well under way, and it would soon claim de Gaulle as a victim. The main thread linking the May movement's disparate groups had been the challenge to their kind of hierarchical system, run by technocrats, that de Gaulle and the other modernizers had created. In April 1969 he proposed constitutional changes to accommodate these demands for more public participation in policy making. When they were defeated in a referendum, he resigned and retired once again, for the last time, to his home in a small country town. That August, as another disappointing tourist season seriously eroded France's dollar earnings, his successors were forced to do what he had stubbornly resisted: they devalued the franc against the dollar.[98]

As Jack Levine's friends had predicted, riots continued to erupt sporadically on the Left Bank, but they hardly discouraged the revival of tourism. They were either suppressed too quickly by the CRS or became tourist attractions in themselves. In June 1970 Janet Flanner reported that a running conflict between the CRS and stone-throwing leftists served as "popular entertainment for the Paris nighthawks and a crowd of tourists, who trailed it faithfully, following its convulsions with the devotion of movie-gang-war experts for once seeing it like it is—except for no deaths, *mirabile dictu*."[99] Later in the decade, *Holiday* magazine's guide to France portrayed the riots as harmless entertainment. It said that Paris was the center of political activity, and "it is here where the great riots occur. . . . At the drop of a flaming epithet the streets will be filled with demonstrators who regard a semiviolent parade as something of a lark: it is the French equivalent of an American football rally."[100] On the other hand, I recall emerging from a Left Bank Métro station one day in 1978 and finding myself in the midst of one these conflicts. I must say that the terrifying sight of the CRS storming down boulevard Raspail mowing down everything in front of them hardly resembled any football rally I have ever seen.

TWELVE

"This Space Ship Is Going to Paris"

When Richard Nixon resigned as president of the United States on August 8, 1974, boarded a helicopter on the White House lawn, and flew off into political purgatory, it marked the climax of a period, lasting from about 1967 to 1976, during which much of the bravado and self-confidence for which Americans traveling abroad were famed dissipated. The Watergate scandal that drove Nixon from office had reinforced the mistrust of government that the uprisings of the 1960s helped foment. Although the New Left collapsed into a heap of self-destructive sects and the counterculture disappeared into a fog of drugs, American culture had absorbed two aspects of their messages. The first, from the New Left, was an antipathy toward large bureaucracies. The second, from the counterculture, was a modern form of romanticism that valued the emotions over the intellect and the individual over the group. This was manifested in everything from wacky California cults and therapies to the revival of evangelical religion, all of which called on individuals to establish a personal relationship with the divinity. The counterculture's rampant individualism also contributed to the rise of the New Right, which echoed the extreme individualism of the nineteenth-century heyday of unbridled capitalism.[1]

One consequence of the new individualism was a marked lowering of expectations from society and government. Not only did the political culture of the New Deal, which looked to government to help bring about the good life, seem futile and out-of-date, but the government now seemed powerless to control important events. There was shock and disbelief in 1971 when it was forced to devalue the dollar, which had been beleaguered by inflation. The media told of American tourists in Europe having to grovel to have their currency accepted. A beggar sitting outside the Sacré-Coeur Basilica in Montmartre was said to have posted a sign refusing to accept dollars.[2] More humiliation came on the heels of the 1973 Mideast war, when an Arab-led boycott sent oil prices soaring. Now the government seemed unable to even assure a supply of inexpensive gasoline, the commodity that had fueled the postwar suburban American dream. Soaring transatlantic airfares seemed to bring an end to hopes for a great new age of mass foreign tourism. *Forbes* declared it "the end of an era." "The schoolteacher from Iowa" would now think twice about flying to Rome, Italy, and might settle instead for a week with her sister in Rome, New York.[3]

Inflation hit Europe as well, forcing American tourists to contend with what the *New York Times* called "the diminishing almightiness of the American dollar." Hotel rooms in Paris in July 1973 cost twice what they did in 1971. One joke making the rounds had a tourist standing with a European friend outside a store window in Paris or Vienna saying, "Look, your inflation isn't so bad. The tag on that pair of trousers is only, uh, $42, and the one on that jacket would be $45," to which the European replies, "But this is a dry cleaners."[4] When Western Europeans began blaming a recession that followed in 1974 on the United States' wasteful energy policies, American youths traveling there began sewing Canadian flags on their backpacks.

As *Forbes* predicted, the slumping dollar led to a steep drop-off in American travel abroad. The number of Americans visiting Europe sank by 20 percent between 1973 and 1975. "Look around and see how many Americans you can spot!" the man presiding over the restaurant in the Eiffel Tower said to a *Time* reporter. "None!" Only the very rich seemed to be arriving at the same pace as before.[5] A young couple interviewed in July in the Tuileries Gardens said, "It is depressing to think that the Arabs are the only ones who will be able to buy anything."[6] The dollar, and tourism, recovered in 1976, but in late 1979 and 1980 the currency plunged again, causing more cutbacks in spending abroad.[7]

Each time the dollar fell, observers would note that American tourists abroad were more subdued than before. Demands to have their bills presented in "real money" were said to have tailed off. "They argue over checks less often," said Jean Bruel, owner of the Bateaux Mouches, whose sightseeing boats did dinner cruises on the Seine. "They now ask you if you speak English before they talk to you in English."[8] A rather Pollyannaish American traveling in France with his family after the 1978 plunge said the weak dollar actually made them feel more comfortable. "We no longer stick out as rich Americans," he said. "The old resentment toward the foreigners with money to throw away has vanished." A French acquaintance agreed, saying, "Things are more in balance and it's better that way."[9] In 1981, after the greenback had recovered, a Londoner told a reporter, "I found Americans a lot nicer when the dollar was down. Before that, they wore those plaid Bermuda shorts that were almost as loud as their voices. In the last couple of years their voices have not seemed as loud."[10]

At the same time, whenever the dollar, and American tourism, suffered a setback, American reporters would discern what *Time* magazine in 1975 called "a refreshing return of the old-fashioned *politesse* on the part of hoteliers, waiters and shopkeepers, who are collectively crying, 'Yankee, come back!'"[11] The next year a *U.S. News & World Report* editor returned from a two-week auto tour of northern France reporting that the rude Frenchman was "a vanishing breed." Salespeople were "not only courteous but amazingly patient in their efforts to understand high-school French and frantic gestures." Even French drivers were courteous, he said.[12] A man traveling with his family in the winter of 1978 wrote of their happy experiences with French service personnel. "At every hotel," he said, "the employees behind the desk were quick to check on museum hours for us, draw maps when we asked directions and make phone calls to our next stop to reserve rooms."[13]

The dollar and tourism marched upward together from 1981 until the summer of 1985, when the dollar that had bought 4.35 francs in 1980 was worth nearly 10 francs. A cover story in *Time* now proclaimed, "MILLIONS GO ABROAD ON THE GREATEST SIGHT-SEEING AND SHOPPING SPREE EVER." A Boston travel agent predicted, "Europe is going to sink under the sheer weight of American tourists." Tour operators reported that so many clients were arriving with extra empty suitcases, to be filled for the return trip home, that there was hardly enough room in the buses for all the luggage.[14] The next year, though, the roller coaster plunged again, and the dollar's drop caused yet another falloff in American tourism. Once again the media told of friendlier Frenchmen. The *Herald Tribune* said "the formerly snooty natives" in Paris's luxury trades "have turned friendly." It quoted one Frenchman as saying, "It has taken away their arrogance."[15]

But the diminishing arrogance was actually part of a long-term process. By the 1970s there was a widespread recognition that a large number of French people's jobs were either wholly or partially dependent on foreign tourism, and that Americans remained an essential ingredient in it. Although the proportion of France's tourist earnings provided by Americans dropped from the two-fifths it had been throughout most of the 1960s to one-fifth in the mid-1970s, individually, Americans remained among the biggest spending of the tourists.[16] The Germans outnumbered them but were much more thrifty. In 1975 the average American tourist spent two and a half times as much per day as the Germans, many of whom arrived with sleeping bags and tents.[17] So, each time American tourism dropped, alarmed French government officials would remind the public of its importance to their economy.[18] Moreover, despite the mid-decade stumble, American travel to Europe, and France, continued to rise in the 1970s and picked up more steam in the 1980s.[19] By 1987, after the dollar had recovered from its latest plunge, France was welcoming (although the term was still debatable) close to 2 million American tourists a year.[20]

— —

By then, the wholesale change in America's political/economic landscape was profoundly affecting tourism to France. During Nixon's presidency, the political power balance had begun tilting dramatically toward the South and Southwest, where a new combination of populism and conservatism coexisted comfortably in a rejuvenated Republican Party. Then the economic landscape was transformed by a new breed of entrepreneurs who oversaw the migration of much of the country's industry southward and overseas, turning parts of the Northeast and Midwest into a desolate "Rust Belt." This politico-economic shift helped erode the cultural influence of two of the groups who had historically been at the core of cultural Francophilia—the old eastern Republican financial and social elite and the liberal Democrat intellectual elite.

The new Sun Belt movers and shakers were not from circles that historically had regarded travel to France as part of the process of acquiring good taste and sophistication. As we have seen, in the 1930s Franklin D. Roosevelt, a Harvard graduate whose social pedigree stretched back centuries, sent his children to travel to France, as he had done, to imbibe its language and culture. (He spoke French fluently.) George W. Bush, scion of another old-line eastern family, was a different story. His father had moved from Connecticut to Texas to join the emerging Southwest power elite, and when George W. went to Yale in the late 1960s, not only did he not take the traditional Ivy Leaguer's trip to Europe; he did not travel abroad at all. A Republican congressman from Connecticut commented, "That's mind-boggling for someone from this district, especially considering his family background."[21] However, the congressman should not have been so surprised, for Europe, and the kind of culture it represented, was hardly on the radar screen of the new elites with whom the Bushes had cast their lot.

— —

Bush's failure to take the trip to Europe is all the more striking because he was in college when young people's travel to Europe boomed. In the early 1960s, the airlines began enticing them to Europe with student discounts. By 1963 almost one in five American tourists to Europe were under twenty-four.[22] A 1965 survey found that 11 percent of college students had already been to Europe, 8 percent of them to France.[23] In 1968 a travel industry journal called the "youth movement" in international travel one of the travel industry's most notable features.[24] By the early 1970s, the average age of American visitors had plummeted since the 1950s, when middle-aged and older tourists had predominated.[25]

Although many of the youngest of the new tourists arrived in group tours, the most noticeable upsurge came from young people traveling unescorted. A former director of the Classrooms Abroad program, which escorted students aged eighteen to twenty-four around France in a program of touring and learning, recalled how in the early 1960s doting parents would accompany their offspring to the departure point in New York City, alerting the guides to such things as their food likes and dislikes. In 1968, however, he saw a complete change. Only half as many young people applied for the program, and those who did showed up alone, without parents. The next year the number of groups was down from four to one, and they were mainly high school students. College students now wanted to strike out on their own.[26]

Their ability to do so was given a boost in mid-1971 when the scheduled transatlantic airlines began introducing very cheap student fares—$220 round-trip—to compete with low charter fares. This contributed to a massive influx of under-thirties.[27] With their backpacks, sleeping bags, hiking boots, and all-weather outerwear, these shaggy-looking specimens were a marked contrast to the traditional image of the American tourist. The changing face—literally—of youthful tourism was reflected at the elegant American Express office on rue Scribe. In the summer of 1952, the company had enlarged the public bathroom adjacent to the marble lobby so that young American hikers and cyclists could have more space to shave and clean up. It was worth the expense, the company said, because they represented "the future executives and wives of executives of America."[28] By 1962, however, young people's falling standards of dress were setting Amex executives to worrying about how this "'beatnik' element" (their term) was affecting its image.[29] By the end of decade, "the 'beatnik' element" was looking positively spiffy in retrospect. Each summer, said a travel guide author, the rails and roads of Europe were "a sea of blue jeans, sweatshirts, backpacks and beards."[30] Now the Amex lobby was packed with scruffy, longhaired, hippie-looking youths, with flowers and peace symbols embroidered on their tattered shirts and jeans—few of whom seemed interested in shaving and cleaning up. Randy Garrett, a young man who dealt in the unofficial used-car market there, recalled that the young tourists, staying in places with "old holes in the floor," were drawn there by the toilets. The street outside the building, he said, became a "vast flea market" and a "nonstop party," a swirling three-ring circus of unofficial commerce where one could buy everything from beads and headbands to used cars and drugs.[31]

The changing nature of young people's tourism was reflected in *Mademoiselle*, a magazine aimed at young women. In 1964 it ran piece called "Where the Action Is in Europe" that assumed readers were traveling with full wallets and impressive wardrobes. It recommended going to exclusive Paris nightspots and discotheques patronized by wealthy jet-setters and to the casino in Biarritz, where "you'll find Spaniards, English, and French 30–40-year-olds in Chanels and Balenciagas."[32] In 1972, on the other hand, it said traveling on a shoestring was now the thing to do. Although traveling in "Europe on Five Dollars a Day" was already an impossibility for adults, students were trying—even competing with one another—to do Europe on half that price.[33] The year before, a *New York Times* reporter leaving Strasbourg picked up three young hitchhikers from California who had spent practically nothing since leaving London. They lived on chocolate bars and the occasional cheap meal and slept in youth hostels for two dollars a night or under the stars. "We'll be three months on the road," said one, "and so far it's been great."[34]

— —

Aside from the American Express office, young people in Paris gravitated to the raffish Latin Quarter, in the 5th arrondissement, which most of the young Americans polled in the summer of 1970 said was their favorite part of Paris.[35] There, said the 1968 *Pan Am's Young Traveler's Guide*,

> everywhere, overflowing into the sidewalks into the streets, are students, young people, and more students. At any hour. It's the young people from the 5th who live and love with such abandon who . . . welcome newcomers who're not out to impress anyone . . . who relax . . . with an exuberance that sets off explosions felt all over Paris, all over France. It's all in the 5th—that's WHERE THE FUN IS![36]

Yet, in fact, France was no longer a special destination for young Americans. Its historic reputation as a place where Americans could immerse themselves in a more civilized environment meant little to them. Its renown for allowing personal and creative freedom to bloom was even further from their horizons. And the kind of fun they were seeking was readily available all over Europe, and in much of the United States as well.

One reason for France's fall from grace among the young was that it played almost no role in the new pop culture that was now central to many

Young tourists waiting in Marseille harbor for a boat to North Africa, where drugs were much more accessible than in France, in 1978. Courtesy of Roger-Viollet.

of their lives. Its popular music was derivative and incomprehensible (the writer Mavis Gallant called it "asthmatic" and "consistently frail"),[37] and few young Americans were interested in the Left Bank *caves* featuring jazz and people playing acoustic guitars.[38] Its young people's clothing was non-descript, and its official attitude toward "soft" drugs was too tough.[39] Amsterdam, where great clouds of pot smoke perfumed warm summer evenings, was far more enticing in terms of "getting high." Morocco and India beckoned those who were more serious about drugs. "Swinging" London, home of great rock music, miniskirts, and outlandish Carnaby Street clothing, held many more attractions.[40] *Pan Am's Young Traveler's Guide* said, "Britannia's mini-skirted granddaughter has lit a fuse under this stony-featured *grande dame* and the whole world has done a double take on England. Put this down to the emergence of Youth." All that the section on France seemed to offer were Left Bank cafés where students did little but talk or stare into each other's eyes.[41]

As for freely available sex, the sexual revolution of the 1960s had moved America much closer to France on that score. Although, as was usually the case in the pre-AIDS era, young people still felt freer to seek out sexual encounters when they were abroad, language barriers usually limited these to other English-speaking tourists. Indeed, if anything, it was too easy to meet other Americans there. In a 1971 article entitled "On the Champs-Elysées: 'Hey Aren't You the Girl Who Sits Across from Me in Abnormal Psych?'" Paul Goldberger, then a twenty-year-old Yale student, wrote of running into one friend from Yale at Chartres, another in the Paris Métro, and, the next day, seeing a friend from high school on the Champs-Elysées. One student suggested that Europe was a better place to meet fellow Americans than home.[42]

The diary of twenty-year-old Rita Roberts, a Canadian student, records what was probably a typical stay there. She and her friend Linda arrived there in July 1981, dragged their suitcases through the Métro, and managed to find the hostel they had been told about. The two went out for a "delicious" dinner at a cheap restaurant, washed down by lots of wine, and then stopped at a café for more wine. Linda "was drunk" and they "walked home and crawled into bed." The next day was a Sunday, and because the stores were closed, they were forced to sightsee. This meant looking at "the Louvre, Eiffel Tower, Seine River, and most of the common sights." They had thought they would be spending Sunday night by themselves, but, wrote Rita, "BOY were we wrong!" At the hostel they met two young Englishmen, one of whom was "a character out of Monty Python," and two Americans, including "Joe" from Louisiana. They all went out for dinner and more wine then "walked down the streets of Paris on a Sunday night. It was alive, with people, clubs, restaurants, unbelievable. We found a cheap bar and had [a] few rounds there. What a circus."[43] When the bar closed, they went to the Eiffel Tower "to pick up somebody's car and [then] drove around." What happened after is unclear, but Rita concluded:

> This Joe, a really sweet guy, was a bit pissed. . . . He wasn't used to all that drinking. It was quite a funny evening. I rolled in about 5:00 am I think. I was just as drunk. . . . Linda saw me come in and didn't give me the 3rd degree. She was pissed too and just as guilty. Weren't you? I crawled up to bed and passed out.[44]

Although driving drunk under the Eiffel Tower must certainly have added a distinctive note, encounters such as this were just as likely to take place in London, Rome, or Amsterdam as in Paris. There is no indication that the young people were at all inspired by the old ideas of the romance of Paris. Indeed, if anything, Paris now seemed old-fashioned and, well . . . just old in this regard. In a 1961 Gallup Poll, France had come out on top by far as the European country young Americans would most like to visit.[45] In the summer of 1971, the *New York Times* ran a series on European cities that were "meccas for young American tourists this summer." They included London, Copenhagen, and Amsterdam, but not Paris.[46] In London a "blond, cheerfully disheveled 18-year-old" from Long Beach, California, told a reporter that his next stop was Copenhagen. Asked why, he replied, "Well, it's groovy, I guess. . . . I've been to Turkey, Iran, Afghanistan and India. I'm washed out. I'm going home, but first I'm off to Amsterdam and then Copenhagen." There was no mention of Paris.[47]

— —

What, then, aside from the hopes of encountering other people their age, impelled so many of these young people to go to France? As Rita's diary would indicate, conventional sightseeing was hardly the main draw. Indeed, sightseeing often made teenagers traveling with their parents sullen and rebellious, rather than grateful for the experience. Russell Baker's teenaged son grudgingly accompanied his parents into the Louvre, but commented that the Venus de Milo was "terribly fat" and dismissed the *Mona Lisa* with, "I don't see what the fuss is about."[48] Thirty-odd years after the event, my neighbor Martin Johns still recalled with disappointment how his two teenaged daughters absolutely refused to enter the Louvre or Chartres Cathedral. They were more interested, they said, in sitting outside and watching the passersby.[49]

As they sat on the steps of the Louvre, they must have envied the crowds of backpacking teenagers passing before them having *real* foreign experiences—ones that did not include sightseeing. One reason these members of what Tom Wolfe called the "Me Generation" slighted sightseeing was that they tended to see foreign travel in terms of the central goal of the 1970s zeitgeist: personal development. This they thought came from encountering different people, such as Rita's Monty Pythonesque Englishman and Joe from Louisiana, and undergoing challenging experiences, such as struggling through the Métro and searching out a hostel with only a modicum of French at their disposal. "Nowadays," said the introduction to a guidebook to Europe for young people, "aware people are traveling to see more than just sights, they are traveling to feel and soak up a foreign culture."[50] Young people's group tours were now structured to avoid sightseeing, offering outdoor activities instead.[51] Randy Garrett still recalls fondly how in the 1970s, "an era of free love," young American tourists would meet at his barbecue stand and sign up for tours of France in his rickety "Magic Bus." Its name, which echoed the West Coast writer Ken Kesey's famed LSD-fueled Magical Mystery Tour, hardly promised a conventional sightseeing trip.[52]

— —

Of course, there were still young people who were seduced by France's traditional charms. Paris was the first stop on what David McFarlane, a recent graduate of University of Toronto, intended to be a year of backpacking and youth-hosteling around Europe. He found himself there only because the cheapest airline ticket took him there and included three nights at a downscale hotel. Many years later, he recalled that on this, his "first encounter with a truly great city," he "pounded around the streets, boggle-eyed." He ended up abandoning his planned tour and stayed for the next eight months in this "exciting and surprising city . . . a city where people stayed up late and did interesting things and experienced first-rate works of art. It was a city where the food and wine were good, and restaurants were everywhere, and people seemed to know how to take full advantage of the pleasures of being alive. It was a revelation."[53] In 1978 Carol Mongo, a young woman from Detroit, also went to Paris on what she intended to be a short visit. She was booked into a cheap hotel whose doors, she was disappointed to discover, closed at 1:00 AM. However, she found a nearby discotheque that opened at 12:30 AM and stayed open until 6:00 AM, by which time the hotel had opened its doors again. "There were "mobs of people there," she said, "who didn't pair off." She recalled being "totally seduced by the city. There were so many more things to do in all aspects of the arts. It was like being in high school. . . . Guys just wanted to show you around the city."[54] She ended up moving there and becoming part of its arts and fashion scene.

The international youth culture that Roberts, Mongo, and the others were part of seemed to reflect the informal, egalitarian norms that many Europeans thought were the most attractive thing about American youth culture. Indeed, there was a common perception, at least among young Americans, that Europeans thought more highly of these disheveled young folk than they did of their wealthier, better-scrubbed elders. The *New York Times* said a clergyman who ran a youth hostel in Paris called them "adventuresome wanderers in search of something they have not yet found—good natured, carefree."[55] A 1971 guidebook for young Americans quoted the director of the Alliance Française in Paris as saying, "I think most Europeans generally like the young American tourists better than the older tourists. The young people are more friendly and natural. They are less snobbish and arrogant."[56] In 1973 the *Underground Travel Guide* advised young people traveling on a shoestring that anti-Americanism was directed, not at them, but at the richer American tourists and GIs.[57] However, young Americans trying to strike up friendships with the French would be rudely awakened to the fact that, unlike Americans, they often do not react well to strangers trying to engage them in conversations. Carol Mongo recalled how, before her first visit to France in 1975, she took a two-month crash course in French and "fantasized about meeting French people and being invited to their homes." She was crestfallen when, on trying to speak to Frenchwomen on trains, she "was suspected of being a lesbian, and given the cold shoulder."[58]

— —

Remarkably, as the 1970s drew on, many of the differences between the older and younger tourists began to blur. In the mid-1970s, as the baby boom generation reached their late twenties and thirties, the major purveyors of consumer culture and products, transfixed by the enormous amounts of disposable income in their pockets, catered assiduously to their tastes and needs. Many older people were also influenced by these marketing efforts, leading to an unusual situation. Previously, as young people aged, they would acquire many of the tastes of the older generation that occupied society's commanding heights. Now quite the reverse was happening: older people were adopting the cultural trappings of the young. Middle-aged people who were at the height of their earning power, when they should have been calling the cultural shots, now followed the lead of the people in their twenties.

The effects of this were readily apparent in the tourist centers of Europe. One of the most enduring of the counterculture's calls was the admonition that one should dress for comfort, rather than style.[59] Older male tourists now abandoned their checked sports jackets and plaid pants in favor of even more informal outfits, such as polo shirts, blue jeans, and shorts—clothes that middle-class, middle-aged Europeans considered inappropriate in urban settings. Women abandoned girdles and exchanged light dresses for tight pants on inappropriate bodies. Carol Mongo recalled being appalled and embarrassed. Not only were the tourists loud and boisterous, she said; "you used to see old ladies in stretch pants."[60] Soon, sneakers became ubiquitous, on men and women, including in some of the most formal restaurants.

Many of the middle-aged tourists were also inspired by the kind of drive for "self-actualization," originating among the young, which Christopher Lasch called the "Culture of Narcissism." Upper-middle-class Americans in particular now searched for happiness by probing ever deeper into their own selves, following a panoply of therapies and ideas that promised to bring well-being through self-absorption.[61] Like the young, they hoped overseas travel would provide the opportunity to learn, not about others, but about themselves. Unscripted personal experiences would liberate one's inner nature. In June 1970 *Holiday* magazine's European travel number began, "Museums and cathedrals are not the sure-fire hit they once were with American tourists." The days when they "regarded Europe as a museum" and were "content to be spectators" were over, it said. Now tourists arrived "determined to participate in European life, not observe it from a discreet distance. . . . The key words are join the fun."[62]

Over the next two decades, the tourists' greater readiness to have unplanned encounters was reflected in the declining proportion of them taking escorted group tours. By 1982 less than 15 percent of Americans arrived in France in such groups. In 1989 the proportion was down to only 6.6 percent. Of course, language difficulties meant that one could not leave the most important things—especially lodging—to chance encounters. Only 18 percent organized their trips by themselves. The large majority—about 80 percent—still arrived with lodging and touring arranged by travel agents or airlines.[63] But it was now mainly the youngest, and the oldest, who took the old "If it's Tuesday, this must be Belgium" tours.[64]

— —

Changes in the French tourist industry helped make individual unescorted tours less challenging. Madame Hamer, the French tour operator, recalled that by the mid-1970s accommodations in most of the country had improved considerably, meaning mainly that there were now many places whose plumbing met minimal American standards. Food was also less of a problem. The French, she said, had begun to eat "more like Americans," and the hotels and restaurants at which the Americans ate had learned to prepare the kind of food that Americans liked. ("They say they want French food but they really don't," she said.)[65] A group tour leader checking his clients into a Holiday Inn told them, "Americans want American-style hotels and American-style food, so that is what you get."[66]

Also, by the 1980s more of the French people dealing with Americans spoke some English. This was increasingly necessary, not only because of the decline of escorted tours, but also because, as Hamer noted, fewer American tourists spoke French.[67] In 1970, 21 percent of the American tourists interviewed at Paris tourist sites said they could speak some French, and 32 percent said they could understand it.[68] Although these were individual, not group, tourists and "understand" has varying meanings, it was still quite a high number. It is unlikely such figures will be seen again. Since then, French-language training has declined steadily in the United States. In 1975 Spanish overtook French as the most popular second language taught in American high schools, and between 1968 and 1990 enrollment in university French courses dropped by about 68 percent.[69] By the 1980s, said Theodore Zeldin, there was probably no Western country in which the French language was less spoken or less appreciated than in the United States.[70]

— —

But if anything, unfamiliarity with the language was no problem to the many tourists who now believed that stumbling through situations without comprehending what was happening around them could still be an educational, culturally uplifting experience. In 1973, 35 percent of American tourists surveyed said that their main motive in traveling to Europe was the trip's "cultural/educational/historical benefits." The surveyors said the next 25 percent, who were the most affluent group, wanted "the cultural/educational benefits of a European trip, but additionally they have high interest in eating/buying/consuming." Only 17 percent—mainly younger males—admitted to being little concerned with culture and history and were mainly interested in "looking to meet young people of their own background."[71]

At first it might seem that high-cultural tourism had made a surprising comeback. The pollsters even labeled the first group "Classic Culture Seekers." But they, and those in the second group ("Culture-Cum-Pleasure Tourists"), had little in common with the previous generations of tourists who sought to imbibe European high culture. A sociological study in the 1980s reported that, unlike earlier generations of nouveaux riches, few new entrants into the upper-middle class "seem to view command of high culture as an important high status signal." Instead, for them culture was part of the quest for self-actualization—the process of developing one's potential by exposing oneself to a variety of experiences. One traveled, not to become more knowledgeable about art, architecture, music, history, or literature, but to "widen one's horizons."[72]

Although in the 1970s many tourists may have taken this to mean exposing themselves to new and unfamiliar situations, by the 1980s this had again been generally reduced to seeing famous sights. A French engineer interviewed in the 1980s said that when his upper-middle-class American acquaintances visited France, they were only interested in the most superficial and stereotypical sights. "They want to take pictures, to be able to say they saw the Eiffel Tower. They are not very curious about [societal] differences."[73] An official from the U.S. Office of Tourism warned a European tourism conference in France that a concern for "general culture" was absent in the education of the average American tourist, who had only the most superficial knowledge of most aspects of culture. However, he said, the tourist was used to being instructed and was willing to turn his European tour into "an educational experience."[74]

Given this cultural void, conventional sightseeing was about the only thing that would provide this kind of experience, and Americans took to it with gusto. They continued to list it as their number one reason for visiting France. Almost 80 percent of the American tourists surveyed in the late 1980s (much more than any other nationality) cited France's museums and historic sights as the main reason for their visits.[75] They also seemed more committed to sightseeing in practice than other foreigners. Most of them (over 60 percent) visited only Paris, where most of the famous sights are (Europeans flocked to the seaside and ski resorts), and they formed a disproportionally large percentage of visitors at the major "monuments" such as the Eiffel Tower, Notre-Dame, and the Conciergerie.[76] There was no concern over these places being "touristy." Instead, as a woman at the Eiffel Tower cheerfully replied when asked why she was there, "Are you kidding? It's because we're *tourists*." Or, as a man responded, "It's the tourist thing to do."[77]

At the same time, they gave short shrift to the hundreds of other French museums, monuments, and sights that were of great cultural and historical interest but were not on the conventional Top 10 lists. In 1986 the ministry in charge of monuments and sites, which was pouring millions into restoring provincial museums and historic sites, lamented that although the number of foreign visitors at the Paris crowd-pleasers, Versailles, and the châteaux of the Loire was satisfactory, "for all the others, it is a desert."[78] But for most tourists, visits to the desert are disorienting and uncomfortable, whereas seeing the famous sights is reassuring. As two sociologists concluded in 1976, travelers abroad are "temporary strangers" who must find ways of managing unfamiliar territory. Seeing well-known landmarks such as the Eiffel Tower and Arc de Triomphe, which they are familiar with from the many images they have seen, is comforting and eases these feelings of strangeness.[79]

— —

There was no indication in the 1970s surveys that significant numbers of Americans were searching for the sexy old Paris. Thanks in large part to the sexual revolution, France had lost the special allure that had drawn successive generations of sex-hungry American men to it. As the head of the *New York Times* bureau said in 1979, "There is really nothing . . . naughtier that Paris can offer visitors . . . than is offered in New York, San Francisco, Copenhagen, Düsseldorf, Tokyo and points in between."[80] The Moulin Rouge and Casino de Paris struggled to stay open. The Folies Bergère became a boring series of naked tableaux, patronized mainly by busloads of "Paris by Night" tourists on their way to Montmartre. In 1974 the French government persuaded the actress Brigitte Bardot, the quintessential "sex kitten," to do a television commercial inviting Americans to come to France, where "you too will feel at home," but any other notions of trying to restore France's sexy image seem to have stopped there.[81] The fact was that it would have been a losing cause, especially among men. Henceforth, it would be mainly American women who were inspired by France's historic image as a sexy, romantic place to visit.

The sybaritic Riviera, on the other hand, staged a bit of a comeback, albeit not as a particularly sexy destination. It had lost much of its luxury luster in the 1960s, as each summer the narrow strip of coast was inundated by larger and larger mobs of European group tourists and campers. In 1966 *The Rich Man's Guide to Europe* said it was "being shunned more and more by sophisticated visitors. . . . The rag trade has superseded the aristocracy. Groups and packaged-deal holidays have caused villa owners and the prewar regulars to look further afield—the Greek Islands, Portugal, the Costa del Sol, Lebanon, anywhere to find a little privacy. The miles of yellow tented campings have spread along the coast like a national epidemic of jaundice."[82] In the 1970s, however, the downscaling was halted. Campers and campgrounds were forced into more unobtrusive areas, and developers began putting up modern luxury apartments, hotels, and villas in practically every nook and cranny of the coast. A new type of tourist was encouraged, particularly in the off-season: business and professional people who took advantage of international conferences to do some touring.[83] In 1972 the New York cardiologist Louis Bishop, now age seventy-one, returned to France with his wife for a medical conference. They spent their first days in Paris and then hired a chauffeur who drove them south to the conference in Aix-en-Provence. His diary for the four days there mentions much eating, drinking, and sightseeing, but nothing about the conference. They were then driven to Cannes, where, appropriately for a cardiologist, they spent much of their time taking long walks through the hilly streets and along the Croisette, the famous seaside promenade.[84] In the years thereafter, Nice and Monte Carlo became the venues for many more international professional conventions. Indeed, in the late 1970s and 1980s, as sending employees to international congresses became a huge tax-deductible way for companies to reward them, France came to occupy second place in the world in terms of attendance at congresses, and Paris ranked number one.[85]

— —

The high-tech and professional American visitors blended in well in France, for in many respects it was now headed down the American road toward becoming a modern mass-consumer society in which technology and professionalism played leading roles. Both the Gaullists and the Socialists, who began alternating in power with them in the 1980s, tried to calm the fears of intellectuals on both the Left and Right that France would be swamped by the kind of mass-cultural "rubbish" that had accompanied the rise of the consumer economy in America.[86] They continued the policies of André Malraux, de Gaulle's culture minister, who sought to restore France as the standard-bearer of Western civilization by shoring up its high-cultural institutions. They also maintained the ambitious program he initiated in 1962 to clean the soot and grime from the facades of Paris's historic public buildings in order to restore French pride in its cultural heritage.[87]

Yet this hardly hid the extent to which American-style values had taken hold, including in the highest circles of France's business and government. Ironically, tourists saw some of the most unfortunate effects of this American-style modernization. Despite his background in tourist development, Georges Pompidou, de Gaulle's successor as president, said he was determined that Paris not become a fossilized museum. One of his government's first acts in 1969 was to tear down the twelve grand mid-nineteenth-century iron and glass buildings of Les Halles, the wholesale food market on the Right Bank, where romantic tourists would eat onion soup and drink café au lait in the early hours of the morning. He commissioned plans to build an office tower there that he said would be "a monument to [his] presidency."[88] The old railroad station in Montparnasse was torn down and a towering fifty-eight-story skyscraper—intended to be the first of many—was erected in its place. The Gare d'Orsay, the delightful Belle Epoque railroad station on the Seine, was also slated for demolition. In 1967, as prime minister, Pompidou had overseen the construction of an expressway along a stretch of the Right Bank of the Seine, obliterating riverside quays that were the setting for countless poems and pictures. Now, he ordered a start on a similar asphalt belt along a four-mile stretch of the Left Bank.[89]

Paris's hotel industry was declared hopelessly old-fashioned and a deterrent to modern business travel. The government aided the construction of new high-rise hotels on the city's periphery in the faceless International Style then favored by American hotel chains. One of these monsters, the thousand-room Hôtel Concorde, built on the site of a historic gate to the city, boasted a new-style convention center with a vast exhibition floor and a stark windowless facade that loomed over an expressway interchange where the old gate once stood.[90] Down the street from it, Air France, the government-owned airline, contributed Le Meridien hotel, a squat concrete structure that an American guest said "has all the Gallic charm of Houston." Other new hotels on the inner city's periphery would have seemed ugly even in London, where Prince Charles claimed that postwar British architects had done more damage than the German Luftwaffe had during the war.[91]

Fortunately for tourism, another sign of Americanization was the American-style reaction that these changes aroused. In the mid-1960s, the demolition of New York City's monumental Penn Station had aroused New Yorkers to organize to preserve other icons of their urban heritage from obliteration by modernizers. In New Orleans and San Francisco, citizens had banded together to stop the construction of expressways that were disfiguring their shorelines. Now Parisians, who for centuries had watched passively as various monarchs and governments had demolished whole neighborhoods to build palaces, fortifications, boulevards, and public buildings, formed a Committee to Save Paris that managed to successfully block further construction of high-rises and expressways within their city. In 1974 a new conservative president, Valéry Giscard d'Estaing, blew the whistle on most of these projects and vowed to restore, not raze, the older parts of town.

Over the next twenty-five years, government support for restoration of older neighborhoods often led to a process of "gentrification" in which poorer residents were forced into the bleak high-rise apartment projects that had been rising in the city's suburbs since the 1950s. People who loved the Paris of lively, close-knit working-class communities, with their thriving marketplaces, tiny cafés, and simple workingmen's restaurants, were dismayed. However, gentrification proved to be a boon to tourists and tourism.[92] The Marais was transformed from a seedy neighborhood with crumbling seventeenth-century buildings into a chic quarter of restored mansions, fashionable apartments, museums, and interesting shops. On the Left Bank, in Saint-Germain-des-Prés, branches of upscale retail chains and renovated apartments replaced the modest shops, used bookstores, and writers' digs of the days of the *Paris Review*. A 1983 *Vogue* article on shopping in Paris now supplemented its roundup of the usual suspects on the Right Bank—Dior, Ungaro, Cartier, and so on—with a long list of expensive boutiques in that quarter, culminating with the only branch of Yves Saint Laurent's Rive Gauche boutique that was actually on the Rive Gauche. Women in the know, it implied, would buy their shoes only in that neighborhood.[93]

— —

Modernization also continued to transform transatlantic transportation, especially in the sense that the word implies mass-produced sameness. In March 1970 Pan Am introduced Boeing 747s, the first of the "jumbo" or wide-bodied jets, on the run from New York to Paris. The first advertisements said, "This space ship is going to Paris" and promised: "You can stretch out, spread out, watch the movie, stroll, quaff, nibble, and enjoy a Paris flight as never before. We even have separate sections for smokers and non-smokers."[94] Of course, passengers wishing to stretch out and spread out would soon be out of luck. After the 1973 Mideast war, soaring fuel prices led the airlines to squeeze their economy-class seats closer together, until the 747s, which at first seated 362, were soon having over 420 people stuffed into them.[95] Even with the additional seating, skyrocketing fuel prices and its inability to compete with more cost-efficient TWA forced Pan Am, the pioneer in transatlantic travel, to abandon the New York–Paris route in 1974.[96] The introduction of lower-cost flights on new all-charter airlines such as Laker cushioned the blow for passengers.[97] In 1978 the scheduled airlines finally responded with discounted rates of their own, but this entailed the elimination of the last of the "frills" that had distinguished them from the charters.[98]

High fuel prices more or less spelled the end for the most comfortable, uncrowded way of getting tourists across the Atlantic, the steamship. The great passenger lines, unable to compete with lower jet fares, had begun abandoning their North Atlantic runs in the mid-1960s, selling many of the liners for conversion into cruise ships. The proud French doggedly persisted in subsidizing the *France*, promoting it as the most pleasurable way to cross and trumpeting the *New York Times* restaurant critic Craig Claiborne's label "the finest restaurant in the world."[99] Finally, however, in 1974, with de Gaulle gone and fuel prices out of sight, the government cut off the line's subsidy and paid off her crew. Three years later she was bought by a Norwegian cruise line and converted into the *Norway*. Her proud transatlantic competitors met sorrier fates. The *Queen Mary* was sold to American businessmen who turned her into a harbor-side attraction in Long Beach, California, while the speedy *United States* was towed to a far corner of Philadelphia harbor, where it still remains, slowly rusting, as of this writing.

Air France, which had replaced the French Line as the main transatlantic French flag carrier, never came close to assuming the French Line's luxurious aura. It spent much of the 1970s living down the reputation it had earned in the 1960s as "Air Chance." (Among other things, American passengers found the sight of the cabin crew delivering cognacs to the cockpit disconcerting, to say the least.)[100] The introduction of the supersonic Concorde, which sped passengers across the ocean in a little over three hours, did little to restore its luster.[101] Although it became the vehicle of choice for celebrities, unlike the great ocean liners, there was no way for the uncelebrated passengers on the jumbo jets behind them to ogle them during the voyage. Now, for those unwilling or unable to pay premium prices, there was no choice but to squeeze into the narrow seats of the behemoths, struggle for control of the small armrests with the large persons beside them, hope that the contents of the small tray placed in front of them would at least be edible, and dread the moment when the seat in front of them tilted all the way back. What used to be called "the crossing," it seemed, had reverted to what it had been in the early nineteenth century: an ordeal to be endured.

THIRTEEN

Bouncing Back: The 1980s

The French think all Americans love them. The Americans think all French hate them. They are both wrong.

—FRANÇOIS FURET, 1990

In 1984 a surprising poll showed that France, which had been the most anti-American country in Western Europe in the postwar years, was now the most pro-American.[1] There were many factors behind this transformation, but certainly the most paradoxical was that President de Gaulle had played a major role in bringing it about. His policy of raising France to America's level in terms of industrial modernization and technology while bolstering pride in its cultural heritage helped erode the sense of inferiority that underlay much of French anti-Americanism.[2] Events abroad also played a role. The end of the war in Vietnam in 1973 and America's subsequent leeriness over foreign military adventures helped dull the French conviction that America was out to conquer the world. The publication the next year of the Russian author Aleksandr Solzhenitsyn's exposé of the huge Soviet network of horrific labor camps bred disillusion with the Soviets, whose stock with the French usually rose in inverse proportion to that of the Americans.[3] Changes in French foreign policy also helped, as de Gaulle's successors abandoned his "go it alone" path, gave up on his aspirations to be one of the world's great superpowers, and began gradually rejoining the Atlantic Alliance.[4]

France's steady transformation into an urbanized consumer society with American-style tastes in popular culture also helped spread more benign views of America. During the 1960s the growing middle class of professionals, white-collar workers, and technicians were able to share in the French version of what had been regarded as the American consumerist dream.[5] By the 1970s a rising standard of living was allowing many of those in the classes below to enjoy the material benefits of mass consumerism as well as the mass culture that accompanied it. Television viewers lapped up American soap operas such as *Dallas* and *Dynasty*, which showed beautiful Americans living in a luxurious consumer's Nirvana.

Hollywood increased its dominance of French movie screens, as French studios were unable to compete with its expensive action movies, with their heavy diet of explosive violence and special effects. America also regained the dominant position in popular music it had briefly shared with Britain in the 1960s. Even Coca-Cola began making inroads.[6] By the mid-1970s, this fascination with American popular culture was helping undermine anti-Americanism, particularly among the working class. A 1979 survey of residents of Châteauroux, whose American air base had aroused such resentment in the 1950s, found most of them now looked back at the days when the Americans were there as the good old days. In a complete reversal of the attitudes of that time, the lower classes regarded Americans more favorably than the higher classes.[7] By the mid-1980s, the French were experiencing the growth of the very aspects of modern consumer societies—giant supermarkets, middle-class suburban developments, and even fast-food outlets—that were most closely associated, in the public mind, with the American Way of Life. Much to the dismay of intellectuals, gourmets, and other guardians of French traditions, they met with broad approval, raising the prestige of American popular and consumer culture yet another notch.[8]

Many intellectuals, of course, continued to denounce America's imperial reach and deleterious impact on French culture.[9] Yet even among them, there was wavering. In 1964 the highly regarded sociologist Edgar Morin had called on the French to reject the kind of European contempt for America "which supposedly expressed our own refinement" and recognize that American liberal values represented the best hope for preserving not only Western civilization, but also the human race.[10] In 1970 he returned from a trip to California, the belly of the dragon—which most French intellectuals regarded as a vulgar, car-crazed, materialistic, intellectual desert—and published a benign view of young Americans struggling to construct an egalitarian society based on love and joy.[11] Surprisingly, although his views provoked the predictable denunciations, it also stimulated some rethinking of America.[12] So did a best-selling book published that year by Jean-François Revel, which argued that far from being the unjust, militaristic juggernaut portrayed by critics, the United States was an admirable anti-authoritarian society that should serve as a model for the rest of the world.[13]

The election of Jimmy Carter to the presidency in 1976 took more of the wind out of the sails of those who denounced the United States as a warmonger out to dominate the world. Although his 1980 defeat by Ronald Reagan puffed some of this wind back in, admiration for Reagan's "free market" domestic policies inspired French conservative intellectuals and business leaders to look more benignly on the United States. As a result, the quality French press began to disseminate less hostile views of the United States. The large numbers of French people who began visiting America in the 1980s to see the beast for themselves also helped dissipate many of the extreme views.[14]

These changing attitudes may have been behind reports, common in the 1980s, that the French were treating American tourists better.[15] However, the better treatment was probably also related to the influx of other foreign tourists. Ernie Ricci, working in a tourist-related position, thought that the French began treating Americans better in the 1980s because their antipathy was redirected toward the many Japanese tourists who, visible mainly behind bus windows, were disliked for segregating themselves completely, and the numerous Germans, who were despised for many reasons, including their frugality and the war. "They had someone else to pick on," he observed.[16]

There is something to be said for this idea. When Western European tourists first began pouring into France in the 1960s, people in the tourist industries began finding them less desirable than Americans on a number of grounds. The West Germans, particularly in groups, took the title of loudest tourists away from Americans and were derided as miserly tippers. The Belgians acquired a reputation for penny-pinching; the Italians, for insensitivity to all around them. "The Americans really aren't so bad," a Paris hotel-keeper told *Business Week* in 1963, "particularly when you see how the Belgians and Germans behave." (The word "behave," the reporter added, was understood to mean "tip.")[17]

Nor did the Americans stand out when it came to boorishness. "The day of the incandescent creature in the incandescent Hawaiian shirt may not have ended," said a *New Yorker* profile of Temple Fielding in January 1968, "but the American rube, once the only traveling boor on the Continent, now has peers from many other nations. European tourists are all over Europe each summer, and one has to hunt for gauche Americans among the competition." Fielding himself went further, saying of American tourists, "They're quiet. They don't complain. They're mannerly. They're honest. They tip well. . . . They dress well, or most of them do. . . . In a hotel, if they're not satisfied, they just move out. The image of the American tourist has completely changed among hoteliers over here."[18] While Fielding surely exaggerated, a 1969 survey of French attitudes toward tourists seemed to confirm that the times were indeed changing. Although Americans were not rated the most likable (*agréable*) of tourists, neither were they the most dislikable. The Italians, Spanish, and Germans all topped them in that regard.[19]

——

Yet changing French views of American tourists were not matched by changes in American tourists' attitudes toward the French. Americans' perceptions that the French were rude, anti-American money-grubbers who delighted in humiliating them remained as strong as ever. A *Newsweek* editor began a 1974 article on how he substituted a trip to Quebec for one to France by saying it would require "some creative paranoia. . . . For beyond fine food and lilting language, a vacation in France should also provide a hint of perpetual put-down for the American tourist. . . . The French-Canadians' reputation for hospitality, plus their perfect willingness to speak English almost anywhere, makes it hard to maintain the fiction of being in France."[20] The humorist Judith Martin ended a *Washington Post* column on how high prices were keeping Americans from France with the assurance that Americans would be back: "And what we'll crave is that fine, indigenous, traditional French commodity we always used to come for. Insults."[21] The *New York Times* humorist Russell Baker told readers who dined in French restaurants in America, "Remember, the waiters are not trying to insult you, they are just trying to be authentic."[22]

Positive articles about France commonly began by saying that the French were not nearly as bad as most Americans thought. In March 1981 a woman wrote in the *Saturday Evening Post* of how she and her husband toured France while trying to abide by the Pritikin diet, an extremely low-fat diet, the mere mention of whose demands would have made previous generations of French chefs apoplectic. "We have always been puzzled by tales of French rudeness or lack of friendliness to Americans," she wrote. "Our experiences in France have been unfailingly agreeable, and never more so than on our Pritikin-plan trip. On more than one occasion, when we unwittingly appeared at a restaurant during the hours when the kitchen was closed, the proprietor himself prepared something for us himself." Even in the South of France, where olive oil reigns supreme, chefs cheerfully put together oil-less meals for the demanding couple.[23] A 1984 piece in *Mademoiselle* said, "Don't listen to anyone who tells you that the French national pastime is sneering at visitors who don't speak the language. . . . The people, like people everywhere, will invariably be as kind, charming, and open as you are—even if your French is clumsy or nonexistent."[24]

Yet many visitors still found the sullenness they expected, especially in Paris. In 1970 only 54 percent of the people, a majority of whom were

Americans, polled at Paris sightseeing spots said that Parisians were courteous to them, while about 41 percent found them "indifferent" and 5 percent thought them "disagreeable." Especially annoying was the Parisians' attitude toward their attempts to speak French. "There is no politeness or good will in making an effort to understand beginners in their language," said one respondent. Another said, "Even though they can tell very well from your accent that you are a foreigner, they do nothing to take this into account. They are even nasty about it, and as for taxi drivers, it's best not to even speak of them."[25] A young American woman interviewed outside American Express in Paris in 1975 said, "France is wonderful. Paris is simply terrific. It's the people I can't stand. I was so sure I'd like them. But they don't like me. Either they don't answer at all or they pretend they don't understand me."[26]

The idea that the French all spoke English but pretended that they did not was also remarkably persistent.[27] A middle-aged American couple from New Jersey who visited France four times in the 1970s and 1980s said they did not like the French because they had "an attitude." Asked to explain, the pair, who did not speak French, said that whenever they spoke English, the French pretended not to understand them. The woman gave as an example going to a small-town pharmacy to get medication for a cold and gesturing repeatedly to explain what was wrong. The pharmacist claimed to be unable to help her, something she thought was a deliberate attempt to humiliate her.[28] In 1985 American travel agencies reported that although the welcome extended to Americans in France seemed to have improved, a very large number (30 percent) of their clients still complained about the poor reception they received there, above all in Paris.[29] In a 1986 survey, 186 American travel agents and tour operators ranked France as the least welcoming of the seven most-visited countries in Europe.[30]

A few years earlier, the food writer Patricia Wells lightheartedly recommended lingering at one of the boulevard Saint-Germain cafés and seeing "that the Paris clichés are still alive and well: the surly waiters and red-eyed Frenchmen inhaling Gitanes."[31] Yet doing so opened the door to another traditional gripe, the high price of drinks in French cafés, which many tourists did not understand presupposed lingering at one's table. "I was robbed in Paris and Italy," said an irate letter to the *New York Times* in 1972. "Did you ever hear of paying 80 or 90 cents for cup of coffee?"[32]

In 1984, on the other hand, when the dollar was riding high against the franc, the old derisory view of French money reappeared. An article from Paris in the *National Review* asked, "Well who can believe in this Frog crepe paper anyhow? Reminds me of the stuff you would roll a nickel bag reefer in." Then, moving on to another traditional inadequacy in the minds of Americans, it said, "And, groan, I've got to take a bath again. How come France hasn't figured out the principle of falling water yet? First time I've been in a tub since Russia in 1975. And how clever of *les Français* to dispense toilet paper by little Sight-Saver-sized squares. All I need is some Scotch tape so I can stick them together."[33]

— —

Yet by then the French needed to please such grumpy visitors more than ever, for tourism was now by far their country's largest single earner of foreign exchange. In 1985 the new head of the government tourism office announced that the profits from foreign tourism had been "a spectacular blow to the recession!" Tourism was the industry of the future, he said. It was based on modern technology, "the cultural evolution of our country," and the new information age. One of his great tasks, he said, was to project France's image as a country that extends a great welcome to foreign tourists, "modern and smiling."[34]

Americans were at the top of the list of those to be impressed. Even though they now comprised less than 10 percent of France's tourists, they were the most prized kind of visitors. They were "long-distance" ones, who stayed many more nights there and spent three times more per day there than visitors from Europe.[35] Moreover, their arrivals were spread more evenly over the year than the Europeans, most of whom headed to the seaside resorts in July and August.[36] At the end of the day, the well over 2 million American tourists who visited in 1985 left behind more than $2 billion.[37]

Yet Great Britain was now surpassing France in the number of American visitors it welcomed, and Italy was breathing down its neck.[38] Since the hotel crisis was now over, it seemed that main culprit had to be the other usual suspect, "the welcome." So, the government mounted yet another "Bienvenue France" campaign to make the French more welcoming to tourists. This time, rather than "smile checks," it involved seminars for people in the tourist industries and newspaper articles and TV slots for the general public.[39] Again, the results were disappointing. In October 1985 an Air France survey of its American customers indicated that they thought of Britain as traditional and friendly and Italy as "a warm and moving environment." France, on the other hand, had a "complex and controversial" image, provoking "very strong reactions, particularly when it came to the French themselves." Perhaps, the airline ventured, the French image would improve if they worked at improving "and perhaps Americanizing [their welcome] a bit."[40]

Then, in early 1986 came more blows, as a sinking dollar and terrorism hammered transatlantic tourism.[41] Hijacks of American airliners had come into vogue in the late 1960s, first to Cuba, then to other locations. Middle Eastern terrorists adopted the tactic in 1973, taking special pains to hijack planes of Pan Am and TWA, the two overseas American flag carriers, and bomb their offices. These tailed off from 1976 until September 1985, when a TWA jet was commandeered and forced to land at the Beirut airport, where, after a prolonged standoff, the hijackers destroyed it, along with some other planes.[42] Then a group of Palestinians hijacked a large Mediterranean cruise ship, the *Achilles Lauro*, and killed a wheelchair-bound Jewish American tourist on it. This was followed on December 27, 1985, by gunmen's attacks on El Al and TWA ticket counters in Rome and Vienna that killed eighteen people and wounded 120. President Reagan did little to calm tourist jitters when, in reply to a news conference question about whether it was safe for Americans to travel to Europe, he said that it was hard to deal with such suicide attacks and that "regular travelers" had told him that they would not plan trips to Europe "under the present circumstances." A wave of cancellations followed, especially on TWA.[43]

The French tourist industry was driven to despair. Tourist officials in Nice bemoaned the Americans' ignorance of geography, citing an American tour operator who blamed the cancellations on his clientele's belief that the terrorist incidents in the Middle East affected all of Europe, "as if Beirut were a suburb of Nice and Tripoli were at the gates of Monte Carlo."[44] But then terrorism struck France itself, in the form of a string of bombings by groups demanding the release of imprisoned Middle Eastern terrorists. These were mainly at Right Bank locales such as the Champs-Elysées and in large department stores that were much frequented by tourists.[45] Then, in March 1986 a number of articles in the American press calling France the most dangerous country for Americans to visit led to the cancellation of hundreds of charter flights and thousands more of planned trips.[46] Dismayed French tourist officials sent a delegation to the national convention of American travel agents to try to counter the cancellations. They returned in gloom, saying the American travel agents said they were simply unable to assure their clients that they would be safe in France. In early April 1986, a bomb exploded aboard a TWA plane as it approached the Athens airport, killing four passengers and wounding a number of others. Thousands of additional Americans now canceled visits to France. Whole floors of the Ritz and Plaza Athénée hotels were said to be closed because of lack of business.[47]

The situation worsened still in mid-April, when the Americans launched major bombing raids on Libya, targeting its leader, Muammar Khaddafi, who it accused of being the major architect of the terrorism. Khaddafi escaped, but his young daughter was killed. The heightened fears of Libyan-backed terrorist retaliation upon Americans abroad led to yet another great wave of cancellations. The Yale Glee Club canceled its annual summertime European tour. Smith College warned its students in Europe to avoid places where Americans congregated.[48] The actor Sylvester Stallone, famed for his portrayals of the hyper-muscular soldier Rambo, the fearless scourge of America's enemies, canceled his upcoming appearance at the Cannes Film Festival out of fears for his safety. A British tabloid rechristened him "Wimpo." In France sales of Rambo T-shirts plummeted and a disc jockey invented the Rambo Rumba, which was danced backward.[49] The director of the American Chamber of Commerce in Britain said Americans were "acting like a bunch of frightened schoolchildren."[50] French tourist officials accused the American press of "brainwashing" the American public. "The smallest car explosion makes page one of the American press," said one.[51]

The Cannes festival passed without incident, but the State Department remained on edge. In mid-July, at the height of the tourist season, it warned that American intelligence services expected Middle Eastern terrorists to mount a wave of "indiscriminate" attacks in Western Europe. The attacks on Americans never occurred. Although there were some more bombings in Paris in July, and again in September, they were in nontouristy places.[52] Yet the summer tourist season was ruined. About 60 percent of the Americans who had reservations at luxury hotels such as the George V and Intercontinental in Paris canceled. Hotels catering to packaged tours also suffered similar cancellations.[53] Those Americans who did come were dismayed at the new look of a city on guard against terrorism. A doctor from Santa Barbara interviewed outside the heavily guarded American Express office in Paris said, "Paris is meant to be fun. But it's not the same feeling when you see armed police walking down every boulevard or when you're searched every time you enter a store."[54]

— —

In June 1986, in the midst of the crisis, the French secretary of state for tourism announced a plan to combat the appalling slump in American tourism. Twelve hundred American travel agents would be invited to a practically free four-day "familiarization trip" of Paris and the provinces. American hotel guests would be given free gifts and rate reductions on July 4, and a major advertising campaign was mounted in the United States. In September 1986, warning that the falloff in American visitors was having "grave" effects on France's balance of payments, he said a new "marketing approach" was needed, beginning with a study of the American image of France.[55]

The study's results were predictable: yet more evidence that Americans thought the French hated them. So was the French response: another attempt to improve the "welcome." This time, though, there was a twist. American Express was enlisted to run the large seminars for people in the travel industries to teach them how to better respond to American wishes.[56] In addition, the tourist department mounted a wide-ranging program to sensitize the entire French public to the importance of being hospitable to tourists. "The welcome," it said, "is the crucial element in clients' choice," and France was generally perceived negatively on that score by foreign tourists, particularly by Americans. In the short term, the French public had to be educated about the economic importance of foreign tourism. In the longer term, it said, the schools should sensitize young people to the importance of "opening up to the outside world, respect for others, and showing hospitality and elementary courtesy to tourists of other nationalities."[57]

The latter suggestion recognized that, as the statement said, "the quality of the welcome reserved for foreign tourists is a cultural phenomenon," and the problems of French culture ran deep in this regard. Still, the government made another gallant effort. Three million "Bienvenue France" pamphlets were printed up and twenty "welcome offices" were set up at the frontiers and major tourist areas. Young language students were hired to translate for foreign tourists in Paris, and free telephone lines were set up to provide information in various languages. A "sensitivity" campaign told of the importance of being hospitable to tourists, and there was a well-publicized national contest to choose the best "ambassadors" of the French welcome.[58]

— —

It is impossible to tell what effect these measures had on the French, but once again they hardly dented the persisting negative image of the French among Americans. Yet, as in the past, despite its unwelcoming reputation, France remained high on the must-see list for most American tourists to Europe. Indeed, 91 percent of the Chicago-area tourist agencies that were asked in 1985 if France were "an easy product to sell," responded: "Yes."

Only 7 percent said no, citing its unfriendly welcome, expensive airfares, and high prices.[59]

There are two conclusions that might be drawn from this. On the one hand, for those of the agents' clients whose main purpose was still sightseeing, it was an indication of the extent to which, in modern tourism, interest in seeing sights is often divorced from interest in the people who live among the sights. But it also reflected changes in tourists' reasons for going abroad. By the late 1970s, falling airfares meant that most tourists no longer regarded their visit to Europe as a once-in-a lifetime proposition. An increasing proportion of visitors were either repeaters or people who intended to return in the not-too-distant future. As a result, they commonly stayed for shorter periods—two or three weeks instead of four or more—and limited their visits to one or two countries instead of doing fifteen countries in twenty-one days.[60]

These repeat visitors, having ticked off the major sights in previous trips, could turn their attention to other attractions. These included, for the first time in the age of mass tourism, gastronomy. In 1985 the French government tourist bureau noted that for some years now American society had been evolving in terms of "sophistication," and there was "a developing interest in gastronomy and wine."[61] It meant, of course, French gastronomy, and there had indeed been a remarkable transformation in this regard. In 1961 the newly inaugurated president John Kennedy and his wife, Jacqueline, helped revive its reputation as elite food by conducting a well-publicized search for a French chef to run the White House kitchen. The next year Julia Child began a public television network show, *The French Chef*, that helped stimulate an appreciation for it among the middle classes. Although trained in Paris's snobbish Cordon Bleu school, Child wanted, she said, "to break down the snob appeal."[62] Instead of a meticulous Frenchman in chef's toque standing amidst a formidable *batterie de cuisine*, viewers saw a tall, amiable woman in a home kitchen who huffed and puffed, dropped things, and insisted that all her recipes could be prepared with supermarket ingredients. Others, such as the *New York Times* food editor Craig Claiborne and the popular cookbook writer James Beard, joined in this effort to bring French cooking to the middle-class American kitchen. Soon middle-class magazines such as *Life* were singing its praises.[63]

In 1965 *Gourmet* magazine began running monthly reviews of Paris restaurants that made then seem as accessible as those in New York.[64] But the vast majority of Francophilic cooks and diners had still not eaten French food in France. Most of the women featured in a 1966 *Ladies' Home Journal* piece showing upper-middle-class women in a number of American cities entertaining with French food said they were inspired by what they had eaten at French restaurants in New York City. None mentioned France.[65] Only 3 percent of tourists surveyed upon returning from France in 1966 listed gastronomy as a reason for going there, and just 12 percent of the tourists said it was one of their favorite things there.[66]

By the end of the 1960s, though, there were enough good French restaurants in major American cities for Craig Claiborne to call it the decade in which French haute cuisine had finally come of age in America.[67] Elsewhere, "Continental" restaurants flourished. Although Calvin Trillin joked that they were usually called something like "La Casa de la Maison House, Continental Cuisine" and speculated that the continent must be Australia (which was then noted for its awful cooking), they usually served French-sounding dishes and had maître d's who cultivated phony French accents. As a taste for French food became, in the parlance of the day, a "status symbol" among the upper-middle class, the media began featuring stories about star French chefs who flew to America to cook at charity functions and do television interviews and demonstrations. In 1973, with sales of her cookbook well past the 1 million mark, Julia Child began fearing that instead of casting a decisive blow against French food snobbery, she had merely helped propagate it. After one particularly orgiastic series of articles on the great chefs in France by *New York Magazine*'s over-the-top food critic, Gael Greene, Child wrote her French collaborator Simone Beck that food was "becoming too much of a status symbol."[68]

But enthusiasts such as Childs and Claiborne also encouraged people to travel to France, not just to dine in a famous chef's restaurant, but to taste the local foodstuffs. In America this was, after all, still the heyday of tasteless battery-raised chickens and iceberg lettuce, when two of the best-selling food products, Wonder Bread and Velveeta cheese, seemed to be made from different kinds of plastic. For many American tourists in France, tasting crusty fresh-baked bread, Bresse chickens, and potatoes, greens, and tomatoes that had discernible tastes was an epiphany. This had little to do with the snobbery that concerned Julia Child. It had much to do with the sorry state of American food in the 1950s and 1960s.

By the mid-1970s, then, upper-middle-class tourists were finally becoming enamored with French food. Some took cooking tours of France, such as that which Julia Child's coauthor, Simone Beck, led to the Riviera in 1976. The wealthiest could sign on for the expensive "gourmet tour" of French wine regions led by Sam Aaron, owner of New York City's most prestigious wine store, which promised twenty-five "connoisseurs" dinners in a number of three-star restaurants along with the winery visits.[69] Most, however, were just more appreciative of French cuisine and the high quality of the ingredients that went into it.

The rise of gastronomic tourism was helped by a turn in French cuisine that made it much more attractive to the American upper-middle class. By the mid-1970s, the "nouvelle cuisine" was transforming many of France's finer restaurants. It rejected the old system, set down by the turn-of-the-century chef Auguste Escoffier, that used two flour-thickened sauces, one white, the other brown, as the bases for innumerable rich and complex dishes. Instead, the innovators emphasized the freshness, taste, and high quality of the ingredients themselves, with sauces that were usually based on reductions of their own juices.[70] The *New York Times* restaurant critic Mimi Sheraton said this "gastronomic revolution" was characterized by the "herbaceous freshness of its dishes with an emphasis on lightness and the elimination of the heavy flour-laden sauces so typical of classic French cooking."[71]

This new light fare was promoted as just the thing for the growing number of weight- and health-conscious Americans. In a fawning article, *Newsweek* quoted Alain Senderens, the leading nouvelle cuisine chef in Paris, as saying, "People must see that too much alcohol, too many fats, too much sugar is not good for them, and that avoiding them can be a marvelously pleasant experience."[72] Despite the weak dollar, Americans began making pilgrimages to restaurants such as his to marvel at their innovative combinations of ingredients and tastes. Although some gourmands might grumble about the meager portions, few could not be impressed by the originality of the brilliant young chefs. The French and American press glowed over these superstars of the kitchen. They seemed to be the gastronomic counterparts of the individualistic New Wave movie director/auteurs who had transformed that art form in the 1960s.[73]

Ironically, though, such hype helped undermine France's status at the pinnacle of the gastronomic world. The glare of publicity surrounding the celebrity French chefs hid the fact that the high quality of most French restaurant food was based not so much on the creativity of famous chefs as on a rugged system of apprenticeship, where young people would labor for years in hot, cramped little spaces while learning the intricacies of a very difficult craft. Just as the New Wave movies were in fact the products of teams of talented craftspeople, so the accomplishments of the great chefs were built on the skills of the people who toiled under them. Now, with the celebrity chefs and their industrious publicity agents giving the impression that their success was based only on their creative genius, there was no reason that Americans might not begin to wonder why they could not produce their own geniuses.

And produce them they seemed to do. In Berkeley, California, Alice Waters managed to blend her New Left ideals with her admiration for traditional French country cooking and turn the modest-looking restaurant she opened in 1972 into a place that was nationally renowned for its cuisine based on foods from a network of local producers of artisanal and non-factory-farmed foods. Other American chefs began turning out such things as "fusion" cuisine, which tried to blend the flavors and techniques of East Asia with those of the West, and "new American cuisine," which followed the trail that Waters and the nouvelle cuisine had blazed in emphasizing the natural flavors of high-quality local ingredients.

The role of food tastes as a status marker shot up. In Los Angeles it was now the latest creations of inventive chefs that determined which were the "hot" places, not just their exclusivity. As each of these American celebrity chefs had his fifteen minutes of glory, France seemed to fade further into the horizon. In 1991 the food historian Laura Shapiro proclaimed in *Newsweek* that "an American Revolution" had occurred—that "our love affair with French food is over, done in by a new passion for our own chefs and ingredients."[74]

French food also met competition from other foreign cuisines and tastes. In the 1970s upscale northern Italian restaurants became popular, as did places serving Chinese regional cuisines. In the 1980s newly adventurous Americans took to eating raw fish in sushi restaurants, green curry sauces in Thai restaurants, and using pancakes instead of forks and knives in Ethiopian ones. Supermarkets began carrying an impressive array of new foods from abroad. In the accompanying outpouring of magazine articles and cookbooks on how to cook and eat these foods, the proportion of attention devoted to French food inevitably declined.[75]

The decline of Francocentrism was evident in *Gourmet* magazine. In the mid-1970s, it dropped its monthly reviews of restaurants in France and replaced them with reviews of California restaurants, only one in ten of which was French. Instead of the old articles on French cooking techniques, there were now ones on Chinese and Mexican cooking. A feature called "Gourmet Holidays" was expanded, but few of the trips were to France. In the five years from 1980 to 1985, out of the two destinations featured in each monthly issue, only one, Lorraine, was in France. The magazine continued to run "Paris Journal," which told of art exhibitions, shopping, new restaurants, and other French attractions, and did features on such things as ballooning in Burgundy, but gastronomic Francocentrism seemed on the wane.[76] Even France's preeminence in fine wine was challenged. In 1976 the tremendous media exposure (in America, not France) given to the results of a blind wine tasting in Paris where French experts ranked some of California's best wines higher than the top wines in France spurred American wine enthusiasts into realizing that other countries, including their own, were now producing excellent wines.[77]

Yet despite all of this, interest in touring France for its food and wine increased. A 1986 *Vogue* article entitled "Why, Oh Why, Do I Love Paris?" acknowledged that "Italy seems to have eroded France's grip on the American imagination and the American dollar: Italian cuisine became *haute*; Americans began sniffing and drinking Italian wines. Armani opened a boutique on Madison Avenue, and New Wave fashions moved to Milan. All roads, trends, and airlines lead to Rome—and Florence and Venice." Still, it said, "Of all the ways to spend time and money in Paris, food is the most satisfying."[78] What had happened, in other words, was not that France had declined as a destination for gastronomic tourism, but that other places had arisen as well. The steady increase in middle-class travel abroad was contributing to a wholesale internationalization of the American diet that made Americans much more appreciative of foreign food.

It was not that foreign travel stimulated a taste for the specific foods of the countries one visited. Rather, it was that it was supposed to make one more amenable to new taste experiences. Now, in contrast to the 1950s, upper-middle-class people who feared new foods were looked down upon. The *Vogue* article on Paris, for example, practically sneered when telling of an American woman who ordered *foie de veau* after her husband correctly translated *veau* as veal, without realizing that *foie* meant liver. When she tasted it, she began to yell, "Oh, God. Oh no. It's liver. I hate liver. You know I'm allergic to liver."[79] Enjoying foreign foods, even innards, had become a sign of refinement. It meant being comfortable in foreign places, of being a "broad" cosmopolitan person. Although the foreign foods one encountered abroad may actually have seemed too unsanitary, too spicy, or too repulsive even to taste, one still gained distinction by returning from trips saying one had tried them. In this context, one could hardly return from France boasting, as Americans used to do, of how they had refused to eat frogs' legs, snails, and the disgusting dishes whose inferior ingredients were camouflaged by sauces.[80] It was no coincidence that in the 1980s the Travel section of the Sunday *New York Times*, which had hitherto concentrated mainly on sightseeing, began regularly running pieces on dining in France.

In 1981 Carol Mongo was surprised to encounter the new attitudes when her father, an African American engineer with Ford in Detroit, came to visit her. Although he arrived with the usual fears ("Can I drink the water?"), he made a concerted effort to shed his conservative eating habits and become an adventurous eater. She watched in amazement as, in a restaurant in Normandy, he ordered the large seafood platter, which was crammed with raw, spiny, strange-looking creatures that few Americans would go near, and devoured it with pleasure and interest.[81]

Another reason for the rising number of people interested in eating their way through France was that although there was some basis for the 1980s reports of French food's loss of hegemony over American gastronomy, the reports of its demise were, as Mark Twain would have said, exaggerated. Indeed, the decade's status-obsessed "yuppie" culture—named after the baby boomers who had now become young urban professionals—provided a tonic for gastro-tourism to France. The wealthiest of them defined themselves more than ever by their consumption habits, and food and foreign travel became, like designer labels, ways of displaying that they had "made it." Being a "foodie" was no longer just associated with upper-middle-class women readers of *Gourmet* and *House Beautiful*. Now, high-flying young financial men, lawyers, and corporate executives exchanged knowledgeable tips on the latest expensive restaurants and hired well-known chefs for their gala gatherings. Boardroom lunches no longer meant three martinis and roast beef sandwiches; they now featured delicately sauced fish fillets prepared by an accomplished chef, accompanied by a fine white Burgundy. Although Italy and other places beckoned as well, France remained a premier destination. The real high-flyers, literally and figuratively, would fly friends to Paris on the Concorde for brief gastronomic expeditions. Susan Gutfreund, wife of the head of Salomon Brothers, made headlines by spending $20 million redecorating her New York apartment and then booking two seats on the Concorde to fly an American-style cake to her husband's birthday party in Paris.[82] Other moguls would fly in French chefs with their *équipes* to cook for their dinner parties in the Hamptons.

Moreover, when the dollar's value surged in the mid-1980s, many Americans discovered that, as Robert Kaiser said in the *Washington Post* in 1983, "You can spend $50 to $200 or more in New York or Washington for an excellent copy of a grand French dinner for two, or you can proceed—right now, don't wait—to Paris and do even better for $75 to $85." Quick trips to Paris to dine at all four of the city's Michelin "three-star" restaurants became the vogue. Many would then travel down to Lyon, to dine at the three-star tables of Paul Bocuse, the Troisgros brothers, and Alain Chapel, each of which were within five miles of the city.[83]

At the same time, high-end French restaurants began retreating from the excessive minimalism of much of the nouvelle cuisine. In 1985 Mimi Sheraton, writing from Paris for *Time*, now hailed the arrival of "cuisine moderne, a blend of the classic and the nouvelle." This was exemplified, she said, by the "exquisite food" of chef Joel Robuchon—who had just shot to Michelin three-stardom in record time—which combined "savory and authentic flavors with lightness and delicacy." Americans flooded Robuchon's forty-five-seat restaurant with requests for reservations, but he turned many away. He tried, he said, for at most a fifty-fifty split between French and foreign customers. "Nobody," he said, "likes to be in a 'tourist' restaurant."[84] Other luxury restaurants, also fearing inundation by Americans wielding bloated dollars, took to denying reservations to anyone with an American accent, even when they had tables open. According to *Le Monde*, they would say that "there was no place, not at lunch or dinner, for the entire month of July. . . . There was some hope for August, if it didn't fall during the restaurant's annual closing."[85]

Predictably, a scandal of sorts ensued, as well-heeled Americans took this as yet more evidence of French arrogance and anti-Americanism. The offending restaurateurs reacted as Robuchon did, arguing that it was more important to retain their regular clientele than to cater to Americans, many of whose visits were prompted by the sagging franc. "To our French clientele, a restaurant full of foreigners has declined into a cheap tourist trap," said one. Another claimed, "If the foreign clientele passes fifty percent the French won't come back again, thinking they are no longer in France." Yet another said, "By accepting too many foreigners I risk losing my French customers, and what's going to happen when the dollar falls? My restaurant will be half empty."[86] Some even claimed to be acting in the Americans' own interests, saying, "Foreigners' pleasure is ruined when they find their compatriots sitting at tables around them." However, Guy Savoy, owner of a top restaurant that did not restrict Americans, recalls the chefs boasting to each other about how many American reservations they turned down, something he thought was "grotesque."[87]

Restaurateurs in hitherto less-frequented places in the provinces were less ambivalent about the American invasion. By 1985 Colette Brossard, who had worked in a Châteauroux hotel during the heyday of the American base there, was the proprietress of a hotel with an excellent Michelin-starred restaurant in Romorantin-Lanthenay, an unprepossessing town in the less-frequented eastern part of the Loire valley. Americans had begun trickling in there in the early 1980s, she recalled, but in 1985, with the franc at twelve to the dollar, this turned into an agreeable flood of high-spenders. It was, she still recalls, a banner year.[88]

— —

There was also a turnabout in tourists' attitudes toward another of France's historic attractions, its art museums. As we have seen, for most postwar tourists, art meant a hopefully brief visit to the vast, intimidating Louvre. For many, it was their first visit to an art museum. (In 1965 a congressman calling for Americans to travel at home asked, "How many Americans have never visited an art museum before arriving in Paris?")[89] They entered the soot-stained palace through a side door and wandered through the endless galleries wondering why they did not at least clean the glass roof of the seemingly interminable Grand Gallery. It was, said Russell Baker, "a building ninety miles square with floors that turn feet into lead and leg muscles into knots of agony."[90] The few who knew something about art could still find it enthralling. Margaret Queneau, a seventy-year-old dietitian from Boston who had studied in Paris in 1931, returned in the winter of 1978–79, when the museum was at its gloomiest, and wrote contentedly in her diary that she "walked miles rushing from one love to another."[91] Most tourists, though, had no "loves" among the Old Master paintings and classical statuary that were its specialty. Instead, if they had favorites, they were among the new superstars of French art: the Impressionists, such as Edgar Degas and Claude Monet, and the Post-Impressionists, such as Vincent van Gogh and Paul Cézanne, whose works were in the small Jeu de Paume, where few of the standard tours ventured.

A small number of American collectors had been among the first to appreciate these nineteenth- and early-twentieth-century artists. Then, in 1934 *Lust for Life*, Irving Stone's best-selling novel about the life of van Gogh, stimulated interest in that artist's work, as well as that of his sometime friend Paul Gauguin.[92] After World War II, the Hollywood movies *Moulin Rouge* (1952), which romanticized the life of Henri de Toulouse-Lautrec, and *Lust for Life* (1956), which starred Kirk Douglas as a riveting van Gogh and the rugged Anthony Quinn as Gauguin, struck a chord that was sympathetic to the times. They portrayed these artists as innovative geniuses whose works were rejected by the dandified "experts" but whose real worth was ultimately confirmed by the marketplace. As a result, French officials noted gratefully, they stimulated an interest in French art among "average tourists."[93]

In the 1970s and 1980s, major changes in the museum industry helped turn more of the Impressionists and Post-Impressionists into posthumous celebrities. Most important was the rise of "blockbuster" art shows: major museum exhibitions devoted to one theme or one artist that attracted large numbers of people who were not normally museumgoers. One of the first of these shows, the Metropolitan Museum of Art's 1968 *Harlem on My Mind*, was a political disaster for the museum, thanks to some anti-Semitic-sounding passages in its catalog, but it was a roaring financial success. The Met followed it with a less controversial, and eminently profitable, show centering on the dead young Egyptian pharaoh Tutankhamen. Soon staid old museums hitherto patronized mainly by small coteries of the social elite were hiring slick public relations firms to promote moneymaking blockbuster shows of their own. The profitable gift shops stuffed with posters, books, catalogs, coffee mugs, T-shirts, and other souvenirs that sprang up at their entrances and exits surely put the lie to Gertrude Stein's remark in 1946 that "the trouble with museums is that you cannot buy anything."[94]

Impressionists and Post-Impressionists (most people lumped them together as Impressionists) proved to be the most reliable of the cash cows. A 1987 show called *Van Gogh in Saint-Rémy and Auvers* brought the Met $1.5 million in poster sales alone.[95] The Impressionists' rise to celebrity status also reverberated in France, where each summer long lines of people, a majority of whom seemed to be American, would wait patiently for hours to get into the Jeu de Paume, which housed the greatest single collection of their work.[96] In 1986 their works were moved from the Jeu de Paume to a huge new museum devoted to nineteenth-century art built in the shell of the Gare d'Orsay, the railroad station by the Seine that had been barely saved from destruction by Pompidouist modernizers. Although the curators insisted that the immense ground floor be devoted to art that was mainstream in the nineteenth century, it was the top floors, housing the Impressionists, that drew the larger, and more American, crowds.

French museum officials also climbed onto the blockbuster wagon, turning the Grand Palais and Petit Palais, monumental relics of the 1900 World Exposition, into venues for these shows. In their first venture into the field in 1967, the King Tut exhibition drew close to 1.25 million people to the Petit Palais.[97] In 1982 a French critic complained that the international competition to put on larger and larger exhibitions ("We have 3,000 visitors a day! We have 4,000!") meant that little attention was paid to deserving smaller exhibitions.[98] But the numbers, and the income, were too tempting, especially when the Impressionists were involved. In 1983 a Manet show drew over 780,000 visitors to the Grand Palais, and in 1985 Renoir drew over 825,000. Van Gogh drew 546,000 to the small exhibition space in the

Musée d'Orsay. On the other hand, large exhibitions of the works of Old Masters such as Raphael, Claude de Lorrain, and even Rembrandt and Vermeer drew far fewer visitors.[99] By the end of the century, a *New York Times* reporter called "the ever-popular Impressionists . . . truly the museum world's most reliable moneymakers."[100]

The heavily promoted shows undoubtedly expanded museum going among the American middle classes. Many of them now arrived in France much less intimidated by art and museums, with definite ideas about which of the Impressionists were their favorites. There was considerable enthusiasm when Claude Monet's house in Giverny was opened to tourism in 1979. About an hour's ride by tour bus from Paris, it had fallen into disrepair and had been bequeathed by his heirs to the government, which, unable to restore it properly, had shipped the paintings there to a small Paris museum, the Musée Marmottan, that was off the tourist track. Then, in 1977 an energetic conservator, Gerald van der Kemp, was put in charge of the shambles. As chief curator of the Palace of Versailles, he had been impressed by the readiness of a group of the old Francophilic eastern elite, led by the Rockefellers, to pour millions into the massive project of restoring it after its wartime neglect. Now, he convinced them to take on Giverny as well, and in 1979 enough of the gardens and house were back in order to open the place to visitors. In accord with the new museology, Monet's atelier, a large barnlike structure, was fitted out as a gift shop selling reproductions of his work, as well as Monet-themed Dior scarves, Limoges china, place mats, and towels.[101] By 1985, when the massive job was finally finished, the site had become a particular favorite of American and Japanese tourists, who would arrive on bus tours, stroll along the gravel paths laid out by the great artist, and pause on the famous little bridge over the lily pond to take photos or videos.[102]

Giverny exemplified the extent to which celebrity culture had come to dominate art tourism, for a visit there put one in touch with the artist, not his art, which is almost nowhere to be found there. In 1992 the American art collector Daniel Terra opened a museum practically next door to Monet's house for his impressive collection of American artists, most of them inspired by the Impressionists, who painted in France. Yet it remained a backwater on the tourist circuit. Even the Musée Marmottan, which was expanded and modernized in 1985 to house an underground gallery devoted to Monet's huge pictures of water lilies in his garden, never made it onto the standard tourist circuit. Among other things, the puzzling pictures, which verge on the abstract, were not what most people expect from Impressionists. Nor did the mansion/museum of the turn-of-the-century sculptor Auguste Rodin, which houses some of his greatest and most sensual work, become a regular stop, even though it is steps from the Invalides, one of Paris's major sights. It was visited mainly by individual tourists with some knowledge of art. The Museum of Modern Art of the City of Paris, whose fine collection has no particular concentration of superstars, was completely off the map for American tourists.

In 1977, though, Paris leaped to the forefront of the museum world with the opening of the Centre Georges-Pompidou to house a large new museum of modern art. It was the first European example of the late-twentieth-century trend in museum building that saw the buildings themselves, rather than their collections, become the major attraction.[103] Initially, the massive glass and metal box with colored pipes and ventilation ducts ranging up and down its exterior was greeted with horror. "Paris has its own monster," said the critic for *Figaro*. "An architectural King Kong," said another. Yet it soon became the most-visited site in Paris, attracting more visitors than the Eiffel Tower or the Louvre.[104] But relatively few tourists ventured inside the building, and fewer paid serious attention to the art collection, even though it is well-endowed with Post-Impressionists. Instead, after watching the fire-eaters, mime artists, and buskers in the large plaza in front of it, they would take a free ride up the glass-enclosed escalator that climbs the front wall to its roof, which has one of the finest views of Paris.[105]

The next great example of this in Paris came in 1989, with the opening of the new entrance to the Louvre, the controversial modern glass pyramid designed by the Chinese American I. M. Pei that sits in the middle of a courtyard of buildings with ornate nineteenth-century facades. Pei's ambitious master plan involved restoring the old palace complex to its former glories while greatly enhancing its use as a modern exhibition space. Yet for most tourists, it was the transparent pyramid, though which one descended by escalator to the entrance hall below, that was the must-see element. Before the pyramid opened, the museum was drawing 3 million visitors a year. The year after it opened, it drew 5 million. The next year, in 1994, the beautifully renovated Richelieu wing was opened. It boasted such brilliant elements as two classical interior courtyards (one of which had been used as a bureaucrats' parking lot) that were turned into magnificent glass-roofed spaces for large outdoor sculptures, a renovation of Napoléon III's dazzling reception rooms, and a chic café/restaurant.[106]

Pei's design also represented a step forward in the commercialization of the French museum-going experience. By the time the pyramid opened, museum gift shops in America had expanded from little stands selling cata-

A rare moment in the Louvre, in 1988, when the *Mona Lisa* was not surrounded by crowds. Tourists were usually surprised by its small size. © Owen Franken/CORBIS.

logs and posters to large emporia selling a wide variety of goods, which were strategically situated where patrons could hardly avoid them. The Pei-designed extension of the Museum of Fine Arts in Boston had boasted such a shop, which was very profitable. Now Pei went this one better. Not only did the new Louvre boast a huge gift shop; the entrance hall beneath the pyramid opened onto a large shopping mall filled with luxury boutiques. Thanks to these changes, the Louvre was soon attracting 6 million people a year. Terrorist threats and staff strikes dented patronage in the years that followed, but it still averaged over 5 million a year. Significantly, Americans constituted a disproportionately large percentage of these visitors—18.5 percent, or about 925,000 a year—about half as many as from all of Europe.[107] Still, in terms of the art they sought out, little had changed. In 2001 the museum's director lamented that although so many people were coming to see the *Mona Lisa* that a special new gallery was being built to display it, the galleries displaying brilliant works by Vermeer, Rubens, Rembrandt, Poussin, and other masters were often empty.[108]

FOURTEEN

Postmodern Tourism

What could I possibly say about Paris that hasn't been said before? You've got your Seine, you've got your fashion and food, you've got your kul-tcha, plus sex galore. I mean, what the fuck else is there?

—DAVID ANDRUSIA, *Gay Europe* (1995)

As the new millennium began, France maintained an enormous lead over all other countries as the world's top tourist destination.[1] It also continued to ride high in the American tourist hit parade. In 2000 it attracted almost 3 million Americans, placing it second only to the United Kingdom, the starting point for most European tours, as an overseas destination.[2] Americans' continuing importance to its tourist economy was reflected in their renting about three-quarters of all the hotel rooms occupied by foreigners in Paris.[3]

By then, both the best hopes and worst fears about the post–World War II rise of mass tourism were coming to pass. The hope that mass American tourism would provide a much-needed infusion of dollars into Western European economies had been more than fulfilled, especially in the case of France.[4] So had the dreams of those such as Pan Am's Juan Trippe that overseas travel would become a matter of course for the middle class. Other hopes, though, had become pipe dreams. Obviously, mass tourism had not brought international understanding and peace.[5] Nor did the arrival of large numbers of ordinary middle-class Americans improve the American image abroad and encourage governments to align themselves with the United States in international politics.

On the other side of the coin, much of the apprehension about the environmental degradations caused by mass tourists—the consequences of what in France were called invasions of the "New Barbarians"—proved to be justified.[6] Each summer the writer Jan Morris's warning that "almost by definition, [mass tourism] attacks everywhere most beautiful" seemed borne out, as mobs of tourists inundated the Côte d'Azur and turned places such as Paris's Notre-Dame Cathedral into three-ring circuses.[7] As one of the characters in David Lodge's 1992 novel about tourism says, "Tourism is wearing out the planet. . . . A hundred and eight people enter Notre Dame every minute: their feet are eroding the floor and the buses that bring them are rotting the stone work with exhaust fumes. . . . The Mediterranean is like a toilet without a chain."[8]

On the other hand, the predictions that mass tourism would bring an essential sameness of experience—of masses of undifferentiated tourists peering at foreign places from man-made cocoons—did not quite pan out. Although the booming cruise ship industry surely bore this out, powerful countervailing forces were also at work. The most important of these was the fragmentation of American popular culture. Cable television undermined the Big Three television networks and opened the way for programs targeted at smaller segments of viewers. A wide variety of opinion leaders came to the fore, each influential in different fields—late-night talk show hosts on the vagaries of politicians, Oprah Winfrey on self-help, MTV on popular music, and so on.[9] Producers of consumer goods began tailoring their products to "niche" markets, rather than trying to turn out "one-size-fits-all" products for an undifferentiated mass market. The all-pervasive styles that had characterized modernism were replaced by individualized juxtapositions of apparently incongruous elements.

In the 1980s literary and social critics began calling this kind of fragmentation, where there is no dominant voice or style, postmodernism. People in the tourist industries, their eyes firmly fixed on their balance sheets, had no need for such theoretical labels. They had begun responding to the new rules of the game in the mid-1970s. In 1975 the European Travel Commission declared that the market was fragmenting and advised government tourist authorities to break down their promotional efforts to appeal to different sections of the market.[10] By the 1980s tourist market researchers were busily trying to "redefine market segments" to allow entrepreneurs to exploit new specialized niche markets.[11]

The fragmentation was clearly visible in American tourism to France. What the trade calls cultural tourism boomed, as colleges, universities, and various cultural institutions became major players in promoting and organizing overseas travel. Colleges opened so many junior-year-abroad programs that by 2000 they were shipping almost 130,000 American undergraduates overseas each year.[12] They scoured France in their search for new locales. Brown University chose Nancy in the west; the University of New Orleans selected beautiful Montpelier, in the south; Oregon hedged its bets, putting some students in urbanized Lyon and others in the small town of Poitiers.[13] They then began offering all kinds of shorter "study-travel" programs for "interested adults," some of whom ranged into their mid-seventies and older. The University of Pennsylvania turned La Napoule, a medieval-style château built near Cannes by a millionaire American artist, into its "campus on the Riviera," offering courses in French literature and "the French environment." Sarah Lawrence College and the University of Michigan joined together to offer a summer session at Lacoste, a village in Provence, where they promised participants could "sculpt in a quarry, paint in Provençal light, live in the village of the Marquis de Sade."[14]

Entrepreneurial French people began running short language courses for adults, involving stays in homes or hotels, in attractive locations around the country.[15] Guidebooks devoted to special-interest tourists proliferated. Women, African Americans, Jews, art lovers, and adventure lovers were each given special advice on how to explore France. *France on Foot* told of how to negotiate France's system of public footpaths with a pack weighing less than twenty pounds.[16] Gay tourism came out of the closet and into the marketplace. David Andrusia, author of *Gay Europe*, enthused that "no doubt about it, Paris is the gay capital of Europe right now. . . . The range and variety of gay life in Paris is . . . second to none." The Marais, he said, was "a focal point of gay life for all of Europe."[17] Alexander Lobrano's *Paris by Night* features a section on "where the boys are" that provides descriptions of a host of male gay bars as well as a smaller one on "where the girls are."[18]

Tour operators began offering a plethora of tours geared to special-interest groups: garden tours, wine-tasting tours, ladies' fashion tours, golf tours, flea-market tours, all-women tours, and even one called "Traveling with Your Grandchildren."[19] In 1995 Out and Abroad Tours offered luxury holidays for lesbians in a Loire valley château.[20] The death of Princess Diana of Great Britain on a Paris expressway in 1998 prompted a "Diana Death Tour" that followed her last itinerary, beginning at the Ritz hotel and ending at the hospital where she died.[21]

Some operators tried to break from dependence on coaches, whose image was now decidedly downscale, by offering alternative modes of transportation: canal boats, horses, balloons, and, of course, foot. They organized bicycle tours in which riders, accompanied by luggage-bearing vans, spent each evening at comfortable country hotels, where, their guilt assuaged by exercise, they could enjoy excellent cuisine. One company combined special-interest touring with alternative transportation by offering a "Gay Biking in Burgundy" tour and a gay men's bike tour of the Dordogne valley with optional hot-air ballooning.[22] In 1998 one tour operator offered to take golfers on the Concorde for a $50,000 two-week round-the-world "Perfect Blend of Golf, Luxury, and Leisure" that stopped in Paris, presumably for the luxury, on the way back to New York.[23]

——

American art museums, universities, and other prestigious nonprofit cultural institutions turned to group tours as fund-raisers. Aside from first-class accommodation and meals, such sponsorship promised to spare tourists from that nightmare of regular tours: being thrust together in enclosed places with tedious people with decidedly different tastes and interests. They also promised a more civilized pace than regular tours. Instead of martinets whose main concern was getting everyone out of the bathroom and back on the bus in time to get to the next souvenir stand, the tours were accompanied by college faculty and other mild-mannered experts who provided informed commentary. The institutions could also help to arrange special viewing hours at art museums, meetings with foreign notables, and entrée into restricted areas. The Smith College alumnae tour group in Paris was invited to cocktail parties in fashionable private apartments and to the American ambassador's residence for tea and a tour of the art collection.[24]

Yet market fragmentation also meant that there were still customers for the old "If It's Tuesday" tours. In 1999 a reporter for *USA Today* joined a seven-day, eight-country whirlwind that began in London. The tourists hardly had time to say, "If it's Tuesday, this must be Belgium," because Belgium flashed by in one hour. After an overnight stop in Amsterdam, they barreled through the German Rhineland, the Austrian and Swiss Alps, and looped into France, making it from Lucerne, Switzerland, to Paris in a day. The next day they were joined by a local guide, who let them debark at Notre-Dame (the reporter had previously learned that "view" in the brochure did not mean "visit") before taking them on a quick spin through the rest of the city's highlights. They were then given the option of taking a $47 afternoon tour of Versailles and $115 evening "can-can dinner show" before heading back to London early the next morning.[25]

Other such guided coach tours were longer, but new expressways cutting through Europe allowed them to use the extra days to add on more destinations.[26] Whatever their length, though, there was always time for stops at shops such as the "perfume factories" of Grasse, outside of Nice, where the guides received a commission on sales. Guides also made money from the "optional" evening entertainment packages such as the ones mentioned above in Paris. There, the Moulin Rouge and Lido paid particularly high commissions, selling the guides tickets at deep discounts, which were then sold to tourists at full price. "Tourists get plucked like pigeons," said one of the guides. "Poor old tourists, they don't know they're pigeons."[27]

One reason for the continuing popularity of such group tours was that people over fifty now comprised a greater proportion of overseas travelers than before.[28] Not only were they an increasing proportion of the general population; they also had the discretionary income and leisure time necessary for an overseas trip.[29] They were particularly concerned about language problems and looked to guided tours to help them navigate through foreign cultures. "When I go to Europe I want to be led by hand everywhere," said one such traveler.[30] Although many naturally opted for cosseting group tours or cruise ships, many also chose more serious kinds of cultural tourism such as Elderhostels, which offered people over fifty-five short academic programs. Even those on the standard sightseeing tours thought of them as educational. The overwhelming response of a sampling of over-65s to a survey asking, "Why do you travel?" was, "To see new sights and scenery." To them, the survey said, seeing "historic sights, museums, landscapes and any places they had not seen before" was an "an educational experience." "Clearly," it concluded, "seniors view travel as a learning experience."[31] Jennifer Burdon, an English-speaking guide in Paris, thinks that her over-sixties clients are the ones most interested in France's history and cultural treasures. "They have the longest attention spans," she says.[32]

Of course, fragmentation only went so far, and overseas travel remained overwhelmingly middle and upper-middle class. In 1999, 75 percent of Americans flying abroad for leisure classified themselves as one of professional/technical, manager/executive, retired, student, or homemaker (in that order). Only 3 percent were in the craftsman/factory worker category.[33]

— —

Perhaps the most paradoxical result of the fragmentation of American tourism was to see France transformed from the quintessential destination for civilized (meaning, in its Latin derivation, urbanized) delights into a place where one could escape into a rustic premodern environment. In the 1990s many Americans, particularly those in the trendsetting upper-middle class, began departing from the sophisticated Paris–Riviera axis to connect with what the French call *la France profonde*, the "deep" France of small old villages and individualistic peasant farmers.[34] Much of the groundwork for this had been laid in the 1970s and 1980s, when the remnants of the counterculture's reverence for people who lived close to nature had merged with

Americans' historic admiration for farmers and others leading "the simple life."[35] The spark was provided by *A Year in Provence*, a 1989 book in which the Englishman Peter Mayle told of how he quit his job as a New York advertising executive and moved, with his new wife, to a small village in the Luberon, an off-the-beaten-track part of Provence. The book chronicles the travails and pleasures that accompanied renovating an old house and tells of the unhurried pace at which the local people worked, or, in some cases, did not work. It is full of amusing stories of the quaint local practices and colorful portraits of the gruff but usually genial neighbors. In it, Mayle seems to have carved out a life that would be the envy of any overworked urbanite, enjoying the area's honest foods, sturdy wines, and lovely sunsets. Hard on the heels of the book's runaway success, he rushed out a sequel, which went into greater detail on how his life was now in tune with the changing seasons and the area's simple gastronomic and oenological pleasures.[36]

Mayle's books set off a rush of tourists to rural Provence. So many poured into his own village looking for his house and the colorful local characters that many of the villagers turned against him. After writing two comic novels playing on the same themes, he moved to less rustic Long Island, New York. However, the tourists still kept coming, especially to Provence and the rest of the South of France, hoping to escape from modern urban pressures. French urbanites caught the bug, too, and all over the South of France people now renovated abandoned town houses and crumbling farm buildings for holiday rentals, equipping them with tastefully furnished living quarters, state-of-the-art plumbing, and even swimming pools. The temporary residents would search out local food markets and small restaurants and, as David Brooks has said, savor living amongst people who did not even have an opinion on Bill Gates. These highly trained, well-off beneficiaries of America's meritocracy were, he said, "suckers for darkly garbed peasants, aged farmers, hardy fishermen, remote craftsmen, weather-beaten pensioners, heavy-set regional cooks—anybody who never possessed or heard of frequent flier miles." To the Americans, their lives "seem[ed] connected to ancient patterns and age-old wisdom."[37]

Shopping locally for food and wine was usually a key element in feeling connected to this stressless premodern world. Writing of renting a small place in a village in Provence, William Grimes, restaurant reviewer for the *New York Times*, said, "At food markets, you enter the daily life of the host country." The profusion and variety of foods at the local market "simply boggled the mind," he wrote. "It was sheer bliss to stand in front of a table and choose from among a dozen kinds of tapenade." These and the other foods he adored—"vegetables, fruit, cheese, meat, charcuterie, honey and olives"—were mainly local and artisanal products, far removed, it seemed, from modern supermarket shelves.[38] Aside from their superior taste, much of the pleasure of buying them comes from feeling that one is getting in touch with relaxing premodern days. A woman who spent a week with her family in one such place in 1995 wrote in her diary that when they left, "we felt we were taking leave of a special little community, far away and in another time. [I] hope that one day we'll get back to there, to the place, the people, and the sense of calm and continuity the old rock has."[39]

— —

Not entirely coincidentally, Americans' new interest in the countryside was accompanied by an increased appreciation for French food and wine. Much of this was fueled by ideas about the "Mediterranean Diet" and the "French Paradox." Throughout the 1970s and 1980s, Americans were warned on all sides about death from heart disease—"America's No. 1 Killer." Then came reports that "Mediterranean" people died from this at about half the American rate. The reason, said a number of the studies, must lie in diet, especially the fact that Mediterranean people ate much more in the way of fruit, vegetables, and carbohydrates than Americans and much less meat, dairy products, and sweets. Some also argued that a key was their high consumption of olive oil.[40] In *Toujours Provence*, Peter Mayle credits the local diet of fresh vegetables and fruits, little meat, a variety of fish and seafood, pasta, "dozens of breads, "cheeses, and olive oil with making him and his wife feel healthier and lose weight.[41]

The diet also had a morally satisfying aspect, for its advocates emphasized the salutary effects of the pleasurable, family-centered surroundings among which Mediterranean people consumed their food—what one called "a sense of food as a fundamentally communal, shared experience."[42] Paula Wolfert, author of a number of Mediterranean cookbooks, said, "The Mediterranean lifestyle is an anti-stress way of living. Life there is centered around the family at the table."[43] People such as Mayle also pointed to the genuine pleasure the French derived from eating—their "national enthusiasm for food"—and there were suggestions that this was also a key to their better health.[44]

The idea of the "French Paradox" stressed the other side of the coin—what the French drank. It became a household word in North America on November 17, 1991, when the television program *60 Minutes* raised the question of why the French, who seem to consume what health-conscious Americans thought were enormous amounts of deadly fats, had lower rates of deaths from cardiovascular diseases than Americans. In it, the presenter, Morley Safer, raised a glass of red wine and said that the answer "may lie in this inviting glass." A number of experts then said they thought this was connected to the fact that the French drank twenty gallons of wine per person per year while Americans only drank two. Also, it was pointed out, unlike Americans, they mainly drank red wine, and did so in the convivial, stress-free atmosphere of mealtime. Clearly, red wine, consumed in relaxed circumstances, seemed to hold the key.

The program's impact was enormous. In the four weeks after it aired, supermarket sales of red wines shot up by 45 percent. In the months that followed, red wine sales continued to climb steadily, followed by white wines, which some experts now said were just as beneficial. The jump in red wine sales was particularly extraordinary in light of the common American belief that red wine, not white, causes headaches.[45]

French foodways were also said to head off the most recent scourge of the American diet—body fat. For years French people visiting America had been struck by the enormous number of obese people one sees there. Now, Americans visiting France noticed the other side of the coin: that French people, despite their apparently fattening diets, seemed much slimmer than Americans. Again, premodernophilia played a role in the explanation: the key element in French success in holding down their weight was said to be their continuing commitment to the old-fashioned family meal. A *Business Week* piece called "Why So Few French People Are Fat" explained that "gathering to eat together in the evening and on weekends is still sacrosanct in most French families and most people eat three balanced meals a day, with very little snacking in between." A quote from a restaurateur in Aix-en-Provence made it seem like a premodern ritual: "In France, eating is like a religion, like a Catholic Mass: At a fixed hour, for a predetermined amount of time, with an unchangeable ritual, we sit down at breakfast, lunch, and dinner."[46]

This satisfyingly rustic aspect of France's image was reinforced by Americans' growing interest in organic farm products and artisanal food products. Now, when the upper-middle classes sought out vacation-cum-cooking classes in France, they went, not to urban cooking schools such as the Cordon Bleu in Paris, but to country towns and rural villages. There, the highlight of the day was usually the daily visit to the local markets, to admire and taste the displays of farm-fresh products and artisanal products, such as unpasteurized cheeses, that they would be hard-pressed to find in the United States.[47]

This was all a reflection of Americans' increasing appreciation of foreign food. *Gourmet* magazine began running so many articles about gastronomic tourism it threatened to become indistinguishable from *Travel and Leisure*. The *New York Sunday Times* Travel section ran a weekly feature, "Choice Tables," on fine dining places around the world. By the end of the millennium, French restaurateurs were recognizing that many of their American customers had very cultivated palates. In an interview in 2000, Guy Savoy, whose eponymous fine restaurant in Paris was a continuing favorite with Americans, said there was no question of him adjusting his food for American tastes. His American customers loved French food and were put off if it was not done in the French way—for example, if their meat was automatically served well done. They were by far the most enthusiastic of his large foreign clientele ("'Best meal I ever had,' they say"), and about 80 percent of them were repeaters. They were just as knowledgeable about wines as his French customers and sometimes knew more about particular wines than his sommeliers.[48] William Ledeuil, the chef and co-owner of an innovative bistro on the Left Bank, said that Americans responded well to his experiments with "fusion" and other techniques. They rarely asked for ketchup, he said, and particularly enjoyed interesting vegetable dishes. Moreover, although they had standard tastes in wine (like the French, he said, who nine times out of ten order a light Bordeaux), they were very open to suggestions.[49] Pierre Piaget, a maître d'hôtel at a brasserie on boulevard Montparnasse, observed in 1999 that Americans were becoming more curious about food and were more willing to try something new, often asking him, "Tell me what it tastes like."[50] Colette Brossard, whose Michelin-starred hotel restaurant in the Loire valley drew a discerning clientele attracted by her son-in-law chef's inventive cuisine, noted an upsurge in what she called American "hobbyists," mainly from the East or West Coasts, who were very interested in food and wine and were willing to try something new.[51] Even first-time tourists with little familiarity with French food would arrive expecting gastronomic epiphanies in France. "Everything seems new and exotic to them," said Olivier Tourlet, the maître d' at a Left Bank bistro with many American patrons. "Chicken and spinach is like truffles and caviar. When you put dessert down on the table they scream. They are like big kids."[52]

Yet for many others, French food remained problematic. The wealthier among them still gravitated to the same expensive restaurants—the Tour d'Argent, Maxim's, Jacques Cagna—where one was assured of a welcome by solicitous English-speaking staff who knew how to steer Americans to dishes that would hardly offend them.[53] Or they would do the steering themselves. "They ask ten questions about the menu and then order steak," said Tourlet. Some of his patrons could not understand why they did not have the usual choice of dressings for their salads—ranch, blue cheese, Thousand Island, and so on—and have to settle for oil and vinegar. When they asked for ketchup with the steaks, he would respond, "It is forbidden."[54]

Others would insist that the French duplicate their favorite dishes back home. Piaget said the staff at his restaurant regularly fielded orders for "surf and turf," an item that they and the kitchen staff regarded as gross. When told it was not on the menu, patrons would provoke sneers in the kitchen by demanding that the chefs take a lobster and a chateaubriand steak, each of which cost a small fortune, and plop one on top of the other. French chefs also continued to brood over Americans' frequent orders for well-done steak, often setting aside their worst cuts of beef, which they cooked to the consistency of shoe leather, for that purpose. ("I warn them it will lead to loss of flavor," said Tourlet.)[55]

Innards, of course, remained off-limits to most, as did fish with bones.[56] Tourlet said that not only are they horrified by fish heads; "they can't handle anything with bones, even chicken." He was amazed to be asked, "Are there bones in that chicken?" Piaget was surprised that Americans were often afraid to order seafood, fearing that it would not be fresh. They seemed unaware that thanks to the marvelous system for supplying Paris with seafood caught the previous day, his fish in Paris is likely far fresher than what they usually see. The most recent puzzlement for the French, though, was the proliferation of food allergies. Ten years ago, said Tourlet in 2002, one encountered this once every six months. Now, ten people a month said they were allergic to grains, seeds, nuts, and/or milk products.[57]

Also, despite the talk of the salutary effects of wine with meals, many Americans still drank coffee and/or Diet Coke with their meals.[58] Jennifer Burdon recalled lunching with an American banker and judge and being embarrassed when they both ordered Coke with their quiche. Piaget said that those who started their meals with coffee were especially frustrated at the difficulty of nursing it through the meal, because the cups are tiny, the coffee is strong, and there are no fill-ups. Yet his attempts to persuade them to also try some wine with their meal were usually to no avail.[59] Burdon recalled one waiter responding to a request for weaker American-style coffee by saying, "We try, but can't quite make coffee as bad as you do." She was also surprised at how many American tourists were still "generally uptight about alcohol" and told of a schoolteacher who complained when, at an overnight stopover at a tour of the châteaux of the Loire, Burdon and the driver drank wine with dinner.[60]

Finally, although some said that American diners are nowhere near as loud as they used to be ("They are no louder than others," said Guy Savoy, "only Quebeckers are") nor as annoying (Burdon said they rarely call waiters "garçon," which, although popular in 1950s movies, waiters find offensive), many Americans still struck French service people as rude.[61] They would commonly omit polite salutations such as "Bonjour, monsieur" before asking questions and still expect that every French person speak English.[62] Olivier Tourlet said, "They speak English right away, even when phoning in reservations, or they come to the door and just say, 'Hi, two.' If you don't answer in English, they are insulted and say, 'How can you not speak English!'" Moreover, he differed from Savoy on the loudness question, saying that once the wine begins to flow, their voices get louder. "The other night," he said, "four ladies at dinner with two bottles of wine got hysterical. The French couple sitting beside them will never come back."[63] On the other hand, like many in the restaurant business, he thought it "bizarre" that the Americans were so intimidated when it came to smoking. Even though smoking was permitted in his restaurant, they were afraid to light up in their seats and would instead go to the bar, or the doorway, or even out on the street to smoke. Sometimes, in a joke, he would follow them outside and tell them, "Sorry, but this is a no smoking sidewalk," or "There's no smoking on this side of the street," but they would often take him seriously.[64]

— —

French cuisine's continuing attraction was not matched by the other artisanal industry that had traditionally drawn visitors, haute couture. At the top levels, Paris did manage to fend off challenges from Milan and New York and cling to its role as the industry's main trendsetter. During the weeklong seasons of fashion shows in the spring and fall, the city remained crowded with buyers, reporters, and TV crews, filming the models slinking down the runways followed by the showers of jubilant air kisses and hugs backstage.[65] Visits to these shows and the fashion houses' shows did remain popular among what a *New Yorker* article called "the international clientele of wealthy American women who were willing to pay $20,000 for a dress they might only wear once."[66] However, Paris was no longer an important destination for the kind of upper-middle-class women who historically would come back from there with trunks full of clothes that would put them in the forefront of style in Chicago or Syracuse. Expensive ready-to-wear clothes and accessories from Paris's top fashion houses were now readily available in boutiques and department stores in major American cities. The only reason to buy them in Paris might be price, which was a factor only when, as in 1985, the dollar soared to nosebleed heights.[67]

Of course, the wider availability of fashionable clothes was by no means apparent in what Americans wore in France. They still tended to wear the same sneakers, warm-up suits, baseball caps, and, in the summer, shorts that they would wear when touring Washington, D.C., Williamsburg, or Disney World. Most seemed unaware or unconcerned that, as the guides Jennifer Burdon and Phillip Redman tried to tell them, the better one is dressed the better one is treated, especially in Paris. The two guides observed that the many American tourists who wore sneakers, "funny pants," jogging suits, and other casual clothes were not "treated well," no matter how rich they were.[68] Journeywoman.com, a Web site for women travelers, is full of warnings to dress well in Paris if one expects good treatment. One woman also advised dressing well and therefore looking "like a Parisienne" as a way of avoiding the infamous *draguers*, the sleazy men who try to pick up female tourists.[69] Olivier Tourlet said he could spot Americans entering his bistro by their dress: they wore sneakers or large walking shoes, even in the evening, and the women would often sport large diamond rings and other expensive jewelry that wealthy Frenchwomen would wear only on special occasions. ("Frenchwomen don't wear those things to bistros," he sniffed.)[70]

— —

Another historic attraction that faded was France's reputation among African Americans as a refuge from racism. Studies done in the mid-1970s and again in the 1990s found that, thanks in part to the civil rights revolution of the 1960s, there were now few differences between African Americans and white Americans in terms of which tourist destinations they found attractive.[71] Randy Garrett says he was inspired to come to Paris in 1973 by a schoolteacher aunt who had once been there and told him of how "cultured" and beautiful it was, with no reference to race.[72] The artist Clarence Major said that when he grew up in the 1950s on the South Side of Chicago, "the presence of Paris was surprisingly vivid." Local painters, singers, and a visit from Josephine Baker herself evoked images of its café life and "the glamour of Paris." So, when he went there in the 1980s, it was not to find freedom from discrimination, but to immerse himself in the "city of grimy bistros, Toulouse-Lautrec-style dance halls ... Henry Miller's postwar Paris."[73] Carol Mongo remembered that her mother, an educator in the Detroit school system, often spoke of her lifelong, and unfulfilled, dream of visiting Paris, but spoke in terms of its beauty, and never in terms of race.

Tourists, in what was by then their typically casual outfits, buying postcards on the Champs-Elysées in 1993. Courtesy of Roger-Viollet.

Mongo herself, who as a commercial artist, designer, and fashion journalist spent much of the 1980s traveling between New York City and Paris, said she far preferred Paris, not because of her race, but because she found it "more enjoyable and interesting."[74]

By the 1990s France's distinctive reputation seems to have receded so much in the African American consciousness that, despite the temptation of low airfares, most of Mongo's black friends and relatives in America could not be coaxed into visiting there. They were "scared of what they might find," she said. She recalled them saying, "I might not find any black people there." "What will I eat?'" In 1999, while running the Parsons School of Design junior-year-abroad program in Paris, she had great difficulty persuading black students to leave New York City for Paris. "They want everything like home," she said. "Fifty channels on the TV, the food the same, and so on." They were even reluctant to come on the summer program. She was also disturbed by the disparaging remarks she overheard from African Americans who did visit Paris, which hardly differed from what one might hear from whites. On the Métro she heard one say, "I'm disappointed. The meat's tough. The wine's sour." At American Express she has heard them say, "What a beautiful city; but where are the *modern* buildings?"[75]

On the other hand, the worsening racial tensions in France, visible in the rise of the racist National Front in the 1980s and increasing clashes between minority youths and police, seemed to have had little impact on African Americans in Paris. This was mainly because, as in the late 1950s and early 1960s, the hostility was mainly directed at North Africans and, to a much lesser extent, black people from France's ex-colonies in sub-Saharan Africa. Clarence Major wrote of the 1980s, "To be sure, there was as much racism in France as in the States, but in Paris I was not the target of French racism. As soon as the French discovered I was not an African or Arab, I was treated well."[76] In 1987 the expatriate African American sculptor Barbara Chase-Riboud even wrote, "The reciprocal love affair between the French and those they see not only as Americans but also as victims of a racist American society goes on."[77] Carol Mongo recalled that during the 1980s and early 1990s African Americans were "much appreciated" by the French. French audiences flocked to shows such as *Ain't Misbehavin'*, *Bubbling Brown Sugar*, and *Black and Blue*, which celebrated black music of the 1920s and 1930s. Jazz festivals continued to flourish on the Riviera, and Paris remained one of the few places in the world where modern jazz was alive and well. Young French people helped keep Haynes soul food restaurant in business and flocked to the Rib Joint, a barbecue place Randy Garrett opened in 1985 in the Latin Quarter. They would join black and white Americans on the large boats Garrett would rent to cruise the Seine on Memorial Day, July 4, and Bastille Day, munching on barbequed chicken and ribs and dancing to a jazz band.[78] In the 1990s a number of young African Americans with literary or artistic ambitions began arriving, seeking to follow in the footsteps of the black writers like Richard Wright, James Baldwin, and Chester Himes and artists such as Beauford Delaney who had thrived in postwar Paris.[79] Still, despite this, Paris remained but a remote blip on the radar screens of most African Americans.

France's loss of its unique role in the African American consciousness paralleled a similar evanescence among the population at large. French-language study continued to plummet. In 1998, 64.5 percent of high school students studying a second language chose Spanish, while only 22.3 percent studied French. The story in higher education was similar. Between 1968 and 1990, enrollment in university French courses dropped by close to 70 percent. This was followed by a 25 percent drop in enrollment in French studies between 1993 and 1998.[80]

All of this seemed to reflect a steady decline in interest France and its culture. At the loftier heights, despite considerable academic interest in trying to decipher French literary and cultural theory in the 1980s and 1990s, few intellectuals felt the kind of need to keep abreast of the latest currents in French thought that was common in the 1940s and 1950s, when people such as Sartre and Camus were on everyone's must-read lists. On the level below, Bertram Gordon's count of the number of articles on France in the *Readers' Guide to Periodical Literature,* which mainly catalogs middle-brow magazines, is aptly titled "Decline of a Cultural Icon," for it chronicles a steady downward drift since the mid-1960s.[81]

In popular culture, the historic image of sexy France dimmed. *Playboy* magazine, which, under the editorship of a French-born American, had enthusiastically helped perpetuate the French reputation for sexiness in the late 1950s and 1960s, was no longer of much consequence.[82] Nor were there any sexy French film stars to match the likes of Maurice Chevalier, Brigitte Bardot, and Jean-Paul Belmondo to keep the ball rolling. Indeed, by the end of the century, France's reputation as a sexier place than America had practically evaporated. About the only thing that now turned American tourists' heads were the topless, and occasionally bottomless, women featured in the advertising posters.[83] In 2002 a reinvented Moulin Rouge was again pulling in busloads of group tourists and others willing to spend $140 on dinner, but this was for a practically sexless show featuring ponies, acrobats, a comic karaoke singer, and dancers doing the can-can. "If you marvel at the choreography on Lawrence Welk reruns, you'll love the Moulin Rouge," said one visitor. It "is not an echo of its glorious, raunchy past. . . . [It] belongs to the France that built EuroDisney. It's a prepackaged, off-the-shelf, sanitized stopover along the same tourist trail that rings the world." He said that even the Montmartre sex shops offered nothing different and were distinguished only by names such as "Dust Live Peep" and "Live Lab Danse."[84] Soon, these and the remaining streetwalkers were threatened by a clean-up campaign that sought to gentrify the quarter, something that was spurred by tourists coming to see the sanitized café featured in the charming movie *Amélie,* which gently played on some of the old themes of romance in Paris.

All in all, then, it seemed that for most American tourists, France had become just another stop on the international sightseeing circuit. The real love affair with those aspects of the country that were distinctively French seemed restricted more than ever to its traditional redoubts among the East Coast social elite and the upper-middle classes. This would prove to be a crucial factor in the brewing crisis in Franco-American relations.

FIFTEEN

Nobody's Perfect

It is perfectly appropriate that [the movie Moulin Rouge*] was filmed in Australia; Paris has always existed best in the minds of its admirers.*

—ROGER EBERT (June 2001)

In April 2002 the satirical late-night television show *Saturday Night Live* did a spoof of a French tourism commercial. It showed a series of images such as the Eiffel Tower, the Louvre, and a little girl carrying a load of baguettes while a sweet female voice-over said, "The French: cowardly yet opinionated, arrogant yet foul smelling. Anti-Israel, anti-American, and, of course, as always, Jew-hating. With all that's going on in the world, isn't it time we got back to hating the French?"[1] The skit was rather too close to home to be funny, for Francophobia was rising again in America. Many American Jews had been dismayed to see Jean-Marie Le Pen, whose National Front had previously appealed to anti-Semitism, come in second in the first round of the 2002 presidential elections.[2] A wave of attacks against French Jews and their religious sites, perpetrated mainly by young Arab French hooligans, exacerbated matters.[3] American Jews now once again condemned France and its government for being soft on anti-Semitism. In early 2002 Edward Koch, the ex-mayor of New York City, took to signing off his weekly radio broadcasts with what he said (incorrectly) were the words Julius Caesar used when he marched off to conquer France: "Omni Gaul delenda est!" (All Gaul must be destroyed!)[4] The Simon Wiesenthal Center, a Jewish human rights organization, called on Jews to avoid travel to France because it was dangerous for them there. Kosher Expeditions of New York responded by canceling all of its tours to France. A Jewish woman canceled her honeymoon trip there, saying, "I love France, I'm a Francophile, and I love French food and wine. But I don't want to go there. Why would I want to give money to people who want to kill me?"[5] The California branch of the American Jewish Congress called for a boycott of the Cannes Film Festival.[6]

However, it was the French government's refusal in early 2003 to go along with the American-led invasion of Iraq that set off the greatest wave of Francophobia. Many of its manifestations, such as the infamous order from a Republican congressman from Ohio to have the word "French" stricken from all House of Representative menus and to have French fries renamed "freedom fries," were too ridiculous to be taken seriously. But there were a number of aspects of this outpouring that are significant for our purposes.[7] First, there was that it appealed mainly to the kind of Sun Belt and midwestern conservatives who, as we saw in chapter 12, sneered at the effete Francophilia of the East Coast elite. Even before the Iraq crisis, these circles had responded enthusiastically to Francophobic sentiments. The self-proclaimed "frog-basher" Jonah Goldberg said that soon after he started writing anti-French pieces in the conservative magazine *National Review* in 1998, he found that "there was a market for it" and turned into a popular "shtick."[8] Now, French consulates reported that midwestern and Sun Belt conservatives were the main source of the nasty messages bombarding the consulates and the calls for boycotts of French products. The director of the French American chamber of commerce in Chicago told *Le Monde* that the bitterness toward France was concentrated in "l'Amérique profonde."[9]

A major part of the "shtick" was how it appealed to American machismo by feminizing France and its men. Although rhetoric such as this was nothing new, it now reflected how in the 1960s and 1970s France had lost its historic reputation among American men as a sexy place full of men satisfying their lusty desires. In late 2001 the conservative theorist Dinesh D'Souza wrote that "the French seem to be outraged by the idea that any single nation, let alone the United States, should enjoy global domination." Fortunately, he said, these views would carry little weight, since "most Americans find it hard to take the French critique seriously, coming as it does from men who carry handbags."[10] One of the conservatives' favorite quotes was from the pundit Robert Kagan, who explained European unwillingness to follow America into war by saying, "Europe is from Venus and the United States is from Mars."[11] When, with the crisis brewing, President Bush, an ex-two-fisted macho drinker, left for a rest at his Texas ranch, he pointedly remarked that it would be a relief to get away from the "wine-swilling" types from the coasts, who presumably, like the French wine swillers, were insufficiently masculine.[12]

Higher-level Francophobia echoed other themes we have heard. Sophisticated commentators such as Thomas Friedman revived the anti-Gaullist rhetoric that portrayed the French as deluded by dreams of grandeur.

France, he said, was a second-rate power that did not belong on the United Nations Security Council. It was "so caught up with its need to differentiate itself from America to feel important, it's become silly." Later he said it was "becoming our enemy," as it nursed the "crazy hope" of assuming its "'rightful' place as America's equal."[13] The secretary of defense, Donald Rumsfeld, gleefully dismissed France as part of a now-irrelevant and powerless "old Europe."[14]

The old canards about World War II were also hauled out again. The *Washington Post* columnist Michael Kelly, who later died while covering the invasion, wrote of "the French foreign minister, whose name is Pétain or Maginot or something."[15] Friedman said, "If America didn't exist and Europe had to rely on France, most Europeans today would be speaking either German or Russian."[16] The *National Review* took pride in popularizing the epithet "cheese-eating surrender monkeys." (It originated on the TV animated show *The Simpsons*.)[17] French ingratitude for being liberated during the war was another favorite target. The conservative *New York Post*, owned by the same corporation as Fox News, featured a front-page photograph of an American military cemetery in Normandy with the headline "HAS FRANCE FORGOTTEN?" One of its reporters told of how, with tears in his eyes, he looked at the cemetery's gravestones and thought of how, "now, as more American kids are poised to fight and die to save the world from an equally vile tyrant," the French were "Hiding. Chickening Out. Proclaiming *Vive les wimps!*" Noting that a poll showed 91 percent of the French were opposed to Bush's policy, he said, "But then again, the French are against everything, including that curious American habit of showering every day."[18] A Republican congresswoman demanded that the bodies of Americans buried in France be repatriated "to patriotic soil, not in a country that has turned its back on the United States and the memory of the Americans who died there."[19]

As we have seen, all of these themes were current among GIs in 1945 and 1946. Even the remarkable absence of hostility toward the Germans, who were much more intransigent than the French in refusing to support military action in Iraq, echoed the old feelings that the Germans were preferable to the French on most counts. However, the French-bashing also went off in some new directions. The main theme of the outpouring of anti-French jokes on e-mail and on Web sites such as www.fuckfrance was that the French opposed the invasion because they were cowards. Many were recycled jokes about the Italian army in World War II that had little specific reference to France. (The most popular was "What do you call 100,000 Frenchmen with their hands up? The Army.") However, a large proportion of them linked supposed French cowardice to its men being feminized and homosexual.[20] This fit in well with attempts to portray American opponents of the war as effete Francophiles who were traitors to masculine American ideals.

This kind of yahooism exemplified two things that were discussed in the previous chapter: The first was the extent to which any real knowledge of France and its culture has practically disappeared in mainstream America. The many Hollywood movies, beginning with *Casablanca*, that portrayed the French as resisting the Nazis were long forgotten. Memories of two generations of macho film stars—Jean Gabin, Maurice Chevalier, Jean-Paul Belmondo, Yves Montand—seemed to have evaporated completely. Moreover, instead of expressing disgust with one of the many things the French eat that Americans have historically found repulsive, people for whom cheeseburgers are a kind of icon resorted to "cheese-eating" as a pejorative.

Second, it shows how Francophilia had become concentrated in the upper-class social elite, upper-middle-class liberals, and women—the people who most enjoyed traveling to France. It was revealing that hardly any of the jokes or Internet tirades contained the kinds of complaints commonly voiced by American tourists to France. Rarely did they refer to French greed or rudeness, and very few even mentioned their reputation for anti-Americanism.[21] Indeed, a rough survey of the many personal messages on the Web site www.fuckfrance turned up no reference at all to an experience, unpleasant or otherwise, in France itself. In contrast to concern about French anti-Semitism, much of this kind of Francophobia seems to have been concentrated among people who never were and never wanted to be tourists in France.

———

This is not to say that the Americans who did travel to France were unaware of the French reputation for anti-Americanism. Indeed, it was practically impossible for anyone who followed the news to be so. In the late 1990s, the American media were full of reports about the anti-American aspects of the French anti-globalization movement. As in other Western countries, the one thing the movement's activists seemed to agree on was that, whatever the consequences that most concerned them—be it environmental degradation, genetic engineering, or *mal-bouffe* (lousy eating)—it was giant American corporate interests and the American government that were behind them. In April 2000 the *New York Times* lamented the appearance of a rash of French books denouncing globalization, American world power, and "deploring the American way."[22]

What was happening was that many of the French, like many others, feared that the disappearance of the Soviet threat was encouraging the United States to use its position as the only remaining superpower to try to impose its system and values on the rest of the world. After an initial wave of sympathy in the wake of the September 11, 2001, terrorist attacks, which prompted *Le Monde*'s famous headline "WE ARE ALL AMERICANS NOW," these fears resurfaced with the United States' unilateral "War on Terror" and its refusal to allow NATO participation in the invasion of Afghanistan. American pundits warned that this was a manifestation of a new wave of French anti-Americanism and cited the usual politicians' and intellectuals' criticisms of American arrogance and mass culture as evidence of this.[23]

The French critics did indeed play on the long-standing anti-American themes, once again condemning the United States' dehumanizing materialism, rapacious individualism, and debased mass culture.[24] What was interesting, though, was that amidst their portrayals of President Bush as a trigger-happy cowboy out to force the world into accepting the American way of life there were few suggestions that in that respect he was typical of most Americans. (Indeed, it was often pointed out that only a minority voted for him in the 2000 election.) Nor was there any suggestion that American tourists in France represented these unfortunate characteristics. Even as the first American troops rolled into Iraq, when French opinion was most opposed to American policy, there were no reports of untoward incidents involving American tourists. A fifty-eight-year-old American woman tourist waiting to meet some friends at the Eiffel Tower told a reporter, "Everyone we're talking to is saying, 'We're friends with the Americans whether we agree with their politics or not.'"[25] When the *New York Post* correspondent weeping in the Normandy cemeteries tried to get an American student studying in France to tell him she had been subject to anti-Americanism, all she could say was, "Nothing has happened to me, but . . . we have been told that if we face any kind of threat, we should say we're Canadians, not Americans."[26]

The main reason for the absence of hostility was that, even more than in previous eras, French anti-Americanism had little to do with individual Americans. Indeed, as had so often been the case, it had much more to do with French politics than with what Americans were really like. In his acerbic analysis of the contradictions in their critiques, Jean-François Revel pointed out how the French anti-Americans of the 1990s attacked the

United States in order to buttress their arguments that France should not abandon its government-directed economy and comfortable welfare state in favor of American-style free-market policies.[27] Even the most virulent opponents of American policies seem to have had little or no animosity toward Americans themselves. In 1999 one of the most notorious of them, José Bové, an anti-globalization leader who was sentenced to prison for helping to destroy a McDonald's outlet, took pains to deny he was anti-American, saying he agreed with another leader who declared, "To be anti-American is idiotic."[28]

Of course, what Bové meant was that he had nothing against Americans as individuals and admired many aspects of American culture. (Indeed, his strategy and tactics owed much to the years he spent at the University of California at Berkeley.)[29] This would seem to have been the case with the large majority of the French. Only 10 percent of the French people surveyed in May 2000 expressed hostility toward the United States, while 41 percent liked it and 49 percent said they neither liked nor disliked it. The main source of popular anti-Americanism, the Communist Party, was withering away, and only a small minority of the working class, who had previously been its bedrock, were anti-American.[30] Indeed, a survey the year before showed more anti-Americanism among older, higher-income people, who were especially alarmed over the popularity of American cultural products among French young people, than among those who were younger and poorer.[31] The young seemed unmoved by denunciations of McDonald's food as "McMerde" (McShit) and flocked to it and other American fast-food chains such as Pizza Hut. Even the Bush administration's appointment of an ambassador, Howard Leach, who spoke no French caused few ripples. ("I wish I could speak their beautiful language," he said, "but I can communicate well with the people.")[32] In a mid-March 2003 poll, taken just before the United States invaded Iraq, three-quarters of the French respondents said that the problems created by America were "mostly Bush," while only a fraction, 15 percent, blamed Americans in general.[33]

— —

Still, throughout the late 1990s and early 2000s, American visitors continued to assume that it was anti-Americanism that impelled café waiters to abuse them and department store clerks to ignore them. So persistent was this idea of implacable French anti-Americanism that American tourists continued to be surprised by signs of French hospitality and decency. The guide Phillip Redman recalled taking a group of 120 Normandy-landing veterans and their families back to Normandy in 1996. When he picked them up in England, they told him, "The French hate us," reflecting, he thought, what they had read in the Americans press. When they arrived in Normandy, though, the French arranged a moving welcoming ceremony in a large town hall and each American family was paired off with a French one. "No one said, 'The French hate us' again," he recalled.[34] A resident of Cape Cod returned from a trip to Paris and told of how, "having heard that the French could be rude to American tourists, especially those who made no attempt to speak French," he and his wife had taken a short evening course at the local high school that equipped them with a few useful phrases. As a result, he said, "The people we met were almost universally kind."[35] A number of Americans interviewed in Paris in the summer of 1995 all repeated the same theme: Parisians were, as one of them said, "nicer and more forgiving" than they expected.[36]

Yet there was still no shortage of Americans experiencing French rudeness. In her 1994 travel guide to historic France, Ina Caro said she was omitting places that were "marvels but where the guides or the townspeople embody those traits of arrogance and rudeness which Americans who think they hate France identify with France . . . those places where the American tourist is likely to be arrogantly or rudely treated."[37] When Sherri Kelly, an administrator at an investment firm in Boston, made her first trip to France with her partner in 2001, she found it nerve-racking to be in the first place she had ever visited where she did not speak the language. Intimidated by the French reputation for rudeness and unable to understand them, she often thought they were insulting and making fun of her. She recalled stopping at a Left Bank café at 3:00 PM and asking a waiter, "Are you open?" He threw up his hands and said, "Don't you see people sitting here? Of course we're open." When she and her partner sat down, the waiter seemed to be talking about them to the other waiters, making fun of them. When he finally came to their table, he was cold, abrupt, and literally looked down his nose at them. "We were told to expect this kind of behavior from the French," she said, but she still felt traumatized by such situations. Her partner, she said, was less perturbed. "That's just the way the French are," he said.[38]

Some observers tried to reassure American tourists that what they perceived as rudeness had nothing to do with their being Americans. An article in the *Boston Globe* said it was difficult for the French to be kind to strangers because they were not taught to be friendly when they were children. It quoted a businessman trying to teach his employees to change their ways as saying, "Being nice is not ingrained in French culture." A *New York Times* article on such efforts was entitled "To Parisians, Nice Is a Place, Not an Attitude."[39] The head of the Paris tourist bureau lamented, "We Latins treat everyone we don't know with suspicion. Not just foreigners. Everyone." Then, perhaps in anticipation of the obvious rejoinder, which is why Italy did not suffer from the same reputation, he added, "Parisians cannot support the notion of service. They are very individualistic and feel they shouldn't have to change their identity for a tourist."[40]

As in the past, the rudeness seemed to be concentrated in Paris. "What few tourists realize," said Alan Riding, a *New York Times* correspondent in Paris, "is that they are not victims of xenophobic discrimination. The rest of France thinks Parisians behave in a pretty uncivilized way. Indeed, Parisians often even treat each other like potential enemies."[41] Government and business leaders apparently agreed, and kept plugging away at their never-ending efforts to, in the words of the Paris tourist authority, "sensitize" Parisians to the importance of being welcoming to foreigners. One of the campaigns told them to "welcome every tourist with a smile" and to apologize, "even if it is not your fault."[42]

There was some evidence that such efforts were finally having an impact. When some French companies began teaching employees to smile, establish eye contact, and try to be helpful to customers, the *Washington Post* reported that "these days employees in hotels, restaurants, and department stores are trained to be not just polite, but downright friendly."[43] Redman and Burdon, the two tour guides, also thought that such efforts were bearing some fruit. Over the past fifteen years, they said in 2000, the French had become more "open, patient, and kind." The provincial hotels where an old crone at a desk looked suspiciously at prospective guests were mainly gone, they said, and everyone had learned "hotel school styles."[44] Even Sherri Kelly felt that the Parisian waiter's rudeness was counterbalanced by the warm, helpful welcome they received at their hotel. "Paris was worth it," she concluded, "even though they were rude."[45]

— —

There was also no consensus on romance in France. The old idea that a visit there might change one's romantic life proved remarkably resilient, but mainly among women. It was Gael Greene, not a man, who said, "What I love about Paris is how often it lives up to my romantic dreams."[46] A French company, L'Oréal, came to dominate the American cosmetics market by associating its products with the beauty and romance of Paris.[47] "You will have pleasure," wrote Heather Mallick of her upcoming trip there with her husband in September 2000.

It is ordained. You will try, and fail, to feel guilty about this. . . . You will cease to care that there are waiters laughing at you behind your back and you will grow so accustomed to Côtes-du-Rhone that sobriety will be sharpish and unnerving. Your tastes will change. . . . You will become a little like the French government, corrupt and unprincipled, but in an interesting way. . . . I want to come back from Paris as a woman who is more fun to be married to. . . . Paris improves the visitor. Even the sex is better in Paris. . . . There is nothing to do in Paris except have sex and go out to eat afterward.[48]

It obviously worked. Later she wrote, "Sex is best of all in a Paris hotel room."[49] Not surprisingly, a 2000 poll found that many more American women than men liked France.[50]

Mallick mentioned the refreshing tisane that was featured in Diane Johnson's novel *Le Divorce*, which was later made into a movie. This is a story about two young American women's interactions with Frenchmen that, while deftly dissecting the French and American middle classes, also helped revivify the classic stereotype of the older Frenchman whose masterful sexual techniques turns the (relatively) innocent young American woman into a mature, pleasurable sexual partner.[51] In a somewhat different vein, *Gay Europe* says, "French men are (often) incredibly sexy and (usually) have no concept of fidelity whatsoever."[52]

But another guidebook warns gay people, "If you're coming from a switched on city like Seattle, Toronto or Miami, the gay scene in Paris may be a bit of a let down."[53] Indeed, for every enthusiastic view, there now seemed to be an equal and opposite one from someone unmoved by French romance and sensuality. A good case in point were two cousins, both in their early forties, who, with their partners and children, shared a house in Provence for two weeks in the summer of 1997 and visited Paris and the Riviera as well. Donna DiFillippo saw the French as the opposite of the puritanical New Englanders among whom she lived. Their lives were full of sensual pleasures, she thought. They cared about beauty and beautiful clothes, dressed provocatively, and acted flirtatiously: "Just being there made me think about sex—romance was in the air." Their culture, she said, was "about pleasure, living for the moment: smoking, drinking wine, enjoying a meal, driving fast," and she loved the leisurely pace of life in the South of France. "All the things I love about myself I could be there," she said. Her cousin Cynthia Croatti, on the other hand, felt none of the above. She saw nothing romantic about France or the French, and thought they were not nearly as open and friendly as the Americans she met on the trip.[54]

Attempts to discern the reality behind these contradictory images also run afoul of contradictions, for the data on sexuality can also be read in different ways. A 2001 sex survey comparing the United States and France undermined the idea that France was the sexier of the two. It found that despite the French reputation for tolerating infidelity and unconventional sexual practices, when it came to actual practice, there was really little to choose between the two nations. Indeed, if anything the French were more monogamous and only somewhat more ready to stray from conventional paths when actually engaged in sex. Yet the study did find a major difference in terms of women over fifty: older American women were far more likely to be sexually inactive than those in France. "French women [over fifty] continue to have sex later in life than Americans," said John Gagnon, the study's lead author, and "continue to see themselves as sexually attractive."[55] This would help explain why people like Donna DiFillippo notice that there seems to be more sex in the air on the streets of French cities. In the words of Mona Levenstein, Donna's cousin and Cynthia's older sister, "Many older Frenchwomen dress and act as if they're still in the game." She thinks this may contribute to American women of a certain age feeling the same when they visit France.[56]

— —

Even the statistics on French-language study in America could be read in two different ways. On the one hand, there was the substantial decline in French-language study mentioned in the previous chapter. On the other hand, when a 1999 report showed that 22 percent of the American secondary school students studying a foreign language took French, critics questioned why so many students were studying a language spoken fluently by only 2 percent of the world's population. "The only answer that makes sense," said one critic, is that French is "just so deeply embedded in our cultural traditions."[57]

Opinion polls seemed to support this contention that, at least before the Iraq crisis, the French language and culture were still highly regarded in America. A Gallup Poll on Americans' perceptions of various countries in the spring of 1999 indicated that 71 percent viewed France "very favorably" or "mostly favorably."[58] A French polling firm that asked a cross section of Americans a similar question in 2000 came up with a similar result. Although nearly half of the Americans chose to answer "neither sympathy or antipathy" or "no opinion," 45 percent said they liked France while only 7 percent said they were antipathetic to it.[59]

On the other hand, in the half-empty-glass category, a sizable proportion (18 percent) of the Gallup respondents did have a "mostly" or "very" unfavorable opinion of France. Moreover, the results showed that not only did they regard France much less favorably than they did Canada (about which, one must grant, they had few preconceptions at all) and Great Britain, they also ranked it behind their ex-wartime enemies, Germany and Japan.[60]

The Iraq controversy, of course, boosted hostility toward France, but not nearly as much as might be expected. While over 70 percent of Americans supported President Bush's refusal to forego invading in the face of the French-led UN refusal to support military action, only a third believed that France should be punished in any way for this.[61] Nor did it seem this would have any long-term effect on American tourism to France, for those favoring punishment came from the same kinds of circles we discussed above who had little interest in traveling there anyway. After returning from a series of speaking engagements in the Midwest just before the Iraq invasion, the Englishman Timothy Garton Ash said, "The predominant American popular attitude towards Europe is probably mildly benign indifference, mixed with impressive ignorance."[62] (Previous studies showing that 20 percent of American high school students thought that Joan of Arc was related to Noah would surely support the latter contention.)[63] However, one is still struck by the resilience of the historic American images of France, both positive and negative. They persist side by side, often in the same mind, leaving a trail of ambiguities.

— —

Of course, by the turn of the millennium, there was a way of indulging in some of France's charms without having to put up with its annoyances. In September 1999 the "Paris Las Vegas," an $850 million hotel-casino designed to look like Paris's Hôtel de Ville, opened in Las Vegas. Significantly, the hotel's theme was the product of focus groups that indicated that while men played a major role in deciding to come to Vegas, it was women who chose which hotels to stay in, and Paris was one of their favorite would-be destinations. The hotel features a fifty-story replica of the Eiffel Tower as well as copies of the Arc de Triomphe (two-thirds the actual size) and the Louvre. The enclosed cobblestoned shopping street is covered with a cloud-specked Paris sky. Croissants are flown in daily from Paris and beret-wearing employees, called "citizens," bicycle around, dressed in striped T-shirts and red kerchiefs, carrying baskets of baguettes and singing "Alouette." There is no need for tourists to feel inferior about their lack of French here. All the "citizens" are taught a tiny bit of French—just enough, Maureen Dowd observed, to make the tourist feel superior. "Bone jer, come on tally view?" her chambermaid said with a big grin. "That means 'How are you?'"[64]

Dowd called Paris Las Vegas "one humongous Gallic cliché," but one wonders whether that is not what most of us want from France, or indeed of any other foreign destination. In this age of mass tourism, where so many of the things we travel to see are subject to overcrowding and physical deterioration, there may be little choice but to pull up some of the most attractive ones from their dying roots and preserve or reproduce them for the delectation of paying visitors. In a 1998 novel called *England, England,* Julian Barnes took this idea to another extreme by having a future tycoon move all of England's favorite tourist attractions into a theme park, located on the Isle of Wight. This enabled tourists to conveniently take in all of them, including the king, in a cleaner, friendlier, and more efficiently seen environment.[65] For Americans, though, Las Vegas would still remain a better bet. There, not only could one have the French experience at the Paris Las Vegas, one could also sit in the shade of Italian trees by an eight-acre Lake Como at the Bellagio and go for a gondola ride at the Venetian Hotel. The Venetian also contained a branch of the Guggenheim Museum (recently closed) whose skylight was covered by a large-scale facsimile of Michelangelo's fresco in the Sistine Chapel of the Vatican. Another hotel features a branch of Madame Tussaud's Gallery, one of London's top tourist attractions. When one adds to these experiences those of the customers for the booming cruise ship industry, who have only the most fleeting interaction with their ports of call, we might be seeing the triumph of the kind of overseas tourism American visitors to France have often wished for: foreign tourism without foreigners.

But, then, tourists would miss out on the kind of thrill that first-time American visitors to France can still feel. In the spring of 2002, the flamboyant hip-hop/rap star "P. Diddy," who was now designing clothes, spent four days in Paris. Soon after his arrival, he made his first visits to the Louvre and Versailles, which he called "some-awe-inspiring shit." Then, as his limousine sped through the half-empty streets of Paris by night, he told a reporter, "This city is so fly. Look at the clocks and the windows and the lights. And those little Smart cars. Even the buses are cool. Can you find a speck of dirt or any garbage on the ground? It's amazing. These people have the food, the clothes, the love. The city is just mad beautiful."[66] He'll always have Paris too.

ABBREVIATIONS FOR FREQUENTLY CITED SOURCES

AAA	Archives of American Art, Smithsonian Institution, Washington, D.C.
ACP	American Cathedral of the Holy Trinity Archives, Paris, France
ATG	*American Traveler's Gazette* (Thomas Cook & Son)
BL	Bancroft Library, University of California, Berkeley, California
BW	*Business Week*
CHS	Chicago Historical Society, Chicago, Illinois
CSM	*Christian Science Monitor*
DU	Perkins Library, Duke University, Durham, North Carolina
DUAA	Advertising Archives, Duke University Web site, Durham, North Carolina
G&M	(Toronto) *Globe and Mail*
GOT	*La Gazette Officielle du Tourisme*
HS	*Hamilton (Ontario) Spectator*
IHT	*International Herald Tribune*
LC	Library of Congress, Washington, D.C.
LM	*Le Monde*
MH	Archives and Special Collections, Mount Holyoke College Library, South Hadley, Massachusetts
MHS	Massachusetts Historical Society, Boston, Massachusetts
NA	National Archives, Washington, D.C.
NT	*Negro Traveler*
NTC	*Negro Traveler and Conventioneer*
NYPL	Archives and Manuscripts Division, New York Public Library, New York, New York
NYRB	*New York Review of Books*
NYT	*New York Times*
NYTM	*New York Times Magazine*
PH	*New York Herald*, Paris edition
PhAA	*Philadelphia Afro-American*
PHT	*New York Herald Tribune*, Paris edition
PhT	*Philadelphia Tribune*
PT	*Chicago Tribune*, Paris edition
RUL	Special Collections, Rutgers University Archives, New Brunswick, New Jersey
SAQ	*Smith College Alumnae Quarterly*

SCA   Smith College Archives, Smith College, Northampton, Massachusetts

SCSLC   Smith College Student Letters Collection, Smith College Archives, Northampton, Massachusetts

SDP   State Department Papers, National Archives, Washington, D.C.

SEP   *Saturday Evening Post*

SHC   Southern Historical Collection, University of North Carolina at Chapel Hill Libraries, Chapel Hill, North Carolina

SL   Schlesinger Library of Women's History, Radcliffe Institute, Cambridge, Massachusetts

SR   *Saturday Review*

SRL   *Saturday Review of Literature*

SSC   Sophia Smith Collection, Smith College Library, Northampton, Massachusetts

TMY   *Travel Market Yearbook*

UM   Archives and Special Collections, Richter Library, University of Miami, Coral Gables, Florida

USNWR *U.S. News & World Report*

WP   *Washington Post*

WSJ   *Wall Street Journal*

NOTES

PREFACE

1. In *Seductive Journey* I say that for most of the nineteenth century, few French people outside of the small political and intellectual elite knew much or cared much about America. Harvey Levenstein, *Seductive Journey: American Tourists in France from Jefferson to the Jazz Age* (Chicago: University of Chicago Press, 1998). Recently, Philippe Roger has written an excellent "genealogy" of French anti-Americanism, tracing it back to Enlightenment thinkers such as Buffon and DePauw and taking it through the political divisions caused by the American Civil War and the 1898 War with Spain. However, he provides no evidence that it penetrated much below these elite circles before World War I. Philippe Roger, *L'ennemi américain: Généalogie de l'antiaméricanisme français* (Paris: Seuil, 2002).

2. By the end of the century, the world's tourists were spending $4 trillion a year on their travels and close to $850 billion had been poured into hotels and other efforts to profit from this in industries employing about 250 million people. *NYT*, April 12, 1998.

3. Although there was a marked falloff in American travel to France in 2003, travel to everywhere else, including major domestic destinations such as Disneyland, dropped as well. Mentioning Disneyland leads to the unrelated question of why there is no mention of the Disneyland outside of Paris in this book. That is because very few American tourists go there.

4. Christopher Endy, "U.S. Tourism in France: An International History, 1944–1971" (Ph.D. diss., University of North Carolina, 2000).

CHAPTER ONE

1. Amanda Vail, *Everybody Was So Young: Gerald and Sara Murphy — A Lost Generation Love Story* (Boston: Houghton Mifflin, 1998), 98–237; Calvin Tompkins, *Living Well Is the Best Revenge* (New York: Random House, 1998), 21–144.

2. F. Scott Fitzgerald, "Babylon Revisited," in *Babylon Revisited and Other Stories* (New York: Scribner's, 1960; repr., New York: Macmillan, 1968), 210–14.

3. In 1927 the Cunard Line estimated that 60 to 65 percent of its transatlantic passengers were female. *NYT*, June 19, 1927.

4. Jan Gelb diary, July 9, 14, 16, 17, 20, 1929, AAA.

5. Francis P. Miller and H. D. Hill, "Europe as Playground," *Atlantic Monthly*, August 1930, 226.

6. Clifton Fadiman, foreword to *Dodsworth*, by Sinclair Lewis (New York: Random House, 1947), v.

7. T. R. Ybarra, "Turistus Americanus," *Outlook*, April 24, 1929, 647.

8. In early 1931 there were 26,000 Americans living in Paris, versus only 8,000 in all of Britain, 5,500 in Italy, and 4,300 in Germany. *PH*, May 8, 1931; Vail, *Everybody Was So Young*, 230.

9. "France is in mighty good shape," the novelist Thomas Wolfe wrote to his brother from Paris in July 1930. "There is no unemployment at all, everyone is at work, and everyone seems to have enough to eat and drink and wear." Thomas Wolfe to Fred W. Wolfe, June 2, 1930, in Thomas Wolfe, *Selected Letters of Thomas Wolfe*, ed. Elizabeth Nowell (London: Heinemann, 1958), 231.

10. Florence Bragdon to family, January 10, 1930, F. Bragdon Folder, "Class of 1931" box, SCSLC.

11. Elizabeth Foster Vytlacil diary, February 19, 1932, in Elizabeth Foster Vytlacil Papers, AAA.

12. *NYT*, July 7, 1933. By October 1934 the expatriate population of France had shrunk to below 13,000, while that of Italy, which had increased by over 5,000 in the past year, stood at twice that number. *NYT*, October 10, 1934. The latter figure can be misleading, however, for many of the U.S. citizens registered with the embassy in Italy were likely immigrants from Italy who had gone back because of the Depression and wanted to retain the option of returning to America when conditions improved.

13. American Library in Paris, "Weathering Hardship to Shape a Lasting Legacy," ALP Web site, August 3, 1997, 6. The library was created in 1920 to take over the twenty-five thousand books the American Library Association had brought to France for the edification of the doughboys.

14. *Le Temps*, December 16, 1934.

15. Gabriel-Louis Jaray, "La crise du tourisme étranger en France," *Revue de Paris* 4 (July–August 1935): 624.

16. *NYT*, August 21, 1930.

17. *NYT*, November 10, 1929.

18. *NYT*, April 1, 1930. See my *Seductive Journey: American Tourists in France from Jefferson to the Jazz Age* (Chicago: University of Chicago Press, 1998), 257–71.

19. *NYT*, March 29, 1931. The number of travelers from America to Europe actually increased slightly from 1929, from 350,000 to 359,000, but this was likely related to immigrants returning rather than tourism. U.S. Bureau of the Census, *Historical Statistics of the United States from Colonial Times to 1970* (Washington, DC: USGPO, 1976), 2:404.

20. *NYT*, June 15, 1931.

21. T. R. Ybarra, "Europe without the American Tourist," *NYTM*, August 30, 1931, 7–8, 18.

22. The *Herald* said that the pavilion "struck an odd and delightfully individualistic note amid the exotic surroundings of pagodas, grass huts, strange temples and grotesque pavilions." Franklin D. Roosevelt visited it and pronounced it "constructed with admirable skill and taste." *PH*, May 3, 8, 13, 1931.

23. For example, W. Howard Sharp diary, July 18–21, 1931, RUL.

24. *NYT*, July 22, 1931; September 6, 1931; December 29, 1931; February 14, 1932.

25. *NYT*, November 30, 1929; January 3, 1930.

26. It also created the new post of undersecretary of tourism to lead the campaign and gave him cabinet rank. *NYT*, March 4, 1930; *CSM*, April 7, 1930.

27. "France Losing American Tourists," *Literary Digest* 106 (September 6, 1930): 13.

28. See Levenstein, *Seductive Journey*, 257–75.

29. Gelb diary, July 13, 1929.

30. A Frenchwoman asking the price of stockings, he said, was told seventy-eight francs. An American woman overhearing this who buys them was told that was seventy-eight francs *apiece*. George Jean Nathan, "Clinical Notes," *American Mercury*, November 1929, 370.

31. Eleanor Kinsella McDonnell, "Plain Tales from the Tourists," *SEP* 202 (April 19, 1930): 10–11.

32. *NYT*, April 7, 13, 1930; Jaray, "La crise," 637. Another source of rage was the grueling test and exorbitant fee to get permission to drive in France, which was also "accompanied by a great deal of palm greasing." *WP*, February 22, 1931.

33. *NYT*, April 20, 1930.

34. *PH*, June 13, 1930; *NYT*, June 13, 14, 1930.

35. *NYT*, June 14, 1930.

36. France, Office National du Tourisme, *Les prix des hotels en France* (Paris, 1929, 1930, 1931, 1932); *WP*, February 22, 1931.

37. France, Commissariat Général au Tourisme, *Les prix des hotels de Paris* (Paris, 1931); Reginald Wright Kauffman, "We Get the Glad Hand," *Collier's* 88 (July 11, 1931): 26.

38. *NYT*, April 13, 1930.

39. *PH*, May 29, 1930; June 22, 1930; August 22, 1933.

40. *PH*, May 23, 25, 1931; June 16, 1931.

41. *NYT*, July 10, 1930.

42. France, Centre National d'Expansion du Tourisme, *France* (Paris, 1937).

43. *PH*, August 9, 1930; May 15, 1931. Ironically, after abdicating in 1936, he spent much of the rest of his life in France.

44. *NYT*, July 7, 1932.

45. A new tourist authority churned out films and promotional material, telling tourists of the new "speedways" that were to be constructed for the tourist trade. *PH*, May 14, 1933; June 23, 1933. Although the effects of the Nazis' anti-Semitic policies—official boycotts of Jewish businesses, attacks on Jewish-owned stores, the banning of Jews from the universities—had already been widely reported and were starkly visible, in the form of Storm Troopers stationed in front of closed stores on the streets of Berlin, in May 1933 Charles Morrison, editor of the *Philadelphia Ledger*, arrived in Paris from Berlin declaring that he was impressed by the "hope" the Nazis had instilled in the Germans and assuring prospective American tourists that "they need have no qualms about visiting Germany this season." *PH*, May 10, 1933. As late as February 1939, an English-language paper in Cannes carried an ad for German resorts whose subhead read: "International Friendliness Established through Tourism." Mary Blume, *Côte d'Azur: Inventing the French Riviera* (London: Thames and Hudson, 1992), 121–22.

46. *PH*, July 31, 1933; *CSM*, July 31, 1933.

47. *NYT*, July 7, 1933.

48. *PH*, August 8, 1933; Blume, *Côte d'Azur*, 119; *NYT*, February 15, 1931. Ironically, in 1930 government policy undermined luxury tourism to the spa towns by allowing Social Assistance to pay for part of the cost of spa cures. This helped flood these towns with ordinary

people, spurring a wholesale desertion of the upper crust for the spas of Germany and Italy. Paul Goujon, *Cent ans de tourisme en France* (Paris: Cherche Midi, 1989), 54.

49. *NYT*, June 14, 1932. The rate cutting had actually begun much earlier. In May 1930 the *Herald* reported that the more expensive hotels had reduced their rates by as much as one-third and that cuts of 20 percent were the norm among other ones "of good standing." *PH*, May 4, 1930.

50. *NYT*, March 1, 1931; March 25, 1934; April 29, 1934.

51. Mark Boxer, *The Paris Ritz* (London: Thames and Hudson, 1991), 92–93.

52. *NYT*, April 29, 1934.

53. Dudley Ann Harmon to Daddy, January 3, 1930, Dudley Ann Harmon Papers, box 1, SCA.

54. Thomas Wolfe to Fred W. Wolfe, June 2, 1930. He told someone else that the French "are creatures from another planet. I never get this feeling with the English, Germans, or Austrians." Wolfe to A. S. Frere-Reeves, June 23, 1930, in Wolfe, *Selected Letters*, 231, 232.

55. For example, although hotels that were 125 francs a night in 1931 were down to 50 or 60 francs in 1934, this meant only a reduction from five dollars a night to four dollars. *NYT*, April 29, 1934.

56. It had been hailed as "the chief new mass movement of Americans to Europe—the thin edge of the wedge perhaps in transforming foreign travel from a leisure class to a popular avocation." "The Swelling Tide of Foreign Travel," *NYTM*, May 6, 1928, 6.

57. Some charged only $192 for tours of two weeks, including crossings, with four days in Paris, and one agency offered a nineteen-day tour with three or four days in Paris for only $145. Arthur Warner, "Travel for a Song," *The Nation* 136 (March 22, 1933): 313.

58. *PH*, May 10, 1933. The *Leviathan* began as the German *Vaterland* but had been seized as reparations by the United States after World War I. It made a brief comeback in 1934 but was soon taken out of service again. It was eventually scrapped as part of a deal to get government subsidies for a replacement, the *America*, which was launched just days before the outbreak of World War II. *PT*, June 16, 1934; *PHT*, August 6, 1937; September 1, 1939.

59. Alexis Gregory, *The Golden Age of Travel, 1880–1939* (New York: Rizzoli, 1991), 207.

60. *PH*, September 25, 1932; May 19, 1933.

61. *NYT*, May 19, 1935.

62. *NYT*, June 23, 1930; August 25, 1936; *PHT*, June 2, 1936; John Maxtone-Graham, *The Only Way to Cross* (New York: Macmillan, 1972), 267–73; Vincent Cronin, *Paris: City of Light, 1919–1939* (London: HarperCollins, 1994), 162–63.

63. *ATG*, January–March 1934.

64. Compagnie Générale Transatlantique, Paquebot "Normandie," "Menu du samedi, 30 avril 1938," "Menu du lundi, 2 mai 1938," at http://www.varsity-nj.com/liners/france; Gregory, *Golden Age*, 209–10; Cronin, *Paris*, 164–65.

65. Gregory, *Golden Age*, 209–10; Cronin, *Paris*, 164–65.

66. Neither did they amount to much in domestic tourism, for few employed workers had paid vacations. This was in contrast to Europe, where annual paid vacations for workers were already common. *NYT*, August 30, 1931.

67. *NYT*, November 10, 1929.

68. The United States Line guessed wrong in this regard. When the *Leviathan* was withdrawn from service, it was replaced by a new liner, the *Manhattan*, whose keel, like that of her sister ship, the *Washington*, had been laid down in 1928, when the boom in middle-class European tourism seemed like it would last forever. They had only cabin-class and tourist-class accommodations. *PH*, May 14, 19, 1933.

69. Brian N. Morton, *Americans in Paris: An Anecdotal Street Guide* (Ann Arbor: Olivia and Hill Press, 1984), 35.

70. Al Laney, *Paris Herald: The Incredible Newspaper* (New York: Appleton-Century, 1947), 169. Actually, the annual rainfall in Nice exceeds that of Paris, which is considered a rainy city. Ibid., 174.

71. For example, *PH*, June 23, 24, 1930; April 3, 1931; May 16, 1931; June 24, 1933; July 17, 1933; July 7, 1934. *PT*, May 15, 1934; June 4, 16, 17, 1934. *PHT*, May 20, 1936; June 11, 1936; July 28, 1937; August 4, 1937.

72. *PH*, June 26, 1933; July 27, 1933.

73. *PHT*, August 28, 1937.

74. *PH*, May 2, 5, 14, 1931; April 29, 1933.

75. Mary Peabody diary, September 16, 1932, Marian Lawrence Peabody Papers, MHS; Theodore Sedgwick III diary, 1836, Sedgwick Papers, "Miscellaneous" box, MHS.

76. The only cultural activity was attending a concert by the child prodigy violinist Yehudi Menuhin in 1933, where she seemed more impressed by the stylishly dressed audience than the playing. Peabody diary, November 12, 1932; May 1, 1933; May 26–June 6, 1933.

77. Joseph Grew, "Rough Notes of Leave of Absence, October 1, 1935 to November 1, 1935," Joseph Grew Papers, MHS. Another version of her background had it that she was an interior decorator. Antony Beevor and Artemis Cooper, *Paris after the Liberation, 1944–1949* (London: Penguin, 1995), 144.

78. *PH*, October 26, 1935.

79. William Harlan Hale, "Grand Tour, New Style: A Young American Discovers His Europe," *Atlantic Monthly* 150 (December 1932): 657–67.

80. *PH*, July 14, 1933; *PHT*, July 16, 1937.

81 Mildred Cox Howes, diaries, 1931, 1933, 1934, 1936, 1937, in Mildred Cox Howes Diaries, MHS.

82. Ibid., August 3, 1931; August 31, 1933; August 15, 31, 1934; November 13–20, 1937.

83. *PH*, May 1, 1930; July 3, 1930; June 14, 1934; September 7, 1938; *NYT*, August 3, 1930; June 9, 1935; *PT*, June 17, 1934; *BW*, May 29, 1937, 15.

84. Paula Ames Plimpton to Mother, December 2, 1930, Ames Family Papers, folder 392a, box 30, MHS.

85. Rather bizarrely, in March 1932 an article in *Good Housekeeping*, a magazine aimed at middle-class housewives, extolled the delights of a one-month chauffeured tour of France for the woman who did not have "an unlimited amount of time or money to spend." Frances Parkinson Keyes, "Motoring through France," *Good Housekeeping*, March 1932, 184–86, 189–91.

86. Paula Ames Plimpton to Mother, June 17, 1930, Ames Family Papers, "Letters from Paris" folder, box 30, MHS.

87. *PH*, May 26, 1930; August 31, 1930.

88. French Government Tourist Bureau, press release, March 23, 1937, in "France Tourisme" box, General Research Collection, NYPL.

89. *PH*, July 12, 17, 1933; August 28, 1933.

90. Eustace L. Adams, *The Family Sees France* (New York: Brewer and Warren, 1931), 68–69.

91. *PH*, June 1, 1933.

92. Blume, *Côte d'Azur*, 101–9; *PH*, May 3, 1931; *NYT*, July 18, 1932.

93. Blume, *Côte d'Azur*, 119; Alain Decaux, *Les heures brillantes de la Côte d'Azur* (Paris: Presses Pocket, 1964), 229–31; Robert Kanigel, *High Season* (New York: Viking, 2002), 183.

94. *NYT*, February 15, 1931.

95. *NYT*, December 1, 1935; February 28, 1937. Even Nice attracted back some of its aging aristocratic clientele. "In a single morning," said a guidebook written in 1935, "you could count a dozen or so genuine princesses, marchionesses, countesses and grand duchesses, with or without their princes, marquises, counts and grand-dukes seated in arm chairs or stretched out in deck-chairs along the Promenade." Eugene Fodor, *Fodor's 1936 . . . On the Continent* (London: Fodor's, 1936), 122.

96. André Rauch, *Vacances en France de 1830 à nos jours* (Paris: Hachette, 1996), 97–126; *PHT*, September 4, 1938.

97. Fodor, *Fodor's 1936*, 135.

98. *PHT*, September 16, 1938.

99. Film buffs will recall the *Rex* as the object of the young boy's fantasies in Federico Fellini's film *Amarcord*.

100. *PH*, June 22, 1936; Fodor, *Fodor's 1936*, 135. Here Edward VIII was reviving the tradition begun by his grandfather Edward VII, who as Prince of Wales had helped make Cannes fashionable.

101. Decaux, *Les heures brillantes*, 231–32.

102. *PH*, July 12, 1931; *PHT*, May 3, 1938.

103. In 1933 Morgan presided over the dignitary-studded opening of the Museum of Franco-American Cooperation in Blérancourt, a reconstructed village about sixty miles north of Paris. She and Vanderbilt also built an inn there for weekend guests. *PH*, June 26, 1933. The museum, a modest affair, is still there, although infrequently visited.

104. *PH*, October 19, 1931.

105. *NYT*, January 25, 1931; April 26, 1936; July 1, 1936; *PHT*, June 20, 1936. Another act of the grateful government, removing a Gothic chapel in a village in Haute-Saône from the list of protected monuments so that he could have it shipped, stone by stone, to another pet project, the Cloisters museum in New York City, was not so well received. Protesting villagers and farmers standing guard over the chapel and an outcry in the Chamber of Deputies forced him to drop the plan. *NYT*, August 5, 1936; November 24, 27, 1936.

106. The Howes stayed at the Hôtel de France et Choiseul in 1937, perhaps at Idie's urging. Howes diary, November 13, 1937.

107. *PHT*, July 28, 1937; October 1, 1937.

108. The *Normandie* and her French Line sister ship, the *Ile de France*, were particular favorites with Broadway and Hollywood stars. *PHT*, August 12, 1937; September 7, 1938. About the only Hollywood star to shun the cameras was the young film star Joan Crawford, who, brokenhearted by the breakup of her marriage to the dashing actor Douglas Fairbanks

Jr., secretly boarded the *Conte di Savoia* in New York in June 1931. She managed to disembark incognito in Cannes and remain there, unnoticed, until mid-August, when she smashed her car into one driven by a touring Englishwoman. *PH*, August 13, 1933.

109. Peabody diary, April 8, 1938.

110. *PHT*, August 30, 1937.

111. Wambly Bald, "Ah Paris," *Lost Generation Journal* 7, no. 3 (Winter 1983): 11.

112. *PHT*, August 12, 1937.

113. *PH*, April 19, 1933. They stayed abroad until October 1935, when they returned to New York to a greeting of blasting boat whistles and tooting tugboats. Herbert Mitgang, *Once upon a Time in New York: Jimmy Walker, Franklin Roosevelt, and the Last Great Battle of the Jazz Age* (New York: Free Press, 1999).

114. *PH*, May 13, 15, 1933.

CHAPTER TWO

1. Most of the tourists still came from the industrialized states east of the Mississippi, especially New York, Pennsylvania, Massachusetts, and Illinois. *NYT*, June 8, 1930.

2. Clara Laughlin, *Traveling through Life* (Boston: Houghton Mifflin, 1934), 289, 299.

3. Bergen Evans, "Grand Tour—Nonstop!" *Atlantic Monthly* 182 (September 1948): 35–36.

4. *NYT*, February 20, 1935; July 1, 7, 1935. Only 178,000 people sailed from the United States to Europe in 1934, compared to 359,000 in 1930. U.S. Bureau of the Census, *Historical Statistics of the United States from Colonial Times to 1970* (Washington, DC: USGPO, 1976), 2:404.

5. *NYT*, July 1, 7, 1935; April 16, 19, 1936; May 17, 1936; August 23, 1936.

6. French Government Tourist Bureau, New York City, press release, December 30, 1936, in "France Tourisme" box, General Research Collection, NYPL.

7. In late 1935 bookstores began reporting 50 to 100 percent increases in sales of travel books, while monthly magazines were suddenly again full of travel articles. Claudia Cranston, "Travel Books for Everyone," *Publisher's Weekly* 129 (January 11, 1936): 113–14.

8. Two more devaluations followed, but price rises still tended to cancel out their impact.

9. It did this with the workers in mind: to save them from groveling for gratuities. Eugen Weber, *The Hollow Years: France in the 1930s* (New York: Norton, 1994), 154.

10. It also reduced visa charges and gave tourists discounts on rail fares. *PHT*, April 24, 1937; *NYT*, April 18, 27, 28, 1937. French Government Tourist Bureau, New York City, press releases, February 25, 1937; March 23, 1937.

11. Edmond Labbé, *Exposition internationale des arts et techniques dans la vie moderne: rapport général* (1940), 11; cited in Weber, *Hollow Years*, 171.

12. Company officials said it looked like "the biggest travel wave since 1926." *NYT*, July 21, 1937.

13. From 1935 to 1937, departures to Europe from America rose from 185,000 to 248,000. U.S. Bureau of the Census, *Historical Statistics*, 2:404. The 200,000 figure, which may be a little high, was the estimate of the French Government Tourist Bureau in New York. *NYT*, December 7, 9, 1937. Sales of French railway tickets in America in mid-1936 were running 60 percent ahead of those for 1935. *PHT*, June 24, 1936.

14. A letter of credit is a document one purchased from one's bank crediting one with a

certain amount of money. Its corresponding banks abroad give one cash against it, deducting the amount from the balance remaining.

15. In the summer of 1937, fares to Europe on these one-class ships were only a hundred dollars each way. *New Yorker*, April 10, 1937, 32.

16. However, she said, he was "one of the few really attractive men aboard." Mary Mahony to Janet Mahony, August 26, 1932, "Class of 1932" box, SCSLC.

17. Mary Mahony to Daddy, August 25, 1930, ibid.

18. R. Howard Sharp diary, June 8–15, 1931, in Thelma P. Sharp Papers, RUL.

19. Glenway Wescott, *Continual Lessons: The Journals of Glenway Wescott*, ed. Robert Phelps (New York: Farrar, Straus and Giroux, 1990), 28. The Canadian Pacific Line captured a lot of American business by advertising its Montreal to Cherbourg route as offering "39% Less Ocean to Europe" because the first thousand miles of which were down what it called "the smooth water comfort" of the St. Lawrence River. *New Yorker*, April 24, 1937, 8.

20. *PHT*, October 1, 1938. The story strikes me as entirely credible. During a severe storm on my first transatlantic sea voyage, as an officer cadet on a small warship, a friend was restrained from doing the same thing only at the last moment. He had thrown his cap in the water and was climbing over the railing to jump in after it (we were trained to wear our caps at all times when outdoors, even, presumably, when drowning) when we grabbed him.

21. Margaret Goddard diary, September 27, 1935, Margaret Goddard Letters and Diaries, box 2106, SCSLC.

22. Goddard diary, September 28, 1935.

23. Jan Gelb diary, July 5, 7, 1929, AAA.

24. Eustace L. Adams, *The Family Sees France* (New York: Brewer and Warren, 1931), 19–20.

25. *NYT*, October 1, 1933.

26. Frank Schoonmaker, *Through Europe on Two Dollars a Day* (New York: McBride, 1927); Sydney A. Clark, *France on $50* (New York: McBride, 1931, 1933, 1934). The latter referred to the cost of one month's travel in France.

27. John Gutknecht diary, July 24, 1934, in John Gutknecht Papers, CHS. "For the first time in the history of touring," the *New York Times* reported, "Americans are generally using buses and subways." *NYT*, August 23, 1936.

28. Gutknecht diary, July 23, 1934.

29. Sharp diary, July 18–31, 1931.

30. Marie Hulsag to Moms, "Spring vacation, 1931," n.d., "Class of 1932" box, SCSLC.

31. "Amex Travel Department Independent Itinerary, Inclusive Tours, for Miss Florence Hearty, March 13, 1931"; Amex contract with Florence Hearty, Paris, March 28, 1931, in Association of Former Juniors in Paris, Junior Year Abroad Collection, box 1133, SCA.

32. Miriam Emerson to Mother and Dad, September 23, 1930, "Class of 1932" box, SCSLC.

33. Specifically, a clerk charged him one pence for a visa application form that he later discovered was free. Then, a clerk at one wicket told him that the charge for the visa itself would be eleven pence, but when he gave a clerk at another wicket a shilling (twelve pence) for it, the clerk would not give him one pence in change. When Kay persisted, insisting that the clerk at the other wicket had told him it was only eleven pence, the recalcitrant clerk finally "tossed the 1 pence in disgust." Colin Kay diary, June 18, 1937, NYPL.

34. Ibid., June 26, 1937.

35. Ibid., June 24–27, 1937.

36. Gelb diary, July 13, 1929.

37. Clark, *France on $50*, 20.

38. He went on to say it was "a constant nightmare that pervades every small hotel room and leaps to the visitor's eye—and olfactory organs—immediately upon his entry, but which every small hotel keeper regards as an important ornament." Eugene Fodor, ed., *1936 . . . on the Continent: The Entertaining Travel Annual* (1936; repr., New York: Fodor's, 1985), 62.

39. Evans, "Grand Tour," 39.

40. Wambly Bald, "Ah Paris," *Lost Generation Journal* 7, no. 3 (Winter 1983): 10.

41. Marie Hulsag to family, August [30?,] 1930, "Class of 1932" box, SCSLC.

42. *PH*, July 23, 1933.

43. Fodor, *1936*, 62.

44. *Smith College Weekly*, October 5, 1938; Florence Bragdon to Mother, September 17, 1929, "Class of 1931" box, SCSLC.

45. Betty Wells to family, October 22, 24, 1933, in Betty Wells Correspondence, MH.

46. Mary Cahill to family, August 31, 1936, "Class of 1938" box, SCSLC. The next week she visited a cookie factory in Dijon and wrote, "The working conditions are simply indescribable. One can easily see why the workers in France are all Communists. The workers here are supposed to be very clean. They take baths 'twice a month.'" Cahill to family, September 6, 1936, ibid.

47. She also enjoyed after-dinner liqueurs ("mmmm," she said in her diary) and was particularly taken by *vin mousseux*, which, unbeknownst to her, is simply any effervescent white wine. She declared it to be better than champagne and subsequently ordered it in Paris restaurants. Gelb diary, July 5, 9, 10, 13, 1929.

48. William Harlan Hale, "Grand Tour, New Style: A Young American Discovers His Europe," *Atlantic Monthly* 150 (December 1932): 657.

49. Marie Hulsag to family, August 30, 1930, "Class of 1932" box, SCSLC.

50. Frances Hurrey, letters home, July 25, 1929–June 6, 1930, Letters of Frances Hurrey, Class of 1931, MH.

51. Betty Wells to family, October 29, 1933, in Betty Wells Correspondence, MH.

52. He was distracted by reports of the crisis caused by the assassination of the Chancellor Dolfuss of Austria. Gutknecht diary, July 25, 1934.

53. Helen Keller, *Helen Keller's Journal* (New York: Doubleday, 1938), 172, January 30, 31, 1937.

54. Clark, *France on $50*, 85–92.

55. *NYT*, August 26, 1936. In 1938 some tour companies began taking tourists to the little dance halls on rue de Lappe, in the predominantly working-class area near the place de la Bastille, but often they would crowd all the French people out, leaving an all-English-speaking clientele. *PHT*, September 25, 1938.

56. Fodor, *1936*, 84.

57. Kay diary, June 27, 1937.

58. Clark, *France on $50*, 91.

59. Jeanne Pinard Bird diary, July 23, 1939, in Jeanne Pinard Bird Papers, MH.

60. Clark, *France on $50*, 92.

61. Phyllis Rose, *Jazz Cleopatra: Josephine Baker in Her Time* (New York: Doubleday, 1989), 142.

62. Sharp diary, July 18–31, 1931. Six years later, after the Folies Bergère lured Baker away, Janet Flanner, in her *New Yorker* "Letter from Paris," said, "Don't miss either Josephine Baker, who has become a real artist, or Maurice Chevalier, straw hat and all, at the Casino de Paris; both theaters house what are unquestionably the most sumptuous shows ever staged in Paris, with beautiful, slender girls, costumes in perfect taste for once, and, as usual, plenty of flesh." *New Yorker*, April 10, 1937, 58.

63. Stanley Karnow, *Paris in the Fifties* (New York: Random House, 1997), 58.

64. Waverley Root, *The Paris Edition: The Autobiography of Waverley Root, 1927–1934* (San Francisco: North Point Press, 1987), 126.

65. Karnow, *Paris in the Fifties*, 58.

66. Root, *Paris Edition*, 130–31.

67. La Rue Brown diary, September 14, 1929, Dorothy Brown Papers, box 11, SL.

68. Helen Josephy and Mary Margaret McBride, *Paris Is a Woman's Town* (New York: Coward-McCann, 1929), 258–70; Clara Laughlin, *So You're Going to Paris! And if I Were Going with You These Are the Things I'd Invite You to Do*, 4th, 5th, 6th, and 7th editions (Boston: Houghton Mifflin, 1929, 1931, 1934, 1938); Clara Laughlin, *So You're Going to France!* 3rd, 4th, and 5th editions (Boston: Houghton Mifflin, 1933, 1935, 1937). Florence Bragdon to family, December 8, 1929; March 5, 1930, "Class of 1931" box, SCSLC.

69. Shari Benstock, "Paris Lesbianism and the Politics of Reaction," in *Hidden from History: Reclaiming the Gay and Lesbian Past*, ed. Martin Duberman, Martha Vicinus, and George Chauncey Jr. (New York: Penguin, 1989), 332–46; Vincent Cronin, *Paris: City of Light, 1919–1939* (London: HarperCollins, 1994), 150–55; Shari Benstock, *Women of the Left Bank, 1900–1940* (Austin: University of Texas Press, 1986), 235.

70. Joseph Barry, *Left Bank, Right Bank: Paris and Parisians* (London: Kimber, 1952), 28.

71. Brown diary, September 14, 1929.

72. Phoebe Elizabeth Adams diary, August 30, 1931, Phoebe Elizabeth Adams Papers, SCA.

73. Mildred Cox Howes diaries, 1931, 1933, 1934, 1936, 1937, in Mildred Cox Howes Diaries, MHS.

74. They catered to "café society," a mixture of entertainment celebrities and faster-living socialites.

75. Amram Scheinfeld, "The European Low-Price Myth," *SEP* 203 (May 9, 1931): 149–50.

76. Evans, "Grand Tour," 36.

77. Sharp diary, July 15, 1931. In 1937 many more American Rotarians would return when the Rotary International held its convention in Nice.

78. Clara Breed diary, November 1936–April 1937, in Clara Breed Diaries, NYPL.

79. Ibid., April–May 1937.

80. Ibid., May 1937.

CHAPTER THREE

1. *NYT*, September 2, 1934.

2. Milnor Dorey, "The Magic Spell of Europe," *ATG*, April–June 1938, 16–17, 43.

3. Cordie Jacob Culp diary, June 28–30, 1932; August 14–18, 1932, in Florence Maude Culp Papers, RUL.

NOTES TO PAGES 42-46

NOTES TO PAGES 42-46

4. Florence Bragdon to family, December 8, 1929, "Class of 1931" box, SCSLC.

5. Jan Gelb diary, July 16, 1929, AAA.

6. Dudley Ann Harmon to Daddy, January 3, 1933, Dudley Ann Harmon Papers, box 1, SCA.

7. *PHT*, October 15, 1937; *NYT*, May 15, 1938.

8. Brian N. Morton, *Americans in Paris: An Anecdotal Street Guide* (Ann Arbor: Olivia and Hill, 1984), 273-74.

9. "Marsh Tours, 1937"; "Marsh Tours, Four Month Sojourn Abroad, January 4th to May 21st, 1939," in Dorothy Marsh Family Papers, Sophia Smith Collection, box 4, SCA.

10. Clara Laughlin, *So You're Going to France!*, 2nd ed. (Boston: Houghton Mifflin, 1932), 630.

11. Clara Laughlin, *So You're Going to France!* (Boston: Houghton Mifflin, 1927), vii; Clara Laughlin, *So You're Going to Paris!: And if I Were Going with You These Are the Things I'd Invite You to Do* (Boston: Houghton Mifflin, 1924), 74-78.

12. Laughlin, *So You're Going to France!*, 2nd ed., 630.

13. "Today," she wrote, "we read and are enchanted; tomorrow, on our rounds, we may walk straight into the frame of that which thrills us with the romance of other days. Nothing is dead in Paris! All the charms of all the pasts are there—not hidden away in dusty libraries, but beckoning us on every hand, no matter where we go. There is no wall between romance and reality; we step from one into the other, freely, continually." Clara Laughlin, *So You're Going to Paris!*, 7th ed. (Boston: Houghton Mifflin, 1938), 69.

14. Bergen Evans, "Grand Tour—Nonstop!" *Atlantic Monthly* 182 (September 1948): 39. The Rubens paintings, a series commissioned by Marie de Médicis portraying her as Diana, Greek goddess of love, had been shocking prudish Americans since the early nineteenth century. See my *Seductive Journey: American Tourists in France from Jefferson to the Jazz Age* (Chicago: University of Chicago Press, 1998), 59.

15. Cook's then suggested that tourists do some serious reading and study before embarking for Europe, but few would follow that advice. Dorey, "Magic Spell of Europe," 16-17, 43.

16. It included a diverse bag of innovators such as Picasso, Matisse, Léger, Brancusi, and Bonnard, as well as so many Jewish immigrants from Eastern Europe such as Chagall, Soutine, Zadkine, and Lipschitz that it was often called the "Ecole juive." William Wiser, *The Twilight Years: Paris in the 1930s* (New York: Carroll and Graf, 2000), 13.

17. Stillman, it seems, was trying to protect a Polish Jewish artist named Aronson who was the main object of Stella's rage. Elizabeth Foster Vytlacil diary, January 24, 1932, in Elizabeth Foster Vytlacil Papers, AAA. Joseph Stella's anger at being excluded was certainly justified. After his prolonged stays in Paris from 1912 to 1919, he had been instrumental in bringing French modernism to American art, including single-handedly introducing futurism to America.

18. Onya LaTour diary, August 10-30, 1934, AAA.

19. Waverley Root, *The Paris Edition: The Autobiography of Waverley Root, 1927-1934* (San Francisco: North Point Press, 1987), 185.

20. John Gutknecht diary, July 24, 1934, in John Gutknecht Papers, CHS.

21. Léon-Paul Fargue, *Le piéton de Paris*; cited in Herbert Lottman, *The Left Bank: Writers, Artists, and Politics from the Popular Front to the Cold War* (San Francisco: Halo Books, 1991), 8.

22. Anton Gill, *Art Lover: A Biography of Peggy Guggenheim* (New York: HarperCollins, 2001), 218–19.

23. John Russell, *Matisse: Father and Son* (New York: Harry Abrams, 1999), 97–98.

24. Jeanne Pinard Bird diary, July 18–28, 1939, Jeanne Pinard Bird Papers, MH.

25. *NYT*, February 13, 1938.

26. *NYT*, June 9, 1935. The nonprofit Office du Tourisme Universitaire de France also organized five- to six-week bus tours for groups of twenty-five that it called "pleasure trips to France as part of summer study programs." *WP*, March 26, 1938.

27. Dean Frank Beekman, undated clipping [1932], in scrapbook, "American Cathedral of Holy Trinity, 1929–1939," ACP.

28. *PH*, July 23, 1933; Vincent Cronin, *Paris: City of Light, 1919–1939* (London: HarperCollins, 1994), 146.

29. However, the hitherto substantial number of medical students plummeted. Pressure from French people angered at foreigners taking up places in medical school led the French to make it well-nigh impossible for foreigners to enroll. Simultaneously, American doctors resentful of Americans receiving high-quality yet inexpensive training in Paris forced state medical societies to bar new French-trained American doctors from practicing. *NYT*, September 9, 1939.

30. James Devine, "Everybody Is Going Abroad," *Educational Review* 75 (May 1928): 307.

31. *NYT*, May 29, 1938.

32. *NYT*, May 19, 1935.

33. The one to France was supposedly to study how Paris was administered, but the real objective seemed to be to make them more sympathetic to the French. *NYT*, May 29, 1938.

34. Delaware, whose program was open to students from forty other colleges, used Nancy as its first stop, while Smith used Grenoble and then Dijon.

35. Dudley Ann Harmon, "Diary of an American Girl in Paris," Harmon Papers, box 1.

36. Harmon to Daddy, February 15, 1933, ibid.

37. Miriam Anderson to Mother and Dad, November 21, 1930, "Class of 1932" box, SCSLC.

38. Florence Bragdon to family, April 19, 1930, "Class of 1931" box, SCSLC. Mothers would also treat their daughters, and themselves, to Paris-made clothes. Mary Mahony to parents, June 6, 1931, "Class of 1932" box, SCSLC; Phoebe Adams to Mum and Father, January 30, 1932; [April?] 1931, Phoebe Adams Papers, SCA; Margaret Goddard diary, June 23–July 2, 1935, Margaret Goddard Letters and Diaries, box 2106, SCSLC.

39. Arthur Warner, "Travel for a Song," *The Nation* 136 (March 22, 1933): 313–14.

40. In Montparnasse she frequently patronized the Dôme café and avoided Le Select, across the road, perhaps because it was known as the favorite of Stalin's vilified arch-rival Leon Trotsky. LaTour diary, August 10, 1934. There were probably more such pilgrims the next year, during the large Communist-sponsored international Writers Congress in Paris, where the Communists first tried to reach out to Socialists and other leftists they had hitherto denounced as tools of fascism.

41. Claude McKay, *A Long Way from Home* (New York: Furman, 1937), 311–12.

42. Joel A. Rogers, "The American Negro in Europe," *American Mercury* 20 (May 1930): 1.

43. *PhT*, April 23, 1931.

44. American Cathedral in Paris, *Bulletin*, no. 16 (November 1934).

45. Tyler Stovall, *Paris Noir: African Americans in the City of Light* (Boston: Houghton Mifflin, 1996), 84.

46. For example, a *Philadelphia Tribune* report on the huge funeral of a prominent African American clergyman in the summer of 1933 noted that the bishop of the church was not there because he was traveling in Europe. *PhT*, July 27, 1933.

47. *PhT*, September 7, 1933.

48. *PhT*, July 19, 1936.

49. Clara Laughlin, *So You're Going to Paris!*, 6th ed. (Boston: Houghton Mifflin, 1934), x.

50. Mary Mahony to Janet Mahony, May 19, 1931, "Class of 1932" box, SCSLC. The term seems to have been a common one for black bands at the time. Betty Wells, a Mount Holyoke student in Paris, asked her parents to send her a recording of "Mood Indigo," adding, "I don't know if it's played by Guy Lombardo or a nigger orch." Betty Wells to family, October 4, 1933, in Betty Wells Correspondence, MH.

51. Stovall, Paris Noir, 82–88; Tony Allan, *Americans in Paris* (Chicago: Contemporary Books, 1977), 46–47; PhT, July 27, 1933.

52. *NYT*, July 9, 1933; January 26, 1935.

53. *PhT*, October 19, 1933.

54. He also said, "In parts of Paris where there are few Negroes living you will, nevertheless, find a number of them in the dens of vice." *PhT*, October 19, 1933.

55. *PhT*, October 19, 1933; *The Jazz Age in Paris, 1914–1940*, traveling exhibition, Smithsonian Institution, Washington, DC, 1998–99; James Lincoln Collier, *Duke Ellington* (New York: Oxford University Press, 1987), 158; Derek Jewell, *Duke: A Portrait of Duke Ellington* (London: Hamish Hamilton, 1977); Stovall, *Paris Noir*, 84–97; Bricktop [Ada Smith Ducongé] and James Haskins, *Bricktop* (New York: Atheneum, 1983), 171–98; William A. Shack, *Harlem in Montmartre: A Paris Love Story between the Great Wars* (Berkeley: University of California Press, 2001), 76–107.

56. Phyllis Rose, *Jazz Cleopatra: Josephine Baker in Her Time* (New York: Doubleday, 1989), 94–180; Stovall, *Paris Noir*, 89–92.

57. Afro-American, February 1, 1936; cited in Rose, *Jazz Cleopatra*, 173.

58. See Levenstein, *Seductive Journey*, 263–66; and Rogers, "American Negro in Europe," 3.

59. He wrote the column under the name "Street Wolf of Paris." *PhT*, July 27, 1933.

60. Sydney A. Clark, France on $50 (New York: McBride, 1934), 253.

61. Vytlacil diary, February 2, 1933.

62. Dudley Harmon to Daddy, n.d. [spring 1933], Harmon Papers, box 1.

CHAPTER FOUR

1. Clara Laughlin, *So You're Going to Paris!: And if I Were Going with You These Are the Things I'd Invite You to Do*, 4th ed. (Boston: Houghton Mifflin, 1929), 423.

2. Joseph Wood Krutch, "Still Innocent and Still Abroad," *Harper's Magazine* 162 (April 1931): 534–35.

3. *NYT*, May 6, 1928.

4. A favorite was the "rosary game." They would gain the confidence of gullible tourists (from whence comes the term "confidence" or "con" man) by asking them to hold some supposedly valuable item for them while they went on some errand. Then they would have the tourist entrust them with a large amount of his own money, supposedly to purchase discounted diamonds or some other such things, with which the charming Frenchman would then disappear. *PHT*, April 24, 1937; April 3, 1951.

5. Thomas Craven, "New Innocents Abroad," *The Forum*, April 1930, 239–43.

6. She said the Rome police, with whom they had a run-in, seemed to regard them as "the annual American barbarian invasion of Rome." Maude Palmer Thayer, "The American Student Leaves the Reservation," *Scribner's Monthly* 102 (August 1937): 41–44.

7. Thyra Edwards, notes, June 30, 1934, Thyra Edwards Papers, box 1, folder 1, CHS. In February 1934 there had been a violent clash, which left seventeen dead and over two hundred injured, when the right-wing Croix de Feux tried to march on the National Assembly. The next week the Communist and non-Communist unions organized a general strike against the fascist sympathizers, which proved to be a step toward forming the Popular Front the next year.

8. Woodson added that those who did stay long enough to become acquainted with the people were too often "the shiftless immigrant, the scullion, or the 'jazz spreader.'" *PhT*, October 19, 1933.

9. Gérard de Catalogne, *Dialogue entre deux mondes* (Paris, 1931), 259.

10. Gilbert Seldes, "Tramps—Are We?—Abroad," *Saturday Evening Post* 104 (June 11, 1932): 21, 64–66.

11. Jacques Chastenet, *L'Oncle Shylock, ou l'impérialisme américain à la conquête du monde* (Paris, 1927). For some, particularly among those working for European unity, the United States came to replace Germany as the greatest threat to France. David Strauss, *Menace in the West: The Rise of French Anti-Americanism in Modern Times* (Westport, CT: Greenwood, 1978), 214–20.

12. Michel Winock, *Nationalism, Anti-Semitism, and Fascism in France* (Stanford: Stanford University Press, 1998), 39.

13. Jean-Philippe Mathy, *Extrême Occident: French Intellectuals and America* (Chicago: University of Chicago Press, 1993), 52–136.

14. Pierre Lyautey, *La révolution américaine* (Paris, 1934), 215–16; cited in Strauss, *Menace in the West*, 230. The most influential indictment of America on this score was Georges Duhamel's *Scènes de la vie future* (Paris, 1929).

15. Robert Aron and Arnaud Dandieu, *Le cancer américain* (Paris, 1931).

16. Krutch, "Still Innocent and Still Abroad."

17. Kadmi-Cohen, *L'abomination américain: essai politique* (Paris, 1930), 264; cited in William R. Keylor, "France and the Illusion of American Support," in *The French Defeat of 1940*, ed. Joel Blatt (Providence: Berghahn, 1998), 217–18.

18. The four Americans who *Le Figaro* asked to comment—Sherwood Anderson, John Dos Passos, H. L. Mencken, and Upton Sinclair—were well-known critics of American culture. They agreed with much of the criticism but said that it applied to France as well. Mencken, for example, agreed that American culture was "brutish, ignorant, vulgar, and even barbarian" and represented a threat to civilization. It was governed by charlatans and dominated by people intent on suppressing fine art and literature. However, he said, it was no worse in those respects than Europe. The spread of French culture would be just as di-

sastrous, he said, for France was suffering from the same thing. The socialist Upton Sinclair, predictably, said that what the French did not like about America was the result of capitalism, and if they wanted to do something about it, they should start by abolishing it in France. De Catalogne, *Dialogue*, 106, 168, 259–71.

19. Elizabeth Bragdon to Mother, September 11, 1939, Florence Elizabeth Bragdon Papers, SCA.

20. Tony Judt, *Past Imperfect: French Intellectuals, 1944–1956* (Berkeley: University of California Press, 1992), 193–95.

21. Eugen Weber, *The Hollow Years: France in the 1930s* (New York: Norton, 1994), 6.

22. Strauss, *Menace in the West*, 237, 245.

23. Volker Berghahn, *America and the Intellectual Cold Wars in Europe* (Princeton: Princeton University Press, 2001), 88–89.

24. "Almost no day goes by without a piece on the New Deal appearing somewhere in the Paris press," a French journalist wrote in the *Washington Post*. "Roosevelt's smile and charming personality have won over almost as many newspapermen in France as they did in America." *WP*, February 11, 1935.

25. Keylor, "France," 224.

26. George Mosse, *Fallen Soldiers: Reshaping the Memory of the World Wars* (New York: Oxford University Press, 1990), 112–13; Harvey Levenstein, *Seductive Journey: American Tourists in France from Jefferson to the Jazz Age* (Chicago: University of Chicago Press, 1998), 225–29. American veterans of the Vietnam War had similar disappointing experiences when they returned to where they had fought. "Everything has changed," said someone who accompanied these tours in 1999. "Almost every time, the vets are disappointed. They can't figure out where anything was." *NYT*, July 7, 1999.

27. Bragdon to Mother, March 5, 1931, Bragdon Papers.

28. Kenneth Davis, "Symbolic Journey," *Antioch Review* 37 (1979): 272.

29. Sydney A. Clark, *France on $50* (New York: McBride, 1933), 155, 224–25.

30. *NYT*, January 12, 1936.

31. Bertha Fanning Taylor, "From Hearth to Palette," 1934, ms., in Bertha Fanning Taylor Papers, AAA.

32. Alvaretta Taylor, "My Trip to France," May 23, 1930; American Pilgrimage Gold Star Mothers and Widows, "General Information for Pilgrims," in Frank Taylor Papers, Eastern Washington State Historical Society, Spokane, Washington; *PH*, May 24, 1930; June 6, 22, 23, 1930; G. Kurt Piehler, *Remembering War the American Way* (Washington, DC: Smithsonian Institution, 1995), 102–4.

33. The last three trips, scheduled for late August and September 1931, were canceled. Colonel Richard Ellis to Dean Frederick Beekman, n.d., ACP.

34. *PH*, July 3, 1933; Piehler, *Remembering War*, 104–5.

35. *PH*, July 23, 1933.

36. Tyler Stovall, *Paris Noir: African Americans in the City of Light* (Boston: Houghton Mifflin, 1996), 87.

37. *PHT*, August 16, 1937; October 3, 1937.

38. *PHT*, August 2, 3, 4, 9, 10, 12, 1937.

39. His first name was Henri-Philippe, but French publications do not normally use first names in identifying military officers.

40. *Le Matin*, October 6, 1937.

41. *PHT*, October 3, 5, 7, 1937. The Pershing statue exactly matched one of the Marquis de Lafayette, who led the French troops in the American Revolution, that was moved from Paris to stand on the other side of the avenue. This prompted *Le Matin* to say, "It was one of the most moving sights to see the great war leader [Pershing] rise amidst his peers to speak in front of his bronze image with Lafayette, who a century before had galloped to the rescue of America, saluting him with his sword." *Le Matin*, October 7, 1937. The next day *Le Matin* wrote movingly of how Pershing, Pétain, and the veterans dedicated the last of the monuments, at Château-Thierry, on the river Marne, where in July 1918, 300,000 fresh American troops helped stop the Germans' last push on Paris. "They were 300,000 happy and brave men! Only 240,000 would return; the blood of the 60,000 heroes can not be spilled for nothing: That was what everyone tried to say yesterday when the monument was unveiled." *Le Matin*, October 8, 1937.

42. *L'Humanité*, October 6, 7, 8, 1937.

43. The summer before, the government had arranged a practically identical tour for nearly five thousand Canadian veterans, who had come to the unveiling of the moving Canadian war memorial at Vimy Ridge. *ATG*, October–December 1936, 10.

44. *PHT*, October 3, 9, 1937.

45. Charles Thompson to Foreign Pilgrimage Committee, October 19, 1937, in French Government Tourist Bureau, press release, November 16, 1937, in "France" box, General Research Collection, NYPL.

46. Gabriel-Louis Jaray, *L'oeuvre du Comité France-Amérique 1909–1938* (Paris: Institut des Etudes Américaines, 1938), 3–12, 19–120.

47. Thayer, "The American Student Leaves," 42.

48. *NYT*, February 28, 1937.

49. French Government Tourist Bureau, "American Philanthropy Museum to Be Opened in France," press release, March 23, 1937, in "France" box, General Research Collection, NYPL.

50. The favorable reporting of the *New York Times* was probably important in this. Robert J. Young, "In the Eye of the Beholder: The Cultural Representation of France and Germany by the *New York Times*, 1939–1940," in Blatt, *French Defeat*, 245–68.

51. Betty Wells to family, October 22, 24, 1933, in Betty Wells Correspondence, MH.

52. He thought Hitler's policies "damnable," though, and wondered how such nice people could follow him. Thomas Wolfe, *The Letters of Thomas Wolfe*, ed. Elizabeth Nowell (New York: Scribner's, 1956), 460. The reader might note that Germans' cleanliness comes first on Wolfe's list of positive qualities.

53. Margaret Goddard diary, July 2, 1935, Margaret Goddard Letters and Diaries, box 2106, SCSLC.

54. The survey said 55 percent of Americans favored the British, only 11 percent the French, and 8 percent the Germans. "Etats-Unis: questions politiques, July 27, 1938," in Archives Nationale, F60, 169; cited in Irwin Wall, *The United States and the Making of Postwar France, 1945–1954* (Cambridge: Cambridge University Press, 1991), 17.

55. *NYT*, April 26, 27, 1938; May 3, 1938.

56. *NYT*, March 13, 1938.

57. *PHT*, September 27, 1938.

58. *PHT*, September 29, 30, 1938.

59. Marilyn Campbell, Kathryn Creed, and Virginia Savage, "L'Association of Former Juniors in France of Smith College: son histoire, sa structure, ses fonctions," in "Mementos," 24, AFJFSC Papers, box 1133, SCA; Sarah Walker Hyde to parents, September 27, 1938, "Class of 1940" box, SCSLC.

60. Sarah Walker Hyde to parents, September 30, 1938, "Class of 1940" box, SCSLC.

61. *PHT*, September 30, 1938; October 1, 3, 1938.

62. *PHT*, August 12, 1947.

63. Keylor, "France," 226–44.

64. *PHT*, July 7, 1939.

65. Christopher Wilson, *Dancing with the Devil: The Windsors and Jimmy Donahue* (New York: St. Martin's, 2001), 102.

66. *PHT*, August 25, 1939.

67. Ibid.

68. *PHT*, August 27, 1939.

69. *PHT*, August 29, 31, 1939.

70. Wilson, *Dancing with the Devil*, 103–5.

71. They only carried about fifteen passengers. *New York Sun* press message, July 11, 1939, in Pan American Airlines Papers, "Winston 'Atlantic Clipper'" folder, box 317, UM.

72. *PHT*, September 5, 8, 1939.

73. *PHT*, September 9, 1939.

74. *Newsweek*, September 18, 1939.

75. *PHT*, September 21, 1939.

76. Ibid.

77. Anton Gill, *Art Lover: A Biography of Peggy Guggenheim* (New York: HarperCollins, 2001), 218–19.

78. It even doubled its spending on publicity to lure foreign tourists to the two areas. *NYT*, November 11, 1939; December 11, 1939.

79. *PHT*, October 9, 1939.

80. Stovall, *Paris Noir*, 119–20. Many probably took advantage of the U.S. embassy's offer to pay the fare of "destitute" Americans. *NYT*, October 13, 1939.

81. *NYT*, October 1, 1939. Trinidad-born, he was a supporter of the Black Nationalist Marcus Garvey, from whom he had derived his colonel title. He also called himself "the Black Lindbergh," for having flown the Atlantic in 1929, two years after Lindbergh. When the United States entered the war, he signed up for the Tuskegee squadron of African American aviators but was dropped before graduation.

82. *NYT*, October 1, 1939.

83. Ibid.

84. *NYT*, January 14, 1940.

85. Dean Beekman, "Prayer, July 14, 1940"; Dean Frederick Beekman and Welles Bosworth to Sumner Welles, July 17, 1940; *Arizona Republican*, May 5, 1941, in American Cathedral of the Holy Trinity Scrapbook, 1929–1939, ACP.

86. Herbert Lottman, *The Fall of Paris* (New York: HarperCollins, 1992), 394–97; Bertram Gordon, "*Ist Gott Französisch?* Germans, Tourism, and Occupied France, 1940–1944," *Modern and Contemporary France*, n.s. 4 (1996): 290–91.

87. Harold Callender, untitled, *NYTM*, June 23, 1940.

CHAPTER FIVE

1. *NYT*, October 17, 1940.

2. Bertram Gordon, "*Ist Gott Französisch?* Germans, Tourism, and Occupied France, 1940–1944," *Modern and Contemporary France*, n.s. 4 (1996): 290–91.

3. Eugen Weber, *The Hollow Years: France in the 1930s* (New York: Norton, 1994), 279.

4. Gordon, "*Ist Gott Französisch?,*" 290–91.

5. Alexis Gregory, *Place Vendôme* (New York: Rizzoli, 1997), 220.

6. Gordon, "*Ist Gott Französisch?,*" 291.

7. *WP*, August 30, 1940.

8. Julian G. Hurstfield, *America and the French Nation, 1939–1945* (Chapel Hill: University of North Carolina Press, 1986), 198; Robert O. Paxton, "Anti-Americanism in the Years of Collaboration and Resistance," in *The Rise and Fall of Anti-Americanism*, ed. Dennis Lacorne, Jacques Rupnik, and Marie-France Toinet; trans. Gerry Turner (Basingstoke: Macmillan, 1990), 55. It did not, as the above say, actually ban jazz. It survived quite well in both the "occupied" and Vichy zones, but played by Frenchmen. Ludovic Tournès, *New Orleans sur Seine: histoire du jazz en France* (Paris: Fayard, 1999), 59–90.

9. Hurstfield, *America and the French Nation*, 31–32.

10. Irwin Wall, *The United States and the Making of Postwar France, 1945–1954* (Cambridge: Cambridge University Press, 1991), 27.

11. Ibid., 25, 27.

12. George Hook, interview by Hilary Kaiser, n.d., in Hilary Kaiser, *Veterans Recall* (Paris: Graphics Group France, 1984), 99. Emlen Etting, an army public relations officer who accompanied the liberating troops into the towns, was offered food, wine, and even a hotel room to sleep in. In Le Mans, "the streets [were] lined with chattering, gesticulating people" and French Resistance members in uniforms from the last war. Emlen Etting diary, August 11, 1944, AAA.

13. Larry Collins and Dominque Lapierre, *Is Paris Burning?* (New York: Simon and Schuster, 1965), 271, 326.

14. Antony Beevor and Artemis Cooper, *Paris after the Liberation, 1944–1949* (New York: Doubleday, 1994), 57.

15. Christopher Sawyer-Lauçanno, *The Continual Pilgrimage: American Writers in Paris, 1944–1960* (New York: Grove, 1992), 35.

16. Collins and Lapierre, *Is Paris Burning?*, 304. Bruce's diary has a somewhat different version, saying they both did a quick head count and ordered fifty martinis, which were not very good. David Bruce diary, August 25, 1944, Virginia Historical Society, Richmond, VA; cited in Beevor and Cooper, *Paris after the Liberation*, 57. Also, it was actually Hemingway's third stop in Paris—he had drinks at the Traveller's Club and the Café de la Paix first—and the Germans had long since departed from the Ritz. Mark Boxer, *The Paris Ritz* (London: Thames and Hudson, 1991), 102–3; Sawyer-Lauçanno, *Continual Pilgrimage*, 12–14, 23.

17. Collins and Lapierre, *Is Paris Burning?*, 338.

18. France, Ministère de Affaires Etrangères, B Amérique, 119, July 28, 1945; cited in Wall, *United States*, 37.

19. Sawyer-Lauçanno, *Continual Pilgrimage*, 55–58; James Lord, *Picasso and Dora: A Personal Memoir* (New York: Fromm, 1994), 18–32; Beevor and Cooper, *Paris after the Liberation*, 230–31.

20. Beevor and Cooper, *Paris after the Liberation*, 85.

21. Ernie Ricci [pseud.], interview by Harvey and Mona Levenstein, Paris, April 22, 1999.

22. Beevor and Cooper, *Paris after the Liberation*, 142.

23. Joseph Gusfield, interview by Harvey Levenstein, Paris, April 27, 2000.

24. "The Paris Review Sketchbook," *Paris Review* 79 (1981): 343.

25. Tournès, *New Orleans sur Seine*, 93–94.

26. Ibid.

27. *Time*, June 18, 1945; L. R. Blanchard, *Les Journalistes Americains See France* (Rochester: Gannet, 1946), 45–47.

28. Mary Blume, *Côte d'Azur: Inventing the French Riviera* (London: Thames and Hudson, 1992), 137; Horace Sutton, *Travelers: The American Tourist from Stagecoach to Space Shuttle* (New York: Morrow, 1980), 201–2.

29. *Time*, June 18, 1945.

30. Soon after the hotel was liberated, General Eisenhower had 650 mines removed from its gardens and hosted a reunion with seventeen of his generals. Before the war ended, 135 other generals had come there for "R & R." Blume, *Côte d'Azur*, 137; Sutton, *Travelers*, 201–2.

31. U.S. War Department, Army Services Forces, Information and Education Division, *Pocket Guide to the Cities of Southern France* (Washington, DC: USGPO, 1944), iv; *Pocket Guide to Paris and the Cities of Northern France* (Washington, DC: USGPO, 1944), iv, 37–38, 69.

32. Clarence Davis to Honey [wife], April 18, 1945, in Clarence W. Davis Letters, DU. Earlier, they had been shown the cathedral in Reims, near where his unit was encamped, but were not allowed to enter it. Davis to Honey, January 10, 1945, ibid.

33. U.S. War Department, Army Services Forces, Information and Education Division, *A Pocket Guide to France* (Washington, DC: War and Navy Departments, 1944), 41, 45–46, 50–52.

34. Ibid., 2, 41.

35. Ibid., 16. It also warned that "many of the so-called French prostitutes right now have been drawn from the dregs of the occupied countries and are deliberately planted Nazi agents."

36. Ibid., 13. The main warning unique to the present war was an admonition not to discuss the French defeat in 1940. It said that the French themselves could not agree on its complicated causes, and "it stands to reason you know less about it than they do." "Don't help the Nazis," who had been "riding them" about this "raw spot" for nearly four years, by "making the French sore." Ibid., 15.

37. Ibid.

38. Horace Sutton, *Footloose in France* (New York: Rinehart, 1948), 42.

39. France, Ministère des Travaux Publiques et le Commissariat Général au Tourisme, *France* (Paris, 1945), n.p.; Canada, Canadian Forces Hospitality and Information Bureau, *Paris Leave Map* (Paris, 1945).

40. *NYT*, June 26, 1945.

41. Marc Hillel, *Vie et moeurs des GI's en Europe, 1942–1947* (Paris: Balland, 1981), 146.

42. Ibid., 146–47.

43. Ibid., 168.

44. Jacques Pernet and Michel Hubert, *1944, il était une fois les Américains: en Champagne, à Reims* (Reims: l'Atelier Graphique, 1994), 119–20.

45. Valérie Moulin, Jean-Michel Harel, and Daniel Baccara, *Le Havre: 16th Port of Embarkation* (Le Havre: Rolland, 1997), 41–45.

46. *PHT*, November 21, 1945.

47. Something of the sort had been done in France after the Armistice in World War I, except that the doughboys had taken their courses in French universities. See my *Seductive Journey: American Tourists in France from Jefferson to the Jazz Age* (Chicago: University of Chicago Press, 1998), 223.

48. Nathan Shoehalter, interview, March 14, 1997, Rutgers Oral Archives of World War II, RUL; Hervie Haufler, "The Most Contented GIs in Europe," *American History* (October 1999), Web version at www.Military.com.

49. *Newsweek*, July 16, 1945.

50. Clarence Davis to Honey, February 25, 1945, Davis Letters.

51. Davis to Honey, April 6, 1945, ibid.

52. *Newsweek*, July 16, 1945.

53. *Life*, November 26, 1945.

54. Sawyer-Lauçanno, *Continual Pilgrimage*, 23–29.

55. "Les Etats-Unis, les Américains et la France, 1939–1945," *Sondages: Revue Française de l'Opinion Publique* 15, no. 2 (January—February 1953): 44.

56. SDP, 711.51/3-945; cited in Beevor and Cooper, *Paris after the Liberation*, 143.

57. *Newsweek*, November 19, 1945.

58. Hillel, *Vie et moeurs*, 156.

59. Robert Kanigel, *High Season* (New York: Viking, 2002), 217.

60. Moulin, Harel, and Baccara, *Le Havre*, 41–78.

61. *PHT*, November 7, 9, 11, 1945.

62. *LM*, November 8, 1945; *PHT*, November 16, 1945.

63. *PHT*, November 8, 1945; *LM*, November 8, 1945.

64. *LM*, November 11, 1945.

65. *LM*, November 15, 1945.

66. *Newsweek*, November 19, 1945.

67. Hillel, *Vie et moeurs*, 171–72.

68. *Ce Soir*, March 6, 1946; Hillel, *Vie et moeurs*, 168.

69. Susan Mary Alsop, *To Marietta from Paris, 1945–1960* (Garden City, NY: Doubleday, 1975), 53.

70. The main reasons given for disappointment with the Americans were insufficient aid, broken promises, imperialist policies, and insufficient toughness on the Germans. The Soviet Union, on the other hand, was widely credited (by 57 percent versus 20 percent for the United States) with having contributed the most to winning the war. "Les Etats-Unis," 3–6.

71. *NYT*, January 31, 1945.

72. *NYT*, January 28, 1945.

73. France, Archives Nationales, F60, 921, Ministère des Affaires Etrangères, telegram, January 15, 1945; cited in Wall, *United States*, 37.

74. France, Ministère des Affaires Étrangères, B Amérique, 119, July 28, 1945; cited in Wall, *United States*, 37.

75. *PHT*, December 1, 1945.

76. *Newsweek*, November 19, 1945.

77. Horace Day diary, June 4, 1945, in Horace Day Papers, AAA.

78. "The fact that France and the rest of Europe has been looted to provide this high standard of living is forgotten," he added. Day diary, June 4, 1945.

79. Julian Bach Jr., *America's Germany: An Account of the Occupation* (New York: Random House, 1946), 271; cited in Rudy Koshar, *German Travel Cultures* (Oxford: Berg, 2000), 180. Koshar goes on to point out that German soldiers judged the countries they were conquering in much the same fashion.

80. Gertrude Stein, "Off We All Went to See Germany," *Life*, August 6, 1945, 54.

81. "France is trying to get back on its feet," he continued, "but what the GI gets to see most are the workings of the sordid, self-seeking interests that prey on soldier and civilian alike. The black market is a major industry." Theodore Singer, letter to the editor, *NYT*, January 5, 1946.

82. U.S. Department of War, [Leo Rosten, au.], *112 Gripes about the French*, n.d. [1945], photocopy of "ditto" copy made by Samuel Stouffer, Harvard University, by Dan Eggleston, [Austin, Texas, 1982], 5, 8, 15–18. In 2001 the editor of a French historical magazine ran across a copy of the pamphlet at an attic sale and translated and published parts of it. In June 2003 the entire pamphlet was translated and published as *Nos amis, les Français* (Paris: Cherche Midi, 2003). It became an immediate best-seller, selling close to fifteen thousand copies. *HS*, August 29, 2003.

83. Hillel, *Vie et moeurs*, 241.

84. Quoted in Moulin, Harel, and Baccara, *Le Havre*, n.p.

85. The comments are interspersed in his letters. In Normandy he said that "gasoline would be milder" than Calvados, the local liquor of choice, which is made from apples, while in Reims, capital of Champagne, he said, "I believe that most of the wine here is made from apples and is not very good. It is about like that sour stuff I made." Davis to Honey, December 12, 1944; February 12, 1945, Davis Letters.

86. Sawyer-Lauçanno, *Continual Pilgrimage*, 213–14.

87. She agreed, saying, "And I explained that American architects I had known had always told me that the place de la Concorde was the most beautiful square in the world, so remarkably harmonious is the sense of proportion in the buildings, the trees, the river, and the perspective, in whichever direction one looks. . . . And so much sky, with a light and colors characteristic of Paris and dear to artists. Somewhere in the U.S. there may be a sky equally beautiful, but if it's over our cities, the buildings hide it. If it's over the desert or the mountains, we don't often get a chance to see it. The way natural and man-made beauty are blended here is comforting." S. Wunder to Laura Puffen Morgan ["Dear Friends"], April 24, 1946, in Morgan-Howes Family papers, folder 39, SL.

88. *WP*, February 7, 1947.

89. Ricci interview.

90. Edward Lindsay, *American Country Editors Abroad* (Decatur: Huston-Patterson, 1946), 30.

91. To make matters worse, when the French asked for American wheat to make up their

shortfall for bread, they were sent tons of corn meal instead, probably because of a translation error by a French official using a British rather than American dictionary. (Corn in Britain meant staple food, which is wheat there. Maize was thus called Indian corn.) Jean-Baptiste Duroselle, *La France et les Etats-Unis: des origines à nos jours* (Paris: Seuil, 1976), 208.

92. "Les Etats-Unis," 3–6.

93. Jacques Thibau, *La France colonisée* (Paris: Flammarion, 1980), 25.

94. Simone de Beauvoir, *La force des choses* (Paris: Gallimard, 1963), 28.

95. Tournès, *New Orleans sur Seine*, 91–94, 344–45.

96. Moulin, Harel, and Baccara, *Le Havre*, n.p.

CHAPTER SIX

1. Emile Servan-Schreiber, "Miami ou Pompeii," *Les Echos*, July 31, 1945; cited in Christopher Endy, "U.S. Tourism in France: An International History, 1944–1971" (Ph.D. diss., University of North Carolina, 2000), 70. Endy shows how, along with the economic benefits, tourism's supporters stressed its importance in spreading French culture, while its opponents thought reviving heavy industry should be central in reconstruction. Ibid., 70–129.

2. The paramount importance of economic considerations in this was indicated by having the campaign directed by the Ministry of Finance, which in May 1945 set up the French Committee to Welcome Allied Armies. Ibid., 94–95.

3. France, Ministère des Travaux Publiques, des Transports et du Tourisme, Commissariat Général au Tourisme, *France* (Paris, 1945), n.p. A subsequent one recommended taking a "flânerie—an aimless walk—through Paris, saying, 'It consists . . . in going as one likes through the streets and across squares as they may lie before us.'" Idem, *How to See Paris* (Paris, n.d. [1946]), n.p. Another was blithely offensive to Jews. In describing the Sainte-Chapelle, which was built to hold the Crown of Thorns, it said that in 1238 Louis IX ("Saint Louis") raised the money to buy the relic "by imposing a tax on the Jews—a proof that the moral training received from his saintly mother had not impaired his sense of humor." Canada, Canadian Forces Hospitality and Information Bureau, *Paris Leave Map* (Paris, 1945), n.p.

4. In 1946, despite French ambivalence about GI tourism, it published a brochure aimed mainly at attracting GIs on leave from Germany. France, Commissariat au Tourisme, *How to see Paris, for the soldiers of the Allied Armies* (Paris, 1946).

5. U.S., Economic Cooperation Administration, *France: Country Study* (Washington, DC: USGPO, 1949), 1.

6. One analysis says the economic toll was worse than after World War I, in part because fighting had raged over much more of French territory. Jean-Pierre Rioux, *The Fourth Republic, 1944–1958* (Cambridge: Cambridge University Press, 1987), 18–19.

7. *LM*, January 5/6, 1947; *PHT*, August 5, 1947.

8. *LM*, January 5/6, 1947.

9. Mary Blume, *Côte d'Azur: Inventing the French Riviera* (London: Thames and Hudson, 1992), 141.

10. Alain Decaux, *Les heures brillantes de la Côte d'Azur* (Paris: Presses Pocket, 1964), 233–34.

11. His technical assistant was the future president Georges Pompidou. Paul Goujon, *Cent ans de tourisme en France* (Paris: Cherche Midi, 1989), 75.

12. Also, because of the shortage of facilities, the number of tourist visas issued that year would be limited to 200,000, with preference given to those from the bigger-spending countries: the United Kingdom, the Netherlands, the United States, Switzerland, Sweden, and Egypt. (The latter was noted for its high-living Francophilic upper class.) *LM*, April 18, 1946.

13. *LM*, April 18, 1946.

14. Harold Callender, "Economics Eclipses Politics in France," *NYTM*, February 3, 1946, 9, 53.

15. For example, there seemed to be no teaspoons in Paris, even at the Grand Hôtel, where the American embassy had set up a mess for visiting American businessmen and journalists. The Germans, it was said, had made off with them all. S. Wunder to Laura Puffen Morgan ["Dear Friends"], April 24, 1946, in Morgan-Howes Family Papers, folder 39, SL.

16. It laid on effusive welcomes for a large group of small-town newspaper editors and brought one hundred high school and college teachers over to take the Sorbonne's summer course in French civilization and other courses. Edward Lindsay, *American Country Editors Abroad* (Decatur: Huston-Patterson, 1946); *NYT*, July 7, 1946.

17. Tyler Abell, "Biographical Note," in *Drew Pearson Diaries, 1949–1959*, ed. Tyler Abell (New York: Holt, Rinehart and Winston, 1974), xiii–xiv.

18. Antony Beevor and Artemis Cooper, *Paris after the Liberation, 1944–1949* (New York: Doubleday, 1994), 436.

19. *LM*, September 19, 20, 24, 1946.

20. Arthur Miller, *Timebends: A Life* (New York: Grove, 1987), 156–57.

21. The British hoteliers, it said, were terrified of the prospect of putting up even this number, fearing that their reputation would never recover from having little more than Brussels sprouts to feed them day after day. The *New York Times* advised that food shortages were less troublesome in France because the French "have ever been able to prepare delicious meals on practically nothing." *LM*, May 13, 1947; *NYT*, April 12, 13, 1947.

22. S. J. Perelman, "Westward Hah!" in *The Most of S. J. Perelman* (New York: Simon and Schuster, 1958), 386.

23. *WP*, August 24, 1947.

24. Martha Churchill to Mom and Pop, October 6, 1948, "Class of 1950" box, SCSLC.

25. *WSJ*, May 14, 1947; *LM*, May 13, 1947.

26. Quoted in Joseph Barry, "Americans in Paris—the More They Change . . ." *NYTM*, August 15, 1948, 43.

27. Avis Berman, "Romare Bearden: 'I Paint Out of the Tradition of the Blues,'" *ARTnews*, December 1980, 66; cited in Myron Schwartzman, *Romare Bearden: His Life and Art* (New York: Abrams, 1990), 168.

28. Saul Bellow, "My Paris," in *The Sophisticated Traveler: Beloved Cities: Europe*, ed. A. M. Rosenthal and Arthur Gelb (New York: Villard, 1984), 169–72.

29. Art Buchwald, *I'll Always Have Paris: A Memoir* (New York: Ballantine, 1997), 2.

30. William Demby, interview by Harvey and Mona Levenstein, Sag Harbor, NY, December 22, 1998.

31. Wright then told of a discussion he had with an American friend regarding why a woman on the Métro had grabbed the zipper on his fly and started laughing uproariously. (Zippers were beginning to replace buttons on flies in America, but not yet in Europe.) Wright and his friend decided it might be because "we pushed our mania for mechanization so far that we even put zippers on pants." Richard Wright, "A Paris les GIs noirs ont appris a connaître et a aimer la liberté," *Samedi-Soir*, May 25, 1946, 2.

32. He added that although the legend had much to support it, it was "unlivable." Yet he spent much of the rest of his life in France, living through a number of *histoires d'amour.* James Baldwin, "A Question of Identity," in *Notes from a Native Son* (Boston: Beacon, 1955), 127.

33. The famed anthropologist Claude Lévi-Strauss, who was cultural attaché at the French embassy in Washington, helped overcome State Department opposition to granting him a passport because of his leftist sympathies.

34. Hazel Rowley, *Richard Wright: The Life and Times* (New York: Henry Holt, 2001), 331–32; Christopher Sawyer-Lauçanno, *The Continual Pilgrimage: American Writers in Paris, 1944–1960* (New York: Grove, 1992), 69–70.

35. In 1948 the United States Lines converted two troopships into "student ships," for people traveling for "cultural and academic purposes." *PHT*, May 10, 1949.

36. Robert Gwathmey to Hudson Walker, n.d. [late 1949?], Hudson Walker Papers, AAA.

37. Thomas Edward Ratcliffe to Robert Frash, October 7, 21, 1949; Ratcliffe to Anita [?], October 21, 1948, Thomas Edward Ratcliffe Papers, series 6, folder 94, SHC.

38. Buchwald, *I'll Always Have Paris*, 8.

39. Ernie Ricci [pseud.], interview by Harvey and Mona Levenstein, Paris, April 22, 1999.

40. *NYT*, February 22, 1998.

41. *PT*, February 4, 1946.

42. Schwartzman, *Romare Bearden*, 162.

43. Ricci interview.

44. *Life*, November 19, 1951.

45. *G&M*, November 13, 1999.

46. Schwartzman, *Romare Bearden*, 162.

47. Romare Bearden to Carl Holty, n.d. [September 1950?], Carl Holty Papers, AAA. He called it working toward a Ph.D., although there is no such degree in France.

48. He added, "During the late forties not to know anyone there was almost better than having acquaintances on arriving." However, he also admitted that the fact that he had previously met Sartre and many other French writers and artists in New York did help. Lionel Abel, *The Intellectual Follies: A Memoir of the Literary Venture in New York and Paris* (New York: Norton, 1984), 160–61.

49. Hillary Mills, *Norman Mailer: A Biography* (New York: Empire, 1982), 96; Carl Rollyson, *The Lives of Norman Mailer* (New York: Paragon House, 1991), 46–50; Mary V. Dearborn, *Mailer: A Biography* (Boston: Houghton Mifflin, 1999), 55–59.

50. She added, "For some reason it seems easier to travel 3000 miles, battle with a foreign tongue, go without creature comforts, and be a foreigner to live this lovely life. Can't yet bring myself to believe this." Cynthia Brants diary, November 5, 1948, Cynthia Brants Papers, AAA.

51. Herbert Gentry, interview by Myron Schwartzman, December 1983; cited in Schwartzman, *Romare Bearden*, 162–63.

52. Ibid., 163.

53. Demby interview.

54. Bearden to Holty, n.d. [September 1950?], Holty Papers.

55. Demby interview.

56. Julian Barnes, *Something to Declare* (Toronto: Random House, 2002), 276.

57. Bearden to Holty, n.d. [September 1950?], Holty Papers.

58. Demby interview.

59. Hightower added that although it did appear that "romantic liaisons do come easier here than at home, the edge is not as overwhelming as you'd think. The post-war slack in morality that tripped up the liberating GIs has been taken up by parental snaffles." Ann Hightower, "If Paris Is Can-Can, New York Is Tom-Tom," *NYTM*, June 26, 1949, 11.

60. Ricci interview.

61. Julian G. Hurstfield, *America and the French Nation, 1939–1945* (Chapel Hill: University of North Carolina Press, 1986), 36.

62. For example, ex–Smith College junior-year-in-France women were split over whether to keep contributing money to the socialites' original organization, French Relief, which distributed it under the auspices of the Pétain government. They eventually decided to contribute and "stay neutral," to keep communications open with the Vichy government. Minutes of meeting, June 26, 1942, in Association of Former Juniors in France of Smith College Papers, "Meetings 1942" folder, box 1133, SCA.

63. Marilyn Campbell, Kathryn Creed, and Virginia Savage, "L'Association of Former Juniors in France of Smith College: son histoire, sa structure, ses fonctions," in "Mementos," 24, Association of Former Juniors in France of Smith College Papers, box 1133, SCA.

64. *NYT*, May 2, 1946.

65. *NYT*, November 21, 1946.

66. *NYT*, November 21, 1946.

67. Ironically, this was the *America*, which had been launched just days before the war began.

68. Horace Sutton, "Europe This Summer?" *The Nation*, May 17, 1947, 571.

69. Ibid.

70. One of the few bright spots the author saw was that the new edition of the Michelin guide indicated which architectural monuments and other sites had suffered war damage. Mary Burnet, "Planning to Visit France?" *Harper's* 194 (May 1947): 459–63.

71. The GIs were deterred by high rail fares and switched to nearer destinations such as Czechoslovakia. *PHT*, July 7, 1947.

72. *WP*, February 22, 1948; *LM*, January 28, 1949.

73. *PHT*, July 7, 1947; Air France advertisements, *New Yorker*, n.d. [1946]; September 27, 1947, n.d. [1948], Ad*Access Web site, DUAA; Horace Sutton, *Footloose in France* (New York: Rinehart, 1948), 17–18.

74. After landing in Paris, Cox boasted of being the first priest to conduct a mass in the air over the Atlantic. *PHT*, July 13, 1947.

75. *NYT*, March 2, 1947. By then, it and the four other transatlantic airlines were flying about twenty round-trips a week.

76. Jean Ginier, "Quelques aspects du tourisme américain en France," *Annales de Géo-*

graphie 397 (1964): 300; Air France advertisement, *Chicago Daily News*, n.d. [1947]; TWA advertisement, *New York Daily News*, n.d. [1948]. In 1948 the airlines began offering reduced return fares for thirty- or sixty-day stays, but this was only for off-peak travel, from October to April. *New York Herald Tribune*, n.d. [1948, 1949], Ad*Access, DUAA.

77. Photos, Pan American Airlines Papers, "Sleeperettes" Folder, box 288, UM.

78. Noise and comfort level based on my recollections of a transcontinental flight on its new and- improved successor, the Super Constellation, ten years later. *NYT*, June 13, 1948.

79. Betsey Schaefer, untitled ms., Pan Am Papers, "2nd Atlantic Flight" folder, box 317.

80. Most Americans were unaware of the rumors that Miller, whose plane was never found, had actually died in a French *maison de tolérance*.

81. Stuart Murray, *A Traveler's Guide to France* (New York: Sheridan House, 1948), 22.

82. Alice Furnaud, "Bon Voyage Doesn't Mean What It Used To," *NYT*, Travel section, October 1, 2000, 37.

83. Pierre et Renée Gosset, "A Penhöet ou l'on achève la refonte de Liberté," *L'Aide Américaine à la France* 32 (November 1949): 1–5.

84. Alexis Gregory, *The Golden Age of Travel, 1880–1939* (New York: Rizzoli, 1991), 214.

85. Martha Churchill to family, September 20, 1948, "Class of 1950" box, SCSLC.

86. Dorothy Brown diary, July 1950, Dorothy Brown Papers, box 11, SL.

87. Furnaud, "Bon Voyage."

88. Brown diary, July 26, 1950; August 7, 1959, boxes 11, 12, Brown Papers; Jennie Barron to Mrs. Daniel Polling, July 26, 1959; Invitation from Chief Engineer, RMS *Queen Elizabeth*, August 29, 1959, Jennie Barron Papers, box 5, folders 87, 88, SL.

89. Quote from *PHT*, May 20, 1936.

90. Alexis Gregory, *Place Vendôme* (New York: Rizzoli, 1997), 220.

91. Christopher Wilson, *Dancing with the Devil: The Windsors and Jimmy Donahue* (New York: St. Martin's, 2001), 147.

92. Brants diary, February 7, 1949.

93. Ibid., November 3, 1948.

94. She added, "New York does this for some people, but not for long." Ibid., November 9, 1948.

95. Wilson, *Dancing with the Devil*, 143, 149.

96. *PHT*, August 26, 1947.

97. Wilson, *Dancing with the Devil*, 149.

98. *PHT*, July 16, 1947. Her outrage at the narcotics story was probably justified—the killing was likely over control of gambling, not drugs, in Las Vegas. However, why she might be on the hit list was never explained.

99. "Women, almost without exception, go bargain-mad in Paris," said Helen Josephy and Mary Margaret McBride in *Paris Is a Woman's Town* (New York: Coward-McCann, 1929), 48.

100. *NYT*, January 20, 21, 1930.

101. *NYT*, September 12, 1937.

102. Beevor and Cooper, *Paris after the Liberation*, 313.

103. Gregory, *Place Vendôme*, 114.

104. Susan Mary Patten to Marietta Tree, February 23, 1947, in Susan Mary Alsop, *To Marietta from Paris, 1945–1960* (Garden City, NY: Doubleday, 1975), 93.

105. Stanley Karnow, *Paris in the Fifties* (New York: Random House, 1997), 275.

106. Brants diary, February 4, 1949.

107. French law prohibited copies from being made for two years, while there were no restrictions on Americans.

108. Brarts diary, January 29, 1949.

CHAPTER SEVEN

1. French Line advertisement, *New Yorker*, July 23, 1949. There were 613 first-class cabins, 489 cabin-class ones, and only 227 in tourist class. *PHT*, May 24, 1949.

2. Horace Sutton, *Travelers: The American Tourist from Stagecoach to Space Shuttle* (New York: Morrow, 1980), 219.

3. Summary of newsreel, [misdated] April 4, 1949, in FilmImages, Paris, France, www .filmimages-archives.com.

4. Initially, the franc went from 119 to the dollar to 214 to the dollar. Later, when rates were allowed to float, it went to 306 to the dollar. Within a year the franc was selling on the black market for 500 to the dollar, but by then inflation had eroded much of its earlier value. Economic Cooperation Administration (ECA), *France: Country Study* (Washington, DC: USGPO, 1949), 39–40.

5. *Time*, May 10, 1948.

6. Quoted in Susan Mary Alsop, *To Marietta from Paris, 1945–1960* (Garden City, NY: Doubleday, 1975), 125.

7. *USNWR*, October 1, 1948.

8. *Time*, May 10, 1948.

9. *WP*, February 22, 1948.

10. He was responding to the astounding suggestion, emanating from Washington, that French hotel chefs be provided with American restaurant expertise. Theodore Pozzy to Henry Ingrand, April 21, 1949, RG 469, NA; cited in Christopher Endy, "U.S. Tourism in France: An International History, 1944–1971" (Ph.D. diss., University of North Carolina, 2000), 149.

11. Peter Grose, *Gentleman Spy: The Life of Allen Dulles* (Boston: Houghton Mifflin, 1994), 447–48.

12. Until 1951 there was no real attempt to coordinate the spending of these operatives. Mario Del Pero, "The United States and 'Psychological Warfare' in Italy, 1948–1955," *Journal of American History* 87 (March 2001): 1304–34.

13. Art Buchwald, *Art Buchwald's Paris* (London: Chatto and Windus, 1955), 15.

14. Unfortunately, his example for this was "and the stores want a hundred dollars for a Picasso original." Carl Rollyson, *The Lives of Normal Mailer* (New York: Paragon House, 1991), 50.

15. Alyce Martin, "France," in *Woman's Guide to Europe*, ed. Eugene Fodor (The Hague: Mouton, 1954), 142.

16. Quoted in Antony Beevor and Artemis Cooper, *Paris after the Liberation, 1944–1949* (New York: Doubleday, 1994), 420.

17. *Newsweek*, January 31, 1949; February 7, 1949. The annual ritual whereby the portly father, the Aga Khan, sat on a large scale and was given his weight in precious jewels by his followers was always a much-discussed feature of movie newsreels.

18. The local government refused Khan's pleas to be allowed to hold it in his palatial villa. *PHT*, May 27, 1949.

19. *PHT*, July 19, 1949.

20. Mary Blume, *Côte d'Azur: Inventing the French Riviera* (London: Thames and Hudson, 1992), 142.

21. Those who, unlike Parsons, paid their own way, were charged an eye-popping fifteen dollars for the dinner and nine dollars for a bottle for champagne. *Newsweek*, June 13, 1949.

22. *PHT*, July 30, 1949; August 16, 1949. The star attraction at the Deauville Casino for Bastille Day, July 14, 1949, was the fine African American contralto Marian Anderson. *PHT*, June 7, 1949.

23. *PHT*, May 6, 1949; July 14, 1949; July 20, 1949.

24. Alain Decaux, *Les heures brillantes de la Côte d'Azur* (Paris: Presses Pocket, 1964), 239–41.

25. *PHT*, April 16, 1949.

26. In 1958, after fourteen straight years on America's "best dressed" list—thirteen of them at the very top—Babe Paley was enshrined in the "Fashion Hall of Fame." The Paleys would also stay in the elegant town house, once owned by Cole Porter, which American friends had bought shortly after the war. Sally Bedell Smith, *In All His Glory: The Life of William S. Paley* (New York: Simon and Schuster, 1990), 329, 339.

27. *NYT*, August 8, 1946.

28. *LM*, May 4, 1948. Among the government efforts to cultivate the American middle class was its support for a number of French organizations that in 1949 organized a "Merci Train" to distribute gifts to the "real" Americans, mainly in the heartland, in thanks for the help extended by the Friendship Train. It was, Drew Pearson wrote in his diary, "the first time any foreign nation has taken any trouble to show its appreciation to the United States and as far as I can see the American people are genuinely grateful." Drew Pearson diary, February 21, 1949, in *Drew Pearson Diaries, 1949–1959*, ed. Tyler Abell (New York: Holt, Rinehart and Winston, 1974), 24.

29. ECA, Special Mission to France, *L'aide américain à la France*, August 15, 1948.

30. ECA, *France: Country Study*, 1–55.

31. Organization of European Economic Cooperation (OEEC), *Tourism and European Recovery* (Paris: OEEC, 1951), 11. See Endy, "U.S. Tourism," 41–55, for a discussion of the attraction of tourism as foreign aid to various interest groups, in and out of government.

32. Henri Lagrand, "Le tourisme français et le tourisme Européen dans le cadre du plan de coopération économique," *L'aide américaine a la France*, May 1, 1949, n.p.

33. *L'aide américain à la France*, August 15, 1948; *PHT*, September 23, 1949; Lagrand, "Le tourisme français."

34. *L'aide américain à la France*, August 15, 1948.

35. Francesco Frangialli, *La France dans le tourisme mondial* (Paris: Economica, 1991), 35.

36. *L'aide américain à la France*, November 1949.

37. *LM*, January 1, 1949.

38. Janet Flanner, *Paris Journal: Vol. 1, 1944–1965*, ed. William Shawn (New York: Atheneum, 1965), 91.

39. *LM*, April 8, 1948.

40. Although only spottily enforced, in the hands of mean-spirited border agents, the

exchange controls, which required visitors to account for the money they took in and out of the country, could drive travelers to distraction. See Cynthia Brants diary, January 1949, Cynthia Brants Papers, AAA. Visa requirements for Americans were not dropped until April 1949. *NYT*, March 30, 1949.

41. Lagrand, "Le tourisme français."

42. *L'aide américaine à la France*, August 15, 1948. The student ships were allowed to undercut the North Atlantic lines' fixed fares in the guise of being open only to students and others traveling for "cultural and academic purposes." *PHT*, May 10, 1949.

43. Lionel Abel, *The Intellectual Follies: A Memoir of the Literary Venture in New York and Paris* (New York: Norton, 1984), 159–61; Buchwald, *Art Buchwald's Paris*, 10; *USNWR*, October 1, 1948.

44. One economist calculated that 220,000—that is, the midway point between the 300,000 in 1929 and the 85,000 in 1938—should be considered the "normal" number of American tourists. *LM*, May 4, 1948.

45. Moreover, they spent only a little over $200 million there, far short of the ECA goal of $500 million. *WSJ*, March 5, 1949; *NYT*, April 5, 1949. Immigrants played a very minor role in American travel to France but continued to represent a large portion of American travelers to the rest of Europe for some years to come. In 1957, for example, 37 percent of the U.S. residents traveling to Europe were foreign born, and 28 percent of all travelers said visiting relatives was the main purpose of their trip. *PHT*, June 28, 1957.

46. *Time*, September 12, 1949; *PHT*, August 12, 1949; *USNWR*, September 16, 1949.

47. *NYT*, December 11, 1949.

48. The same luxury hotels in Biarritz where room and board cost eight dollars in 1948 now charged eighteen dollars for room alone. *USNWR*, September 16, 1949.

49. *Time*, September 12, 1949; *PHT*, July 22, 1949; Horace Sutton, "'400,000 'Diplomats' on the Loose," *SR*, January 13, 1951, 75.

50. Flanner, *Paris Journal: Vol. 1, 1944–1965*, 106.

51. Sutton, "400,000 'Diplomats,'" 77.

52. Martha Churchill to family, January 16, 1949, "Class of 1950" box, SCSLC.

53. Deirdre Bair, *Simone de Beauvoir: A Biography* (London: Jonathan Cape, 1990), 325–33.

54. French existentialist women often wore long flowing skirts, while the males wore blue jeans. Ibid., 360.

55. Thomas Edward Ratcliffe to Anita [?], October 21, 1948; November 23, 1948, Thomas Edward Ratcliffe Papers, series 6, folder 94, SHC.

56. See my *Seductive Journey: American Tourists in France from Jefferson to the Jazz Age* (Chicago: University of Chicago Press, 1998), 74–79.

57. Martha Churchill to family, October 4, 1948, "Class of 1950" box, SCSLC.

58. *PT*, August 27, 1949.

59. Flanner, *Paris Journal: Vol. 1, 1944–1965*, 92.

60. *PHT*, May 15, 1949.

61. Thomas Ratcliffe to Anita [?], October 21, 1948, Thomas Edward Ratcliffe Papers, series 6, folder 94, SHC.

62. *Time*, July 11, 1949.

63. Georges Ravon, "Les Américains chez nous," *L'aide américaine à la France*, May 1, 1949, 10.

64. Herbert Lottman, *The Left Bank: Writers, Artists, and Politics from the Popular Front to the Cold War* (San Francisco: Halo Books, 1991), 233.

65. The article, not actually aimed at the tourists, was by Soviet writer Ilya Ehrenburg, in *Les Lettres Françaises*, February 10, 1949; cited in Lottman, *The Left Bank*, 254.

66. Bair, *Simone de Beauvoir*, 402–3; Flanner, *Paris Journal: Vol. 1, 1944–1965*, 92.

67. Louis Bishop diary, August 31, 1950, Louis Bishop Papers, RUL.

68. *PHT*, May 15, 1949.

69. Ravon, "Les Américains," 10.

70. Christopher Wilson, *Dancing with the Devil: The Windsors and Jimmy Donahue* (New York: St. Martin's, 2001), 147. In 1949 the actor Marlon Brando, holidaying in Paris after his Broadway triumph in *Streetcar Named Desire*, is said to have fallen for the beautiful young African American singer Eartha Kitt while watching her perform at Le Boeuf sur le Toit.

71. William Barrett, "New Innocents Abroad," *Partisan Review* 17 (March 1950): 274–75.

72. Ibid., 281.

73. Herbert Gentry, interview by Myron Schwartzman, December 1983; cited in Myron Schwartzman, *Romare Bearden: His Life and Art* (New York: Abrams, 1990), 162.

74. Minna Citron to [?], July 10, 1947, Minna Citron Papers, AAA.

75. Bearden to Holty, n.d. [April 1950?], Holty Papers, AAA.

76. Brants diary, November 3, 1948.

77. Robert Gwathmey to Hudson Walker, n.d. [November 1949?]; Gwathmey to Walker, n.d. [October 1949?], Hudson Walker Papers, AAA.

78. Bearden to Holty, n.d. [April 1950?], Holty Papers, AAA.

79. James Lord, *Picasso and Dora: A Personal Memoir* (New York: Fromm, 1994), 72–73.

80. Ned Rorem, *The Paris and New York Diaries of Ned Rorem, 1951–1961* (San Francisco: North Point Press, 1983), 6.

81. Quoted in Schwartzman, *Romare Bearden*, 169.

82. Decaux, *Les heures brillantes*, 241.

83. Horace Sutton, "Only for Americans," *SR*, August 13, 1949, 32.

84. "Paris 'Soul Food' King," *Ebony*, June 1968, 54–57.

85. Trevor Christie, "Notes for a French Postcard," *SR*, May 1, 1948, 34.

86. *PHT*, April 22, 1950.

87. P. E. Schneider, "In France, Only the Americans Wear Berets," *NYTM*, June 17, 1962, 49.

88. Stanley Karnow, *Paris in the Fifties* (New York: Random House, 1997), 41.

89. Sutton, "400,000 'Diplomats,'" 70–74.

90. Beevor and Cooper, *Paris after the Liberation*, 437–38.

91. They remained loyal to the latter, even though after one dinner there, Bishop got sick during a performance of *Lohengrin*. They went to some of the finer restaurants only when being entertained as part of a medical convention that Bishop attended for a few days. Louis Bishop diary, August 1950; September 2, 6, 8, 9, 1950.

92. OEEC, *Tourism and European Recovery*, 23–25.

93. Ogilvy said, "In truth, few readers of the *Saturday Evening Post*," which was known as a more solidly middle- and lower-middle-class magazine, "are interested in foreign travel." Geer to David Ogilvy, July 11, 1951. Ogilvy to W. S. Blair, March 4, 1951, David Ogilvy Papers, boxes 44 and 45, LC.

CHAPTER EIGHT

1. *USNWR*, September 16, 1949; *Time*, September 12, 1949.

2. "When they come home they will be very influential with Congress on the question of aid to Europe," he said, "and the impression they get will be very important." *PHT*, September 23, 1949.

3. See Christopher Endy, "U.S. Tourism in France: An International History, 1944–1971" (Ph.D. diss., University of North Carolina, 2000), chap. 4, for a very good discussion of their disappointments and divisions on this score.

4. *L'Humanité*, January 26, 27, 1949; cited in Endy, "U.S. Tourism," 116.

5. *Action*, October 6, 1949, in Jean-Pierre Bernard, *Paris Rouge: Les Communistes français dans la capitale* (Seysell: Champ Vallon, 1991), 71; cited in Antony Beevor and Artemis Cooper, *Paris after the Liberation, 1944–1949* (New York: Doubleday, 1994), 434.

6. *Time*, September 12, 1949.

7. *PHT*, July 14, 1949.

8. *PHT*, June 1, 1949.

9. From 1947 to 1950, well over half the films shown in France were American, and they attracted close to 45 percent of the audience. Patricia Hubert-Lacombe, "L'acceuil des films américains en France pendant la guerre froid (1946–1953)," *Revue d'histoire moderne et contemporaine* 36 (April–June 1986): 301–5; Antoine de Baeque, "Paris et l'accueil des cinéastes américains (1945–1960)," in *Le Paris des étrangers depuis 1945*, by Antoine Marès and Pierre Milza (Paris: Publications de la Sorbonne, 1994), 429–40.

10. Ludovic Tournès, "L'américanisation de la culture française," *Historiens et Géographes* 358 (July/August 1997): 66–67; Michel Winock, "The Cold War," in *The Rise and Fall of Anti-Americanism: A Century of French Perception*, ed. Denis Lacorne, Jacques Rupnik, and Marie-France Toinet; trans. Gerry Turner (Basingstoke: Macmillan, 1990), 73; Irwin Wall, *The United States and the Making of Postwar France, 1945–1954* (Cambridge: Cambridge University Press, 1991), 114–19; Arnold Rose, "Anti-Americanism in France," *Antioch Review* 12 (December 1952): 469.

11. *Action*, December 16, 1949; cited in Denis Lacorne and Jacques Rupnik, "La France saisie par l'Amérique," in *L'Amérique dans les têtes*, ed. Denis Lacorne, Jacques Rupnik, and Marie-France Toinet (Paris: Hachette, 1986), 29.

12. Richard Kuisel, "Coca-Cola au pays des buveurs de vin," *L'Histoire* 44 (November 1986): 24.

13. Wall, *United States*, 113–24; Kuisel, "Coca-Cola," 22–28.

14. Kuisel, "Coca-Cola," 24, 27.

15. Sartre had previously been a fan of Hollywood movies, but he now explained that the war had deprived Hollywood of its intelligent European audiences and as a result it had turned mindless. Ironically, after about 1953, French cinephiles such as Henri Langlois, founder of the Cinémathèque Française, and future "New Wave" directors such as François Truffaut and Eric Rohmer began to appreciate the genius of films by directors such as Howard Hawks, Fritz Lang, John Huston, John Ford, and Alfred Hitchcock, which were condemned as vulgar "B" grade movies in the late 1940s. Baeque, "Paris et l'accueil," 440–47.

16. Pierre Nora, "America and the French Intellectuals," *Daedelus* 107 (Winter 1978): 326.

17. Jean-Philippe Mathy, *Extrême Occident: French Intellectuals and America* (Chicago: University of Chicago Press, 1993), 156; Marie-Christine Granjon, "Sartre, Beauvoir, Aron: An Ambiguous Affair," in Lacorne, Rupnik, and Toinet, *Rise and Fall*, 116–21; Herbert Lottman, *The Left Bank: Writers, Artists, and Politics from the Popular Front to the Cold War* (San Francisco: Halo Books, 1991), 260.

18. Winock, "Cold War," 71.

19. Nora, "America and the French Intellectuals," 326.

20. Jean-Baptiste Duroselle, *France and the United States from the Beginnings to the Present Day* (Chicago: University of Chicago Press, 1978), 195.

21. "Les Etats-Unis, les Américains et la France, 1939–1945," *Sondages: Revue Française de l'Opinion Publique* 15, no. 2 (January–February 1953): 62.

22. Rose, "Anti-Americanism," 469.

23. Ibid., 471.

24. Gérard Louchet, "Apprenez à connaître les gouts des touristes étrangers à l'hôtel," *L'Hôtellerie*, July 15, 1950; cited in Endy, "U.S. Tourism," 145.

25. The surprising thing is that this was in an American-subsidized magazine designed to promote the Marshall Plan. Renée et Pierre Gosset, "Les touristes à Paris," *Rapports France-Etats-Unis* (April 1950): 32–33.

26. Stanley Karnow, *Paris in the Fifties* (New York: Random House, 1997), 116. Escargots did indeed constitute a formidable barrier. Only after having lived in France for over eight years could Ollie Stewart, an expatriate African American who loved almost everything about France, including frogs' legs, bring himself to try them—and pronounce them delicious. *PhAA*, April 7, 1956.

27. Duroselle, *France and the United States*, 199.

28. Or, the author said, he was "the son of an immigrant vaguely curious about 'the old country,'" something that did not apply to France. *LM*, August 19, 1950.

29. Tony Judt, *Past Imperfect: French Intellectuals, 1944–1956* (Berkeley: University of California Press, 1992), 200. The term had first become current among the opposition to the influx of American films following the Blum-Byrnes agreement. Tournès, "L'américanisation," 265.

30. Ellipses in original. "Confidential Security Information," "Public Sentiment in France," n.d. [1950], RG59, 651.00/4-852, SDP.

31. Ernie Ricci [pseud.], interview by Harvey and Mona Levenstein, Paris, April 22, 1999.

32. It was cheaper than Britain and every other European country except Spain and Austria. *LM*, September 20, 1951.

33. Horace Sutton, "Only for Americans," *SR*, August 13, 1949, 32–33.

34. A. Piater, *Une enquête de l'AIT sur les dépenses des touristes étrangers en France* (Berne: AIT, 1952), 22.

35. David Ogilvy to Steve and Roger, September 14, 1953, David Ogilvy Papers, box 45, LC.

36. Janet Flanner to Natalia Danesi Murray, October 12, 1952, in Janet Flanner, *Darlinghissima: Letters to a Friend*, ed. Natalia Danesi Murray (San Diego: Harcourt Brace, 1986), 172.

37. Beevor and Cooper, *Paris after the Liberation*, 437.

38. Stephen White, "The Pleasant Mist of Dollars in French Eyes," *Look*, November 21, 1950, 2.

39. She described herself as a "sometime expatriate." Alyce Martin, "Take It or Leave It?" in *Woman's Guide to Europe*, ed. Eugene Fodor (The Hague: Mouton, 1954), 36.

40. Quoted in Beevor and Cooper, *Paris after the Liberation*, 437.

41. Frances Stillman diary, July 16, 1952, Ary Stillman Papers, AAA.

42. Pan American World Airways, *New Horizons Guide*, 10th ed., rev. (New York: Simon and Schuster, 1961), 63.

43. Lee Bouvier Radziwill and Jacqueline Bouvier Onassis, *One Special Summer* (New York: Delacorte, 1974), n.p.

44. They had met the schoolteacher on the crossing. Dorothy Brown diary, "Italy, Switzerland, France and England, June 1 to August 14, 1959," Dorothy Brown Papers, box 12, SL.

45. *PhAA*, February 18, 1956.

46. "U.S. Tourists: Good or Ill-Will Envoys?" *NYTM*, September 1, 1957, 45.

47. Yves-Henri Nouailhat, "Aspects de la politique culturelle des Etats-Unis à l'égard de la France de 1945 à 1950," *Relations Internationales* 25 (Spring 1981): 96–104; American Library in Paris, "Weathering Hardship to Shape a Lasting Legacy," ALP Web site, August 3, 1997, 5; Tournès, "L'américanisation," 73; Howard C. Rice, "Seeing Ourselves as the French See Us," *French Review* 21 (1948): 432–41. See Volker R. Berghahn, *America and the Intellectual Cold Wars in Europe* (Princeton: Princeton University Press, 2001), for the European context of these efforts.

48. Naima Prevots, *Dance for Export: Cultural Diplomacy and the Cold War* (Hanover, NH: University Press of New England, 1998). American cultural leaders supported this to show that no longer did they need to defer to Europe in high culture. In order to avoid the charge of propaganda, much of this activity was run by private philanthropies, most notably the Ford Foundation. Volker Berghahn, "Philanthropy and Diplomacy in the 'American Century,'" *Diplomatic History* 23 (Summer 1999): 393–419; Berghahn, *America and the Intellectual Cold Wars*, 168–77.

49. The pamphlet then lists some of things the Marshall Plan had aided in France—gasoline imports, hospitals, factories, and so on. *L'homme au cigar entre les dents* (Paris: Rapports France-Etats-Unis, 1950), n.p.

50. Georges Ravon, "Les Américains chez nous," *L'aide américaine à la France*, May 1, 1949.

51. He also said, less convincingly, that it was wrong to think that he eats poorly at home. Just because most American restaurants did not serve sweetbreads, duck à l'orange, frogs' legs, and escargots did not mean that Americans did not eat well. Even their hot dogs, hamburgers, ice cream, and great variety of milk drinks were not to be disdained. Pierre Daninos, "Le touriste et vous, suggestions et conseils," *Rapports France-Etats-Unis* (July 1950): 33–37.

52. Raoul Bertrand to Bonnet, November 4, 1952, vol. 238, sous-série Etats-Unis, Amérique 1952–63, France, Ministère d'Affaires Etrangères, Paris; cited in Endy, "U.S. Tourism," 117.

53. Ralph Reed, *American Express: Its Origins and Growth* (New York: Newcomen Society, 1952), 27.

54. Horace Sutton, "400,000 'Diplomats' on the Loose," *SR*, January 13, 1951, 72. The slogan the European Travel Commission used to promote American travel to Europe, "Understanding through Travel Is the Passport to Peace," was the product of a compromise between ECA officials who wanted to emphasize going to Europe to see the Marshall Plan in action and advertising executives appalled at the idea of having to use that as an enticement to tourism. Endy, "U.S. Tourism," 215–16.

55. *Time*, April 9, 1956.

56. Joseph and Naomi Barry, "A Primer on Etiquette for Innocents Abroad," *NYTM*, July 23, 1950, 12.

57. U.S. Information Agency, "What Should I Know When I Travel Abroad?" (1952); cited in Endy, "U.S. Tourism," 265–66.

58. Sinclair Weeks, "Importance of International Travel in Advancing World Peace," *Department of State Bulletin*, July 18, 1955, 106–8. At the same time, though, it vigorously enforced its bans on tourist travel to China, actively discouraged visits to Soviet bloc countries, and deprived leftist Americans of their passports.

59. *NYT*, July 26, 27, 1957; R. L. Duffus, "Still 'The Innocents Abroad,'" *NYTM* August 2, 1959, 14; Charles E. Wilson, "Peace through Understanding," *ASTA Travel News* 27 (July 1958): 26–28; cited in Endy, "U.S. Tourism," 272–73.

60. Frances Knight, "Don't Be an Ugly American," *Parade*, June 5, 1960, 4. The irony is that Knight herself probably did much more harm to the American image abroad than the tourists. A close associate of the most extreme anti-Communists in Congress and of J. Edgar Hoover, the paranoid head of the FBI, she caused the United States untold embarrassment abroad by refusing to issue passports to Americans to travel to Communist countries and by ensuring that visitors' visas were refused to hundreds of eminent foreigners who were suspected of harboring Communist sympathies.

61. Horace Sutton, "Our Dollars and Manners Abroad," *SR*, May 13, 1950, 20–21.

62. Sutton, "400,000 'Diplomats,'" 70–74.

63. There was a widespread belief, said the survey's author, shared by many Europeans, that although Americans may have been the masters of "technique," the "fundamental thoughts" all came from Europe. Jacques Freymond, "America in European Eyes," *Annals of the American Academy of Political and Social Science* 295 (1954): 35–37. This latter idea, first popularized by Georges Duhamel in the 1920s, was not unlike what Americans said twenty-odd years later when the Japanese began threatening them in various industrial fields.

64. Travel Development Section, "Results of a 'Pilot' Survey Made by OSR Travel Development Section, Paris," Records of Chief of Department of Commerce Travel Bureau, Herbert Wilkinson, 1948–1951, Travel Development Section, RG 469, box 1, NA; cited in Endy, "U.S. Tourism," 199.

65. *Congressional Record*, 82 Cong., 2nd sess., May 15, 1952, vol. 98, pt. 10: A9275–76.

66. "Every American passing through France asks about how the French feel about his compatriots," said a French polling organization. "Ce que les Français pensant des Américains," *Réalités* 91(August 1953): 18–22.

67. Rita Hamer, interview by Harvey and Mona Levenstein, Paris, April 27, 2000.

68. Hamer interview.

69. Donovan Richardson, "An Air-Conditioned Look at France," *CSM*, December 15, 1950.

70. Temple Fielding, citing National Geographic Society, in *Temple Fielding's Guide to Europe* (New York: Sloane, 1963), 442.

71. Martha Churchill to family, September 20, 1948, "Class of 1950" box, SCSLC.

72. Gordon Cooper and Walter Hackett, *France on Your Own* (New York: Cortina, 1954). 3.

73. He noted that the Amex office in London "doesn't draw half as well." *PhAA*, November 8, 1958.

74. Hamer interview.

75. Gosset, "Les touristes à Paris," 34.

76. Hamer interview.

77. Temple Fielding, *Fielding's Travel Guide to Europe: 1953–54 Edition* (New York: Sloane, 1953), 326.

78. Dorothy Marsh to George Brownell, January 20, 1958, Dorothy Marsh Papers, box 1023, SCA.

79. Sylvia Plath, *The Unabridged Journals of Sylvia Plath, 1950–1962* (New York: Random House, 2000), March 26–April 5, 1956, 265.

80. Rachelle Girson, *Maiden Voyages: A Lively Guide for the Woman Traveler* (New York: Harcourt Brace, 1967), 131–32.

81. Louis Bishop diary, August 1950, Louis Bishop Papers, RUL.

82. It left their hotel in Paris very early in the morning, stopped in Reims, where they had a quick look at the cathedral, and pressed on to Nancy in time for dinner. There was hardly time for an after-dinner walk, though, because they had to arise early the next morning for the ride to Strasbourg. After a brief stop there, they were back on the bus, across the German border, and deep into the Black Forest in time for lunch in a small town. They exchanged money there and climbed back in the bus to push on to Stuttgart, and so on. Bishop diary, August 1950.

83. Ibid.

84. "In the beginning," said one, "they looked at us as if we were from Mars. Then they became very friendly when our guides and hotel people showered us with special attention. Their desire to discuss the racial situation in America gave us a chance to tell them a few things they've probably never heard before." *PhAA*, June 14, 1958.

85. Hamer interview.

86. Virgile Barel, "Tourisme et Plan Marshall," *L'Hôtel-Café-Restaurant et le Travailleur des H.R.C.B réunis de la région parisienne* 33 (March 1949); cited in Endy, "U.S. Tourism," 110.

87. In 1952 almost three-quarters of Nice's hotel guests stayed in basic bottom-rung hotels. Robert Kanigel, *High Season* (New York: Viking, 2002), 206.

88. Stillman diary, July 18–July 30, 1952.

89. *PHT*, June 28, 1957; Bennet Travel Co., "Itinerary for Mr. and Mrs. La Rue Brown, July, 1959," Brown Papers, box 12.

90. *Time*, April 9, 1956.

91. James Baldwin, "A Question of Identity," in *Notes of a Native Son* (Boston: Beacon, 1955), 128; reprinted from *Partisan Review*, July–August 1954.

92. Some responses add up to over 100 percent because of multiple responses. "Ce que les Français," 18–22.

93. For example, *Business Week*, admitting the poll showed that most did not agree with the "u.s. go home" signs, still emphasized that only 11 percent wanted them removed. However, 40 percent had said they had not even seen them and 8 percent gave no response to the question. In fact, 85 percent of those who saw and disapproved of them wanted them removed. "Sightseeing without Insults," *BW*, September 26, 1953, 200; "Ce que les Français," 19.

94. Fielding, *Fielding's Travel Guide to Europe: 1953–54 Edition*, 321.

95. Plath, *Unabridged Journals*, August 26, 1956, 260.

96. *PHT*, June 6, 1963. By then, Buchwald had moved to Washington, but when he was on vacation, the *Herald Tribune* ran his Paris columns from the 1950s.

97. Bob Sage, "Yankee Come Over!" *SR*, March 13, 1957, 52.

98. All it took, Steinbeck said, was for one of them to get drunk, or one to be a "loud mouth," and all of these people who "have come to see and learn and carry away the impressions of the greatness and beauty of Europe . . . paying their respects to the roots of their culture" were treated with contempt. John Steinbeck, "One American in Paris," in *Holiday in France*, by Ludwig Bemelmans (Cambridge: Houghton Mifflin, 1957), 148.

99. Edgar Wiggins to Claude Barnett, June 1, 1946; Barnett to Wiggins, June 11, 1946, Claude Barnett Papers, box 199, folder 1, CHS.

100. *PhT*, August 27, 1949.

101. Phyllis Rose, *Jazz Cleopatra: Josephine Baker in Her Time* (New York: Doubleday, 1989), 209–10. When she opened a new show at the Folies Bergère in 1951, its publicist thought there was enough potential African American patronage to solicit advertisements for its program from *Ebony*, the African American magazine. A. E. Whily-Tell to John H. Johnson, July 7, 1951, Barnett Papers, box 198, folder 6.

102. Richard Wright, "A Paris, les GIs noirs ont appris a connaître et a aimer la liberté," *Samedi-Soir*, May 25, 1946, 2.

103. Hazel Rowley, *Richard Wright: The Life and Times* (New York: Henry Holt, 2001), 348.

104. James Campbell, *Exiled in Paris: Richard Wright, James Baldwin, Samuel Beckett, and Others on the Left Bank* (New York: Scribner, 1995), 247.

105. He did warn that this was being threatened by the racism imported by white American GIs, who had clashed with civilian African Americans in Paris, and by white American tourists, "laden with dollars and racist psychology, [who] have forced a few French hotels to enforce racial practices for the first time in recent French history." He was probably thinking of the writer Chester Himes's story of having been refused accommodations in some Paris hotels that then rented rooms to white people. He also denounced large American corporate offices in Paris and the American Hospital there for not hiring any African Americans. Richard Wright, "American Negroes in France," *The Crisis*, June–July 1951, 381–83.

106. Joseph Barry, "American in Paris—the More They Change . . . ," *NYTM*, August 15, 1948, 42.

107. Campbell, *Exiled in Paris*, 245–46. His African American fellow-expatriate friend, the cartoonist Ollie Harrington, later said, "I've never met a black person who did *not* believe that Richard Wright was done in." Rowley, *Richard Wright*, 525.

108. William Demby, described him as "holding court" there. William Demby, interview by Harvey and Mona Levenstein, Sag Harbor, NY, December 22, 1998.

109. Essentially, Baldwin said that by concentrating only on his hero's individual acts of rebellion, he provided little insight into the kinds of ties blacks developed among themselves to cope with racism. The piece was later revised and published in America as "Many Thousands Gone," *Partisan Review*, November–December 1951, and reprinted in Baldwin, *Notes of a Native Son*, 85–116.

110. Derek Jewell, *Duke: A Portrait of Duke Ellington* (London: Hamish Hamilton, 1977), 62.

111. Demby interview.

112. Romare Bearden to Charles Alston, March 9, 1950; cited in Myron Schwartzman, *Romare Bearden: His Life and Art* (New York: Abrams, 1990), 165.

113. Demby interview.

114. *PhT*, August 27, 1949.

115. Demby interview. During the Depression most of the school districts that did not already have restrictions on married women teaching enacted them. As a result, well into the late 1950s most women teachers were single.

116. Chester Himes, *The Quality of Hurt: The Autobiography of Chester Himes*, vol. 1 (Garden City, NY: Doubleday, 1972), 187–88; Himes, *My Life of Absurdity: The Autobiography of Chester Himes*, vol. 2 (Garden City, NY: Doubleday, 1976), 34. Himes, somewhat defensively, said that in the 1950s African American women tourists would have nothing to do with a poor black writer like him. Ibid., vol. 2, 37.

117. *PhT*, March 11, 1950.

118. Hazel Scott, "What Paris Means to Me," *Negro Digest* (November 1961): 60–61; reprinted from *Ebony*, no citation given.

119. *G&M*, October 20, 2001.

120. *PhT*, October 29, 1955.

121. "Europe on a Budget," *Ebony*, May 1962, 61.

122. The best of these required annual memberships, effectively excluding most tourists. Art Buchwald, "Seeing Paris after Dark," in New York Herald Tribune, European Edition, *The Herald Tribune Guide to Paris* (Paris, 1952), 37.

123. Miles Davis, *Miles, the Autobiography* (New York: Simon and Schuster, 1989), 126.

124. Tournès, "L'américanisation," 66. Bechet died in 1959.

125. Ludovic Tournès, *New Orleans sur Seine: histoire du jazz en France* (Paris: Fayard, 1999), 134–40, 224–28; Edward Kennedy Ellington, *Music Is My Mistress* (New York: Doubleday, 1973), 141–44, 188; Sidney Bechet, *Treat It Gentle* (New York: Hill and Wang, 1960), 191–99.

126. *PHT*, July 8, 1958.

127. *PhAA*, November 17, 1958.

128. James Baldwin joked that if he ever wrote a memoir of his years in Paris, he would call it "Non, nous ne jouons pas la trompette" (No, we don't play the trumpet). Campbell, *Exiled in Paris*, 103.

129. Duke Ellington spent eight weeks in Paris writing the music for the movie. Ellington, *Music Is My Mistress*, 143. Tyler Stovall pointed out that the 1957 novel upon which it was based, written by a white writer, had the black musician as the central character, whereas the movie reduced him to Paul Newman's sidekick. Tyler Stovall, *Paris Noir: African Americans in the City of Light* (Boston: Houghton Mifflin, 1996), 242.

130. *Newsweek*, September 21, 1964.

CHAPTER NINE

1. *BW*, September 26, 1953.

2. Belgium and Britain came next, followed, curiously, by Yugoslavia. *CSM*, May 15, 1956.

3. In 1951, 75 percent listed France as their preferred destination in Europe, while Britain, the next favorite country, trailed far behind. A. Piater, *Une enquête de l'AIT sur les dépenses des touristes étrangers en France* (Berne: AIT, 1952), 22. In 1958, much to the chagrin of the British Travel Authority, twice as many still preferred France as did Britain. Bill Blair, "Comments on Potential Travel Market for Europe in the U.S.A.," in David Ogilvy to Leonard Lickorish, n.d. [1958], David Ogilvy Papers, box 45, LC.

4. Jean Ginier, "Quelques aspects du tourisme américain en France," *Annales de Géographie* 397 (1964): 317.

5. Gordon Cooper and Walter Hackett, *France on Your Own* (New York: Cortina, 1954), ix.

6. Joseph Barry, *Left Bank, Right Bank: Paris and Parisians* (London: Kimber, 1952), 9.

7. *PHT*, June 12, 1951.

8. Bertram M. Gordon, "The Decline of a Cultural Icon: France in American Perspective," *French Historical Studies* 22 (1999): 625–51; Christopher Endy, "U.S. Tourism in France: An International History, 1944–1971" (Ph.D. diss., University of North Carolina, 2000), 175–76.

9. Endy, "U.S. Tourism," 189; Art Buchwald, "The Night Life," in *Holiday in France*, by Ludwig Bemelmans (Cambridge: Houghton Mifflin, 1957), 61.

10. *PHT*, May 29, 1951. Her trip helped quell prospective tourists' fears that Europe was about to be invaded by the Soviets. *LM*, June 19, 1951.

11. *PHT*, June 20, 1951.

12. Horace Sutton, "Paix as You Go," *SR*, May 12, 1979, 50.

13. *PHT*, July 10, 1954.

14. Although the mere mention of their names struck terror in the hearts of embassy employees, they caused considerable merriment in the French press, which reported that during their previous stop in Munich they had managed to investigate the loyalty of one thousand employees of Radio Free Europe in half an hour. James Campbell, *Exiled in Paris: Richard Wright, James Baldwin, Samuel Beckett, and Others on the Left Bank* (New York: Scribner, 1995), 100.

15. Janet Flanner to Natalia Danesi Murray, April 23, 1953, in Janet Flanner, *Darlinghissima: Letters to a Friend*, ed. Natalia Danesi Murray (San Diego: Harcourt Brace, 1986), 197.

16. Flanner to Murray, n.d. [December 1957], in ibid., 207.

17. One correspondent, said Bradlee, had "bitten the dust" solely because the large limousine he hired to take the editor-in-chief and his wife to the Windsors' country estate was too wide to fit between the pillars guarding the mile-long driveway and the couple had to walk through pouring rain and mud to get to the couple's château. Ben Bradlee, *A Good Life: Newspapering and Other Adventures* (New York: Simon and Schuster, 1995), 187.

18. The conditions of the huge federal subsidies that financed her dictated that she be readily convertible to wartime troopship duty, preventing her from excelling in terms of lux-

urious fittings. Her paneling, for example, had to be made of fireproof plastic and Formica instead of wood.

19. J. Driscoll, "Passenger Journal," 1953, http://www.flare.net/e9ee52a/Passenger Journal.htm.

20. *PHT*, April 13, 1951.

21. *PHT*, May 14, 1954. Virginia Creed and Henry Milo, *All about Paris and Its Environs* (New York: Duell, Sloan and Pierce, 1955), 4.

22. Elizabeth Church, "How to Make a Cook's Tour," *House Beautiful*, September 1951, 178.

23. "Flying a Pan Am Stratocruiser," http://www.flare.net/users/e9ee52a/Pan%Am%/20Sratocruiser.html.

24. Eugene Fodor, ed., *Woman's Guide to Europe* (The Hague: Mouton, 1954).

25. *PHT*, April 5, 1957.

26. Temple Fielding, *Fielding's Travel Guide to Europe: 1964 Edition* (New York: Sloan, 1964), 514.

27. John McPhee, "Templex," *New Yorker*, January 6, 1968, 49.

28. Stephen Watts, *The Ritz* (London: Bodley Head, 1963), 22–23, 13–14.

29. *PHT*, May 26, 1954.

30. *PHT*, August 16, 1954.

31. He was speaking of the Duke of Windsor, formerly the Prince of Wales. Fiercely loyal to his good customer, he refused to acknowledge the drop in rank that resulted when the ex-prince gave up his throne. Alain Decaux, *Les heures brillantes de la Côte d'Azur* (Paris: Presses Pocket, 1964), 238–39.

32. *PHT*, August 16, 1954.

33. Raymond Gatti, *Taxi de guerre, taxi de paix* (Cannes: private, 1988), 132.

34. Alan Jay Lerner, *The Street Where I Live* (London: Hodder and Stoughton, 1978), 129.

35. "Riviera," telex, n.d. [March 1957?], Pan American Airlines Papers, "Press Flight 1957" folder, box 322, UM.

36. Decaux, *Les heures brillantes*, 238–41.

37. A 1953 guide for young American tourists in France tells of two boys standing at the balustrade, one of whom tells their father, "We were talking about suicide. . . . David was telling me how after they've lost their money gambling in the casino the people come out here and shoot themselves." Alexander Reid, *The Young Traveler in France* (New York: Dutton, 1953), 125.

38. Marsh Tours, "Conducted Tours: Europe, 1957" [brochure published in 1956], Dorothy Marsh Papers, box 4, SSC.

39. Mary Blume, *Côte d'Azur: Inventing the French Riviera* (London: Thames and Hudson, 1992), 144.

40. Decaux, *Les heures brillantes*, 239–40.

41. Peter Stone, in "I Love Paris in the Fifties," *Paris Review* 150 (Spring 1999), on http://www.parisreview.com/history/iloveparis/iloveparis.htm, n.p. Most reporters were barred from the festivities, but several managed to infiltrate themselves among the six hundred guests by disguising themselves as cassocked priests. Art Buchwald wangled an invitation after writing a column saying he wasn't going to be invited because the Grimaldis

and Buchwalds had been feuding for five hundred years. Art Buchwald in "I Love Paris," n.p.

42. Blume, *Côte d'Azur*, 144.

43. Leavitt Morris, "Travel Editor's Diary," *CSM*, April 24, 1957.

44. Mary Hulsizer diary, October 26, 1957, in Mary Burr Hulsizer Papers, RUL; Dorothy Marsh Tours, "Minutes of 1964 Tour Conductors Meeting," November 28, 1964, in Marsh Papers, box 4.

45. "Riviera," "Nice," telexes, n.d. [March 1957?], "Press Flight 1957" folder, Pan Am Papers, box 322.

46. Blume, *Côte d'Azur*, 145.

47. Miles Davis, *Miles, the Autobiography* (New York: Simon and Schuster, 1989), 127.

48. Karal Ann Marling, "Americans in Paris: Montmartre and the Art of Pop Culture," in *Montmartre and the Making of Mass Culture*, ed. Gabriel Weisberg (New Brunswick: Rutgers University Press, 2001), xiv.

49. New York Herald Tribune, *The Herald Tribune Guide to Paris, 1952* (Paris: Herald Tribune, 1952), 37.

50. Temple Fielding, *Fielding's Travel Guide to Europe: 1953–54 Edition* (New York: Sloane, 1953), 348–49.

51. *PHT*, 1952, passim.

52. They were so tall that many Americans believed, with good reason, that they could not be French and must have come from elsewhere in northern Europe. *PHT*, June 28, 1957; *Time*, May 20, 1957; Stanley Karnow, *Paris in the Fifties* (New York: Random House, 1997), 204–6; Marie and Aldo Croatti, interview by Harvey and Mona Levenstein, Boston, MA, December 23, 2000.

53. In addition to the closing of the *maisons*, he cited stricter regulations of the music hall shows.

54. Jean Ginier, *Les touristes étrangers en France pendant l'été* (Paris: Genin, 1969), 336–37.

55. *PHT*, June 28, 1957; Karnow, *Paris in the Fifties*, 199–206; *Time*, April 9, 1956.

56. *PHT*, June 28, 1957; Karnow, *Paris in the Fifties*, 199–206.

57. Dorothy Brown diary, August 19, 1950, Dorothy Brown Papers, box 11, SL.

58. Louis Bishop diary, July 3–18, 1963, Louis Bishop Papers, RUL.

59. "An Artist's Impressions of American Tourists," *NYT*, May 5, 1950.

60. Phillip Andrews, "Two Terrific Weeks," *Mademoiselle*, October 1956.

61. *PhAA*, July 11, 1959.

62. Why the actor Anthony Perkins, who was also at the dinner, did not join the excursion is open to speculation. Janet Flanner to Natalia Danesi Murray, November 12, 1960, in Flanner, *Darlinghissima*, 286.

63. *PhT*, August 27, 1949.

64. Ibid.

65. Bishop diary, September 7, 12, 1950.

66. Buchwald, "Night Life," 62.

67. Naomi Barry, "Everybody's Going to Europe," in *Woman's Guide to Europe*, ed. Eugene Fodor (The Hague: Mouton, 1954), 31.

68. *PHT*, July 7, 1954. For example, Countess de la Falaise, "'My Choice' of the Paris

Collections," *Look*, October 10, 1950, 69–72; Gordon, "Decline of a Cultural Icon," 642–43.

69. *PhT*, August 22, 1958.

70. Paul Deutschman, "How to Buy a Dior Gown," in Bemelmans, *Holiday in France*, 77–78.

71. *PhAA*, March 15, 1958.

72. Alyce Martin, "France," in Fodor, *Woman's Guide*, 135–79. Eloise Henkel, shopping columnist for the *Herald Tribune*, was even more practical. Her 1950 guidebook gave instructions on how to sell dollars on the black market, recommending her newspaper's daily reports on the currency's "unofficial fluctuations." Eloise Henkel, *How to Save Money in Paris* (New York: Doubleday, 1950), 15–18.

73. Pan American World Airways, *New Horizons Guide*, 10th ed., rev. (New York: Simon and Schuster, 1961), 63.

74. It continues, "Should you be the guest of a certain countess, one evening, you will find yourself chatting with men of widely divergent interests: [the novelist] André Maurois, [secretary-general of the United Nations] Trygve Lie, [the Spanish philosopher] Ortega y Gasset, [British army commander] Marshall Montgomery." Martin, "France," 140.

75. Naomi Barry, "How to Be a Lady," in Fodor, *Woman's Guide*, 55.

76. Martin, "France," 142–43.

77. When, in 1950, *Life* ran a chart cataloging the different tastes of status groups, food was only mentioned with regard to tastes in salads, with the higher groups preferring greens with an oil and vinegar dressing while the lower-middle-brows liked iceberg lettuce and store-bought dressing. Tom Funk, "Everyday Tastes from High-brow to Low-brow," *Life*, April 11, 1949, 100–101.

78. Craig Claiborne, interview by Harvey Levenstein, East Hampton, NY, February 23, 1989; *NYT*, January 28, 1966.

79. Julia Child, interview by Harvey Levenstein, Cambridge, MA, December 28, 1988.

80. One time he was driven seventy-five miles to a famous restaurant in Normandy, where he ate two complete lunches (the first, lobster; the second, duck) and then returned to Paris, where he sat down to a fine multicourse dinner. Sally Bedell Smith, *In All His Glory: The Life of William S. Paley* (New York: Simon and Schuster, 1990), 327.

81. Lee Bouvier Radziwill and Jacqueline Bouvier Onassis, *One Special Summer* (New York: Delacorte, 1974), n.p.

82. Earle MacAusland, preface, in Gourmet Magazine, *The Gourmet Cookbook* (New York: Gourmet, 1950), 8.

83. Its 1950 cookbook, for example, had a forty-three-page chapter called "Dozens of Sauces," devoted almost solely to the classic French sauces. Ibid. From 1955 to 1957, it ran monthly lessons on cooking the classics of French cuisine by the French chef Louis Diat, beginning with bouillon and ending with frogs' legs. *Gourmet*, indices, 1951–55, 1956–60.

84. *Gourmet*, indices, 1946–50, 1951–55, 1956–60, 1961–65; Anne Mendelson, "The 50's," *Gourmet* (September 2001): 113.

85. Art Buchwald, "Gay Night Life and Fine Food," *PHT*, June 12, 1951; Church, "How to Make a Cook's Tour," 176–78. It also said that eating "combines ideally with shopping and sightseeing, for they fill in the times between meals, and are conducive to building

up an appetite and slimming the waist." Also, since most French shops and museums closed at midday, it meant women need not fret over "wasting time" over a long meal. Ibid., 178.

86. Alexander Watt, "V.I.P.'s in Paris Restaurants: Who Eats What and How to Cook It," *Vogue*, May 15, 1955, 80–81.

87. Alexander Watt, "6 Secret Paris Bistros," *Vogue*, October 1, 1958, 186.

88. *PhAA*, September 6, 1958.

89. Romare Bearden to Carl Holty, n.d. [April 1950?], Carl Holty Papers, AAA.

90. Beauford Delaney to Lawrence Calcagno, December 22, 1955, Calcagno Papers, AAA. In 1953, 124 of them got together to plan a big group show, which never came off. *Time*, May 4, 1953.

91. Man Ray to Paul Wechser, November 15, 1954, Wechser Papers, AAA.

92. Taki Theodoracopulos, "It Really Was Yesterday," *National Review* 25 (March 2, 1973): 259.

93. Ibid. It later became an upscale restaurant.

94. Shaw arrived in 1951, originally intending to stay only for the summer, but liked it so much, and so abhorred the McCarthyism that threatened his career in the States, that he stayed on. Jones arrived in 1958, intent on emulating the Lost Generation writers of the 1920s. Christopher Sawyer-Lauçanno, *The Continual Pilgrimage: American Writers in Paris, 1944–1960* (New York: Grove, 1992), 212–32.

95. Terry Southern, interview, *Smoke Signals* 20 (n.d.), http://www.carminestreet.com/smoke_signals.html.

96. Ibid.

97. Lee Hill, *A Grand Guy: The Art and Life of Terry Southern* (New York: Harper Collins, 2001), 36–38.

98. "Classic Upstart," *Guardian* (London), November 17, 2001.

99. George Plimpton, in "I Love Paris," n.p.

100. Gay Talese, "Looking for Hemingway," *Esquire*, May 1963; cited in Harold Hayes, ed., *"Smiling through the Apocalypse": Esquire's History of the Sixties* (New York: McCall, 1970), 863.

101. Campbell, *Exiled in Paris*, 115.

102. Fonda did contribute a line drawing of a coffee urn to it. George Plimpton, "The Paris Review Sketchbook," *Paris Review* 29 (1981): 316–48. So many young American women passed through there that one of the male staff gave up on learning their names and decreed that they should all be called "Apetecker." Talese, "Looking for Hemingway," 868.

103. Tyler Stovall, *Paris Noir: African Americans in the City of Light* (Boston: Houghton Mifflin, 1996), 182–215.

104. *New York Herald Tribune*, November 5, 1949; cited in Campbell, *Exiled in Paris*, 114.

105. Campbell, *Exiled in Paris*, 122–23; Plimpton, "Paris Review Sketchbook," 336; Sawyer-Lauçanno, *Continual Pilgrimage*, 133–35; Mike Golden, "The Next Man to Go: An Interview with 'Accursed Publisher' Maurice Girodias," Instant Classics 1999, http://www.instantclassics.com/ic_html/next_man.html.

106. *Guardian* (London), November 17, 2001.

107. Barry Miles, *The Beat Hotel: Ginsberg, Burroughs, and Corso in Paris, 1958–1963* (New York: Grove, 2000), 12–16.

108. Ibid., 66.

109. Sawyer-Lauçanno, *Continual Pilgrimage*, 264.

110. Ibid., 271. A German officer friend told of how taken aback he was when, in Paris in December 1941, Céline had told him "how surprised and stupefied he is that we soldiers don't shoot, hang, exterminate Jews." Herbert Lottman, *The Left Bank: Writers, Artists, and Politics from the Popular Front to the Cold War* (San Francisco: Halo Books, 1991), 173.

111. Miles, *Beat Hotel*, 71.

112. William Demby, interview by Harvey and Mona Levenstein, Sag Harbor, NY, December 22, 1998.

113. According to the Institute of International Education, in the academic year 1956–57 over seven thousand young Americans visited Europe "in the formal pursuit of knowledge." John Garraty and Walter Adams, *From Main Street to the Left Bank: Students and Scholars Abroad* (East Lansing: Michigan State University Press, 1959), 2. Many more went to France than any other country.

114. Ibid., 145.

115. They were so conscientious about preserving this atmosphere, she said, that they were sometimes more concerned about preserving French traditions than the French themselves. Henriette Nizan, "Quand la jeunesse Américaine vient respirer l'air de Paris," *Rapports France-Etats-Unis* 38 (May 1950[?]): 45–46.

116. Anne Rittershofer to parents, September 17, 1956, "Class of 1958" box, SCSLC.

117. Rittershofer to parents, September 28, 1956, ibid. Picasso was in Arles for its bullfight season, which was popular among nostalgic exiles from Franco Spain even though French law prohibited the killing of the bull.

118. Garraty and Adams, *Main Street*, 4.

119. Tracy Quayle, "Reflexions d'une élève de la class '65," in Association of Former Juniors in France of Smith College, "Memento," 18, Association of Former Juniors in France of Smith College Papers, History folder, box 1133, SCA.

120. Anne Rittershofer to parents, December 19, 1956, "Class of 1958" box, SCSLC.

121. Vasiliki Galani-Moutafi, "The Self and the Other: American Students in Greece," *Journeys: The International Journal of Travel and Travel Writing* 2 (2001): 109–11.

122. Garraty and Adams, *Main Street*, 5.

123. Ibid. The father of one of the Smith students who visited her in Paris saw another psychological benefit: "Most of the foreigners she has met [in America] have been from a lower social strata," he said, "like the local fruit man, for instance." In France, though, she was "meeting foreigners who not only sell fruit but who paint pictures, study in famous schools and are perhaps better educated than she is. It is both an exhilarating and somewhat humbling experience. . . . She'll no longer be a snob." Thomas Page Smith, "I Saw Your Daughter in Paris," *SAQ*, February 1949, 85.

124. Quayle, "Reflexions," 18.

125. Nizan, "Quand la jeunesse Américaine," 47.

126. The courses were usually too specialized for American undergraduates, presupposing the kind of basic knowledge they generally acquired in introductory courses, which were absent in the French system. Americans enrolling in a course on French thought in the eighteenth century would find themselves attending a weekly lecture on Voltaire's *Candide*. Frances Stokes, "The *Moi* in Me," *SAQ*, November 1960, 13. The Sorbonne considered completing the first two years of American college as the equivalent of passing the *bac*, the French university entrance exam, and would only allow students who were at least in their

third year of college to take courses there. Joanne Dauphin, interview by Harvey and Mona Levenstein, Paris, April 19, 2000.

127. Garraty and Adams, *Main Street*, 68–73.

128. "Internationalist" was defined as supporting American participation in the United Nations and NATO. The major difference was with older interviewees who had been in the prewar junior-year program of the University of Delaware, who were much less tolerant and internationalist. C. Robert Pace, *The Junior Year in France: An Evaluation of the University of Delaware — Sweet Briar Program* (Syracuse: Syracuse University Press, 1959), 25–51.

129. F. J. McGuigan, "Psychological Changes Related to Intercultural Experiences," *Psychological Reports* 4 (1958): 55–60; cited in Garraty and Adams, *Main Street*, 148.

130. Pace, *Junior Year in France*, 40–51.

CHAPTER TEN

1. John Steinbeck, "One American in Paris," in *Holiday in France*, by Ludwig Bemelmans (Cambridge: Houghton Mifflin, 1957), 148.

2. Not only were tourists to Europe more highly educated than the general population; they were better educated than the average of their income level. Bill Blair, "Comments on 'Potential Travel Market for Europe in the USA,'" in David Ogilvy to Leonard Lickorish, n.d. [1959?], David Ogilvy Papers, box 45, LC.

3. "Topics," *NYT*, November 17, 1960; cited in Christopher Endy, "U.S. Tourism in France: An International History, 1944–1971" (Ph.D. diss., University of North Carolina, 2000), 249.

4. David Ogilvy, "Notes for Talk to European Travel Conference, February 13, 1962," Ogilvy Papers, box 45. Emphasis in original.

5. John Lansing and Dwight Blood, *The Changing Travel Market* (Ann Arbor: Survey Research Center, University of Michigan, 1964), 6–10.

6. Thorstein Veblen, *The Theory of the Leisure Class* (New York: Macmillan, 1902); Robert S. and Helen Lynd, *Middletown, a Study in Contemporary American Culture* (New York: Harcourt Brace, 1929). *Middletown*, which much to its left-wing authors' chagrin became a kind of bible to the advertising industry, skirted around the term "class." The term fell further out of favor in America in the 1950s because of its Marxist connotations. See Olivier Zunz, "Deradicalizing Class," in *Why the American Century?* (Chicago: University of Chicago Press, 1998), 93–111.

7. One of the decade's most persuasive American historians ascribed pre–World War I populism, progressivism, the Ku Klux Klan, and McCarthyism to status insecurity. Richard Hofstadter, *The Age of Reform* (New York: Knopf, 1955).

8. Vance Packard, *The Hidden Persuaders* (New York: McKay, 1957); *The Status Seekers* (New York: McKay, 1959).

9. Ogilvy, "Notes for Talk to the European Travel Conference, February 13, 1962."

10. *PhAA*, March 17, 1956; August 11, 1956.

11. *PhAA*, March 17, 1956.

12. The other reason was "people to people" exchanges to promote world peace. "Travel—the New Status Symbol," *Ebony*, March 1962, 84.

13. The significant thing, of course, is not what they actually did, but what they thought they should reply. *NYT*, March 24, 1957.

14. Ed Berrol, "Memorandum: BTA Media and Copy Implications from Recent Research [1961]," Ogilvy Papers, box 45.

15. The division into four categories, rather than the usual three, was first proposed by the popular sociologist Russell Lynes.

16. Steinbeck, "One American in Paris," 150–51.

17. High-brows liked ballet, "little magazines' criticism of criticism, avant garde literature," and had recordings of "Bach and before, Ives and after." Tom Funk, "Everyday Tastes from High-brow to Low-brow," *Life*, April 11, 1949, 100–101.

18. Thirty-seven percent cited culture. Far fewer thought of "having a good time," which was more associated with travel within the United States. Lansing and Blood, *Changing Travel Market*, 6–10.

19. *PhAA*, June 7, 1958.

20. Rita Hamer, interview by Harvey and Mona Levenstein, Paris, April 27, 2000.

21. "Tourists' 'Likes and Dislikes,'" *ASTA Travel News* 25 (October 1956): 116–18; cited in Endy, "U.S. Tourism," 247.

22. Art Buchwald, in "I Love Paris in the Fifties," *Paris Review* 150 (Spring 1999): n.p.

23. Joseph Wechsberg, "The American Abroad," *The Atlantic*, November 1957, 266.

24. He added, "And many of them are quite young [and] out for a good time." Extracts from letter in David Ogilvy to Paul Biklen, June 6, 1961, Ogilvy Papers, box 45.

25. P. E. Schneider, "In France, Only the Americans Wear Berets," *NYTM*, June 17, 1962, 48.

26. By 1956 the Holland America Line alone had five vessels plying between New York and Le Havre. *SR*, March 16, 1957, 53. In 1959 over 880,000 people crossed by boat, more than double the number who did so in 1946. Jean Ginier, "Quelques aspects du tourisme américain en France," *Annales de Géographie* 397 (1964): 299. Horace Sutton gives a much higher figure, saying that in 1957 the ships carried 1,032,400 passengers to Europe. Horace Sutton, *Travelers: The American Tourist from Stagecoach to Space Shuttle* (New York: Morrow, 1980), 246.

27. Patrick Robert, "Le comportement des étrangers face au produit France," *Visages de France*, September 1968, 3.

28. Ogilvy, Benson, and Mather, "British Travel and Holidays Association: Proposals for Advertising in the United States, 1958–1959," September 1957, Ogilvy Papers, box 45; Ginier, "Quelques aspects," 300–301; France, Commissariat Général au Tourisme, *Bulletin Statistique* 5, no. 11 (November 15, 1968): 11.

29. Ginier, "Quelques aspects," 300–301.

30. These figures exclude the 37 percent of travelers who were foreign-born returning on family visits, who spent less and stayed longer. Wechsberg, "The American Abroad," 264.

31. Arthur Frommer, *Europe on 5 Dollars a Day* (New York: Frommer, 1957), 9.

32. Blair, "Comments on 'Potential Travel Market.'"

33. "The question is never asked outright," he said. "Usually the person asking the question gets very friendly and confidential, then sort of hints that it must be pretty expensive to be vacationing in Europe—and hitting only the fine places." *PhAA*, July 25, 1959.

34. Natalia Danesi Murray to Janet Flanner, April 1959, in Janet Flanner, *Darlinghissima: Letters to a Friend*, ed. Natalia Danesi Murray (San Diego: Harcourt Brace, 1986), 241.

35. Ginier, "Quelques aspects," 299, 317.

36. In 1960 more than 90 percent of the Americans arriving in France were over twenty-five and few of them were over sixty-five. Ibid., 297.

37. Lansing and Blood, *Changing Travel Market*, 33.

38. Ginier, "Quelques aspects," 297; Berrol, "Memorandum."

39. "Report from Paris," *Rotarian*, June 1953, 20–22; "A World of Friends on the Champs-Elysèes," *Rotarian*, July 1953, 34–37.

40. "1956 Kappa Kappa Gamma Tour," Dorothy Marsh Papers, box 4, SSC.

41. *PhAA*, August 15, 1959; September 19, 1959; December 5, 1959; *PT*, August 22, 1959; October 20, 1959.

42. Blair, "Comments on 'Potential Travel Market,'" Ogilvy Papers, box, 45; Memo: "Lickorish," [1961], ibid.; "January–February 1963 Survey: Preliminary Summary," ibid.; "American Express: Overall Operating Plan for the Travel Division," November 23, 1963, ibid., box 49.

43. Stephen Watts, *The Ritz of Paris* (New York: Norton, 1964), 144.

44. Mary Hulsizer diary, October 27, 1957, in Mary Burr Hulsizer Papers, RUL.

45. Robert C. Doty, "Not Adaptable Enough," *NYTM*, September 1, 1957, 47.

46. R. L. Duffus, "Still 'The Innocents Abroad,'" *NYTM*, August 2, 1959, 14, 26.

47. Schneider, "In France," 49.

48. The peripatetic traveler, who lived for much of the year in Spain, never learned a foreign language. John McPhee, "Templex," *New Yorker*, January 6, 1968, 32–67.

49. In 1931 Gilbert Seldes said, "Loudness is, in fact, the first thing people mention in the list of the American [tourist's] crimes." Gilbert Seldes, "Tramps—Are We?—Abroad," *Saturday Evening Post* 104 (June 11, 1932): 65.

50. Wechsberg, "The American Abroad," 267.

51. Cornelia Otis Skinner, "It's Ridiculous!" *Reader's Digest* 64 (April 1954): 105–8; cited in Endy, "U.S. Tourism," 251.

52. Doty, "Not Adaptable Enough," 45, 47.

53. Stanley Karnow, *Paris in the Fifties* (New York: Random House, 1997), 44.

54. Ginier, "Quelques aspects," 297.

55. "Notes on American Express," March 23, 1962, Ogilvy Papers, box 49; Elliot Detchon to Esty Stowell, April 18, 1962, ibid.; "American Express: Overall Operating Plan for the Travel Division," November 23, 1963, ibid.

56. The student version, whose itinerary was similar, cost $136 less because the accommodation for that group, traveling on the same ship, was tourist class.

57. Marsh Tours, "Conducted Tours: Europe 1957" [brochure], Marsh Papers, box 4.

58. Schneider, "In France," 48.

59. Duffus, "Still 'The Innocents Abroad,'" 26.

60. Quoted in Doty, "Not Adaptable Enough," 47.

61. *PhAA*, August 15, 1959.

62. Dorothy Marsh to George Brownell, January 28, 1958, Marsh Papers, box 4.

63. He added, "And the language barrier was there—as usual. One woman said she became ill and almost had to die because she did not know how to say 'sick' in French." *PhAA*, December 5, 1959.

64. *PhAA*, September 3, 1955.

65. Dorothy Marsh Tours, "Minutes of 1964 Tour Conductors Meeting," November 28, 1964, Marsh Papers, box 4.

66. John Offner, interview with Christopher Endy, September 9, 1998; cited in Christopher Endy, "A Most Unusual Type of Work," *American Diplomacy* 4 (Winter 1999), http://www.unc.edu/depts/diplomat/AD_Issues/amdipl-endy.html.

67. Alexander Reid, *The Young Traveler in France* (New York: Dutton, 1953), 58.

68. Doty, "Not Adaptable Enough," 47.

69. Hamer interview.

70. Schneider, "In France," 49.

71. Ben Bradlee, *A Good Life: Newspapering and Other Adventures* (New York: Simon and Schuster, 1995), 188.

72. David Ogilvy to Roger Lloyd, August 18, 1955; Ogilvy to Lloyd, September 2, 1955, Ogilvy Papers, box 44; Ogilvy to Cliff Field, June 17, 1957, ibid., box 45.

73. Despite his previous campaigns touting British beef, it also rated British food (and weather) very low, causing Ogilvy to back down from mentioning it in ads. Survey, [January–February 1963], "Preliminary Summary," March 1963, Ogilvy Papers, box 45.

74. Ibid.

75. One of them said that he tried to explain to his groups that the French were a proud people who were "individualists." He prepared them for a cold reception in Paris by telling them that it was "like a beautiful woman who does not wear her heart on her sleeve." Marsh Tours, "Minutes of 1964 Tour Conductors Meeting."

76. Nowland Organization, *Le public étranger et les bureaux de tourisme français* (1960); cited in Ginier, "Quelques aspects," 298.

77. "L'acceuil des voyaguers de groupes," *Revue Technique des Hôtels* 152 (June 1961): 13–15; cited in Ginier, "Quelques aspects," 306.

78. Quoted in Ginier, "Quelques aspects," 297.

79. *PHT*, June 4–5, 1960.

80. Two books on the incident estimated the number killed as 30 to 50 and 265. Philippe Bernard, "Paris Recalls Murder of Algerians in 1961," *Guardian Weekly* (London), October 10, 2001, 30. An official investigation said there were a minimum of 246 victims, most of whom were strangled, bound, and drowned in the Seine. *Libération*, August 11, 1999.

81. William Demby, interview by Harvey and Mona Levenstein, Sag Harbor, NY, December 22, 1998.

82. Christopher Sawyer-Lauçanno, *The Continual Pilgrimage: American Writers in Paris, 1944–1960* (New York: Grove, 1992), 94–95, 116–17.

83. Lionel Abel, *The Intellectual Follies: A Memoir of the Literary Venture in New York and Paris* (New York: Norton, 1984), 187.

84. Demby interview.

85. *PhAA*, December 13, 1958; October 10, 1959; October 15, 1960.

86. Charles Boggs to Lawrence Calcagno, April 30, 1960, Ogilvy Papers, box 45.

87. Temple Fielding, *Fielding's Travel Guide to Europe: 1964 Edition* (New York: Sloane, 1964), 432–33.

88. *NYT*, May 27, 1953. In late 1950 it was decided that the port of Bremen, in Germany, which had been the main depot for supplying the troops in Germany, was too vulnerable to the Red Army. Ginier, "Quelques aspects," 315.

89. François Jarraud, *Les Américains à Châteauroux, 1951–1967* (Arthon: private, 1981), 14–16; Ginier, "Quelques aspects," 315; Jean Ginier, *Les touristes étrangers en France pendant l'été* (Paris: Genin, 1969), 353.

90. *WSJ*, June 14, 1951.

91. Simone de Beauvoir, *La force des choses* (Paris: Gallimard, 1963) 1:348.

92. Richard Wright, "American Negroes in France," *The Crisis*, June–July 1951, 382.

93. U.S. Department of Defense, *A Pocket Guide to France* (Washington, DC: USGPO, 1951), 3, 24.

94. It did add that, as in every country, "you can get chummy with a special sort of hard-boiled dame who, for obvious reasons, is sitting alone at a café." Ibid., 34–35.

95. Ibid., 44.

96. *NYT*, May 27, 1953; *LM*, August 2–3, 1953.

97. *NYT*, May 27, 1953.

98. *LM*, August 1, 1953.

99. *LM*, August 2–3, 1953.

100. *NYT*, May 27, 1953.

101. Although some of the people in the "bourgeois" (higher circles) of the southwest did open their houses to some American officers and their families, many of the more "traditional" ones, such as the old Protestant circles in La Rochelle, "remained closed to them." *LM*, August 5, 1953.

102. The French reporter concluded that the consensus among the French was that the Americans behaved neither better nor worse than French soldiers would under similar circumstances. *LM*, August 4, 5, 1953.

103. For the highest-ranking officers, the air force rented lovely country mansions, including a few châteaux surrounded by lovely parks. Jarraud, *Les Américains*, 30–37.

104. Philippe Mauffrey, ed., *Phalsbourg Air Base: histoire de la base de Phalsbourg: periode américaine, 1953–1967* (Drulingen: Scheur, 1990), 115.

105. Ibid.

106. Colette Brossard, interview by Harvey Levenstein, Romorantin-Lanthenay, April 23, 2000.

107. Mauffrey, *Phalsbourg Air Base*, 121.

108. Quoted in Jarraud, *Les Américains*, 88.

109. Jean Fourton, *Les Américains et les coutumes de France* (Paris: Rabelais, 1961), n.p.

110. *La Marseillaise*, October 8, 1953; cited in Jarraud, *Les Américains*, 88.

111. Jarraud, *Les Américains*, 88–89.

112. Ibid., 39, 70.

113. Brossard interview.

114. Jarraud, *Les Américains*, 70–72.

115. Fourton, *Les Américains et les coutumes*.

116. Jarraud, *Les Américains*, 71–72.

117. Brossard interview.

118. Mauffrey, *Phalsbourg Air Base*, 72.

119. Jarraud, *Les Américains*, 70.

120. Ibid., 115.

121. Brossard interview.

122. Mino Monicelli, "Au Revoir with a Shrug," *L'Europeo* (Milan), trans. *Atlas*, September 1966, 34–35; cited in Paul Hollander, *Anti-Americanism: Critiques at Home and Abroad* (New York: Oxford University Press, 1992), 384–85.

123. Allen A. Broussard, interview, chapter 5, "U.S. Army, 1954–1956," in "A California Supreme Court Justice Looks at Law and Society," University of California Black Alumni Series, BL.

124. Jarraud, *Les Américains*, 55.

125. This included those stationed in Germany and other countries, whose first goal, said the *New York Times*, was a jaunt to Paris. *NYT*, May 30, 1954. It is not clear whether it included the 20,000-odd sailors from the Sixth Fleet who would periodically descend en masse on the Riviera. *WSJ*, July 18, 1952.

126. Ginier, "Quelques aspects," 315; Ginier, *Les touristes étrangers*, 353. An increase in independent touring in 1958 was ascribed in part to the number of relatives and friends coming over to visit servicemen and therefore staying in more off-the-beaten-track places. *CSM*, November 7, 1958.

127. Interview with anonymous airport limousine driver by Harvey Levenstein, Boston, MA, October 2000.

128. Quoted in Robert Kanigel, *High Season* (New York: Viking, 2002), 217.

129. John Garraty and Walter Adams, *From Main Street to the Left Bank: Students and Scholars Abroad* (East Lansing: Michigan State University Press, 1959), passim.

CHAPTER ELEVEN

1. *Newsweek*, June 12, 1961. Wearing the Givenchy creation was particularly symbolic because it had already been announced that she would wear an off-the-shoulder yellow organza gown by the American designer Oleg Cassini, who had been one of her husband's early supporters. *Newsweek*, June 5, 1961.

2. It was obviously written before November 22, 1963, when Kennedy was assassinated. Temple Fielding, *Fielding's Travel Guide to Europe: 1964 Edition* (New York: Sloane, 1964), 434.

3. Janet Flanner diary, March 11, 1964, in Janet Flanner, *Paris Journal: Vol. 1, 1944–1965*, ed. William Shawn (New York: Atheneum, 1965), 578–81.

4. Flanner diary, June 4, 1964, in ibid., 591.

5. Luc Boltansky, "America, America . . . Le plan Marshall et l'importation du management," *Actes de la recherche en sciences sociales* (May 1981); cited in Ludovic Tournès, "L'américanisation de la culture française," *Historiens et Géographes* 358 (July/August 1997): 74.

6. Although often regarded as a sign of Americanization, the push to inexpensive, widely advertised kitchen appliances for the masses was started by a Frenchman, Jean Mantelet, founder of Moulinex, whose low-cost electric coffee grinders were an immediate success when launched in 1956. Tournès, "L'américanisation," 264.

7. Kristin Ross, *Fast Cars and Clean Bodies: Decolonization and the Reordering of French Culture* (Cambridge: MIT Press, 1985), 177–78; Michael Harrison, "French Anti-Americanism under the Fourth Republic and the Gaullist Solution," in *The Rise and Fall of Anti-Americanism: A Century of French Perception*, ed. Denis Lacorne, Jacques Rupnik, and Marie-France Toinet; trans. Gerry Turner (Basingstoke: Macmillan, 1990), 174–77.

8. *LM*, July 2, 2001.

9. In 1962 these included the African-American National Association of Fashion and Accessory Designers and governing councils of the National Council of Negro Women, the National Association of Business and Professional Women, as well as the Rinkeydinks—wives of prominent African American orchestra leaders and entertainers, who met in Paris. *Ebony*, March 1962, 84.

10. The total number of American tourists dropped a bit in 1957 and 1958, due to French involvement in the Suez War in 1956, the political crisis of 1958, and rising French prices, but after 1959, when the franc was devalued, it rose again in 1960, to over 437,000. France, Commissariat Général au Tourisme, *Bulletin Statistique* 5, no. 11 (November 15, 1968): 11.

11. *TMY 1971/1972*, 66.

12. From 1960 to 1975, the number of New Yorkers applying for passports to travel to Europe increased by only 31 percent, while the number applying to go there from Texas increased by over 400 percent, and those from California, Ohio, Michigan, Illinois, and Pennsylvania doubled or more than tripled. *TMY 1976/1977*, 63.

13. In the early 1960s, Americans accounted for one-quarter of all the hotel rooms rented in Paris, and 60 to 70 percent of those in the three highest categories of hotels: deluxe, four star, and three star. France, Commissariat Général au Tourisme, *Bulletin Statistique* 5, no. 11 (November 15, 1968): 11; Jean Ginier, "Quelques aspects du tourisme américain en France," *Annales de Géographie* 397 (1964): 312. On the Riviera in 1960, they spent twice as much per day as the British and French and represented four in ten of the foreign guests at the top-flight hotels. Robert Kanigel, *High Season* (New York: Viking, 2002), 225.

14. *New Yorker*, March 1961, 86–87; J. W. Hartman Advertising Collection, Duke University Library; cited in Christopher Endy, "U.S. Tourism in France: An International History, 1944–1971" (Ph.D. diss., University of North Carolina, 2000), 318.

15. David Ogilvy to John Mawson, September 28, 1960; February 16, 1962, David Ogilvy Papers, box 45, LC.

16. Ginier, "Quelques aspects," 316; Francesco Frangialli, *La France dans le tourisme mondial* (Paris: Economica, 1991), 177; *LM*, August 14, 1968.

17. Endy, "U.S. Tourism," 333.

18. Gladys Pratt diary, Gladys Pratt Papers, MH.

19. *LM*, August 14, 1968.

20. Then, following the "modernizing" theme, it mentioned "the outpourings of countless industries . . . the phenomenal advances of French scientists." Advertisement in the *New Yorker*, October 31, 1959, 21; cited in Endy, "U.S. Tourism," 316. Endy has a perceptive discussion of the divisions among the French, particularly between the representatives of the older, labor-intensive "artisanal" tradition of hotel- and restaurant-keeping and the modernizers who sought to replace these seemingly inefficient tradition-bound ways. Endy, "U.S. Tourism," chap. 6.

21. Pierre Py, *Droit du tourisme* (Paris: Dalloz, 1991).

22. *PHT*, May 7, 1963.

23. François Corre, "Comment on reçoit les touristes américains à Paris," *Le Nouveau Candide*, August 7–13, 1963; *PHT*, August 8, 1963. After the Paris brouhaha, the *London Daily Telegraph* sent a reporter to pose as an Eastern European tourist in London with

markedly different results. Taxi drivers and restaurants were honest, there were no demands for tips, and people were polite and helpful. *PHT*, August 16, 1963.

24. *Time*, April 23, 1965.

25. "The Worm Turns," *Newsweek*, September 7, 1964.

26. Fielding, *Fielding's Travel Guide to Europe: 1964 Edition*, 491.

27. *GOT*, December 1, 1964.

28. Ibid.; *GOT*, April 10, 1965; *Time*, April 23, 1965; Crane Brinton, *The Americans and the French* (Cambridge: Harvard University Press, 1968), 107–8.

29. *Time*, April 23, 1965.

30. *NYT*, May 18, 1965.

31. The first beneficiaries of this were a puzzled group of Italians on a pilgrimage in Nantes. *LM*, July 21, 1966.

32. The other was that they were usually in too much of a hurry to appreciate the subtleties of what seemed to them to be an "exotic" cuisine. The best tippers were said to be the British, followed by the Japanese and the Germans. Jean Ginier, *Les touristes étrangers en France pendant l'été* (Paris: Genin, 1969), 173.

33. *LM*, September 1–2, 1968.

34. Lilian and Philip Van Doren Stern, *Beyond Paris: A Touring Guide to the French Provinces* (New York: Norton, 1967), 18; Sydney Clark, *All the Best in France* (New York: Dodd, Mead, 1967), 3–4.

35. "Gaullism Empties Bistros," *Newsweek*, September 2, 1967.

36. Carol Denis, interview by Harvey and Mona Levenstein, Paris, April 28, 2000. De Gaulle also put off potential Canadian tourists by championing Quebec independence and British tourists by blocking Britain's entry into the European Common Market. *Newsweek*, September 2, 1967.

37. They decided against the boycott "at this time," the president of I. Magnin explained, because "France is a unique position and exports unique products—couture, perfume, and fabrics. There just isn't really a choice." *BW*, December 30, 1967.

38. Ibid.

39. *NYT*, January 26, 1969.

40. In 1965 tourists who insisted on going to Europe were admonished to at least fly on one of the two American-flag carriers, Pan Am and TWA. Ginier, *Les touristes étrangers*, 343.

41. *BW*, December 30, 1967.

42. *LM*, July 31, 1965.

43. *TMY 1969*, 91; Endy, "U.S. Tourism," 341–42.

44. *NYT*, January 14, 1968.

45. *LM*, January 16, 1968.

46. Endy, "U.S. Tourism," 341–66.

47. *LM*, January 17, 1968.

48. *Newsweek*, June 3, 1968.

49. In June 1947 the influential book editor Clifton Fadiman wrote a foreword to a reprint of Sinclair Lewis's 1929 novel *Dodsworth*, in which the nouveau-riche midwestern protagonist undertakes a European tour in a quest for culture and respectability. Only one of the book's themes had lost its point, said Fadiman, and that was "the Henry Jamesian fairy-tale vision we have played with for fifty years, of a Europe possessing some magical secret, some snake oil Happiness-and-Culture, unpurchasable within domestic boundaries.

The Europe we no longer believe in. If it ever existed, the last war had bled it white; the next will tread its corpse into the ground." Clifton Fadiman, foreword to *Dodsworth*, by Sinclair Lewis (New York: Random House, 1947), v.

50. *Time*, October 12, 1981.

51. Laurence Bertrand-Dorléac, "De la France aux *Magiciens de la terre:* les artistes étrangers à Paris depuis 1945," in *Le Paris des étrangers depuis 1945*, by Antoine Marès and Pierre Milza (Paris: Publications de la Sorbonne, 1994), 408–11.

52. "Before the war," Pierre Loeb, a Paris gallery owner recalled, "four out of five of the big dealers were Jewish. So were four out of five of the big collectors. After the war, all that was altered. Most of the dealers, and most of the collectors, had disappeared. Others had left France." Pierre Loeb, 1964, quoted in John Russell, *Matisse: Father and Son* (New York: Harry Abrams, 1999), 261.

53. Cynthia Brants diary, November 12, 1948, Cynthia Brants Papers, AAA.

54. Ibid., February 19, 1949.

55. Robert Gwathmey to Hudson Walker, n.d. [October 1949?], Hudson Walker Papers, AAA.

56. He added, "The dead painters are much classier competition." "ND." to Jackson Pollock, n.d. [1952?], Jackson Pollock Papers, AAA.

57. Lee Krasner to Jackson Pollock, n.d. [July 1956], Pollock Papers, AAA. Not every visiting modernist was impressed by its architectural treasures. In the spring of 1950, Romare Bearden wrote a friend about how the abstractionist Mark Rothko, whom Bearden said was "a fool," had declared that while Chartres cathedral's renowned stained glass was "fair enough, he felt the rest of the church was like St. Patrick's cathedral. He was mad at himself for liking a crumbling city like Paris. For after all one couldn't paint in such a manner. And he wanted to be in charge for awhile so he could tear down the Place de la Concorde." Romare Bearden to Carl Holty, n.d. [April 1950?], Carl Holty Papers, AAA.

58. *Time*, October 17, 1955. Calcagno vigorously protested the anti-French spin *Time* put on the story, saying that, contrary to what the story implied, he had benefited greatly from his Paris sojourn. Lawrence Calcagno to Joe Downing, November 8, 1955, Lawrence Calcagno Papers, AAA.

59. David Bowers to Larry Calcagno, n.d. [December 1964], Calcagno Papers.

60. Bearden to Holty, May 28, 1960, Holty Papers.

61. Larry Rivers, interview by Myron Schwartzman, June 1984, in Myron Schwartzman, *Romare Bearden: His Life and Art* (New York: Abrams, 1990), 164.

62. Bertrand-Dorléac, "De la France," 405–7, 413–18. Rauschenberg himself was not a pop artist. The elite French public, still persuaded by Communist criticism to deplore abstract art, clung to the idea that modern American art was in bad taste for somewhat longer. Tournès, "L'américanisation," 258.

63. Gay Talese, "Looking for Hemingway," *Esquire*, May 1963; cited in Harold Hayes, ed., *"Smiling through the Apocalypse": Esquire's History of the Sixties* (New York: McCall, 1970), 864.

64. Saul Bellow, "My Paris," in *The Sophisticated Traveler: Beloved Cities: Europe*, ed. A. M. Rosenthal and Arthur Gelb (New York: Villard, 1984), 175.

65. Edmund Wilson, *Europe without Baedeker* (New York: Farrar, Straus and Giroux, 1966), 361.

66. Lionel Abel, *The Intellectual Follies: A Memoir of the Literary Venture in New York and Paris* (New York: Norton, 1984), 187.

67. Michael Kammen, *American Culture, American Tastes: Social Change and the 20th Century* (New York: Knopf, 1999).

68. P. E. Schneider, "In France, Only the Americans Wear Berets," *NYTM*, June 17, 1962, 22, 48–49.

69. Harvey Levenstein, *Seductive Journey: American Tourists in France from Jefferson to the Jazz Age* (Chicago: University of Chicago Press, 1998), 246; *Time*, July 26, 1963.

70. *Time*, July 26, 1963. Fielding said he was motivated to write his book when he looked up some travel guides before a trip to Europe in 1946: "None of these books is worth a good God damn," he said to his wife. "I'm learning nothing. Everything is either picturesque or Romanesque and I want to know where to go, how to get there, what the hotels are—good and bad—and where the restaurants are, how many cigarettes to take." John McPhee, "Templex," *New Yorker*, January 6, 1968, 65.

71. *Time*, July 26, 1963.

72. The song, "The Shadows of Paris," by Henry Mancini, was rarely heard again.

73. There is a French singer in it, but rather than sing, he is part of a scheme to smuggle heroin into New York City.

74. *Newsweek*, September 29, 1969.

75. The agency's ads in response to this, which featured Britain's thatched cottages, Beefeaters, and other "Olde Worlde" themes, were roundly criticized by British "modernizers" for presenting a country "embalmed in the past." Lord Mabane to David Ogilvy, November 8, 1962, Ogilvy Papers, box 45; transcript of BBC broadcast, "Is This Really Britain?" October 9, 1962, ibid.

76. Schneider, "In France," 22, 48–49.

77. Janet Flanner to "My darlinghissima," June 19, 1964, in Janet Flanner, *Darlinghissima: Letters to a Friend*, ed. Natalia Danesi Murray (San Diego: Harcourt Brace, 1986), 355.

78. By 1963 close to 40 percent of the Americans visiting Europe stayed for three weeks or less. *TMY 1967*, 141. (It was not that they preferred such short vacations. A 1969 survey of readers of *Harper's* and *Atlantic Monthly* showed that the large majority thought the "ideal" holiday was one lasting from twenty-two to over ninety days. *TMY 1970*, 101.)

79. Ginier, *Les touristes étrangers*, 326, 333.

80. Ibid., 338.

81. Rochelle Gerson, *Maiden Voyages: A Lively Guide for the Woman Traveler* (New York: Harcourt, Brace and World, 1967), 20.

82. Ginier, "Quelques aspects," 313. In 1964 only two nights was said to be the norm. *Newsweek*, September 7, 1964. However, it is difficult to separate business and convention travel from tourism in such statistics.

83. The survey reported that 98 percent of the respondents intended to or had visited the Eiffel Tower; 85 percent, Notre-Dame; and 79 percent, the Invalides, where Napoléon's tomb is located. However, it was biased toward those who would be interested in such things, as it was conducted at a number of tourist sights, such as the Arc de Triomphe. "Les visiteurs de Paris," *Paris-Projet* 6 (1971): 77.

84. David Ogilvy, "Draft," May 31, 1961, Ogilvy Papers, box 45; Ginier, *Les touristes étrangers*, 333–34, 344.

85. Gallup Poll, May 17, 1961, cited in draft memo, May 31, 1961, Ogilvy Papers, box 45; *NYT*, November 17, 1968; *GOT*, December 1, 1968. In the 1968 poll, it tied for fourth place with Scandinavia.

86. Patrick Robert, "Le comportement des étrangers face au produit France," *Visages de France*, September 1968, 10–14.

87. Institut Français d'Opinion Publique, "Le tourisme en France vue par les Français," ms. (Paris: Commissariat Général au Tourisme, 1969), x–xi.

88. "Le tourisme à Paris," *Paris-Projet* 6 (1971): 81.

89. *LM*, May 22, 1968; June 16–17, 1968.

90. *Newsweek*, June 3, 1968; *NYT*, June 2, 1968.

91. Raymond Gatti, *Taxi de guerre, taxi de paix* (Cannes: private, 1988), 110.

92. The number of Americans arriving in France for the entire month of May (10,360) was about half of what it was the previous year. *LM*, August 23, 1968. They returned in greater numbers in July, but still remained 15 percent below that of the previous July. Patrick Robert, "Saison 68: les incidences d'une crise," *Visages de France*, December 1968, 3–5.

93. *Newsweek*, June 3, 1968.

94. *LM*, August 23, 1968. Many parents of students on junior-year-abroad programs in Paris were worried sick, especially since students living in French homes could not use the telephones for overseas calls. Sweetbriar College set up a special communications center in Virginia to help keep them in touch. Joanne Dauphin, interview by Harvey and Mona Levenstein, Paris, April 19, 2000.

95. *NYT*, June 23, 1968; July 20, 1968; *LM*, August 14, 1968.

96. Jack Levine to Isabel Bishop, October 13, 1968, in Isabel Bishop Papers, AAA.

97. The number of Americans registered in Paris hotels dropped from 432,000 in 1967 to 314,000 in 1968. France, Commissariat Général au Tourisme, *Bulletin Statistique* 5, no. 11 (November 15, 1968): 11; Robert, "Saison 68," 3–5.

98. The government devalued the franc by 12.5 percent. *NYT*, August 9, 1969.

99. Gênet [Janet Flanner], "Letter from Paris," *New Yorker*, June 13, 1970, 97–98.

100. Holiday [magazine], *The Holiday Guide to France* (New York: Random House, 1979), 9.

CHAPTER TWELVE

1. Although he does not call it romanticism, Bruce J. Schulman makes a good case for the individualistic link between believers in New Age, Christian revivalism, and the New Right in *The Seventies: The Great Shift in American Culture, Society, and Politics* (New York: Free Press, 2001), 92–101.

2. Christopher Endy, "U.S. Tourism in France: An International History, 1944–1971" (Ph.D. diss., University of North Carolina, 2000), 368.

3. *NYT*, April 15, 1974; "Tourism: End of an Era," *Forbes*, September 1, 1974, 44.

4. *NYT*, July 12, 1973.

5. *Time*, August 4, 1975.

6. *NYT*, July 7, 1975.

7. *Newsweek*, May 26, 1980.

8. *Time*, August 4, 1975.

9. Paul Lancaster, "Holding Down Costs: A French Recipe," *NYT*, Travel section, February 25, 1979.

10. *Newsweek*, May 26, 1980; May 18, 1981.

11. *Time*, August 4, 1975.

12. Orr Kelly, "Vanishing Breed: The Rude Frenchman," *USNWR*, November 8, 1976. Not a resident correspondent, he did not apparently take into account that it was in Paris, not the provinces, that the reputation for rudeness rested.

13. Lancaster, "Holding Down Costs."

14. *Time*, April 22, 1985.

15. *IHT*, July 11, 1986.

16. Robert Languar, *L'économie du tourisme* (Paris: PUF, 1983), 46; *Time*, August 12, 1974.

17. *NYT*, August 25, 1974; *Time*, August 4, 1975.

18. "Tourism: End of an Era," 44; Endy, "U.S. Tourism," 378.

19. Région Ile-de-France, *Le tourisme étranger en Ile-de-France: septembre 1985* (Paris: Institut d'Aménagement et d'Urbanisme de la Région de l'Ile-de-France, 1985), 3–4.

20. In 1987, 1,802,000 American tourists arrived, staying 25,477 nights. France, Conseil Economique, *Pour une industrie touristique plus compétitive* (Paris: Journal Officiel de la République Française 1988), 25.

21. Nicholas Lemann, "William Jennings Bush," *New Yorker*, September 10, 2001, 47.

22. In 1963, 18 percent of American overseas travelers were twenty-four or younger, compared to 13 percent in 1956. *TMY 1967*, 98; "Travel to Europe among U.S. College Students," *Travel Europe*, November 1957, 32–35; cited in Endy, "U.S. Tourism," 246.

23. "Travel to Europe," cited in Endy, "U.S. Tourism," 246.

24. *TMY 1969*, 102.

25. *TMY 1975/1976*, 58.

26. Adrien Cartier [pseud.], interview by Harvey and Mona Levenstein, Paris, April 27, 2000.

27. British authorities expected over 3 million young visitors in the summer of 1971, including 750,000 Americans. *NYT*, June 1, 1971.

28. Harry Hill, "Things Happen in Paris," *Travel Europe* 5 (November 1967): 32–35; cited in Endy, "U.S. Tourism," 245–46.

29. "American Express Overseas Free Services," January 2, 1963, memo in David Ogilvy Papers, box 43, LC.

30. Robert A. Liston, *Young Americans Abroad* (New York: Messner, 1971), 24.

31. He arrived there in the early 1970s. Randy Garrett, interview by Harvey and Mona Levenstein, Paris, April 25, 1999.

32. Katherine Davis Fishman, "Where the Action Is in Europe," *Mademoiselle*, March 1964, 92–93.

33. "Cheapest Ways through Europe," *Mademoiselle*, May 1972, 76.

34. *NYT*, August 1, 1971.

35. It was followed by its rather raffish Left Bank neighbor, Saint-Germain-des-Prés, and Montmartre, which also had downscale connotations. Seventy percent of the American respondents were under thirty and half of them were students. "Les visiteurs de Paris," *Paris-Projet* 6 (1971): 81.

36. Excerpts in "Where the Fun Is," *Mademoiselle*, February 1968, 167–68.

37. Mavis Gallant, "The Taste of a New Age," *Atlantic Monthly*, April 1981, 12.

38. "Where the Fun Is," 167.

39. Some young Americans received a rude shock when they discovered that the French police did not distinguish between "soft" and "hard" drugs, and that those charged with possession normally endured three to four months of pretrial confinement. Gay Bryant, *The Underground Travel Guide* (New York: Award Books, 1973), 163.

40. French young people poured in there as well, hoping to plug into the latest trends. *BW*, September 2, 1967.

41. "Where the Fun Is," 165–69.

42. Paul Goldberger, "On the Champs-Elysées: 'Hey, Aren't You the Girl Who Sits Across from Me in Abnormal Psych?'" *NYT*, Travel section, June 13, 1971.

43. What was probably unbelievable was the Sunday activity, for the Lord's Day Act still prevented such things in Ontario.

44. Rita Roberts [pseud.] diary, July 1981, photocopy in possession of author.

45. Forty-two percent of those between twenty-one and thirty-four had named it, versus only 27 percent for second-ranked Italy. David Ogilvy, "Draft," May 31, 1961, Ogilvy Papers, box 45.

46. *NYT*, June 19, 26, 1971; July 2, 1971. French tourist experts continued to delude themselves in this regard, taking heart in a 1971 survey showing that 88 percent of college-educated American between eighteen and twenty-five said they'd like to visit France, versus 76 percent who listed Britain and 62 percent who said Italy. "Le tourisme à Paris," *Paris-Projet* 6 (1971): 68.

47. *NYT*, June 1, 1971.

48. *NYT*, April 8, 1969.

49. Martin Johns, interview by Harvey and Mona Levenstein, Hamilton, Ontario, June 12, 1998.

50. Bryant, *Underground Travel Guide*, 7. The twenty-seven-year-old author was the fiction editor of *Penthouse*.

51. Among the replacements were pursuits such as pony-trekking in Scotland or sailing on the Zuider Zee. Goldberger, "On the Champs-Elysées."

52. Garrett interview.

53. *G&M*, September 30, 2002.

54. Carol Mongo, interview by Harvey and Mona Levenstein, Paris, April 23, 1999.

55. *NYT*, June 1, 1971.

56. Liston, *Young Americans Abroad*, 25. This was probably wishful thinking on his part. A survey done two years before did indicate that there was much more positive feeling toward American tourists among the fifteen to twenty-four age group than among the population at large. Twenty-one percent of the young people polled ranked the Americans among the two "nicest" (*plus agréable*) tourists versus 16 percent of the sample as a whole. However, more of the young people also disliked American tourists. Twenty-one percent listed them among the two least "nice" (*moins agréables*) tourists versus 17 percent of all those over fifteen. (Italians were ranked at the bottom of both groups as the least likable.) Institut Français d'Opinion Publique, *L'acceuil aux touristes étrangers en France* (Paris: Commissariat Général au Tourisme, 1969), 17.

57. "You'll probably find the French anti-American," it said. "It's understandable, for they are both bourgeois and independent and they have had many rich and vulgar tourists

tramping through their land (in addition to the GI influx) since the days of World War II." Bryant, *Underground Travel Guide*, 163.

58. Mongo interview.

59. Charles Reich, one of the movement's few theorists, called this one of its most important contributions. Charles Reich, *The Greening of America* (New York: Bantam, 1971).

60. Mongo interview.

61. Christopher Lasch, *The Culture of Narcissism: American Life in an Age of Diminishing Expectations* (New York: Norton, 1979).

62. "Travel Europe: 1970," *Holiday*, June 1970, 30.

63. About 25 percent of the sample were there mainly on business. Région Ile-de-France, *Le tourisme étranger: septembre 1985*, 7–12; *Le tourisme étranger en Ile-de-France* (Paris: Institut d'Aménagement et d'Urbanisme de la Région de l'Ile-de-France, 1993), 4–43.

64. The elderly tended to dominate the spring and fall tours to Europe, while the summer tours attracted a more mixed bag, mainly because they could cost half the price of individual tours. Jay Miller, "A Group Travel Convert," *NYT*, Travel section, January 5, 1975.

65. Rita Hamer, interview by Harvey and Mona Levenstein, Paris, April 27, 2000.

66. This was in (French-speaking) Luxembourg. Miller, "A Group Travel Convert."

67. Hamer interview.

68. "Les visiteurs de Paris," 81.

69. Bertram M. Gordon, "The Decline of a Cultural Icon: France in American Perspective," *French Historical Studies* 22 (1999): 626.

70. Theodore Zeldin, foreword to *The Rise and Fall of Anti-Americanism: A Century of French Perception*, ed. Denis Lacorne, Jacques Rupnik, and Marie-France Toinet; trans. Gerry Turner (Basingstoke: Macmillan, 1990), xi.

71. The surveyors said that the "Culture-Cum-Pleasure Tourists . . . travel in style and want their trips to be thoroughly planned. While they tend to take shorter trips, they add to their attendance at cultural exhibits patronage of good restaurants, night spots and auctions, eschewing only sports events." Another 12 percent, of little importance in France, were "The Family-Oriented Roots Seekers." Only 4 percent admitted to being "Status-Conscious Bargain-Hunters," who seemed mainly interested in inexpensive but classy-sounding places to ski. *TMY 1975/1976*, 65.

72. Michèle Lamont, *Money Morals and Manners: The Culture of the French and American Upper-Middle Class* (Chicago: University of Chicago Press, 1992), 165, 99, 107.

73. Ibid., 97.

74. Martin Garay, *Le tourisme culturel en France* (Paris: Documentation Française, 1980), 73.

75. Région Ile-de-France, *Le tourisme étranger en Ile-de-France en 1989*, 18. There was many a slip between good intentions and trudging through museums. Forty-eight percent of the foreigners surveyed when they entered France in 1984 said they had "a cultural motivation," whereas only 10 percent of those leaving the country said they had visited a museum or attended a festival. *GOT*, August 12, 1986.

76. Région Ile-de-France, *Le tourisme étranger en Ile-de-France en 1989*, 7; "La fréquentation des monuments historiques parisiens par les étrangers," *Paris-Projet* 6 (1971): 76–81.

77. Maxine Feifer, *Going Places: The Ways of the Tourist from Imperial Rome to the Present Day* (London: Macmillan, 1985), 267.

78. *GOT*, August 12, 1986.

79. John Gagnon and Cathy Greenblat, cited in Jack Horn, "Tourists—Strangers in a Strange Land," *Psychology Today* 10 (December 1976): 26.

80. Flora Lewis, "The Night Life of Paris Retains Its Spicy Savor," *NYT*, Travel section, June 10, 1979.

81. *NYT*, April 15, 1974.

82. Charles Graves, *The Rich Man's Guide to Europe* (Englewood: Prentice-Hall, 1966), 55.

83. A regional group, Provence-Riviera-Congrès, was very successful in promoting such meetings in Provence and the Riviera. In 1978 half of the half a million foreigners who spent 2 million nights at conferences spent them at meetings outside of Paris. Garay, *Le tourisme culturel*, 89.

84. Louis Bishop diary, 1972, Louis Bishop Papers, RUL.

85. The French tourist department was so impressed by the importance of these kinds of "business tourism" that it set up a special office in Chicago to promote such meetings. *GOT*, October 1985, 3.

86. Edgar Morin, *L'esprit du temps* (Paris: Grasset et Fasquelle, 1962), 19.

87. Equally important, but less visible to Paris-oriented American tourists, were the law's regulations prohibiting destruction of the old quarters of cities and towns such as Lyon, Lille, Strasbourg, and Colmar, mandating that they be restored instead and turned into "living museums." Paul Goujon, *Cent ans de tourisme en France* (Paris: Cherche Midi, 1989), 82–84.

88. Thomas Carlson-Reddig, *An Architect's Paris* (Boston: Little Brown, 1993), 112; *Time*, November 4, 1974. Eventually, a small park and enormous sunken shopping mall went in there, prompting an unimpressed American journalist to write, "Les Halles has been leveled and, *voilà*, they've set up Paramus Shopping Mall instead." D. Keith Mano, "The Last Time I'll See Paris," *National Review* 36 (March 9, 1984): 59.

89. *LM*, July 20, 2002; Taki Theodoracopulos, "It Really Was Yesterday," *National Review* 25 (March 2, 1973): 259.

90. "Le tourisme à Paris," 72–74.

91. Ibid.; Theodoracopulos, "It Really Was Yesterday," 259. The 1967 Jacques Tati comedy *Playtime* anticipated much of this by portraying a bewildered tour group of Americans expecting to see Paris's historic beauty who instead see a series of places that are ultramodern, automated, and dehumanized.

92. Richard Cobb, "The Assassination of Paris," *NYRB*, February 7, 1980, 16–21.

93. Kathleen Madden, "Shopping: Map of Pleasures," *Vogue*, October 1983, 306, 309, 312–13.

94. *NYT*, February 24, 1970; March 2, 1970.

95. *NYT*, February 13, 1970. In 2001 Air Canada, whose configurations were about average for major international airlines, had 421 seats in its Paris-bound 747s.

96. *BW*, August 31, 1974. It did not resume Paris service until 1981, when it tried to revive recollections of its famed first-class sleeping berths by calling the reclining chairs in the first-class cabin of its L-1011s "sleeperettes." Press release, March 3, 1981, New York–Paris folder, box 148, Pan American Airlines Papers, UM.

97. This helped London, where most landed, surpass Paris as the main gateway for American tourists to Europe. *TMY 1979*, 21–22; *TMY 1980*, 27–28.

98. *NYT*, December 1, 18, 31, 1978. Initially, they tried to discriminate by serving discount passengers smaller meals and allowing them less carry-on baggage than full-fare passengers, but this backfired. Full-fare passengers did not notice the difference, but discount ones did and complained. *NYT*, December 31, 1978.

99. *Negro Traveler and Conventioneer*, November–December 1970, 8–10.

100. John McPhee, "Templex," *New Yorker*, January 6, 1968, 63.

101. Horace Sutton, "Paris, Paris!" *SR*, June 23, 1979, 46.

CHAPTER THIRTEEN

1. Jacques Rupnik and Muriel Humbertjean, "Images of the United States in Public Opinion," in *The Rise and Fall of Anti-Americanism: A Century of French Perception*, ed. Denis Lacorne, Jacques Rupnik, and Marie-France Toinet; trans. Gerry Turner (Basingstoke: Macmillan, 1990), 79–96.

2. Michael Harrison, "French Anti-Americanism under the Fourth Republic and the Gaullist Solution," in Lacorne, Rupnik, and Toinet, *Rise and Fall*, 174–78. In 1986, when another poll showed that 44 percent of the French considered themselves pro-American and only 15 percent thought of themselves as anti-American, a reporter for the leftist newspaper *Libération* said, "As ironic as it sounds, Americans should thank de Gaulle. He made the French feel comfortable with themselves." *CSM*, April 8, 1986.

3. Michel Winock, "'US Go Home': l'antiaméricanisme français," *L'Histoire* 50 (November 1982): 18.

4. The widespread perception that Jimmy Carter, the president from 1977 to 1981, was "peace loving" also helped. So did a remarkable turnabout in views of his successor, Ronald Reagan, who was initially regarded as a dangerous warmonger but was later viewed as an effective foreign policy leader. Rupnik and Humbertjean, "Images of the United States," 79–94.

5. Kristin Ross, *Fast Cars and Clean Bodies: Decolonization and the Reordering of French Culture* (Cambridge: MIT Press, 1985), 170–75.

6. Jacques Thibau, *La France colonisée* (Paris: Flammarion, 1980), 84–87; Richard F. Kuisel, *Seducing the French: The Dilemma of Americanization* (Berkeley: University of California Press, 1993).

7. François Jarraud, *Les Américains à Châteauroux, 1951–1967* (Arthon: private, 1981), 185–96.

8. Denis Lacorne and Jacques Rupnik, "La France saisie par l'Amérique," in *L'Amérique dans les têtes*, ed. Denis Lacorne, Jacques Rupnik, and Marie-France Toinet (Paris: Hachette, 1986), 36–38, 44.

9. A 1984 survey showed that "a relative majority of those polled had no worries about American cultural influence with respect to cinema, language, music, dress, advertising and the like. The largest contingent to think this way are the under-34 age group, followed by managerial personnel and professional people." Rupnik and Humbertjean, "Images of the United States," 93–94.

10. Edgar Morin, introduction to *La foule solitaire*, by David Riesman (Paris: Arthaud, 1964); cited in Pierre Nora, "America and the French Intellectuals," *Daedalus* 107 (Winter 1978): 330.

11. Edgar Morin, *Journal de Californie* (Paris: Seuil, 1971).

12. Indeed, excerpts from it were first published in a journal, *Esprit*, that had hitherto

been quite solidly "Third Way" and anti-American. Diana Pinto, "La conversion de la intelligentsia," in Lacorne, Rupnik, and Toinet, *L'Amérique*, 128; Winock, "'US Go Home,'" 18.

13. Jean-François Revel, *Ni Marx ni Jésus: de la seconde révolution américaine à la seconde révolution mondiale* (Paris: R. Laffont, 1970).

14. Lacorne and Rupnik, "La France saisie,", 36–38, 44.

15. *GOT*, May 20–30, 1986, 1–3.

16. Ernie Ricci [pseud.], interview by Harvey and Mona Levenstein, Paris, April 22, 1999.

17. "In Europe, Tourists Beat the Beaten Paths," *BW*, May 25, 1963.

18. John McPhee, "Templex," *New Yorker*, January 6, 1968, 44.

19. The general public ranked the Belgians, the English, and the Germans as the nicest (*les plus agréables*). However, "tourist professionals" ranked the Germans as by far the nicest. In the least-nice category, almost half the professionals ranked the Italians as the worst. The Americans tied for the second spot with the Spanish, with 20 percent each, while only 5 percent of them listed the Germans as the worst. Institut Français d'Opinion Publique, "Le tourisme en France vue par les Français," ms. (Paris: Commissariat Général au Tourisme, 1969), 15–18.

20. David Alpern, "Canada: France on the Cheap? A Little Imagination Helps," *NYT*, International Travel section, February 23, 1975.

21. *WP*, August 17, 1975.

22. *IHT*, May 28, 1986.

23. Barbara Harris, "France along the Diet Route," *Saturday Evening Post*, March 1981, 126–28.

24. Ellen Schoen, "Travel on the Cheap in London, Paris, and Rome," *Mademoiselle*, March 1984, 244.

25. Nor were they any more impressed with French plumbing than were earlier generations. It was almost certainly an American who said, "I am very put off by the rudimentary and often filthy state of the public toilets, as well as those in cafés and restaurants." "Les visiteurs de Paris," *Paris-Projet* 6 (1971): 81.

26. *CSM*, September 19, 1975.

27. All through the 1950s and into the 1960s, successive editions of Pan Am's overseas guide said, "After two wars shared by the French with G.I.'s and 'Tommies,' almost every Frenchman not only can understand English but can even understand an American trying to speak French." Pan American World Airways, *New Horizons Guide*, 10th ed., rev. (New York: Simon and Schuster, 1961–62), 60. When she first went to France in the 1980s, Carol Mongo was told not to bother learning French as "everybody" there spoke English. Carol Mongo, interview by Harvey and Mona Levenstein, Paris, April 23, 1999.

28. Anne and Joe Frank [pseud.], interview by Harvey and Mona Levenstein, Whitehouse Station, NJ, December 21, 1998. A French pharmaceutical company executive who stayed with them tried to explain that the French were really just intimidated by Americans speaking English, but they were unconvinced by this.

29. This was in a French Travel Service survey of Chicago travel agencies. *GOT*, October 1985, 6–7.

30. *LM*, February 8, 1986.

31. Patricia Wells, "Where to See and to Be Seen," *NYT*, Travel section, June 6, 1982.

32. (Miss) Betty Aurich to Travel Editor, Travel section, *NYT*, August 27, 1972.

33. D. Keith Mano, "The Last Time I'll See Paris," *National Review* 36 (March 9, 1984): 59.

34. *GOT*, January 1985.

35. *GOT*, October 1985; September 15, 1986.

36. They arrived steadily from March to September, while most of the others poured in during the already overcrowded months of July and August. France, Ministère du Commerce, d'Artisanat et du Tourisme, *Touristes étrangers en France, touristes français a l étranger* (Paris: La Documentation Française, 1985), 27.

37. *GOT*, June 20, 1986.

38. In 1985, 2.9 million Americans arrived in Britain, versus 1.9 million in France and 1.1 million in Italy. The French government said the preference for Britain was "for the obvious reasons of language and cultural attachments," but it had not always been thus. It also would not admit that a major reason was government-owned Air France's refusal to allow the low airfares to France that one could get to Britain. *GOT*, October 1985.

39. France, Ministère du Tourisme, "Direction de Industries Touristiques," "Compte du Tourisme, 1990," November 1993, 163; *GOT*, January 1986; May 20–30, 1986.

40. It also discovered that Americans were terribly ignorant of French geography, thinking that it consisted of Paris on its northern frontier, the Riviera on it south, and "some prairies and vineyards in between." *GOT*, October 1985.

41. In mid-July 1986, the dollar was worth one-third less than it had been the previous summer. *IHT*, July 19–20, 1986.

42. *GOT*, March 1, 1986. There had previously been a serious incident in France, on August 9, 1982, when two gunmen from the Abu Nidal group attacked the Goldenberg restaurant in the Marais, Paris's old Jewish quarter, killing six people and wounding twenty-two. *G&M*, August 19, 2002.

43. *NYT*, January 8, 1986.

44. *LM*, February 6, 7, 1986. They were probably not far off the mark. In 1982 the American Association of Geographers discovered that only 40 percent of American college students could locate the United States on a map. Lewis Lapham, *Money and Class in America* (New York: Weidenfeld and Nicholson, 1988), 194.

45. *NYT*, April 2, 1986; September 16, 1986.

46. *GOT*, March 15–25, 1986.

47. Ibid.; *IHT*, May 20, 1986.

48. *NYT*, April 19, 1986.

49. *Newsweek*, May 19, 1986.

50. *LM*, June 12, 1986; *Newsweek*, May 19, 1986. Stallone denied backing out, saying that he had not planned to go in the first place. *NYT*, May 7, 1986.

51. *GOT*, July 10–20, 1986.

52. *IHT*, July 14, 1986; *NYT*, September 16, 1986.

53. *CSM*, June 10, 1986; *NYT*, September 14, 1986. The French economy was seriously harmed by the American defections. An increase in European visitors made up for the drop in their numbers, but not in their spending. *GOT*, September 15, 1986; January 15, 1987.

54. *WP*, September 19, 1986.

55. *GOT*, June 20, 1986; September 15, 1986.

56. Participants could stick an official "Bienvenue en France" sticker on their doors and

vote for the participant who, in their opinion, "best represented the welcome in their region." Ultimately, ten seminars, each with about 150 people, were held in Paris and the provinces. *GOT*, February 10–17, 1987; October 1987.

57. *GOT*, October 1987.

58. *GOT*, December 15, 1986.

59. *GOT*, October 1985.

60. *TMY 1979*, 21. From 1970 to 1979, the average length of stay of all American travelers to Europe and the Mediterranean fell from twenty-seven days to twenty days. *TMY 1981*, 31. A 1985 survey of American tourists by Air France indicated that 71 percent stayed less than twenty-one days, and 36 percent were there for only seven to thirteen days. *GOT*, October 1985.

61. *GOT*, October 1985.

62. Julia Child, interview by Harvey Levenstein, Cambridge, MA, December 28, 1988.

63. For example, E. Graves, "Ballet of Flames for Christmas," *Life*, December 16, 1966, 108–9; "Napoleon and Friends," *McCall's*, January 1966, 88–90; E. Alston, "Napoleon's Chicken Marengo," *Look*, September 9, 1969, 30–31.

64. Anne Mendelson, "The 60's," *Gourmet*, September 2001, 133.

65. "How America Entertains," *Ladies' Home Journal*, October 1966, 99–112.

66. This is of the nine out of ten who said that would like to return. Thirty-three percent cited French gaiety, shows, and joie de vivre. Twenty-six percent chose "cultural attractions," which would mean sightseeing; and 13 percent the countryside. Jean Ginier, *Les touristes étrangers en France pendant l'été* (Paris: Genin, 1969), 348.

67. *NYT*, March 3, 1970.

68. Julia Child to Simone Beck, November 12, 1973, Avis DeVoto Papers, box 2, SL.

69. The cost of Beck's eight-day tour was $960 per person, including airfare, whereas Aaron's prices for eight days started at $2,500, excluding airfare. *NYT*, January 18, 1976.

70. It is interesting that the major criticism that proponents of the new cuisine leveled against the older cuisine was not much different from that of unsophisticated American tourists: that it camouflaged inferior ingredients. Claude Fischler, *L'homnivore* (Paris: Odile Jacob, 1990), 239–41.

71. Quoted in an obituary for Henri Gault, who, with his partner Christian Millau, played a leading role in popularizing nouvelle cuisine in their restaurant guide to France. *NYT*, July 12, 2000.

72. "Star Wars," *Newsweek*, March 20, 1978. His was the first nouvelle cuisine restaurant to achieve three-star status in the Michelin guide to France. Nouvelle cuisine was often confused with *cuisine minceur* (dieter's cuisine), a much more complex way of cooking developed by Michel Guérard for his expensive spa in the southwest of France.

73. Susan Heller Anderson, "Beyond the 'Nouvelle Cuisine,'" *NYTM*, March 4, 1979, 62–66.

74. Laura Shapiro, "An American Revolution," *Newsweek*, December 16, 1991.

75. Bertram Gordon, "Going Abroad to Taste," *Proceedings* of the 25th Annual Meeting of the Western Society for French History, 1998, 162–65.

76. Gourmet Magazine, *Indices*, 1971–75, 1976–80, 1981–85.

77. Not surprisingly, it was *Time* magazine, which had long delighted in putting down the French, that led the charge, while there was little coverage in the French press. Harvey Levenstein, "La memoire à deux vitesses," *L'Amateur de Bordeaux* 96 (1996): 15–19.

78. Jay McInerney, "Why, Oh Why, Do I Love Paris?" *Vogue*, April 1986, 236–38.

79. Ibid., 238.

80. I discuss the relative roles of immigration and travel in bringing about this change in "Immigration, Travel, and the Internationalization of the American Diet," in *From Genes to Culture*, ed. Harvey Anderson, John Blundell, and Matty Chiva (Paris: Danone Institute, 2002).

81. Mongo interview.

82. Adam Smith, review of Edward Chancellor, *Devil Take the Hindmost* (New York: Farrar Straus and Giroux, 1999); *NYRB*, July 18, 1999, 10.

83. *WP*, July 24, 1983; *NYT*, June 12, 1985; *WSJ*, December 20, 1985.

84. Mimi Sheraton, "The Moderne Touch," *Time*, September 16, 1985.

85. *LM*, July 12, 1986.

86. Ibid.

87. Guy Savoy, interview by Harvey Levenstein, Paris, April 29, 2000.

88. Colette Brossard, interview by Harvey Levenstein, Romorantin-Lanthenay, April 23, 2000.

89. Congressman Albert Ullman of Oregon, *Congressional Record*, 89th Cong., 1st sess., March 29, 1965, vol. 111, pt. 5: 6277; cited in Christopher Endy, "U.S. Tourism in France: An International History, 1944–1971" (Ph.D. diss., University of North Carolina, 2000)," 355.

90. *NYT*, April 8, 1969.

91. "Rough draft of notes," December–January 1978–79, Margaret Queneau Papers, folder 16, box 1, SL.

92. Cynthia Saltzman, *Portrait of Dr. Gachet* (New York: Penguin, 1998), 234.

93. They also credited popular magazines such as *Life* magazine and the movie *An American in Paris* with this. Georges Bernier, "Venez en France," *Rapports France-Etats-Unis*, February 1953, 41.

94. Joseph Barry, "The Most Glamorous Half Mile in the World," *SR*, September 12, 1970, 100.

95. Saltzman, *Portrait of Dr. Gachet*, 259.

96. At the height of the tourist season, it was receiving eight thousand people a day, "the majority of them apparently American." *NYT*, August 18, 1986.

97. Pierre Py, *Le tourisme: un phénomène économique* (Paris: La Documentation Française, 1992), 162.

98. Michael Gibson, "Paris: Machines that Manufacture History," *Art News*, January 1982, 139.

99. Paris, Préfecture de Paris, *Dix ans de tourisme à Paris, 1980–1990* (Paris, 1990), Annexe II.

100. Ralph Blumenthal, "Painting by Numbers," *NYT*, June 6, 1999.

101. Gerald van der Kamp, preface to *Claude Monet: Life at Giverny*, by Claire Joyes (London: Thames and Hudson, 1985), 7–11; *NYT*, October 19, 1980.

102. By then, Americans had put up virtually all of the $7 million cost of restoring the place. In addition, two private Franco-American associations, the Friends of Vielles Maisons Françaises and La Demeure Historique, were raising $400,000 annually to restore other historic French buildings. *NYT*, May 21, 1987.

103. This kind of tourism actually began years before, when Frank Lloyd Wright's

Guggenheim Museum in New York City became in itself a major attraction. Its high point, though, came late in the century, with the Frank Gehry–designed art museum in Bilbao, Spain. Each year over 1.5 million visitors made special trips to this out-of-the-way city to see the museum, many with hardly the faintest idea of what it exhibited. Around the same time, the new Jewish museum in Berlin became an instant attraction, even though disputes over what it should contain left it empty of exhibits for some years.

104. Most of the serious visitors were French, many of them young, who among other things were attracted to the large library, which was the first major one in the country to offer that unheard-of luxury—open shelving. Martin Garay, *Le tourisme culturel en France* (Paris: Documentation Française, 1980), 83; Cathy Newman, "Pompidou Center, Rage of Paris," *National Geographic* 158 (October 1980): 469; Py, *Le tourisme*, 162.

105. It was free until 2002, when a small fee was initiated, with little apparent effect on ridership.

106. *LM*, Musexpo (www.musexpo.com), April 4, 1999.

107. All told, 63 percent of the visitors are foreigners. Not surprisingly, to anyone who has seen the mobs of school tours arriving there, almost 40 percent are less than twenty-five years old. *LM*, April 1, 1999.

108. *NYT*, April 12, 2001. The large crowds at the art museums also helped camouflage France's continuing decline as a center of contemporary art. By the 1970s France had been supplanted as a center of modern art not just by the United States, but also by Germany and even Great Britain, which had always stood in France's shadow when it came to the visual arts. By the end of the century, few French artists were internationally recognized and it ranked far behind Germany, the United States, and Switzerland in terms of the number of art exhibits. In 2001 a French study concluded that it now occupied only a "minor" place in the world of contemporary art. *LM*, June 8, 2001.

CHAPTER FOURTEEN

1. In 2001 it welcomed considerably more visitors—75 million of them—than its entire population. France, Ministère de l'Equipment, des Transports, du Logement, du Tourisme et de la Mer, "Données publiques du tourisme: chiffres clés du tourisme," http://www .tourisme.gouv.fr.

2. U.S., Office of Travel and Tourism Industries, "Select Destinations Visited by U.S. Resident Travelers 1999–2000"; and "2000 Profile of U.S. Resident Traveler Visiting Overseas Destinations," http://www.tinet.its.doc.gov/view.

3. France, Ministère de l'Equipment, des Transports, du Logement, du Tourisme et de la Mer, "Le tourisme étranger en France en 2000"; France, Direction du tourisme, "Les clientèles du tourisme urbain," 4, http://www.tourisme.gouv.fr.

4. Pierre Py, *Le tourisme: un phénomène économique* (Paris: La Documentation Française, 1992).

5. The authors of a study examining attitudes toward tourism and peace were surprised to discover that people who had visited a foreign country were much less positive about tourism's contribution to world peace than those who had not. Turgut Var, John Ap, and Carlton Van Doren, "Tourism and World Peace," in *Global Tourism: The Next Decade*, ed. William Theobald (Oxford: Butterworth Heinemann, 1994), 35.

6. "Tourisme de masse: les nouveaux barbares," *Le Point*, August 3, 1987; Robert

Spizzichino, *Les marchands de bonheur* (Paris: Dumond, 1991), 79–80. The analogy was not new. In 1959, when Americans dominated tourism in Europe, Nancy Mitford wrote, "The Barbarian of yesterday is the tourist of today" and said that the growing number of tourists, "far more surely than any war, will be the end of Europe." Nancy Mitford, "The Tourist," *Encounter* 13 (1959): 3, 7; cited in Malcolm Crick, "Representations of International Tourism in the Social Sciences: Sun, Sex, Sights, Savings, and Servility," *Annual Review of Anthropology* 18 (1989): 308–9.

7. Jan Morris, "When Paradise Becomes a Tourist Trap," *G&M*, August 26, 1998.

8. David Lodge, *Paradise News* (London: Penguin, 1992), 76.

9. Michael Kammen, *American Culture, American Tastes: Social Change and the 20th Century* (New York: Knopf, 1999), 159–60.

10. *TMY 1976/1977*, 52.

11. Joseph A. Mazanec, "Constructing Traveler Types," in *Changes in Tourism: People, Places, Processes,* ed. Richard Butler and Douglas Pearce (London: Routledge, 1995), 138–39.

12. *NYT*, April 4, 2001.

13. The Lyon program exposed the female students to some big-city-style sexual harassment, as well as tensions with Arab men. Harold Turnquist, "Cultural Conflicts in International Exchange Programs: Oregon Higher Education Programs in France" (Ph.D. diss., University of Oregon, 1994), 81–86.

14. *NYT*, March 2, 1975. Although they assiduously avoided being labeled as tourism (the announcement of a two-week University of Southern Mississippi summer course on "regional culture in Mediterranean France" in Arles in 2000 bore the slogan "Why is it called tourist season if you can't shoot them?" [H-France site, winter 1999–2000, copy in author's possession]), geared as they were to temporary visitors traveling in search of cultural uplift, they surely fell within the traditional definition of tourism.

15. *NYT*, April 8, 2001.

16. Will Nixon, "Guidebooks to the Diaspora," *American Visions* 6 (December 1991): 52–56; Bruce LeFavour, *France on Foot* (Saint Helena, CA: Attis Press, 1999).

17. David Andrusia, *Gay Europe* (New York: Berkeley, 1995), 83, 93.

18. Alexander Lobrano, *Paris by Night* (New York: Macmillan, 1996), 73–75.

19. The Service, Bureau d'Etudes en Voyages et Tourisme, Paris, "Special Interest Tours, 2000." "All-Women Tours of France" at www.traveloffthebeatenpath.com.

20. *Our World* (January/February 1995): 29.

21. *Guardian Weekly* (London), August 8, 1998.

22. Harry Matthews Jr., "Gaily through the Vines: Gay Biking in Burgundy," *Our World,* July–August 1991, 33–34, 46.

23. Advertised in 1998 as www.concordegolf.com.

24. Marylin Bender, "The Bonuses of Touring with Groups," Travel section, *NYT*, May 5, 1979.

25. *USA Today*, November 15, 1999.

26. Two-week tours originating in London would venture into southern Italy, while three-week ones would sometimes make it to Greece. Even on twenty-six-day tours, tourists would be lucky to have one full day in Paris. Cosmos Tours, European tours brochure, 1993.

27. Jennifer Burdon and Phillip Redman, interview by Harvey and Mona Levenstein, Paris, April 17, 2000.

28. The average age of Americans traveling overseas by air for leisure is about forty-five years old. U.S., Office of Travel and Tourism Industries, "1999 Profile of U.S. Resident Travelers Visiting Overseas Destinations Reported from: Survey of International Air Travelers," http://tinet.ita.doc.gov/view/f-1999-101-001. Factoring in cruise ship passengers would almost certainly cause the average to rise.

29. *G&M*, June 30, 1997.

30. Jan Van Harssel, "The Senior Travel Market: Distinct, Diverse, Demanding," in *Global Tourism*, ed. Theobald, 368, 372.

31. Ibid., 370.

32. Jennifer Burdon, interview by Harvey and Mona Levenstein, Paris, April 27, 1999.

33. U.S., Office of Travel and Tourism Industries, "1999 Profile."

34. France, Observatoire National du Tourisme, *Touristes étrangers en France, touristes français à l'étranger en 1991* (Paris: Observatoire National du Tourisme, 1993), 198. In the rural areas, they were far outnumbered by the English, Swiss, and Germans, most of whom stayed for a week in simple, inexpensive *gîtes*. In 1993 the average American's rural stay was 11.6 days. France, Observatoire National du Tourisme, *Les touristes non-residents en France: donées par espace* (Paris: Observatoire National du Tourisme, 1993), 129–30.

35. David E. Shi, *The Simple Life: Plain Living and High Thinking in American Culture* (New York: Oxford University Press, 1985).

36. Peter Mayle, *A Year in Provence* (New York: Knopf, 1989); *Toujours Provence* (New York: Knopf, 1991).

37. David Brooks, *Bobos in Paradise: The New Upper Class and How They Got There* (New York: Simon and Schuster, 2000), 206. Mayle's books were popular in France as well, and the 1990s saw many French people buy and renovate abandoned rural buildings into holiday homes. However, they were also building on a long tradition of urban French people holidaying in or near the rural villages from which their families originated.

38. William Grimes, "Perfecting the Art of the Tasty Escape," *NYT*, Travel section, July 21, 1999.

39. Tahida Hambleton diary, "Easter 1995, France," photocopy in possession of author.

40. Nancy Harmon Jenkins, *The Mediterranean Diet Cook Book* (New York: Bantam, 1994), 17–21.

41. Mayle, *Toujours Provence*, 233.

42. Jenkins, *Mediterranean Diet Cook Book*, 12.

43. *NYT*, July 6, 1994.

44. Mayle, *Toujours Provence*, 233.

45. Harvey Levenstein, "The Paradox of the 'French Paradox' in America," paper at "Confiance Publique et Science de l'Alimentation," Entretiens Franklin, Paris, April 27, 2001, to be published by Entretiens Franklin, Paris. The French, on the other hand, tend to think that white wine produces headaches because of the sulfites that are used to clarify it.

46. Thane Peterson, "Why So Few French Are Fat," *BW*, July 3, 2001. A more credible, and complex, explanation is provided in Peter Stearns's interesting comparison of American and French attitudes toward food and body fat in *Fat History: Bodies and Beauty in the Modern West* (New York: New York University Press, 1997).

47. *NYT*, August 30, 1998.

48. Guy Savoy, interview by Harvey Levenstein, Paris, April 29, 2000.

49. William Ledeuil, interview by Harvey Levenstein, Paris, April 17, 2000.

50. At a table for a family of four, he said, the parents will now try something different, but not the children: "They are pandered to." Pierre Piaget [pseud.], interview by Harvey and Mona Levenstein, Paris, April 27, 1999. Jennifer Burdon was present at this interview as well.

51. Like the others in the French restaurant business, her impression is that they are mainly from New York and other East Coast cities, with a smattering from California. Colette Brossard, interview by Harvey Levenstein, Romorantin-Lanthenay, April 23, 2000.

52. The French "don't respect them for this," he added. "They don't seem serious." Olivier Tourlet, interview by Harvey and Mona Levenstein, Paris, April 12, 2000.

53. Jennifer Burdon, interview by Harvey and Mona Levenstein, Paris, April 17, 2000.

54. Olivier Tourlet, interview by Harvey and Mona Levenstein, Paris, April 12, 2000.

55. This section is based on observations from a number of French people in the restaurant business.

56. Brossard interview.

57. Brossard, Tourlet (April 12, 2000), and Piaget interviews.

58. Ibid.

59. Piaget interview.

60. Burdon interview, April 27, 1999.

61. Savoy interview; Burdon interview, April 27, 1999.

62. A guidebook for women tourists said Paris's reputation for being rude to tourists was undeserved, and that one gets a better reception when you at least try to speak the language. "How would you react," it asks, "to someone who came into your office or place of employment and started speaking French to you? This is exactly what many Americans do in France." Linda E. Ledray, *The Single Woman's Vacation Guide* (New York, Fawcett Columbine, 1988), 320.

63. Tourlet interview, April 12, 2000.

64. Olivier Tourlet, interview by Harvey and Mona Levenstein, Paris, April 25, 2000.

65. *NYT*, March 11, 2002.

66. Michael Specter, "I Am Fashion," *New Yorker*, September 9, 2002, 219.

67. "Paris: Where Everything's a Bargain This Year," *Glamour* 83 (September 1985): 310–12.

68. Burdon and Redman interview. An American woman who lived on a houseboat in Paris for nine months made a similar point, but from a feminist perspective. She complained of Parisians' "blatant discrimination by appearance. The conventions of neatness, tidiness, and feminine prettiness are rigidly upheld. It seems if you can't or don't wish to conform to the high-heeled, well groomed, perfumed, and decorated image, then you must expect to meet the sharp end of snubbery and snobbery." Louise Hume, "Afloat in Paris," in *Women Travel: A Real Special Guide*, by Miranda Davies and Natania Jansz (New York: Prentice Hall, 1990), 158.

69. "GirlTalk Paris," Journeywoman.com (2002), http://www.journeywoman.com/girltalk/girl_talk_paris.html.

70. Tourlet interview, April 12, 2000.

71. Steven F. Phillip, "Racial Differences in the Perceived Attractiveness of Tourism Destinations, Interests, and Cultural Resources," *Journal of Leisure Research* 25 (1993): 290–304.

72. Randy Garrett, interview by Harvey and Mona Levenstein, Paris, April 25, 1999.

73. Clarence Major, "And an Artist with Paris on His Mind," *NYT*, February 10, 1996.

74 Carol Mongo, interview by Harvey and Mona Levenstein, Paris, April 23, 1999.

75. Ibid.

76. Major, "And an Artist."

77. Barbara Chase-Riboud, "Why Paris?" *Essence* 18 (October 1987): 66.

78. Garrett interview; Mongo interview.

79. Paule Marshall, "Chez Tournon: An Homage," *NYTM*, October 18, 1992, 28–34; *NYT*, February 18, 1996; December 27, 1998; Major, "And an Artist"; Shay Youngblood, *Black Girl in Paris* (New York: Riverhead, 2000), 1–4. An important work in inspiring this was Tyler Stovall, *Paris Noir: African Americans in the City of Light* (Boston: Houghton Mifflin, 1996).

80. *NYT*, December 27, 1998; Bertram M. Gordon, "The Decline of a Cultural Icon: France in American Perspective," *French Historical Studies* 22 (1999): 626.

81. The only breaks in the fall came from surges in interest in French food in the 1970s and couture in the 1980s, when the dollar was very strong. Gordon, "Decline of a Cultural Icon," 630–46.

82. I am indebted to one of the publisher's anonymous readers of the manuscript for this point.

83. Catherine Cullen, *Virago Woman's Travel Guide to Paris* (Berkeley: Ulysses Press, 1993), 23. "The constant barrage of exploitative images in advertising remains one of the more disturbing aspects of a first-time visit to the country," said a disapproving guidebook for women travelers. Davies and Jansz, eds., *Women Travel*, 157.

84. Bruce Thorson, "Montmartre for the Masses," *G&M*, March 25, 2002. On the other hand, Gary Smith, the ballet and theater critic at another Canadian newspaper, recommended the new shows at the Moulin Rouge and Lido (both now owned by the same impresarios) as the finest kind of vaudeville: "brilliantly over the top" examples of the "great art of the cabaret revue." Rather than Lawrence Welk, for him it evoked memories of the best of Ed Sullivan. Gary Smith, "Parisian Cabaret Is Brilliantly Over the Top," *HS*, August 2, 2002. However, the *Ed Sullivan Show* was hardly sexier than *Lawrence Welk*.

CHAPTER FIFTEEN

1. *NYT*, July 6, 2002.

2. The fact that he received less than 20 percent of the vote then, and in the subsequent runoff, did little to assuage their fears. Nor did his apparent support for the right-wing government of Israel and the clear indications that his support derived from his anti-Arab, rather than anti-Semitic, stance.

3. That there was a marked increase in anti-Semitic incidents was confirmed the next year, when the French human rights commission reported that there were six times as many such incidents in 2002 as in the previous year. *LM*, March 28, 2003.

4. *NYT*, July 6, 2002. He seems to have muddled Caesar's inoffensive "Gallia est omnis diviso in partes tres" (All of Gaul is divided into three parts) with Cato the Elder's demand, 150 years later, at the end of each of his Senate speeches, that "Carthago delenda est" (Cartage must be destroyed). E-mail from Prof. Richard Talbert, University of North Carolina–Chapel Hill, to author, April 22, 2003.

5. *New York Newsday*, May 12, 2002.

6. *NYT*, July 6, 2002.

7. *NYT*, March 3, 2003.

8. Timothy Garton Ash, "Anti-Europeanism in America," *NYRB*, February 13, 2003.

9. *LM*, February 19, 2003.

10. Dinesh D'Souza, *What's So Great about America* (New York: Regnery, 2002); cited in Louis Menand, "Faith, Hope and Clarity," *New Yorker*, September 16, 2002, 102.

11. Robert Kagan, "Power and Weakness," *Policy Review* 113 (July 2003); Robert Kagan, interview on *The Big Story with John Gibson*, Fox TV News, February 6, 2003.

12. *WP*, August 23, 2002. His association of wine drinking and effete liberalism echoed his father's dismissal of his critics as Chardonnay sippers. Bush Jr. also voiced suspicions that the journalists covering him were nibbling on French cheese. Julian Borger, "Washington Diary," (London) *Guardian Weekly*, February 16, 2003. It was a source of some embarrassment for the "hawks" when it was revealed that Richard Perle, a wealthy consultant who was one of their most brilliant advocates, was a well-known gourmand who had a house in Provence. *NYT*, March 23, 2003.

13. *NYT*, February 9, 2003; September 18, 2003.

14. This was in contrast to the nations of "new Europe," such as Slovakia and Hungary, that fell in behind the United States.

15. *NYT*, July 6, 2002.

16. Quoted in Borger, "Washington Diary."

17. Ibid.

18. *New York Post*, February 10, 2003.

19. *G&M*, March 14, 2003.

20. Along with the usual drivel, there was much shock, outrage, and glee expressed over a posting saying that an application had been submitted to have a "pink" channel on French cable TV.

21. The absence of references to greed and rudeness might be connected to the homophobia, for these are macho traits.

22. Thomas Frank, *One Market under God* (New York: Doubleday, 2000), 75–78; *IHT*, April 10, 2000.

23. *LM*, January 5, 2002. The May poll indicated that anti-Americanism was much more prevalent among professionals and white-collar workers in the public sector than among those who worked in the private sector or as independent professionals. It was also more common among the Left than the Right, although, surprisingly, many more Communists declared they liked America than disliked it (34 percent vs. 23 percent). Gerard Corman, "France-Etats-Unis: regards croisés," June 16, 2000 (SOFRES poll for French-American Foundation), http://www.sofres.com/etudes/pol/160600_france-eu.htm.

24. I discussed those that came to the fore in the 1920s in chapter 14 of my *Seductive Journey: American Tourists in France from Jefferson to the Jazz Age* (Chicago: University of Chicago Press, 1998). Philippe Roger has a long analysis of these and those of the nineteenth and early twentieth centuries in *L'ennemi américain: généalogie de l'antiaméricanisme français* (Paris: Seuil, 2002).

25. *NYT*, March 30, 2003. The *Times* reported similar responses from Germany, where public opinion was also largely opposed to American policy. Indeed, it found no increase in anti-Americanism anywhere in Europe.

26. "Now that's just fine," he wrote (as if this had already happened). "Americans in France having to pretend they're not Americans. If they had done this in 1944, the French would have replaced 'La Marseillaise' with the Nazi 'Deutschland Uber Alles.'" *New York Post*, February 10, 2003. He did not explain how Americans pretending they were Canadians, who also contributed a major force to the landings, would have led to such dire results.

27. Jean-François Revel, *L'obsession anti-américain* (Paris: Plon, 2003). As Tony Judt has pointed out, while his analysis of the contradictions of current French anti-Americanism is astute, the rosy picture he paints of the United States is as far from reality as that of the anti-Americans. Tony Judt, "Anti-Americans Abroad," *NYRB*, May 1, 2003.

28. Roger, *L'ennemi américain*, 574–75.

29. Roger sees him as importing Ralph Nader into France. Ibid., 574.

30. Corman, "France-Etats-Unis." The poll asked if people felt "sympathie" and "antipathie" toward the two nations.

31. "Un Sondage CSA-Libération sur la perception de Etats-Unis en France," *Libération*, April 10, 1999. This poll, done at the height of controversy over the American role in Kosovo, showed more opposition to America than the next year's one, cited above, but this seems to be mainly because the questions were oriented toward foreign policy concerns.

32. BBC TV News, *Newsnight*, October 28, 2002.

33. *NYT*, March 18, 2003.

34. Jennifer Burdon and Phillip Redman, interview by Harvey and Mona Levenstein, Paris, April 17, 2000. By the end of the century, training foreigners in American hotel and restaurant techniques had become a major source of income for the 180 American colleges and universities with hotel and restaurant schools. *NYT*, May 6, 1998.

35. Ernest Dickinson, "Our P'town Parlez-vous Goes to France," *The Cape Codder*, May 19, 2000.

36. *NYT*, August 5, 1995.

37. Ina Caro, *The Road from the Past* (New York: Doubleday, 1994), 4.

38. Sherri Kelly, interview by Mona Levenstein, Boston, MA, May 2002.

39. Lynne Terry, "Paris Musters a Gallic Shrug for Rudeness," clipping, undated [1996?], from *Boston Globe*, in author's possession. Alan Riding, "To Parisians, Nice Is a Place, Not an Attitude," *NYT*, August 5, 1975.

40. *NYT*, August 25, 1995.

41. Ibid.

42. Jean Perrin, "Le tourisme à Paris et en Ile-de-France," September 4, 1997, Chambre de Commerce et d'Industrie de Paris, http://www.ccip.fr/etudes/arch/rap97; Riding, "To Parisians."

43. Ann Swarsdon, reprinted as "France Sheds Rude Attitude, Recognizing Tourism Demands Service," in *HS*, December 7, 1996.

44. Burdon and Redman interview.

45. Kelly interview.

46. Gael Greene, "A Short Tour of France," *New York Magazine*, July 23, 1990, 44.

47. *G&M*, January 9, 2003.

48. Heather Mallick, "Even the Sex Is Better in Paris," *G&M*, September 16, 2000.

49. Heather Mallick, "A Hotel Room in Calcutta," *G&M*, March 10, 2001.

50. Fifty percent of women versus 39 percent of men said they liked it. Also, young people, Democrats, and the more highly educated were more favorably disposed toward it than their counterparts. These were practically the reverse of how French opinion of America was divided. Corman, "France-Etats-Unis."

51. Diane Johnson, *Le Divorce* (New York: Dutton, 1997).

52. David Andrusia, *Gay Europe* (New York: Berkeley, 1995), 80.

53. He did note, though, that "there are signs that things are picking up a bit." Alexander Lobrano, *Paris by Night* (New York: Macmillan, 1996), 73–75.

54. Donna DiFillippo, interview by Mona Levenstein, Hanover, NH, June 12, 2002. Cynthia Croatti, interview by Mona Levenstein, Prides Crossing, MA, June 14, 2002.

55. *NYT*, May 29, 2001.

56. Many interviews with Mona Levenstein by Harvey Levenstein.

57. *G&M*, January 7, 1999.

58. Gallup Poll, Gallup Social and Economic Indicators, "Perceptions of Foreign Countries," (1999), http://www.gallup.com/poll/indicators/indforeign.asp.

59. Corman, "France-Etats-Unis."

60. Gallup, "Perceptions."

61. *WP*, March 18, 2003.

62. Ash, "Anti-Europeanism."

63. *HS*, November 15, 1997.

64. *G&M*, September 11, 1999; *NYT*, September 5, 1999.

65. Julian Barnes, *England, England* (New York: Random House, 1998).

66. Quoted in Michael Specter, "I Am Fashion," *New Yorker*, September 9, 2002.

INDEX

Page numbers in italics refer to illustrations.